D0041440

TRUE LIFE IN GOD

Volume I

Vassula: Conversations with Jesus

[Revised]

Published and Distributed by:-

J.M.J. Publications
P.O. Box 385
Belfast BT9 6RQ
United Kingdom
Fax: (01232) 381596

His Holiness Pope Paul VI has confirmed on October 14, 1966, the decree of the Sacred Congregation for the propagation of the Faith, under number 58/16 (A.A.S.), permitting the publication of writings about supernatural apparitions, even if they do not have a "nihil obstat" from ecclesiastical authorities.

True Life in God

Vassula Rydén 1991
© All rights reserved worldwide
© U.S. Copyright No. TX 3 677 390
ISBN No. 0 9519973 1 9
Printed in Canada

No part of this publication may be reproduced or transmitted in any form or by any means without permission.

First Printing, United Kingdom, November 1991 (10,000)
Second Printing, Canada, March 1993 (10,000)
Third Printing, Canada, February 1995 (10,000)

See back for the addresses of distributors

ՊԱՏՐԻԱՐՔԱՐԱՆ ՀԱՅՈՑ

ARMENIAN PATRIARCHATE

№ Թուական Date

Ms Vassula Ryden

Dear Ms Ryden,

It is an occasion of great pleasure and personal satisfaction for us to recognize in you a new catalyst of spiritual rejuvenation who can talk to our present generation in a most persuasive language, through the books you are publishing.

Your inspired mission of bringing the message of Christ to others is a source of profound joy to the Church. And your indefatigable zeal of drawing strength from and seeking regeneration and reinforcement in your Greek roots, should set an enviable example of dedicated fidelity, to our tortured youth.

In our days, at at time when crass materialism has taken such a deep root in the hearts of men, it is refreshing to know that all is not lost, that there still are among us people like yourself who are in communion with the Creator, and able to transmit to us the benefit of your inspiration.

We take pride in encouraging your ecumenical mission and pray for your success.

We look forward to reading your next book.

Meanwhile, we send you our blessings from the Holy City of God. and ask the Lord to keep you and guard you.

Archbishop David Sahagian

Archbishop David Sahagian
Chancellor & Grand Sacristan

ՓՈՍՏԱՐԿՂ 14235 ՀԵՌԱՁԱՅՆ 894866 ԵՐՈՒՍԱՂԷՄ ԻՍՐԱՅԷԼ
P.O.BOX 14235 PHONE: 894866 JERUSALEM ISRAEL

I am He who seeks your heart.

Jesus, June 1st, 1989

Love desires love. Love thirsts for love. Love begs from you a return of love.

Jesus, July 14th, 1989

I do not come as a Judge, not yet. I come to you as The Beggar, in rags and barefoot, with parched lips, imploring and lamenting for some love, for a return of love...

Jesus, May 1st, 1989

I beg you: come back to me and love Me. Learn to love Me; learn to love Me. Make peace with Me; make peace with Me. I will not reject you. I Am Love, and I love you everlastingly.

Jesus, May 1st, 1989

TABLE OF CONTENTS

INTRODUCTION

Patrick de Laubier

In the gardens of God, the marvellous variety of flowers never ceases to surprise one, and it can create a sort of wonder of disbelief. The history of Christian mysticism is still filled with cases of surprising people who are at first rejected in the name of a tradition that is more human than divine. It is only later that they become a point of reference for the future.

It seems legitimate to speak of a kind of expansion in the fullness of spiritual gifts which is not simply due to the response of creatures. Rather it stems from a mysterious plan of God that the Fathers of the Church called the "economy of salvation".

What attracts our interest in the case of Vassula is not so much the response of the creature as the role of the Creator. In the writings that are presented here, we do not find another autobiography like that of St. Theresa of Lisieux, what we do find is the account of a loving initiative that comes from God. Here one finds a teaching, a message, even more, a declaration and a yearning - one might even dare to say a supplication from God, which is addressed to His creatures.

The appeal is not new; it echoes down the ages and finds its response in attentive souls. What is new, instead, is the manner and the tone. We are presented with the case of a woman who for almost thirty years hardly thought at all about God. Then suddenly, in the midst of total worldly well-being, she finds herself addressed by an angel who prepares her during three months for a direct encounter with Christ. All this happens through the writing of notebooks, with visions and supernatural presences on an almost continual basis.

Other examples do come to mind. We could mention Frances of Rome in the fifteenth century, Anne Marie Taïgi in the nineteenth century, and in the twentieth century, Maria Conception de Armida, Gabrielle Bossis, and Marie Sevray. In each of these cases, ordinary lay-women, usually married, live in spiritual intimacy,

i

without ecstasy, in the presence of Christ, the Blessed Virgin, and the Angels. They do not all have visions, but each of them is called to write inspired messages, which make them privileged witnesses. One could say that each is a chosen prophetess of the interior life in the midst of the most common of daily occupations.

In the case of Vassula, the eruption of God into her daily life is similar to that of St. Frances of Rome: for the details of daily life are intertwined with teachings on the destiny of our world, as well as astonishing visions of heaven, purgatory and hell. We become witnesses, almost in a clinical way, of successive astonishing manifestations of an interlocutor who is both human and divine, who recalls both His message and His Name while always respecting the freedom of choice of the one He has chosen. And though Vassula sees and experiences this presence, which is both so near and so intense, not even she is dispensed from the necessity of making an act of faith.

We are witnesses here to scenes from an ordinary life which has become amazingly wonderful through an incomprehensible and concrete Presence. Vassula is accepted as she is in her daily life: the attractive, athletic-looking mother of a family. Yet within this very ordinary situation, a prophetic message has been proclaimed to the world.

Each individual soul is invited to intimacy, while the world as a whole is called to conversion in preparation for the coming of the Kingdom. In the Gospel, Christ has given us a way of discerning: we must judge the tree by its fruits. From the beginning till now, the reading of these messages has been the instrument for dozens of conversions, reaching especially those who might have seemed to be the least prepared to accept the message of Christ by the usual means. Some of those who were already believers also find a new fervor in this call to conversion.

This message is only understandable in an attitude of faith which reaches the conclusion that Love is more inventive then we had thought. A more elaborate discussion of the matter would never convince the skeptics and would risk burdening the reading of the text itself. I hope you will permit here a personal testimony. It is one thing to read mystical writings and quite another to meet one who writes them. Thus, I have been able to see for myself that grace does not destroy nature when God grants a mission that goes in such an evident way beyond the human possibilities: Vassula remains a woman of our times with whom anyone can converse and so come to understand that the love of God appeals to all of us, and that we are loved for more than we could have imagined. St. Paul had an expression to describe this reality: the folly of God, or more literally the folly of the cross.

1991

I really must express here my gratitude to my family, my spiritual director, and all my faithful friends who have made possible the preparation of this book. I want to mention in particular Father René Laurentin for his enlightened support, and François de Guibert, the director of O.E.I.L. for immediately accepting this unusual manuscript. The epilogue is from a Russian Orthodox friend, Vladimir Zielinski. For me it is prophetic.

Vassula Rydén

The text presented in this volume is the original English. At Vassula's request, there have been some abbreviations and additions which were necessary either due to the personal nature of a message or to clarify the sense of certain passages.

Fr. Michael O'Carroll, CSSp

EDITORS NOTE

I would like to thank Moira for her dedicated and untiring work in preparing the text for all the writings to date, as well as the Prayer Book (desired by Jesus). I would also like to thank Bernard and Christine for their work in preparing these writings for publication.

C. Lynch, B.E.M., January 1993

I AM THE LIGHT

Bangladesh, September 20, 1986

Peace be with you.
Can I be with You?
Yes, you are with Me; I am the Light.
Can I be near You?
You are near Me; you are in Me; I am the Light.
Can you shelter me?
You are sheltered by Me.
Can I lean on You?
You can lean on Me.
I need Your Strength to keep my Faith.
You are given Strength.
I need Your love.
You are loved by Me.

I am the Light and shine for everybody to see. Have no fear; My Path is straight; My Path will lead you to Me. I will meet you and you will recognize Me, for I radiate Peace and Love. ♥ ♥ *Come to Me. Can you see Me? Can you hear Me? Do not be afraid; do not just stand there in the dark. See, your limbs are healed,[1] you can walk again. See your sight is back. I healed you; I have healed your shame, and your sins are washed by Me. Use your limbs to walk to Me, your eyes to see Me, your faith to meet Me. I am your Redeemer, your Peace. I, Jesus, love all of you.*

I AM YOUR REDEEMER

September 27, 1986

Peace be with you, Vassula. Come to me. I am your Redeemer, your Peace. I lived on earth among you in flesh; I am God's Begotten Son. Come to Me and lean your head on Me. I am your Consoler. When you feel miserable, remember, I am near you.

---

[1]Jesus speaks symbolically.

Recite with Me this Prayer:

♥   *Help me Father and lead me to Your pastures of repose,*
       Where everlasting pure water flows.
       Be My Light to show me the Way;
       With You, by Your side will I walk,
       With You illuminating me, will I talk.
       Father, Beloved, remain within me to have Peace,
       To feel your Love.
       I will follow you in Your footprints,
       With You I will remain;
       Enlighten me, love me,
       Be with me here and forever after.
       Amen.

Jesus had come to teach me this prayer.

I AM THE WAY

September 28, 1986

Today Jesus gave me a clear (intellectual) vision of myself in nowhere, my surrounding looked like I was in marshlands with no one around, and my spirit seemed lost. Among the dry trees, I saw Jesus looking for me.

I am here; it is I, Jesus. I have found you. Come, let Me show you the way back. Hear Me; I, Jesus, am the Way. Every time you feel lost, call Me; I will come to you, and I will show you the way. I am the Way.

I GOD EXIST

September 30, 1986

Peace be with you, daughter.
Please, Jesus, give me light to be able feel you and write.
♥ ♥ *Vassula, lip service means the call is meaningless.*
I realized my mistake; I asked Jesus this favor without love, without thinking, without really feeling it. I repeated it, but really meaning each word and raising my soul to Him.

Deliver your call to Me feeling Me, like this time. I, God, feel; I feel all! I must receive from your call, love from the depths of your soul, needing Me, loving Me, meaning every word you say. I, God, exist, and I feel! Any call which is lip service might as well stay buried. Lip services are calls bellowing from graves. Remember I exist and feel. I wish that all my children work, giving Me joy!

I AM NOT BEYOND REACH

October 5, 1986

I'm reading a book in which many people reported "experiences with God". But almost all of those people are told by "experts" that they should forget what they experienced because it's not from God, telling them also that only highly elevated souls get experiences from God, and one has to be highly elevated too.

All this book explains that to get to God, one has to be a saint, and as I know I'm none and far from good, I decided to stop these meetings by writing with God. I might as well "pack up" the whole thing. They seemed to make me understand that to reach God, you have to be a saint, and they made me believe God is so far. So I will drop the whole thing, leaving my hand, writing for the last time what it wants, led by the force who wrote all these months.

Vassula, do not leave Me; beloved, be calling on Me and be learning with Me; remember: I am beside you all the time; I, God, am living in you; believe Me, I am the Almighty, the Eternal God.

No, It can't be; it can't be God. These who know, would prove to me that it is not God. Only highly and pure souls who are worthy, God reaches, giving such graces.

♥ *I am not beyond reach, Vassula! I do not refuse anybody. I blame all those who discourage My countenance to My children to come to Me.* ♥ *Whoever teaches that to be able to be with Me or be accepted by Me one should be pure or worthy are those who are damaging My Church. Any man having found Me, but is discouraged by others, I, who am Infinite Strength, will support him, giving him My Strength. Why, why do I have men who call themselves experts, judging whether I am or not, banning every possibility, leaving my children disconsolate and helpless and disillusioned; disregarding all My Graces, pulling away My children from me; why are all My given blessings rejected, blessings that I gave. I am Infinite Wealth.*

Daughter, when you finally found Me, I was full of happiness; I was careful not to frighten you away. I was being gentle, treating you like a mother handling her infant. I made you approach Me. I was full of happiness, calling you and meeting you, having you near Me, sharing everything I have, My beloved; and now, you come telling Me that you are thinking of leaving Me, because I, God, am impossible to reach, and that you were given information that only worthy souls can reach Me, and that you are below the standard required! I never deny any soul. I offer My Graces even to the most wretched. Delight Me and meet Me in this way. I bless you, daughter, I am guiding you; you are eating from Me. ♥ Vassula, read today Peter I,[1] read attentively, then I will relate it to you. Read the first chapter. Live with faith. Peter teaches you to have faith. ♥

Jesus made me understand many things with the word faith; that one can make mountains move by faith. One has to believe blindly, if you wish.

I AM PEACE

October 10, 1986

I am the Light; I, Jesus, want to warn you: never ever fall into traps set up by evil; never believe in any message which brings you unrest; do understand why evil is trying very hard to stop you. The devil is trying once again to stop you and discourage you. I, who am Your Saviour, am confirming to you that all the Messages bearing calls of love and peace, leading those that are lost to find their way back to Me, are all from the Father and Me, so do not get discouraged; have faith in Me. Remember, do not believe any Message which will leave your heart worried. I am Peace, and peaceful you should feel.

I AM YOUR CREATOR

October 12, 1986

Peace be with you. Light is giving you guidance, beloved, live peacefully.
I want to tell you that I felt in peace and comfortable with Dan. (My guardian angel.) I felt nostalgia for my angel.
Leave him, for he is but My servant. I am your Creator, God Almighty.
I must tell you that I did feel in peace with Dan and that I love him.
I know; leave him.
He told me once: "No man ever loved his angel as much as you do." Did he say this? Did he mean it?

---

[1] First epistle of Peter in the Bible.

He meant it. Leave him now and be with Me; lean your head on Me; feel how I love you; you are My daughter. I am your Heavenly Father, and I bless you; you are Mine; I am Yahweh, and I will never let anyone harm you. Feel My love I have for you. Listen to Me; I watched you grow from your tender childhood. I held you close to Me and saw you were pleasing to My Eyes. I looked at you grow like the wild flowers I created. My heart was filled with joy to watch you live in My Light. I remained near you; My bud started to blossom; you reached the time to be loved. I felt you, and you delighted Me. I felt your heart and blessed you. I read your wishes, and I loved feeling them. I remained near you, helping you to keep up your beauty. I saw you had flowered, so I called you, but you did not hear Me. I called again, but you ignored Me. You came to see Me now and then, and My Heart rejoiced to see you. These few times you came to see Me,[1] I was filled up with joy; I knew you were Mine, but you seemed to have forgotten Me. You never even felt that I was near you.

Years went by, your fragrance left, your leaves exposed in the harsh winter winds began to fall, your head was bent and your petals lost their velvety freshness and their beauty, the sun had started to scorch you, your feelings grew hard. Hear Me; I watched you with pity, I could not bear it any longer. Many a times I approached you, feeling you, but you were too far gone, you could not recognize Me, you knew not anymore the One who was bent over you, holding you and calling you by name. I lamented to see your beauty gone, to see that I held in My Arms a wretched child, deplorable to look at. Your sight made my heart cry, for I could still see in your eyes a faint light of love, the love of your youth, you had once for Me. I lifted you to Me, your little hands clutched on Me; I felt relieved to see my child needing Me. I took you back home and healed you with all My Love. I gave you water to quench your thirst, I nourished you and I slowly nursed you back to health. I am your Healer, I am your Redeemer; I will always be, I will never leave you, I love you. I God will never leave you lose yourself again. Delight Me now and stay with Me. I raised you up beloved, lean on Me, turn to Me and look at Me. I am God, your Heavenly Father; realize why I am with you.

I God will do the same to all My other sons and daughters, for you are all Mine. I will not leave them scorch in the sun, I shall protect them and restore them, I will not wait to see their leaves scatter, I will not wait to see you thirsty. Remember, I God love all of you; I am going to reunite you all.

---

[1] In church.

I AM FULLY AWARE OF YOUR CAPACITY

October 16, 1986

Peace be with you. Beloved rest, do not, do not burden yourself more; I can feel how you are straining.
I felt your Presence; were you emphasizing your Presence, Jesus?
I Am; I emphasized My Presence so that you understand. Vassula, I am fully aware of your capacity.

That day I was particularly tired, but I could not stop reading and working. I felt Jesus' Presence everywhere, and He was trying to tell me something.

I AM YOUR TEACHER

October 22, 1986

I, God, delight to have you near Me. I love you daughter, have faith in Me. In less than two months, you will be hearing Me distinctly,[1] I will give you the support you want. My aim is to guide you. You will progress enormously in less than two months, for this is My Will. I am your Teacher. All My teachings will enlighten your soul. Remain near Me. Vassula, every time you feel miserable, come to Me and I will console you, for you are My beloved. I never want to see any of My children miserable; they should come to Me, and I will console them.

WHICH HOUSE NEEDS YOU MORE?

October 23, 1986

Vassula, which house needs you more? I want you to choose.
Jesus, if you are asking me, meaning what is more important, your House or mine, I would of course say your House. And to choose, I choose your House. ♥ *I bless you.*

Jesus seemed so pleased!

---

[1]Prediction which came to reality: six weeks later I could hear His Voice.

I will guide you little one. Come, take with you My Cross and follow Me. Remember, I will help you; ♥ you will be My disciple. I will help you to reveal Me. I am Holy; I am Holy, so be Holy; live Holy. I will give you My support. Vassula, are you willing to work for Me ?

Name yourself again.

Jesus Christ.

Yes, I will work for you.

I love you; call Me when you wish.

I was agreeing without really realizing what it means to work for God. Since I love God, I wanted to please Him. I never realized my incapacity!

Hear Me. Listen to My cries; listen to My cries; can you see My Cross ? I am Jesus who brings forth this vision.[1] I call; I am suffering because I am counting you, My beloved, and I see you scatter and unaware of the dangers the devil has laid for you. My Heart lacerates to see you so far away from Me!

Jesus, for a whole month, was giving me images of His Cross. Wherever I turned my head and looked in any direction, a huge, dark brown Cross was standing. If I lifted my eyes from my plate while eating, this enormous Cross was there. If I looked from within my mosquito-net, the Cross again. If I walked and went to another room to sit or something, the Cross followed me, and it was there. For a month, it was as if haunting me. Then another thing started to haunt me: that all that's happening is perhaps not from God. But, then, if it is from the devil, how dumb can he get? I started to fear what people would say about all this. What will happen to me? I will be mocked!

Daughter, daughter, live in peace!

I was suspicious.

Who is it?

It is I, Jesus. Remain near Me; I have been calling you for years. I wanted you to love Me, Vassula....

Jesus, when was it, the first time you called me?

The time you were going to Lebanon. I called you in your sleep. You saw ♥ Me. Remember how I pulled you towards Me, calling you ?

Yes, I remember. I was very frightened; I was about ten. I was frightened by Your Force that pulled me. It felt like a strong current, like a magnet pulling a small magnet. I tried to resist and pull away, but I couldn't until I found my self stuck on you; then I woke up.

---

[1] It was a huge, dark cross.

I found it strange that Jesus reminded me of this dream, and of how I could remember it still.

THE CRUCIFIXION

November 9, 1986

Peace be with you. I am here; I am Jesus Christ. I am before you; I am your Teacher, and I love you. Evil was conquered by sacrificing Myself. Sleep not, because I am soon with you; I am the Revelations; I have tidings that will talk. Talk to Me about My Crucifixion, Vassula.
What shall I say? Shall I think before or during Your Crucifixion?
Before.

Jesus gave me an image of the scourging.

Having scourged me, they spat on Me, and gave several hard blows on My Head, leaving Me dizzy. They kicked Me in My stomach, leaving Me breathless and falling to the ground, moaning with pain. They took sport in Me, kicking Me by turns. I was unrecognizable; my body was broken, and so was My Heart. My flesh which was ripped off, hung all over My body. One of them picked Me up and dragged Me because My legs would not carry Me any longer. Then they clothed Me with one of their robes; they hauled Me forward, repeating their blows, hitting Me across My face, breaking My nose[1], harassing Me. I listened to their insults, daughter. With such hatred and mockery their voices resounded, augmenting My Cup. I listened to them saying: "Where are your friends mustering while their king is with us; are all Jews as treacherous as these ones? Behold their king!" And they crowned Me with a woven crown of thorns, daughter. "Where are your Jews to hail you? You ARE king are you not? Can you mimic one? LAUGH! Do not cry; you are king are you not? Behave like one then."

They tied up My feet with ropes, and told Me to walk to where My Cross was. Daughter, I could not go since they had My feet tied, so they hauled Me to the ground and dragged Me by My hair towards My Cross. My pain was intolerable; parts of my flesh which hung from the scourging was ripped off. They loosened the ropes off My feet and kicked Me to get up and lift My burden on My shoulders. I could not see where My Cross was, for My Eyes were filled up with My Blood,

---

[1]Cartilage was fractured, not bone (Holy Shroud experts confirm this with one voice).

which was streaking down My Face from the thorns which had penetrated My Head. So they lifted My cross and laid it on My shoulders, pushing Me towards the gates.

Daughter, O how heavy My Cross was which I had to bear! I felt My way to the gate, led by the scourge behind Me; I tried to see My way through My Blood, which burned My Eyes. I then felt someone wiping My Face. Women in agony came forth, washing My swollen Face; I heard them weeping and mourning; I felt them, "Be blessed," I uttered. "My Blood will wash away all sins of mankind; behold, daughter, the time has come for your salvation." I dragged Myself up; the crowds turned wild; I could see no friend around Me; no one was there to console Me; My agony seemed to grow, and I fell on the ground. Fearing that I would expire before the Crucifixion, the soldiers ordered a man called Simon to bear My Cross. Daughter, it was not a gesture of kindness or compassion; it was to save Me for the Cross.

Arriving on the Mount, they thrust Me on the ground, tearing off Me My clothes, leaving Me naked for every eye to see Me; My wounds, opening again, and My Blood flowing out on the earth.
The soldiers offered Me wine mixed with gall. I refused it, for deep inside Me, I had already the bitterness given to Me by My foes.

They quickly nailed My Wrists first; and after allowing the nails to set in My Cross, they stretched My broken Body, and with violence, pierced My Feet through.
Daughter, O daughter, what pain, what agony, what torment of My Soul. Forsaken by My beloved ones, denied by Peter, upon whom I would found My Church, denied by the rest of My friends, left all alone, abandoned to My foes, I wept, for My soul was filled with sorrows.
The soldiers erected My Cross, setting it in the furrow. I gazed upon the crowds from where I was, hardly seeing from My swollen Eyes. I watched the world; I saw no friend among those who mocked Me; no one was there to console Me. "My God! My God! why have you forsaken Me?" Forsaken by all those who loved Me.

My gaze fell on My Mother; I looked upon Her, and Our Hearts spoke: "I am giving You My beloved children to be your children too. You are to be their Mother." All was ending; salvation was near; I saw the heavens open, and every angel stood erect; all stood in silence: "My Father, into Your Hands I commend My Spirit; I am with You now."

I, Jesus Christ, dictated to you My agony. Bear My Cross, Vassula, bear it for Me. My Cross cries out for Peace and Love. I will show you the Way, for I love you, daughter.

YOU ARE SPIRIT AND I AM ALSO SPIRIT AND HOLY

December 4, 1986

Still I'm amazed and have enormous doubts of how this is happening; how could this happen? I mean, how can't I not control my writing hand? It is like I'm being used by another force. But, I'm too realistic; that's why I doubt, and yet, it's happening. I'm confused.

I am here. It is I, Jesus. Daughter, remember you are spirit, and I am also Spirit and Holy; I live in you, and you in Me. Remain in Me. I, Jesus, am with you always; understand this. ♥ Be in My Light; for I am the Light, and through Me you are receiving Knowledge; you are progressing.

All right, you have convinced me that it is You. You have reached Your two goals: that I love You was one, and second, You convinced me that You are meeting me this way. You have seduced me. I know that I am not more schizophrenic than the rest of the world, or psychotic than the psychiatrist himself. I know too that it is not from the devils, since I know how one feels when attacked by them: giving you a disquieting feeling of torments (that is , when I was attacked before, so that I would abandon the writings).[1] I have not chosen to receive Your calls since I was totally aloof to You. You willed it, My God. I do not regret; how could I, since I am seduced now!

Child, I elevated you to enable you to be with Me, I taught you to love Me. Are you happy to be with Me in this way?
Oh yes!
I bless you from the core of My Heart. ♥

December 8, 1986

Can I be in Your Light ?
You are in My Light; I am Jesus your Saviour. Wearing My Cross means bearing with you My sufferings daughter.

Jesus meant the cross one wears around the neck.

---

[1]One week.

BE HOLY

December 10, 1986

Daughter, will you follow Me? Do not wander astray; lead a holy life. ♥
Jesus, can't I be like I am? (Leading a jazzy life, but also trying to be a disciple.)
Hear Me; list Me one person of holy creed who never chose the Church; list Me one person who was partial!
I can't think of any.
No, there were none.
Jesus seemed to wait that I say something.

You want me "complete"?
Yes, I do. Fear not, what are you caring for daughter?
I must have sighed.

What happens if I stay the same?
Remain always the same, and you will discover that I will not stop calling you to Me!
Can I ask you a question?
You may.
Do you really care if I change?
I do!
Is there a difference if I change, I mean, to be holy like you say?
Yes, there is a difference; turn to Me and remain with Me.
Can you see right now in the future?
I do, beloved.
Can I ask you a question?
You can.
Since you see in the future, I would like to know something. If you don't want to answer me, just draw me a heart. Will I disappoint you in the end.?
No, you will not disappoint Me.

I was relieved.

How would you feel?
I, God, will feel glorified.
You would?
I would. Do not fear! Why are you fearing to be holy? Remember, you are in the beginning of My call.
What does this really mean?
It means that you are still learning from Me. I will be teaching you and showing

you My Works. I am only in the beginning of my call; you will discover later on how I work. I will call you later on at the appointed time to find Peace. Are you fully aware of what Peace means?

I'm not really sure; Peace could mean death, could mean Church. I do not know quite.

I am Peace. I am here near you. My Right Hand holding your writing hand, My left Hand on your left shoulder. I am present, and you feel Me. I am your Teacher, daughter, walk with Me! Work with Me, for I have appointed you to be My bearer. Do not let discouragement come from men. Many of them do not understand, for the darkness might have closed their heart, eradicating all understanding. Have peace. I, God, love you to distraction; courage, daughter.

ARE YOU WILLING TO BE HOLY?

December 11, 1986

Daughter, are you willing to be holy? Do not fear.

Jesus came back to the same subject of the previous message.

What is it exactly to be holy?
To be holy is to be pure and completely devoted to Me; holy is to work with love for Me; holy is to love Me and stay near Me; holy is to obey the Law; holy is to be like I am.
Can one be holy in heart only?
Yes!
Is the heart what counts more than the holy clothes?
Yes, the heart is what is important. Remain near Me, remain near Me;[1] you are not near Me like I wish! I feel you are evading Me.
Jesus was not happy...

I am Holy, so I want you to be holy.
I really want to be nearer You!
Do you really mean it? Are you really seeking Me?
Do not abandon me!
I will not!
Never?

---

[1] "Remain near Me" means that I was not concentrating on Him.

Never! Daughter, do not fear; are you fearing that the habit[1] give you sorrows? Go on, say it!

I took all my courage.

I will tell you, I don't really want to wear garments of nuns; I love You as I am also....
♥ *You finally had the courage to say it! Daughter! I am pleased with you for being truthful! I, God, love you; you realize you would have been lying in My Face if you would have said the opposite.*
I felt God so pleased, but He might be sad too for the result.

I am not sad! Listen to Me, I want you to be holy in heart, not in the habit.

What is partial? Wouldn't it be partial not wearing the garments?
Partial again teams up with the same meaning; one does not need holy garments to be holy. What worth are holy garments when the heart is unholy? It is like salt having lost its taste. I am going to teach you to be nearer to Me. I will bring you closer to Me. Feel loved by Me, do not fear Me; I am Peace. I, Jesus, guide you, I lead you. Pray more and work with Me in this way, augment your faith in Me; need Me; be watchful for the time is near.

HOLY IS TO BE LIKE I AM

December 13, 1986

Daughter, do you feel I have trapped you? I love you, beloved; do not fear Me; you seem to fear that I am trapping you!

True, I mentioned to my friends this and used the word "trap".
I know; I wished that you love Me.
Are you angry?
No, I am not.
Shall I be frank?
Be.
You wanted me to love you?
I did.
You have reached your goal?

---

[1]Nun's dresses.

I have.
You seduced me, and I like it!
Are you happy this way?
I am, very! I wish I would be less blunt!
You are learning; eat from Me; be blessed.
Is it possible that I bless you too?
It is.
Then have my blessings, Jesus Christ!
♥ *I love you; I have brought you up to be My bearer. I wished that you love Me. Since you are going to be My bearer, I wish you to be holy, since I am Holy and you are willing to follow Me and work for Me. Do not fear of being holy; why are you fearing it so much?*
Are you angry?
No, I am not angry. Holy is to be pure and to live in Me, holy is to follow Me, loving Me, holy is to be like I am. I will teach you to be holy if you are willing.
I am willing to do as You wish since I love you.
I will teach you then, daughter. Remain near Me, and you will learn; trust Me, and have faith in Me; believe Me when I tell you that I am happy to have you near Me, you will learn. Go in peace and remember: feel loved by Me.

I AM YOUR CONSOLER

December 14, 1986

I am your Consoler.
Tell me, Jesus, what good is this guidance, and what for?
It will lead many to Me; it will revive My children to come back to Me and read My Word. I am your Good Shepherd who calls you to Me. Believe Me, daughter, look at Me; look at Me. I have revealed My Face to you, do not feel uncertain; believe in Me. Have you forgotten how I work? Have you not heard of My Works? Do not let your era destroy you. Stay, daughter, as you are;[1] do not let them convince you, now that you are awake and abiding in My Light. Stay near Me.
Jesus, please, will you stop them if they try to do this?
I will; ♥ *I will not let anybody destroy you. Hear, all those that have ears; be watchful for the time is near.*

---

[1] Easy to convince me to believe just about anything! These people are called naive in our circles.

ALL WISDOM COMES FROM ME

December 15, 1986

Daughter, all Wisdom comes from Me; do you want Wisdom?
Yes, Lord!
I am going to give you Wisdom. Hear Me, you will acquire Wisdom. I am the Lord Almighty, and I will teach you. Cling to Me, and you will learn; have faith in Me. <u>Awake</u> My children; daughter, live in Peace, for every step you take, I, God, bless. <u>Full, you shall be many.</u>[1] <u>Go in peace.</u> ♥

YOU WILL HAVE TO ACQUIRE WISDOM

December 16, 1986

It took me a day to realize what You offered me! I was amazed with myself for just accepting without thinking what you have offered me! I want to thank you, Lord.
♥ *Peace be with you; are you realizing its importance?*
Slowly, yes! But I am not worthy for such a grace!
You will have to acquire Wisdom. Do not get discouraged though; I will teach you to earn it. You are in My Light, and being in My Light, you will learn. Listen to My Voice; try and recognize Me; I am Jesus Christ, and I am your Teacher. I have taught you to work through the Holy Spirit, I have taught you to love Me. I have poured out My Works on you to enable you to understand Me. I am your Strength. You will be given Strength to surmount your oppressors, who will be many, My child.[2]

God seemed a bit sad.

Why? Why?
Because many do not believe that I work in this way too; some do not believe in Me at all; daughter, I have to warn you;[3] I am telling you this so that you are prepared and aware of these people, since they are deaf and blind and have closed

---

[1] Full, you shall be many, means: Filled up with the Holy Spirit, I shall be able to witness and thus bring many souls to the Lord.
[2] This scared me because God's voice suddenly became grave and sad.
[3] God spoke in a very fatherly way and intimately.

their hearts. They will want to justify their cause; they will tell you that this is not Me, that all this comes from your mind; they will feed you with venomous theories; they will find ways of showing you that you are wrong; they will let you read their theories[1] to prove to you that you are wrong. So I am warning you, daughter, do not let men discourage you; do not let your era destroy you.

Lord, what can I do? Unless You protect me with Your Hand!

I will be near you all the time; do not feel abandoned. I will teach you to be strong, and you will overlook all your oppressors. I am preparing you; I will feed you to be full; have My Peace and abide in Me, JESUS CHRIST. IXθΥΣ
◁✕

BE MY BRIDE

January 8, 1987

Peace be with you, Vassula; it is I, Jesus. Come to Me, come and live in the middle of My Heart.

Do you want <u>me</u>, Jesus?

O I do! I eagerly want you, I want to entice you!

But I'm not worth anything.

I love you as your are...be My bride Vassula.

How could I!

I love you.

I don't know how to be Your bride. Jesus?

I will teach you to be My bride, beloved.

Do I carry a symbol for this Lord?

I will let you bear My Cross; My Cross cries out for Peace and Love.

I want to make you happy, Jesus.

Give Me happiness by never leaving Me; give Me happiness by loving Me; give Me happiness by awakening My children.

I need Your strength for all this, especially the last one!

Look at Me.

I looked at Him; He was radiating strength like an aura.

I am Strength. I will help you; be blessed.

Are you happy with me? I never asked you before.

I am happy with you; all the time I feel loved by you.

I wish I could see You materialize!

---

[1]Prediction which came true after a week or so.

♥ *Ask, and it shall be given to you. Augment your faith in Me.*

I decided to show the writings to a Catholic priest here. He condemned them saying it's the devil, and that I should stop. Jesus had asked him if he wanted to bear the Cross of Peace and Love with me. I told him that. He said it was evil. He gave me to read: Saint Michael's prayer, and the Memorare of Saint Bernard, and the Novena of confidence to the Sacred Heart. He told Me to read these prayers for the following days and then see what happen's. I did. I let my hand write, and it came out: "I, Yahweh, am guiding you." four days in the row.

Lord Jesus, I have done the priest's will; I stopped writing except letting these five words which came out after praying. I stopped You from writing to obey the priest. I want to ask you Lord, why, why did You ask him since you knew what will happen and what a lot of sufferings he would give me !

♥ *I am with you, daughter, I asked him because I want him to learn. I want him to start to understand My Riches. I am Infinite Wealth!*
"Learn that I, Jesus Christ, am giving this guidance for My children. It is I, who is guiding Vassula. Do not reject My given blessings. My messages cry out for Peace and Love, I want My children to fill up My sanctuaries, I want them to turn to Me. I want them to live holy. I come to shine on this dark world; I want to revive them and tell them that My Word is Alive! I want them to remember My Word which they put aside, I want to remind them how much I love them. I want to enkindle their hearts; I want to tell them to love each other as I love them. I love you, son; understand that by trying to stop Vassula, you are unwillingly damaging My Church. I am the Lord Jesus Christ whom you love. I know you are doing this in good faith, but so was Saul before I came to tell him that what he believed right ♥ *was but persecuting Me; you believe that the charisma I, Jesus, gave to My daughter is from evil; believe Me, son; do not feel frightened, for I am telling you again that it is My Will having Vassula learning from Me. She is flourishing now; and later on her fruits will feed many lost souls. You will one day understand son.[1] I, Jesus Christ, love you."*

The priest after having read this, blamed me saying its evil and divinations.

I know, narrate Me by saying to him: "Divinations are for fools; inspirations are for blessed children. Divinations bear no fruits; inspiration bear good fruits feeding many". Regain your courage, daughter; Wisdom awakes My children. I God love you.

---

[1]Prediction came true.

The priest gave me a lot of sufferings like God predicted to me on the 16th, he sent me pamphlets with all sorts of theories, to prove it's evil. He also sent me as God predicted a theory about subconscious mind, and occultism and satanism, plus a letter telling me to destroy the writings and warn people that it was all from evil, for my good and for the others. I told him that I obeyed his wish, his wish to pray those three prayers and that I did not write to see the result. But I do not think he believed me, because he went to tell the other priest (who believes they are from God the writings and who supports me) that the writings are satanic, and that I am not even reading the three prayers he asked me to! He alarmed a lot the other priests, so the one who supports me asked me to leave him the latest two books to read. The following day, having made his own opinion, told me to continue writing. Yet I know the one who believes it's evil, I know he does it because of the love of the church, to protect the church. I only wish he would see clearer, he wants to save me too believing it is evil. I hope one day he will understand.

I pray to St Mary.

What am I doing wrong?
O daughter, how I pain for you!
Am I doing wrong if I desire the others to love God and show them His message?

No, you are doing nothing wrong. I am Mary, Mother of Sorrows; Vassula, I am near you always. Be with Us; come to Us for consolation. They do not understand Our Riches. They have closed their hearts forever. You are one of the many signs we have given them, but they do not seem to understand. God encouraged you to hear His call. Vassula, every time you bring a soul near God, God is pleased with you. My Son Jesus and I are always beside you. Be careful, because evil is furious with you. Evil is trying to discourage you. Their way of fighting you is to add wrong words to mislead you. Remember always this, and never forget it; it is their weapon against you. I am near you protecting you. ♥
Would I be able to recognize the evil?
♥ I will always tell you; trust Me, Jesus has trained you to recognize Him. ♥
Why am I attacked?
I will explain this to you. ♥ My child, understand that you are being exposed in Hades[1] because your love to God is healing many lost[2] souls; that is why you are attacked.[3] I am near you protecting you; I have now told you this so that you may understand why you receive the wrong word. You are healing them with your love you have for Jesus and your Holy Father.
Am I working in this way too?

---

[1]Purgatory.
[2]Strayed and still living on earth.
[3]I am attacked by demons while writing.

Yes, you are healing them with your love. Do not let men influence you to submit in their theories; every time you are told to stop writing, remember how you were unaware and living in darkness. Many of our children do not recognize Our signs anymore. God has chosen you to be His bearer; please Him and hear Him. ♥

Thank you Saint Mary. May God bless you.
Peace be with you.

YOU ARE FREE TO CHOOSE

Jesus?
I Am.

Vassula I love you to a degree you are unable to grasp. How I suffer to watch my children so arid. How can they forget the love I have for them. I laid out My Life for them. Beloved, be near Me and feel Me. I will come to you in the appointed time to deliver you, but first you have a task to accomplish. I, God, have already revealed Wisdom to bless all mankind. O daughter, one day you will understand fully how I work. Do not fear, for I, God, love you.

Daughter, it is I, Jesus. I want you to read the three prayers every time before you write with Me, because they keep away evil. Believe Me, they are powerful prayers. ♥ Do you still want to work for Me?

Jesus, if I say no, what will you do?
You are free to choose. Do not fear. I will not take away the charisma I gave you. I will always meet you to tell you how much I love you. ♥
No, Jesus. I have already said that I am willing to work for You. Why should I change my word, you remember?
I am pleased with your answer, daughter; remain near, Me, and I will guide you.
Jesus, have I hurted You at anytime?

Yes, you have. I was hurt when you forgot how I came to save you from darkness, but I have forgiven you. I know how much you love Me. ♥ I am your Bridegroom, do not forget; do not forget either that by being My bride we share everything. Vassula, I am bearing My Cross of Peace and Love on My weary shoulders. Take It, beloved, for a while. I will place It on your shoulders, liberating Me from My burden. I want you near Me, so that I am able to unload My Cross on you. I want you near Me, because I know you understand how I suffer. ♥ *When you will feel My Cross, you will suffer too. I am your Bridegroom, and I will share My sufferings too with you. I will feel rested whenever you liberate Me from My burden. Before you accepted Me, I was near you all the time, watching every movement you made. Beloved, I called you so many times, but you were unaware of my Presence. Now, finally you heard Me and came to Me; why then do you doubt.?*

Doubts after my contact with the priest.

Every time you are weak, doubting; remember what I have just told you. Bear My Cross of Peace and Love, and do not leave Me. Come and pray with Me.

Jesus prayed with me. He was looking upwards while praying.

Jesus, You know how much I love You. I will help You carry Your Cross and unburden You. We can share it.

Daughter, how I always wanted to hear you tell Me this. Come, beloved, let us continue our way. ♥

Jesus was <u>so</u> pleased, happy.

Next day, I heard my name. Jesus was calling me incessantly. I was painting. I threw the brushes in the air; got up; and ran to the desk.

Vassula, Vassula, Vassula, I, Jesus, called you. O Vassula, how I love you! Glorify Me, be with Me always. Every time you love Me with such fervor, I feel glorified. Delight Me always, hearing Me like now. ♥ *Remember, I am with you soon. I am going to take you near Me soon, beloved, because I love you to a degree you can never imagine. But first you must deliver My Message to all nations as you are doing now; then I will soon fetch you. I will take you here where I am and will have you near Me forever. I, Jesus Christ, love you.* ♥ *I have given you this Grace, Vassula; I have blessed you; I will never take away what I give. Daughter, will you revive My Church?*

Oh Jesus, You ask me something that I am unable to do for You!

Trust Me!

I will cling on You and depend on You entirely; You're my Teacher.

Glorify Me. I will lead you. ♥

I HAVE CHOSEN YOU TO BE MY BEARER

January 23, 1987

O Vassula, how I love you! Come to Me. I am your Eternal Father. Feel My Love I have for My children! I guided you to love Me; I it is, who showed you the Way. I am a God of love, I am a God of Peace, I am God of Mercy, I am Meek, ♥ *I am the Good Shepherd, I am a Forgiving Father. How could I see you lost without coming to your rescue? I count each one of you. The Good Shepherd will lay down His Life for His sheep. I am an Abyss of Forgiveness; I will never abandon you.* ♥

Later:

If I stopped writing, Jesus, what happens?

Vassula, even if you stopped writing, I am always with you, guiding you. I gave you this charisma to meet Me in this way and teach you. I have asked you if you want to work for Me, and your reply pleased Me. Vassula, I like it when you hesitate. You are beginning to learn to think before deciding. I am your Teacher; accept My guidance. I am guiding you to stay aware of evil seeking the ruin of souls by feeding them her vanity. I am teaching you to understand how treacherous evil can be. I will teach you to accept; I will teach you to be humble, honest with yourself, faithful to Me. I will feed you with humility. ♥ I am reminding you that I am not favouring you from others. My guidance, is to teach you to improve and purify your soul. Do not think for one moment that I gave you this charisma because I love you more than the rest of My children. I gave you this Grace to feed you and others who are in <u>desperate need</u>. ♥ I am the Lord, Jesus Christ, the Good Shepherd who watches over His flock. I come to show you the way back; I come to shine on you and give you hope. Vassula, it is true; I have assessed you before you were born. I have chosen you to be My bearer, revealing My Message to all mankind. ♥ Are you hesitating because I asked you before to be My bride?
Yes, Lord.
You have already accepted, remember?
I know, Jesus. But on second thought, I can't, not that I don't want to, but I'm not worthy to be your bride. How! how could I have accepted just like that, without realizing its value!
Vassula, I can teach you to become worthy of Me. ♥
Even if I am worthy, that's not enough.
Why?
Because it's not just being worthy; there is more than that.

I know, to be worthy is not enough, but I will teach you to be worthy and holy. You will have to work and earn it. ♥ Come, I will help you. You are going to remain My bride, a bride who needs forming. I have accepted you as you are because I love you, but you must let Me form you as I want you to be. I will feed you to grow. I have revealed to you how evil works, delivering amounts of

information[1]. ♥ *I want you to stay awake reading them carefully.*
Learn to accept. Every time I see you weak, bound to fall into traps I will rush to
your rescue. Do not take my guidance as a treatment of penitence; I am guiding
you so that you do not fall. I do not want to lose you; invoke Me in your prayers;
pray more. ♥

WERE YOU ABLE ON YOUR OWN TO LOVE ME?

January 24, 1987

Vassula, Vassula, little one, beloved of My Sacred Heart, do not fear. I love you.
Daughter, were you able on your own to love Me?
No, Jesus.
You have learned to love Me because I approached you, enlightening you. I
converted you by awakening you. Vassula, do you know why I love you?
No, I don't know Jesus.
I will tell you then. I love you because you are helpless, wretched, and guilty.
Children are My weakness. I love them because they let Me form them. Vassula,
come and abide in My Sacred Heart, where in its depths you will find Peace and
will feel My ardent Love I have for all of you. You will be able to tell them of My
Love for them. Behold, every day that goes by, you come closer to Me!

CHILDREN ARE MY WEAKNESS

January 30, 1987

Peace be with you. Every time you feel weak, come to Me and I will give you
Strength. Vassula, do you know why I chose you?
No, I don't, Jesus.
I will tell you then; I chose you because you are helpless and by far the most
wretched from any man I know of. Wretchedness attracts Me because I can console
you. You are helpless and insufficient, unable of mastering any language.
Lord, if I am that bad, why have you chosen me to take this guidance?
Have I not told you before? Children are My weakness because they let Me form
them. I have chosen you to manifest My Love through you, a frail flower unable

---

[1] Pamphlets sent by the priest whom Jesus uses as His instrument, sending me the
books Jesus wants me to read.

to grow on its own. A flower which I found in the middle of wilderness and which I took and transplanted in My garden of delights, letting it grow under My Light. All I ask from you is love. Love me and be faithful to Me. I want fidelity from you; I want every drop of love you have in your heart to fill up My Heart. I thirst for love, for I am Master of Love, so all I ask from you is to love Me. When you love someone, do you not burn with desire to be with him every second of your life?

Yes, that's true.

So what more natural than giving yourself entirely to Me? Come, come to Me. I am your Father; I know you are helpless without Me, wretched when left by yourself, and weak on your own. Let Me form you so that through you I may deliver My Message. O daughter, how much you will have to learn!

I know. I know, I know nothing.

Vassula, I love you, have no doubt, I will answer your question. I do not only choose those who are My brides by choice; I also come and choose those who do not know Me. I come and knock on every door. I knock and wait, hoping that I would be heard. Vassula, I long for every soul to receive Me and welcome Me. I love you all.

I thought you prefer to be among religious souls who make you feel always happy.

Vassula, I love My religious souls and My priests and nuns as much as My other children. I love everyone including sinners and those who persecute Me. Vassula, I approach everyone irrespective to what they are and how much knowledge they have acquired in their lifetime. I can raise the dead with My Power. I am giving you My Strength to meet Me in this way; for I am Lord, and the smaller you are, the easier I can handle. You know quite well that I Suffice by Myself. Your insufficiency will glory My Suffice. Your wretchedness is of little account in My Eyes. Leave yourself to Me, and let My Hands form you. I have not chosen someone of authority, for My Authority suffices in Itself. My appeal for Peace and Love will come through you, showing My Mercy to all mankind. I will manifest Myself through you. I ask nothing of My children that they have not already. If they have but faults and sins, let them give them to Me, and I will purify them; I will unburden them; I will forgive them; I will not blame them, I will only love them. I love all those who fall and come to Me asking for forgiveness; I love them still more. I will never reject them even if they fall millions of times; I will be there to forgive them and wash in My Blood their iniquities, never will I weary in pardoning them, for I am a God of Love and Mercy. I am full of pity for the weak. My Heart is Holy and an Abyss of Forgiveness.

Do no more, daughter. I love you. Trust Me, Vassula, and all I have to say will be written.

I HAVE CHOSEN A NOTHING

Later On:

Do you know that I am happy to have you near Me? I, Jesus, love you from the depths of My Heart, and because of this Love I have for you, evil hates you. They will be setting traps for you. I will be near you to warn you.
I don't want to fall!
I will not see you fall; I will be near you to sustain your falls.
I don't understand why I received messages before my "formation".
Vassula, I, God, gave you My Messages so that many would profit from them. If you only knew how valuable souls are to me.[1] I know what you have in mind; I will answer your question. Hear Me, I have come to you to give My Message of Peace and Love. I have chosen a mere child, unfit for My task, helpless and small, without prestige, <u>a nothing</u>, to manifest through you My passionate Love and teach those that still do not understand the Riches of My Heart. I suffer to watch My teachers so withdrawn from what is heavenly, and their indifference they give to My Blessings; ♥ for charisma is a blessing. How their hearts have become coarse, leading to spiritual deafness and aridity. Once more I come appealing for Peace and Love; but how many more will reject Me? How many more of you will not respond? How many of you, especially My teachers, would turn away their eyes in the other direction, looking for Me?
O men of little faith, how little do you know Me! Have you forgotten that I am Infinite Wealth? Why are you surprised at the kind of instruments I use? My Power is great and limitless, and I will let My words be known through wretched souls.
Vassula, many will ask Me for a sign that this guidance comes from Me, but the sign that I will give is you.
I have delivered you from evil, awakening you; I raised you up and lifted you to My Heart, pouring on you many of My Works. Accept what I give you, for Wisdom is leading you. Vassula, I love you; little one, you are Mine. Daughter, give Me love and give Me rest; let Me rest in your heart; accept Me Vassula, do not deny Me Vassula. Do you know how many years I was waiting for you to accept Me? Oh How alienated you were from My Heart. Have I ever told you how I felt then?
I don't really remember, Jesus.
I will tell you. I have been fearing for you. You had drifted away from Me, and My Heart was utterly torn with sorrow. Vassula, how then could you resist My appeal, beloved? I have been waiting for you <u>so</u> many years, Vassula; accept My love; My love heals you.

---

[1] It seem like God did not want to spare a minute.

It's not that I refuse you Jesus; I just feel more comfortable to give and love rather than to receive. I think you know me.

I felt sad because I hurt Jesus without willing. Jesus immediately felt this.

Come with Me; I have a secret I want to tell you. ♥ *Vassula, do you know why I love you?*

Yes, you told me already.

There is still one more reason; I love you because you love My children. Come now nearer to Me; will you let Me enter your heart?

Yes, do, Jesus.

How happy you made Me, for I know I can rest in you. Do not deny Me again, for I but long to enter hearts.

You will probably find stains.

All impurities I will find, I <u>will</u> wash away. Beloved, My Blood will purify you.

MY HEART IS AN ABYSS OF LOVE

February 1, 1987

Vassula, it I Jesus Christ. I love you. Any messages bearing blames or harsh words, know that it is not coming from Me. I am Love, Love, Love. My Heart is an Abyss of Love. The guidance I am giving you, is adjusted for you. Regard yourself as a toddler who has but started her first steps; no one expects a toddler to walk with confidence and self-assurance. My guidance is for a beginner; I teach you in gradual steps, and every step you take with Me I bless. I am your Father, helping you and teaching you, My child, to walk with Me. Here is My answer to your thought: I love you all in the same way.

You speak of specially chosen souls.

Are you not a chosen one? I love you all. Daughter, I have longed to have you near Me. How I longed for you to love Me! How I long for the rest of My beloved children to love Me! I call them; I spend all day and night behind their doors, waiting, hoping for a response. I watch them incessantly, My Eyes never leaving them; I watch them, filled up with sorrow. If they only knew in what state of poverty their souls are; if they only knew how they are damaging and hurting their souls!

I am near you; I am calling you to come to Me; do not be afraid; I will not reproach you; I do not call you to reproach your sins; I call you to meet Me, if it is but for just a few minutes; come to Me, you poor souls; come and meet Me and get to know your loving Father. He Himself will feed you with His own Body, He will slacken your thirst with His own Blood; He will heal you if you are sick, He will comfort you if you are distressed; He will envelop you with His Love, and warm you if you feel cold. Do not refuse Me. I am Love, and I love you in spite of your wickedness. I say I love you even if you despise Me. I am a God full of pity, always ready to receive you and let you live in My Heart.

Daughter, how I pain to watch them slumbering while they are slowly sinking deeper and deeper in vile depths of sin. If they could only know how their iniquities render their souls!

I tell you that your life on earth is but a passing shadow, but your life in Heaven is forevermore. There, you will live eternally near your Creator in His Glory, for let Me remind you that you are His own children. ♥

Vassula, I will call all those who persecute Me and defile My name in My following Message.

Yes Lord.

MY FATHER CREATED YOU BECAUSE OF LOVE

February 2, 1987

O daughter, all I ask from all of you is love. My Father created you because of Love; He gave His only Son because of Love. I suffered for you and died on the Cross for Love; I saved you from dying because of love; so why, why do some of you hate Me and persecute Me? Are you hating Me because of My given Laws? Am I preventing you to live free and fall into rebellion? Have you perhaps not heard of Me because no one was there to teach you? Thus developing your own laws, languishing for earthly wealth and pleasures, following your own inclinations? Children, beloved ones, this is the beginning of your hatred for Me; it is because you do not know Me. Come then, and meet Me; I am Love; believe in Me. If you tell Me that you do not know Me, I tell you that I knew you before you were born, and I have consecrated you. If you tell Me that you hate Me, I tell you I love you. If you have sinned, I have forgiven you. If you have profaned My Name, I have shown My Mercy on you. If you have wounded Me, I still love you and offer you to share My Kingdom in Heaven. In spite of your iniquities, I forgive you fully.

Vassula, I love you; have rest; I will continue dictating to you later on. ♥

MY LAW IS A LAW OF LOVE

Later On:

I am here; it is I, Jesus Christ. Let Me dictate to you, daughter, My Words. Hear Me now and discern Me.
Are you fearing Me? Are you denying Me because My Eyes see through you and can read all that your soul has done? Do not fear Me, for I have already forgiven you. My Blood was shed for your salvation. I was on earth in flesh; I lived among sinners, healing the sick and raising the dead. I have not forsaken you, for I am still among you, healing you. Come to Me to be healed. I will raise your souls to Me, I will teach you to love Me and to love one another. If you are weak, My Strength will sustain you, if you are lost, I will be there and show you the Way. My Law is a <u>Law of Love</u>; follow it; by following it, I will open your hearts to be able to receive Me. I will inspire you, I will teach you how to love, how to forgive, how to be holy and live holy. Come then, beloved ones; come and learn from Me; I am Love; I am Peace; I am Mercy; I am Meek and Humble; I am Forgiveness; I love you all. ♥

I AM YOUR DEVOUT KEEPER

February 3, 1987

Lord, I feel void empty, not as usual, cold as a stone.
Vassula, I it is who trims your branches, giving strength to you. I am your Devout Keeper. By trimming you, I strengthen you so that your fruit may be plenty.

LITTLE ONE, DO YOU KNOW WHY I LOVE YOU?

February 4, 1987

Little one, do you know why I love you? Here is one more reason: because you are My flower, allowing Me to trim you, allowing Me to feed you, and allowing My Light to shine on you. I am helping you to grow to bear the fruits of Peace and Love. I am your Lord and Master.

PURIFY YOURSELVES, FOR THE TIME IS NEAR

February 5, 1987

Beloved, I am Yahweh, and My ecclesiastical Messages are from Me; I have fed you; I am forming you, daughter. I am the Almighty; have no fear. Listen, daughter; fulfil My Word. I came and delivered you from evil to be in My Light, for you are to be My bearer. I will give you strength, I am always beside you; never have any doubt.

My incapacity is great, and I am afraid of the circumstances.

You need not fear, for My Power will envelop you, thus giving you My Strength to tread on My foes. Be on your guard, for many will try and discourage you, saying that this guidance is not from Me. I know how little you are and helpless, so be near Me and let Wisdom lead you. All authority will come from Me. Understand that Wisdom comes from Me. All those that have eyes, let them see; all those that have a heart, let them understand that it is I, Yahweh Sabaoth who speaks. I have never forsaken you; I am delivering Wisdom to re-establish My given Word. I come to remind you all of My Love for you, blessing you all. I do not want to see you lost. Woe to the unwise! Purify yourselves, for the time is near. Listen to My Words, for in doing what I ask you, I will forgive you. I am guiding you to live in Peace and Love, for I am a God of Peace and Love. Live holy; pray for forgiveness, and I will bless you. You are all My children whom I have created with Love. Come, bind My words in your hearts, for it is I, Yahweh, who guides you.

Lord, I am helpless and do not know anything. I only see a big mountain in front of me.

Fear not, Vassula, for you are not the first helpless messenger I raised, giving My word. Have faith in Me; trust Me; I am guiding you.

LET THEM KNOW, TELL THEM OF MY LOVE

February 9, 1987

Peace be with you. I love you, child, I am Yahweh. I have chosen you mainly because I willed it, but also because you are so helpless.

I love you Father, very much.

I know, and I love you too, daughter. Hear Me; have you felt as happy as now before you loved Me?

No, never!

Love Me, Vassula, I it is who taught you how to love Me. ♥ *Are you willing to progress?*

Yes, Father, so that I am able to glorify you. I want to do all that you ask, because I do want you glorified.

Vassula, I will progress you. I want to warn you of evil. They hate you and are constantly setting traps for you. I am near you, guarding you, so do not fear. Vassula, I love you and I love all My children. My love is like a consuming flame, constantly ablaze! My Love is a jealous love. I thirst for love. Fear not, for it is Love I am talking about, little one. I hold you, and your littleness delights Me. Little one, through your frailty, I will manifest My appeal for Peace and Love. I will fill you with My words; I will breathe into you My revelations. Little one, cling to Me, trust Me, and love Me with fervour. Let them know, tell them of My Love I have for them.

MY FATHER DELIGHTS IN CHILDREN

February 10 1987

♥ *Vassula, it is I, Jesus Christ. I am with you, beloved. Do you know that I am guiding you through Hades?[1] Have no fear; My Light is on you, protecting you from evil.[2]*
Having you exposed in Hades, many souls are healing. I have taught you to love Me. Your love for Me is healing them. I use your love as a remedy to cure them. Heal them, Vassula; heal them; you are bearing My Cross with Me, Vassula; these works are Heavenly Works that My Father is revealing to you. Many Heavenly Works are still hidden and are but mysteries to you.

Many people will not accept this, Jesus; they will blame it on my fantasy.

Vassula, how many among them have understood fully My Father's Work on earth?

Some Works are not understood and are still mysteries.

How then will they understand what is Heavenly? Vassula, all Wisdom is given to mere children. My Father delights in children. Be happy, daughter, and praise My Father for being good to you. Daughter, be His bearer and glorify Him. Do not worry; I am guiding you; work in this way; I am your Teacher. I will continue forming you, beloved; I am forming you as well as My other children. Go in peace, and remember that you are guided by Me; hear Me; I love you, and I want you to be with Me.
Vassula, I am pleased that your faith has augmented. Purify yourself by eating Me and drinking Me.

I will, Jesus; I will go to Holy Communion.

---

[1]Purgatory.
[2]When Satan wants to attack me all the time and stop me from writing this revelation.

Come to Me; all My Love covers you; I love you, child.
Jesus, I love You, and I'll fight for You.
Fight I do not want! For I am Peace, and you will work with peace, for Peace. Fill Me with joy, remaining as close to Me as possible. Will you kiss My Feet?

I took a picture of Jesus, kissing His Feet.

I love you; go in peace.

I SUFFICE BY MYSELF

February 11, 1987

Vassula, it is I, Jesus Christ. Daughter, your sufferings will be Mine and My Sufferings will be yours. You will share all that I have, yes, even My Sufferings. I will be near you, consoling you when you need Me; but I want to be consoled in return when I am suffering.
Jesus, You don't really <u>need</u> anybody, especially me!
No, I do not need anybody; I suffice by Myself, but do I not share everything I have with you? I am your Saviour, your Healer, your Father, your Spouse; I am your God who will never, ever abandon you.

In the evening, while in the hall downstairs and about to climb the stairs, with my hands full of glasses, I very clearly discerned a huge, dark cross on the upper level of the stair-case; huge it was. Jesus hanged on it, moaning with agony, covered in bruises and blood. I had to go by it; I didn't know what to do while passing it, I heard Jesus call, saying: "Oh, help Me, Vassula; come near Me."
I ran quickly up; left those glasses on the table, and ran and took my scrapbook, and Jesus wrote:
"My agony is great; My sufferings are many; will you not help Me, I who died for you? I am nailed on My Cross, and I can not come to you; so come, I want you nearer. Vassula, how I love you all; heal My children; call them; have them love Me. Be blessed, be near Me; I love you".

While He wrote this down He made me feel all alarmed, and I had not realized that in a few seconds I was covered with sweat.

Vassula, I, Jesus suffer, and you discerned fully My Cross and I on It. I want you to feel My Agony; suffer with Me; daughter, live in Me, and I will let you feel My pierced Heart, wounded by the lance, and wounded by so many beloved souls. I love you; would you deny Me? I who suffered and died for you; will your heart have the courage to resist Me? I have suffered for Love; I have called you out of love; I blessed you; I fed you; so now, since I chose you, I will expect you to console Me, to love Me ardently; I will expect you to respond to Me. Vassula, have no fear; abandon yourself fully to Me; yes, surrender completely, abandoning yourself entirely to Me, and leave Me free to do with you whatsoever I want to.

I have already agreed to work for you, so now you can do what you please with me, Lord.

Yes, surrender; I love you; it pleases Me to hear you surrendering; never, ever refuse Me, for My Love for you is unlimited. I will continue My teachings in giving you a secret. Vassula, take your scrapbook; fear not, for My Teachings come from Wisdom; all mysteries have not yet been revealed. All Works are given to those who know how to love Me.

I will take my scrapbook now... Jesus gave me the secret. Then he said: *"I will reveal many more hidden Works to you."*

That was the third secret.

Every day that goes by, you come closer to Me.

What does this mean?

It means that I will soon be with you.

Death does not scare me at all!

I AM TEACHING YOU STEP BY STEP

February 12, 1987

God Almighty, I do not want to fall into vanity or self-interest. I ask you to help me! I want to remain a nothing; I want to remain plain and give You all the glory!

Vassula, I am Yahweh; I love you. All authority will come from Me, little one. I will always remind you of your littleness; I will let you understand how I work; find peace, Vassula; I am soon with you.

I felt relieved knowing that God will always remind me of my nothingness!

I had an awful day: only doubts that this is quite impossible, and that the whole thing is untrue. I felt that what is happening is not happening, yet I heard God calling me; it is like it's absolutely real, and yet nothing real. I suddenly felt like as really the most wretched among men. What is really happening?

Vassula, have you forgotten how you were a year ago? My beloved, let Me remind you: when I, Yahweh, was passing among the dead,[1] I saw you there among the wicked; they were holding you, tormenting you. I saw you lying there struggling on your own, your soul close to death. I felt full of pity for you[2]. You remembered My works of old times; and you realized then that I could be your Refuge, and so I heard your plea from earth. Daughter, I always loved you, but you had forgotten Me. I yearned to be loved by you, to hear you call Me "Father"; for how many years I have been outside your door waiting, waiting that one day you might hear Me.... I was at hand's reach; yes, I was so near you; then, My Heart could not resist your plea. I came full of joy. Finally, you called Me; I lifted you to My Breast, daughter, and I healed your wounds. I taught you how to love Me, I taught you how to receive Me by elevating you, and I let My Light shine upon you. My flower, do not despair; I am teaching you step by step, with the vocabulary that you understand. You are asking Me why has part of My guidance been written before your formation. I will answer your question after you reply to My question: do you know how valuable just one single soul is to Me?

I know it is valuable, but how much, that I do not know My God.

I will tell you then how valuable souls are to Me, thus replying to your question. A soul for Me is as valuable as to have written part of My guidance[3] just for that single soul who would have had no other opportunity before his departure. Do you understand now?

Yes, I do, and I know whom You mean.

I love you, daughter; have no <u>doubt</u> that this guidance is from Me. I will always remind you who awakened you from your slumber. ♥ I love you; be always sure of My Love. Work in peace and do not forget Me.

ALL I WANT FROM YOU IS LOVE

February 13, 1987

Peace be with you. I am here; it is I, Jesus, who guides you; have no fear. Unite in Me, Vassula; all I want from you is love.

I am worrying about the Messages. I feel responsible. I don't know how to work.

I am Self-Sufficient, and I am able to help all My children without your help, but as a Spouse, I want to share everything. Do not worry, for I am Strength; beloved, lean on Me, and let <u>Me</u> lead. Remember that it is I who give you this force to meet Me. I ask from you to love Me faithfully; love Me fervently; comfort Me when I

---

[1] Spiritually dead.
[2] At the beginning of this, I was three months among the wicked, who tried to chase me away, dismaying me.
[3] A guidance that took me around six month.

ask for comfort, for there are many among you who wound Me; such a multitude of sins are committed daily, grieving My Soul, embittering Me, filling up My Chalice with sorrows; how have they forgotten Me! Vassula, when a Spouse feels grieved, where would he turn to for consolation, but to his bride who loves him.
I will console you if I can, but what to do? I who is, I know, unworthy, probably hurting you unwillingly, insufficient, and embarrassed to talk to you, filled with indignity!

♥ *I know that all that you said is true, but have I not chosen you, knowing all your weakness? I love you, Vassula, and all I want from you is a response to My Love.*
I love you a lot. You are constantly in my mind. I live for You. I love You; I cannot measure how much, but you can. I can only ask You to teach me to love You more, so that it becomes immeasurable.
Beloved, pose your head on Me, and let Me anoint you with Purity to become one of My saturated flowers, having absorbed Me. Come, I will feed you, from My Hand you will eat. I will teach you to love Me more.

WISDOM HAS BROUGHT YOU UP

February 14, 1987

After reading "The Memorare" of Saint Bernard (a small prayer to Saint Mary).

All the guidance is from God. Vassula, can you hear Me? Listen again, Vassula, it is I, Saint Mary; do not fear Me, Vassula, I know your difficulties to realize that all this is really happening, but I ask from you to trust God, augment your faith. He is working in you, child; do not restrain yourself from submission; abandon yourself in His Hands; and do what He asks from you. I am near you, helping you; have peace, for He is guiding you. Vassula, Jesus is forming you to become strong to be able to resist temptation. He feeds you, giving you all that you are lacking. Remember, daughter, Wisdom has brought you up; do realize why.
It is not just for me all this, it is meant for others too?

Yes, you are being formed to be God's bearer.
I do not know how to be God's bearer.

God has preached to you and has taught you to love Him. Trust Him, for His Riches are innumerable and His Mercy unfathomable; He loves you with ineffable tenderness and watches over you with loving Eyes. Every Heavenly word lives forever.

I have to learn to love You more.

I will teach you; have peace.

I GIVE EVEN TO THE MOST WRETCHED SOULS

Later on:

Vassula, it I, Jesus. I am giving you Strength to meet Me. Progress with Me, for I will institute My given words, so that many can read them and profit from them. Daughter, when My given guidance will be established, I shall prepare you to meet Me; I long to have you near Me. Vassula, look at Me.

I looked in Jesus' Face. He looked straight at me.

Are you happy meeting Me in this way?
Yes, very; I don't deserve this charisma at all.
Accept it. *Accept what I give; I give even to the most wretched souls.* *Vassula, have you heard that I give Wisdom to mere children and not to the learned and clever.*
Yes, I have; why is this?

Because children are My weakness; they let Me form them. I choose unworthy souls to form, ones who know little or next to nothing. I will supply you, Vassula, for I am wealthy; with Me you will lack nothing. I love you; do you realize how happy you make Me every time we meet? I feel happy having you finally near Me. Would not a father rejoice having found his lost child? You were lost, and My Heart was utterly torn with sorrow; you had wandered away, leaving Me in despair. I went to look for you and found you. How then would I not rejoice having you near Me? Vassula, near Me you will learn; I will teach you all virtues to enable you to glorify Me. My child, learn to absorb the Dew of Righteousness; learn to glorify Me; learn from Wisdom. I love you; leave now in Peace, and call Me when you wish. Let us pray together.

We prayed.

♥ *Be now My companion and keep Me in your heart.*

BE MINE ENTIRELY

February 15, 1987

I love you, but maybe I love you in the wrong way. What is right or wrong, I don't know. I worship you.

Vassula, love is love; I want you to love Me without restraint. I am your Holy Father who loves you intimately; approach Me and love Me intimately; I want to be intimate with you. Do not fear; I want all your love. Vassula, I want you today to repent.

Should I repent to You now?

Yes, repent; I am listening.

I did.

Yes, daughter, I forgive all your sins, for they are many. Vassula, do you know that I am He who taught My teachers to repent? They are My instructions; I have given to My teachers the authority to have My children confess to them. Child, I wrote it.

I tried to erase "confess"; I was against confessions, but my hand was blocked by God.

Vassula, refuse Me nothing. I will demand from you many things. Are you ready to follow your God and Saviour?

I will, as long as I <u>recognize</u> that it is coming from You. I will follow you because I love You.

Vassula, never fear Me, trust Me. I am preparing you to face bigger trials. Are you ready to follow Me?

With your help, I will be.

Have no fear, for I am near you, supporting you. Daughter, leave yourself entirely in My Hands; let Me use you, beloved, for healing souls. Let Me bind you to Me with love's chains; let Me feel you are entirely Mine; let Me who is your Creator possess you. I have longed for your love; let My love enkindle your heart now. Be Mine entirely. I longed for you; I long for you; do you never long for Me, Vassula?

I do, or I think I do.

Vassula, beloved, by giving yourself to Me will both glorify Me and purify you. I now bind you to Me. I, God the most High, will be with you till the end. I tell you, truly, that I have chosen you, knowing you are nothing, helpless, wretched and sinful; but in spite of all your faults, I love you. Yes, I love you all in spite of your iniquities.

Lord, did you bind me now?

Yes, I have, I love you. It is out of Love I want you always near Me. Beloved, hear Me; My bonds are bonds of Love; they are bonds of purity. I love you; let My children understand how much I can love them. My clemency has no limits; My Love is a consuming Flame, enkindling every heart which receives Me. Daughter, leave now and remember that I am leading you; remember who purified you.

I couldn't understand, so I hesitated.

Have you forgotten? Have I not anointed you Myself?

Yes, Lord, on the thirteenth.

Vassula, I have Myself given you My Bread and Wine; remember, I chose the time for you to purify you, child.

True: for in church, I fully discerned Jesus by the Tabernacle chanting with the others. He Himself gave me the Bread and Wine, taking the place of the priest.

Love Me; let us work together.

This reminded me of the first time I took Holy Communion in this church. Again it was done in a mystical way. I was with Karl the priest; God had sent me to him to get Holy Communion. He was not sure whether he should give it to me or not because it was asked in this mystical way. Then Karl said that he will talk to God, pray but not aloud, so that I won't hear what he says, and I should let my hand write from God the answers. God wrote: *"I will"*. I asked Karl what he asked. He said he had asked God whether he should make me give my confession to him. God answered that He will.[1] Karl, without hesitation, told me to simply come for Holy Communion in four days. In the meantime God asked me to repent. I did not know how, so he explained to me what to say. I did it with Him. Then, the next day I had Holy Communion.

I WANT YOU TO BE INTIMATE WITH ME

February 16, 1987

I started to realize that really I can't live without God anymore. I think He really attached me.

I am Yahweh; child, I it is; turn to Me. I love you, and because of this great love I have for you, I hold you. Do not fear, child; hear Me; because of My elate love

---

[1] Exceptionally this time.

I have for you, I bind you to Me. Lean on Me; I want you to need Me, Vassula.
Do you love us so much?
O daughter, have you not felt My love?

Yes, of course I did, it's unbelievable!

*My Love for you wants to consume you. I feel glorified to feel how attached you
are to Me. I, for My part, love you inexhaustibly, and I will not part from you
ever, but I have also made sure that neither will you. I made sure of our union,
see? I delight to have prevailed. I desired us to be united for ever, you needing Me,
loving Me, and bound forever to Me; and I bound to you, leaving Me free to love
you without restrain and reign over you. I who created you, and I who nursed you,
I who consecrated you, and I who was first to lay eyes on you, I who filled you
with My Spirit, willed it; for I, Vassula, am your God, Yahweh, who brought you
up. ♥ I made sure that the bonds I have attached you to Me, are for eternity; you
will be unable to detach yourself from Me, for I am the Most High.*
It is frightening even though I love you, Lord. Your Power and Wisdom are great!
*Why Vassula, what have you to fear? Am I not Lord of Love? I will care for you;
I will soothe you if in pain; I will cover you with My blessings; I will provide what
you lack; I am Infinite Wealth. You need not fear with Me. I am He who holds the
earth's foundations; leave Me free to do with you whatsoever I want. I am so
happy having you near Me, you so frail and weak, for I know that your heart will
leave Me do as I please with you. Fear not, for I am your Heavenly Father, and
I love you beyond any human understanding. I am Yahweh, and if you have not
heard afore, I am telling you now that I am known to be Faithful, and My word
stands secure. Child, I have revived you from death to let My word be written. I
have brought you up to be My bearer. Since you are to be My bearer, you have to
be formed; you must learn how I feel, how I work, and how My Love enkindles
hearts. How else would you be able to tell My beloved children? Come, feel My
Presence the way I have taught you. I love you, little one; discern Me; I want you
to be intimate with Me, Vassula. Tomorrow I will dictate you a Message teaching
My children how to be with Me. Go now and fulfill your other duties. Go in peace.*

Later on:

Vassula, write.
*You are now united with Me; you will work with Me; you will suffer with Me; you
will help Me; yes, I will share everything I have with you, and for your part, you
will do the same. Being united is being forever together, because My bonds are
eternal bonds, My elate love binds you forever to Me. My love enkindles even the
hearts out of stone and puts them ablaze, consuming them. Daughter, I have
prevailed; you need not fear, I have won your heart, beloved, and I made sure that
you will forever be Mine. O Vassula, how I longed to thrust you in the depths of
My Heart and let all the Flames of My Love utterly consume you, leaving you in*

total rapture for Me, your God.
Do You love me as much as that to have done this?
Have I not laid out My Life for you? I laid out My Life out of love; I sacrificed Myself for your salvation, out of love; I shed My Blood for you out of love. Now I made sure that you are bound to Me.
Why?
Why, have you forgotten that I am All Faithful? Having you bound to Me, I will be sure that you too will remain faithful to Me. Now that we are united, we will continue working together. I will use your love for Me to heal many souls who are bound to be engulfed in Satan's flames. You and I are going to help these souls. All you have to do is love Me fervently. There will be times where I will come to you, entrusting you with My Cross.
But I am nothing!
Vassula, remain nothing and let Me be everything you lack. Wherever I go, you will follow. Alone you will never ever be; you are now united to Me. Grow in spirit, Vassula, grow, for your task is to deliver all Messages given by Me and My Father. Wisdom will instruct you.
Yes Father!
How beautiful to hear you call Me "Father"! I longed to hear from your lips this word: "Father".

I AM FATHER OF ALL HUMANITY

February 17, 1987

Vassula, why, why were you avoiding calling Me Father? Vassula, I love being called Father. I am Father of all humanity. ♥
I love you Father.
I love you too.

HEAVENLY WORKS ARE FROM WISDOM

February 18, 1987

Peace be with you. Vassula, you need not rush; learn that I work gently. Keep close to Me. My Light covers you. Anyone who approaches you cannot touch you or harm you; My Light is upon you as a Halo of All Redemption. Your love for Me heals and saves many lost souls who are in perdition.[1]

Vassula, they are like little children left on their own, not knowing which direction to take; they are lost. When I am with them, I feed them giving them love. Some of them then follow Me; you are helping them to love Me and follow Me. I am using you, Vassula, in this way.

Should I then be patient and pray daily?

Yes, have patience with them, for they are beloved to Me; heal them; Love them, Vassula.

I am teaching you Wisdom; Heavenly Works are from Wisdom.

Understand when I am teaching you. Come, lean on Me. Do you wish to leave now?

No, Jesus, we go on.

O daughter, I love you; beloved, work with Me and glorify Me. I love your littleness; you are My saturated flower, having absorbed Me fully. Child, need Me always, for without Me, you will perish. I will give you all that you lack till the end. Let Me completely free with you, for I know what your needs are.

I felt as though I will be unable to take down God's guidance, for it is difficult, as I have all the time interruptions and insults from evil. Sometimes I feel as though God abandoned me completely to be their sport. The more it advances, the worse the insults. For a moment, I thought God left me. The insults are the worst words one can tell!

Vassula, will I ever abandon you? I am All Faithful; have you forgotten My words?

It's my fault; I am weak!

Give Me now your weakness, and My Strength will dissolve it. Come, I will sanctify you Myself; I have with you reached My Heaven, for in you I find My rest. Remember, we are united, and our bonds are bonds of Peace and Love. These cords which attach your wrists and feet to Mine, are for eternity, for, beloved, you are Mine. I Myself have purified you, uniting you to Me; I have triumphed over you. I wished that you love Me; have no fear, for I am Jesus holding you with Me. You are to be and feel My Presence. All I ask from you is love. Do you love Me?

You know I do, Jesus.

Love Me without measure; look at Me; have My peace. Is there something you want to tell Me?

Yes, Jesus. (I felt guilty for having to say this to Him.) Jesus, although I love to be with you and take this guidance, I must do other things too!

Vassula, happy are those who withdraw from their occupations and follow Me. You are indeed devoting a lot of your time writing with Me, but let Me tell you

---

[1] On earth.

something else too. I also love to see you work and accomplish minor duties, duties of small importance, as long as you do them with love. Every little work you do, no matter how small and meaningless, becomes great in My Eyes and pleases Me, as long as these small acts are done with love. Be blessed.

In the evening, we had guests, and I was counting plates, napkins, etc. I thought I had everything on my tray. I hesitated and asked, knowing Jesus was with me, "What do we need more?" He answered me without hesitation: *"We need love, Vassula."*

MY HEAVEN IS IN YOU

February 19, 1987

Vassula, allow yourself to suffer; all My chosen souls suffered. By suffering, your soul is purified. Like gold is purified in fire, so is the soul. Your suffering is in your guidance.
How in my guidance, Jesus?
Although I allow you to call Me anytime in this way, and thus be together, I also allow the gates of evil to be left open. Your guidance will not be an easy task, for you will have evil fighting you by discouraging you, in giving you the wrong word.
But Lord, Your guidance can mislead me!
No, it will never mislead you or anybody else. I have taught you to recognize Me, Vassula. I have chosen someone with an incapacity of mastering any language, one who will depend on My given words. I have taught you to hear Me; I am training your ear. Come, be patient; learn to accept; learn from Me.

I started to worry.

Vassula, all <u>will</u> be perfect! Edit: It is I, Jesus....

Doubts again!

O come! I long to tell you something. My Heaven is in you, because I feel glorified and rested.
Jesus, I love you, yes, a lot too, twenty-four hours a day. I do; even when I wake up in the night, my first thought is You. I eat, it's You; I work at home, it's You; I drive, it's You; I play tennis, and You are in my mind, and love is in my blood for You, since my body aches from love. But I cannot accept that I can give You rest, or that You find heaven in me, for what am I? A speck of dust, impossible I am; and

when You tell me this, I feel even worse in Your Presence and ashamed.

All that you said about yourself is true, but I love you and I do find rest in you. I have irrigated your heart with My Blood and placed it in Mine; I have purified it and given it My Peace and Love, beloved. Vassula, I who came to you, always wanted your love; now I have prevailed. I delight in you. Love Me without restraint, making up for those who forget Me and are but multiplying My Wounds; love Me, Vassula, healing My beloved souls, be My Heaven.

My God, I realize it is You, yet I do not think I fully realize.

Vassula, you will one day.

If I do, I think I will faint!

When My word will be established, Vassula, I have always been known to keep My word. I, Yahweh, come from above. Heaven is made by My Grace. I will fulfill My word, trust Me, Vassula, do not worry too much, beloved. Be near Me, feel Me, love Me and glorify Me. Leave the rest to Me; live in peace. I am forming you with Wisdom; have My Grace. Weary not in healing souls. Are you happy being now united to Me?

Yes, Lord, I am very happy to feel I am united to You, although I could not dare think of it.

Why, Vassula?

Why? because of my not being fit for You.

Vassula, I always longed to be united with you and be intimately close to you; nevertheless, never forget that I am your God and Holy. Vassula, will you still work for Me?

I have given my consent already. I am willing to continue working for Yahweh.

I am Yahweh, be blessed.

AMEND FOR THOSE THAT EMBITTER HIM

February 20, 1987

I read the prayer to Saint Mary, "The Memorare" of Saint Bernard.

Daughter, it is Jesus who guides you. Do not fear, Vassula. My daughter, listen to Me, your Holy Mother. I am here, present, near you; I am helping you; I love you. I will help you understand the way Jesus works, do not worry. Jesus has united you now to Him. Rejoice, Vassula. You must believe Me when I tell you that your soul heals other souls in Hades. Vassula, do as Jesus asks you; He knows your needs; all He wants from you is love. Love Him without restraint; glorify Him; amend for those that embitter Him; call Him always, telling Him you love Him; forsake Him not; accomplish all your other duties too with Love,

for love; for acts of love are what counts most for Him; no matter how little and meaningless they appear to you, they are of great value in His Eyes, and thus become great. Follow Him and repair for others who neglect Him.

Daughter, by being now united to Him, you will feel His Cross; you will feel his Heart; He will ask you to share His feelings; He will ask you to help Him; He will ask you for rest; He will ask you to share His Cross. Suffer when He suffers; rejoice when He rejoices; your sufferings will be His; comply with His wishes, for He is God. Learn to recognize Him; remember all that He taught you, for He is a Loving God, All Merciful. He loves you all with ineffable tenderness; He will never demand from you anything that would harm you. He is gentle and good; learn to recognize Him, Vassula. He is a God full of Love, never harsh; He will watch over you, protecting you from all evil; He will never abandon you Vassula. Courage, daughter, call Me when you wish. I love you.

I love you too, Mother. Teach me to love you more!

Jesus, I love You.

I am here, beloved; it is I, Jesus.

I surrendered all over again.

I love you. Give Me your little heart in which I will sow the seeds of Peace and Love. I will form you like I desire you to be; nothing will go in vain. All will be for saving My children. Do not fear, let Me lead you, daughter.

WILL I HAVE TO REVEAL MYSELF WITH WRATH?

February 21, 1987

My love for Jesus was at its full this morning; also a fear that He'll abandon me, since I'm "nothing", and a "nothing" loving God is probably profaning His Holy Name.

O daughter, I love you! Be with Me; I will never leave you. O My little one, few are those that glorify Me as you do. Vassula, My Vassula, I care for you. When I have delivered My guidance, I shall not wait further. My Heart longs for your little soul. O how I myself suffer to have you down on earth. I shall take you back to Me, delivering you and rejoicing My Heart, for I burn with desire to have you again with Me. Have My Peace; I am with you soon.

Vassula, do you want to take in writing My next Message?

Yes, Lord.

Are you ready?

I had avoided this message for a few days, but now I felt ready for it. Jesus had talked about it already some time ago.

Yes, Lord.
Do you Love Me?
Very much; you know I do.
Do you desire that others love Me too?
Yes, this is my wish now.
Work then with Me, and write down all that I tell you. Yes, Vassula?
I just wanted to say that this is like a miracle, being able to be guided in this way, Lord.
I willed it, Vassula. I have chosen you to show the world that I need neither authority nor holiness. I have chosen a mere child, helpless and sinful, with no authority and knowing no one in power, to manifest through this weak instrument with My Grace, My Peace and Love I have for you all. I want to convey to this dark world My Message, thus showing My effusions to the world, for My Mercy is ineffable, and My affection beyond any human understanding.
Heaven above with all its Glory, reigns forever in Peace and Love, and I shall see that on earth too, all peace and love prevails evil. My Peace will cover the earth like mist, spreading from the heights to the depths and from one end of the globe to the other end. I come to proclaim My Message to you all and turn you away from your evil doings. My Word will be like a cedar, spreading out its branches like arms, healing your wickedness, feeding your misery, and delivering you from evil. I come once more to enlighten this dark world and revive this flickering flame about to extinguish and cover you with My Peace.[1] I love them, Vassula; O this love I have for them! Have I not sacrificed Myself as a lamb for them to liberate them? I suffered for them.
My beloved ones, was My Blood shed in vain? I have poured out my Blood that your sins may be immersed in It and that you may be purified. I have bathed you in the torrents of My Blood to conquer evil and deliver you. I am among you all, but, nevertheless, Satan is escorting you, for he has found means to seduce you and make you fall into his impious nets; I, God, cannot see you heading into perdition; I am here to untangle you from his vices. It is thus I stand before you, that you may know who your Saviour is. I come once more with My Heart in My Hand, offering it to you. Will you refuse it? Will you refuse My Peace? I come to call those who conform My children into bloodshed. I want them to hear My call, for My Word will come like a hammer, shattering the rock,[2] penetrating every heart. I ask you, have you forgotten your God, or is He of little account in your eyes? Have you no fear of Me? I weary with your lofty aims! I have taught you to

---

[1] Through my mind, a thought passed; I was thinking: "But with those sort of people, it's not worth the trouble; they'll never listen.
[2] One day, suddenly God enlightened me to understand that the <u>rock</u> is our hearts, our hearts covered with stone.

love Me, but also to fear Me, for I am the Almighty. So what have you done? You are gnawing down your own graves, by having sown seeds of wickedness, dispersing them around the world, reaping them now and feeding yourselves upon its fruits of evil. Learn that My whole Kingdom reigns in Peace, the whole of My creation was created in Peace and Love.

My eyes have grown tired watching you slaughtering one another. I care for you, for I am your Father who loves you. Behold, I come with all My Sovereignty, I, who am your God; I come to you offering you My Heart. Here, take It. All of It is yours. My Heart rends and lacerates; feel It; all of It is but one big wound...you have torn the Heart of your God; you have pierced it through again and again. Leaders of war, will I have to come and tread on you showing you My power? Will I have to reveal Myself with wrath? My chalice of Mercy has brimmed over, and My chalice of Justice is full! I who breathed in you Life and consecrated you, I, God of all creation who bathed you in My Holiness, come to you with My Peace, exhorting you to convert yourselves and live in My Peace; I will cover the entire universe with My Peace, letting it reign over you, for I am Peace and Love and All Wisdom. My appeal is addressed to all nations. They must know that Peace reigns in My Kingdom. I come in spite of their wickedness to bless them and shine on them, for they are My beloved sons and daughters.

Listen to this Heart your God is offering you, a Heart you have forgotten and know no more, a Heart who loves you and seeks you out to impart life. Cease to do evil! Cease rebelling against Me! Are you afraid of My Law? My Law is not a law of rebellion; My law is a law of Peace and Love. Follow My given Law; respond to It, and salvation will be yours. Your weakness is to ignore My Laws, bigoted by your own, thus leading mankind into destruction, antagonizing your neighbors; your laws are based on violence.

O children! Have I implanted in your soul hatred? My Soul is the Source of Love and Life in Itself, and from It, came all into being.

Vassula, do no more; I love you; trust Me; let your love cover My Heart; unite, love and work with Me.

I will, Father; help me be worthy, so that I may be able to glorify you.

DIANG VILLAGE

February 26, 1987

Beatrice and I flew to Chittagong, and from there crossed the river to find the village Diang, where we could meet Raymond Dujarrier, who is a French semi-hermit, mystic, Catholic priest, (...)to exchange a few ideas and show him the writings. He called them: Divine Revelations of the Heart. What he said corresponded very much to the idea of the revelations and their purpose: that they are not for me only but for the benefit of others. Our whole trip went perfectly smooth as if someone had programmed it. I forgot to mention that the day before our departure for Diang, I had a feeling of great distress and was asking myself why I am going to Diang, to show what, to show rubbish? The whole day passed in agony. Then early the same day of our departure, the first word appeared:"A liar was guiding you; collect everything and burn it." I knew then that evil from the day before was trying to stop my trip. A few seconds after this message, I felt God's presence and He wrote: *"I will be with you till the end; we are united forever. Let My Light shine on you, child, I am Yahweh guiding you. Glorify Me by loving Me".*

AMEND

March 1, 1987

Today, several times a day, Jesus told me (while I discerned Him around me): *"Never weary of writing."*

Vassula, I desire that My words be known by many, words that come directly from My Lips, for all the revelations I breathed into you are from Me. I work in this way too. Now and then I come and refresh all that has already been taught by Me. I am your Saviour always near you, always ready to withdraw you from evil. I come, hoping that My word will penetrate hearts and rest in them. Vassula, will you amend for others?
What does "amend" mean here exactly, Lord?
Amend means to compensate for others who give no response to My love. Repair for others. All you do is love Me with all your heart and mind.
I love You! But I want to learn to love You without measure, to be able to amend more.
Come, I will teach you; have I ever been known not to keep My word? Daughter, I am your Teacher, and from Me you will learn everything; I will progress you.

I am unworthy of all that You give me; I know for a fact when I compare myself to the humble and so dedicated people.
I am not proud of myself for having been chosen as the most wretched person, and by far too, from the before last one, to be given this guidance. I know that I have not been chosen for my qualities; on the contrary, I have been chosen because of my wretchedness; You have confirmed it, Lord!

♥ Have My peace, Vassula; wretched you are, but I love you anyway. Give Me all your wretchedness and My Mercy will consume it. Feel loved by Me; come, lean on Me; hear Me; keep Me company; do not forget that I am your Holy Companion.

I AM ALL IN ONE

March 2, 1987

♥ ♥ *Glory be to God the Father for delivering you from evil.*
Who is it?
It is I, Jesus, why?

Here I felt embarrassed. I still do not understand who is the Father and what is the difference between Father and Jesus. If He refers to God the Father, then how could Jesus say He is also Father?

Listen, Vassula; give your attention to Me; learn that God and I am One; I am the Father and the Son. Now do you understand? I am One; I am All in One; I am All in One.
You are All in One?!
I am. ♥
And the Light?
I am the Light too. Hear Me.

Here I thought it would be difficult to understand and write down, as also the question of the Holy Spirit was in my mind too.

Let us try; the Holy Spirit comes from Me; do you understand now? All in One. The Holy Trinity is One; you can call Me Father too. Wisdom comes from Me; I am Wisdom too.
It is I, Jesus. Every time you doubt, come to Me.
But I feel embarrassed to still have now and then doubts after having completed 11 copy books of revelations. Anybody would not be like me; by now anybody would have turned into a saint!
Every time you feel embarrassed, I love you more. Vassula, come; you are My beloved, and I love resting in you. Do you love Me?
You know I do, Lord, but at times I feel as cold as a stone! How ungrateful I must be!
Every time you have this feeling, it is I who use your love to warm up other souls who are in need of warmth, souls who are cold towards Me; do you understand now? Daughter, write these words now:

I understand that this is the following of the Peace Message.

I, Yahweh, will cover you with My Love, giving you all My Peace, proclaiming My Word to all nations, for behold, within Me abideth Love, Peace, Mercy and

Wisdom. I will establish My Kingdom on earth as it is in Heaven.
Vassula, this is only part of My message, write the rest later on. ♥ *Come, stay near Me.*

CAN YOU WORK WITH LOVE FOR LOVE?

March 3, 1987

It is I, Jesus.
Forgive me for all my sins.
I forgive you. Come, I delight in you. Do you remember the day I showed you My Glory?
Yes!
Do you wish to follow it up? ♥ *Yes?*

Father, can't I wait a little?

I felt insecure.

♥ *Be it. I will later on ask you again. I would like to show you more of My Glory, so that you are able to describe to My children how My Kingdom is. As for My previous Message, when I feel you are ready to write it down, I shall let you know. Vassula, will you let Me use you today?*
In which way Lord?
By using the essence of the love you have for Me. So love Me fervently, Vassula. I wish to save a very special soul from falling; she is one of My chosen ones. We can still save her, Vassula. I will leave two pure drops of My Blood on your heart. These two drops will be enough to cover your entire heart and make you feel My sorrow.
What shall I do?
Can you work with love for Love?
I will try, Lord.
Unite with Me; we will restore her soul today; we will strengthen her. I will teach you how I work, for these are Heavenly works. All Holy works are from Me. Wisdom is instructing you. Never forget this; you are My flower which I leave to grow in My Light. I will purify your soil and give you what you lack. I will come back and let you know about My special soul's heart. I love you; love Me Vassula, for so many depend on this love.

Later on in the afternoon, I was attacked by evil blaming me. I knew it was not God since I learned that He will never blame me.

♥ I bless you, daughter; I will never blame you for what I, Yahweh, have given you. I delight in you; I have chosen you to reveal My Face. Meditate, My Vassula; feel, feel this love I have for you. Shortly you will be seeing Me; yes, I will come.
Lord, when you take me, I do not expect anything since I have done nothing and am incapable of doing anything. Again ending with the word "unworthy"! Yet how I wish to be near You!
Vassula, feel My Hand, My Hand is trying ever so hard to get hold of you and keep near you Me. I am longing to shelter you; I love to take you, thrusting you in the depths of My Heart, and hide you there, all for Myself. ♥ You seem to forget My words; have I not bound you to Me for eternity? Have we not been united by Me, placing a wreath of love upon it? My beloved, we are working together; I am your God and Leader.
My Lord, I am weak and need you; I need to be strengthened in everything, so that I will be able to glorify You.
Vassula, watch My hands; place your hands in a way that you fingertips touch Mine.

I saw like lightening coming out from His fingertips, like electricity. I placed my hands and touched His fingertips. This was done in discernment and meditation.

Feel My Holiness; My Strength is penetrating through your fingertips. Such works are Heavenly works. I bless you. Lean on Me; you have now absorbed Me; keep your hands in Mine, feeling My warmth.

Later on:

Vassula Hear Me; now we have saved her from falling. Rejoice! I have used the essence of your love; ♥ we are working together, helping and healing souls. Never weary, daughter, in healing them.

I was again attacked by evil. They said: "Will you disappear from here."

Vassula Come; approach Me; have My love. Do you understand why they hate you? You are snatching from evil My beloved souls, bringing them back to Me.
Lord, what about all the love other people give you; does it help too?
Yes! All love is used for restoring and healing souls. My Kingdom will spread and keep growing with the love given.
♥ ♥ ♥ I am telling you truly that all My sufferings will not be in vain; with tremendous Glory I will prevail over all evil. I will enkindle every heart, thus spreading out My seeds of Love and Peace, uniting My children. Over the entire universe My Light will be shed, for thus is My will. Honour Me, Vassula, by loving Me. Kiss My Hands.

I did it in discernment as well as on a picture.

♥ ♥ *Glorify Me always; I love you all. Come, beloved, nearer to Me, for My love for you is more than you can ever imagine.*

I felt so much happiness from God; God was so happy!

WE HAVE BONDS TOGETHER

March 4, 1987

As I know myself so treacherous, I fear I might one day, out of weakness, abandon you. The thought is awful; I can't see how this might happen, but I don't want it to happen, or you to leave me either!

Vassula, I, Yahweh, love you; do I ever abandon you? We have bonds together, and being bound to each other, you will be unable of abandoning Me. See? I have taken care of our union; we will stay united till the end, you needing Me and loving Me fervently, and I free reigning over you and loving you without restraint, never without the desire of delivering you to Me.

Did you say that My God?

I have said it. Are you going to ask Me your question?

I don't dare!

Why? ♥ *Do not fear Me.*

I knew that he knew, but I did not want it on paper.

Please God!

Come, let us learn; I am the Almighty, and I know what is best for your soul. If one of you asks Me a question or a favour, I will answer. My answer will be the best in which the soul can be nourished. It is like I would select from all fruits, the ideal fruit which could give best results for her. Have you heard how many times I can forgive?

Yes, Lord, but some books say that although You do not want to answer them (in a supernatural way,) You do, but disliking it, and You are angry.

♥ *I, Yahweh, tell you this: "My way of thinking is not Your way of thinking, and My ways are not your ways. "[1]* ♥ *Vassula, I am a God Most Merciful, a Loving, Holy Father to you; I know your needs and weakness. My Love to you all is a jealous love. Come, come nearer to Me; I, Yahweh, take all opportunities to reach you.* ♥

My Father, when I am with You, I feel so loved by You and My love to You but grows, yet I am afraid to fail You since I am full of sin.

---

[1] Meaning that this theory is wrong.

Vassula do I not know all this? You are a pinch of dust whereupon if I blow on it, you will disappear. I know how frail you are, for after all, you are but a passing shadow on earth; yet in your nothingness and in your wretchedness, My eyes never leave you; I look upon your weaknesses with Compassion and Love. Do not fear, for I will strengthen you; your sins I take, and give you My forgiveness. Vasula do no more today, ♥ I will call you tomorrow. Have My peace. ♥

AS A SPOUSE I WILL PROVIDE YOU

March 5, 1987

Peace be with you, Vassula. Do you love Me?
I love you, Yahweh, my God, with all my heart; near You I wish to stay.
I love you too. I will never abandon you.
I am King and Sovereign of Peace and Love; before you I am, revealing My Holy Face to you all.
This is the beginning of My call of Peace and Love. Daughter, I will instruct you more with Wisdom; I am well pleased with you; delight Me, hearing My calls, and writing them down; weary not writing; come, all will not be in vain. I give you My blessings; come, lean on Me; ♥ glorify Me by loving Me, daughter. Seek Me always; deny Me never; amend for others; fulfill My words; have My everlasting Peace

Vassula, stay near Me. I will remind you that as a Spouse I will provide for you with great abundance all that you lack. I love you. Every word I say will be written, we will work together. Weary not writing. ♥

I read Saint Michael's prayer to Him. Saint Michael answered me.
With God's Power, I, Saint Michael, will cast into hell Satan and all the other evil spirits that ruin souls.

I then read the "Memorare" of Saint Bernard.

Our Lady:

Beloved daughter, I will help you. Have My everlasting Peace; I am near you until the end. Fulfill the Message, Vassula; fulfill God's word. Lean on your Holy Father, for He is Most Powerful. Love Him and glorify Him. Will you do all this? Stay near us. ♥ I love you.

MY BREAD WILL FILL YOU

March 6, 1987

Vassula, it I, Jesus, your Saviour. Are you hungry?
In fact, Jesus, I am right now.
Always be, be hungry for My Bread. Come, My Bread is free, and when you eat from Me, you will be filled.
Jesus, I was talking about earthly bread.
I know, Vassula, but which would you prefer to have?
Both, Jesus.
♥ *Your bread will only satisfy you for a while, but when you eat from My Bread, you will be filled.* ♥ *Anyone who eats from My Bread will live forever.* ♥ *I will feed you, Vassula.*
I love you, Jesus.
O daughter, how I long to hear these words from every lip! "I love you Jesus." Do you want to feel My Heart?
Look at Me, before you I stand
I looked at His Heart. All His Breast was lit.

My Heart is ablaze with fervent love; My Heart wants to consume you in It's love; My Heart wants to entice you and forever be Mine! Come, daughter, cry out for love; cry out for peace; be united to the end with Me. Come, let us revive the others; love Me with all your soul and with all your mind to be able to glorify Me, beloved.
Jesus, loving You is painful, because one wants to be with You; I mean: rid of the body and be near You. That's why it is painful to love.
♥ *I suffer too because of My Great Love for all of you. I cruelly suffered because of love; I still suffer when I do not get any response to the love I have for you. Can you imagine how I feel? Beloved, I need souls who truly love Me, souls who could repair for those who ignore Me. Tell them; let them know how it feels to love someone, having layed out My life out of love, and yet I get no response, no love! Weary not of bearing My Cross of Peace and Love. Bearing it for Me, rest My weary Soul. I need to rest beloved.*
Jesus, I will do what You want and try to understand what You are telling me.
In the evening my soul was heavy and sad.

USE THE WORD "US" - A VISION OF HELL

March 7, 1987

Vassula, I, Jesus, love you; beloved, I have rested. Come, I am pleased; ♥ *believe Me, I feel rested! Let us work with love and repair. Come, I will teach you to repair. I am the Elixir of Life, I am the Resurrection.*

Jesus, How I wish that every soul loved you! It must be awful not to get a response to a love so Great as Yours!

My wish is already implanted in your soul. Daughter, fill Me With joy and learn to say: "Let us go and work; let us do this or that." Use the word us; we are united forever! ♥ *Delight Me by saying, "Father, may your will be done"; refuse Me nothing. Daughter, today you will follow Me in the dark dominion of My foe to see how those souls who refused Me suffer.*[1]

Jesus, are they lost?

Those in hell are, but those in Purgatory are saved with love by My beloved ones who repair and amend. Do not fear, for My Light protects you, and I am with you.

I saw myself underground. It looked like an underground cave, dark, lit only by fire. It was damp, and the ground was sticky. I saw several souls in a row. They were tied, and only their heads shown, faces of agony. It was very noisy; it sounded like iron machines at work: lots of clamouring, hammering, shrieks; it was very busy. In front of those heads was someone standing, his hand outstretched, and inside his palm was lava. His arm waved from right to left, pouring, splashing the hot lava across those faces which were swelled up from burns. Suddenly this man, whom I understood was Satan, noticed our presence and turned around.

Satan speaks: "Look at her!" And he spat on the ground with disgust and fury at the sight of Jesus' presence and mine. "Miserable worm, look at her. We even have worms nowadays, coming to suck out our blood, go and f... off." He said to me: "Look," and he threw hot lava again across those faces. I heard them cry out:"Oh let us die...." Then Satan, who looked exactly like a mad-man, fuming with rage called out:"Creatures of the earth, hear me, to me you will come!" I just thought that although he was menacing, he was a fool to believe that in the end he would win. He must have read my thoughts of contempt, and very menacingly said: "I am not a fool!" Then with a malicious laugh and with irony, he said to those poor souls: "Have you heard? She called me a fool. Dear, beloved souls, I will make you pay for her sayings." He was ready to take new lava to throw. I turned to Jesus in despair, asking Him to do something! to stop him! Jesus replied: "I will stop him." The minute Satan had lifted his arm to throw the lava, it gave him great pain, and he screeched with pain, cursing Jesus, he said to me: "Witch, go! yes go; leave us!"

---

[1] In hell and in the nearest Purgatory.

Voices from souls found at the gates of hell were crying:"Save us, save us"![1] Then someone came forward; I understood it was one of Satan's demons, and Satan asked him: "Are you on your duty? Are you doing what I have asked you to do? Hurt her; destroy her; discourage her". I knew Satan was referring to me. He wanted this demon to discourage me from meeting with Jesus by giving the wrong word or destroying the message I get. I asked Jesus if we could leave. He said:

Come, let us leave; I want you to write all this down; I will edit for you. Be near Me, beloved. I want My children to understand that their souls live, and that evil exists. All that is written in My Blessed Word is not a myth; Satan exists and seeks to ruin your souls. I suffer to see you slumbering and unaware of his existence. I come, giving you warnings, giving you signs, but how many of you will read My warnings like fairy-tales? Beloved, I am your Saviour; do not deny My word; turn to Me and feel the pangs of love I have for you. Why, why are you so willing to thrust yourselves at Satan's feet? O come! All of you who believe no more in Me; come to Me, all who have forsaken Me! Come and behold, for this is the time to listen. All you who wound My Soul, arise, revive, and see My Light. Do not fear Me; I have forgiven you; I will take your sins, and My Blood will wash them; I will condone your weakness and forgive you. Come and absorb the Dew of Righteousness, restoring your souls which are heading for perdition. I come to look for you; I come in search of My lost sheep. Will I as the Good shepherd see you lost and remain indifferent? ♥ Vassula, are you willing to pray for all those in perdition?

Now, Jesus?

Yes, now.

I wouldn't know what to say, Lord.

I will teach you; listen to Me and repeat after Me:

> *O Holy Father, by Thy Power and with Thy Mercy,*
> *I implore You, gather all your sheep;*
> *Forgive them and let them return to Your Beloved Home;*
> *Look upon them as your children,*
> *And with Thy Hand bless them. Amen.*

Come in My Heart, Vassula, for therein is profound Peace.

---

[1]Souls at the gates of hell, in a very low Purgatory can be "lifted" by our prayer, raising them to less torment.

WHY REFUSE ME A PLACE IN YOUR HEART?

March 8, 1987

Beloved one, I want to remind you again that I am not favoring you from My other children, for your merits are none and your worthiness even less in My Eyes, but I love you even so. I gave you this Grace, for this is My Will. Be My bearer, and through you, I will manifest Myself. Do not think that I am contradicting Myself. My Love for you is boundless, and you are My beloved one since I chose you. Do not think for one minute that because I point out your weakness I love you less. I am your Holy Father who knows you, and if I do not point out your mistakes, then who will? You are My frail flower which I form, letting you sip My Strength that you may grow, Vassula.

I want to remind you that the Revelations I am breathing in you are not just for your own benefit; they are meant for others too who are in desperate need of My Bread. I come to feed all of you who are hungry. My Message is one of Peace and Love, and to remind you of your foundations and who created you. I come tell you that <u>My Body is My Church,</u> YES! My Church which fills the whole creation. I come to show this world My Mercy. You, Vassula, were one among those multitudes who wounded Me, who never responded to My Love, embittering Me. What is more embittering than receiving no response to a Love so thirsty and so great as Mine?

Instead, in your wilderness you sought after daily material pleasures, symbolizing them as gods, idolizing them, alienating yourself even further from Me, embittering Me and wounding My Heart: a Heart of a living God, so unsought and so unloved by you, a God completely forgotten.

Daughter, was I that far away from you?

Come, come and feel My Heart. My Heart is crying out for you all.

My sons, My daughters, come…come nearer to Me; turn to Me; allow Me to hold you; let Me thrust you deep inside My Heart; and let It engulf you, giving you profound Peace.

Come and enter My Spiritual World of Peace and Love. Come to Me and eat from My Body, for My Bread is pure and will purify you.

My Body[1] cries out for you! Come and see Me, I, who spend day and night at the Tabernacle, waiting for you to feed you. Do not dread or fear Me; do not disown Me. Why refuse Me a place in your heart? Come and get to know Me and you will love Me, for how could you love someone you do not know or know only imperfectly? Endeavour to know Me well, and you will love Me fervently.

Vassula, you had gone astray and thus detached yourself from Me; you turned away from the truth, transforming good into evil and being attached more to evil

---

[1] The Eucharist.

rather than good.
Come then, all those who still are evading Me and bring forth your sins, that I may pardon them. Come and eat from Me; come and empty your hearts to Me, and let Me fill them up with Love. I know you are weak, but allow me to act in all of you. Give Me your consent, beloved ones. Let Me uproot all your iniquities, casting them away, and sow in you My seed of Peace and Love. Let Me purify you.
Vassula, do no more; I will continue later on. Do not forget My Presence; remember, always: us, we.
I will remember; I will try, Lord.
♥ ♥ *Let us go.*
Let us.

Later on:

Come and get to know Me; I am not beyond reach; we walk side by side. You live in Me and I in you; we are never parted. ♥ Never. Come and derive from My Infinite Goodness, and let your inclemency dissolve in My Purity.
O daughter, in spite of having many of My beloved children made holy by Baptism, there are only very few who know Me as I am. They forget to look upon Me as a loving Father. Many of them leave Me thinking that I am beyond reach. Many of them think of Me, in their own manner, attributing permanent feelings of despicable inclinations. ♥ Some think of Me only in fear; others doubt of My Infinite Love.

Here I was interrupted. The photograph I ordered of the Holy Shroud arrived. I contemplated on it and came back to writing while I was looking at it.

Remember, I am still suffering. Vassula, how embittered I am. Why, why are so many of My sheep scattered? Look at them. Was it in vain, My Sacrifice? Daughter, how displeased I am. How utterly shattered My Soul is. I suffer. Feed My sheep, weary not of writing.
No, Lord, I will not weary.
I will give you the Strength you need. Come, let us work; ♥ let us continue. I am your Teacher. Fill Me with joy, and do not forget My Presence.
Vassula, you felt my Presence. Indeed, I was sitting at the corner of your bed. Let Me edit what I wrote: It is I, Jesus; I am sitting now, but at this very instant I will arise since you too will arise.

He hardly finished writing when the door knocked urgently, and I jumped up; I stood there quite perplexed. Jesus was emphasizing His Presence to me that evening very much...at the door was my employee telling me something.

I love you; weary not of writing, giving Me this freedom is what I desire.
Jesus, You are wonderful!

Be always cheerful when I am cheerful. Follow Me. You will grieve Me if you forget My Presence. Never forget My Presence. Never!

But, Lord, it is difficult; sometimes I have to drive my car; I have to concentrate on the road. I converse with friends on trivial subjects; I help my son in his homework, so how could I constantly have Your Presence in my mind? It is almost impossible!

Vassula, My flower, when you are in that way, you only have to remember the virtues by being humble, devoted, gentle, graceful, truthful, loving. Yes, being virtuous is remembering Me. Come, let us go.

I wish to make it known to you that I do approach in a supernatural way giving My Messages. Do not forget that I am a God of Mercy, and in spite of your wretchedness and the indifference you had towards Me, I love you.

I gave you this charisma so that you learn directly from My lips. Vassula, resting in your heart feels good.

Later on: again, the wave of doubt covered me.

Come, suffering purifies you; lean on Me; accept to suffer. Amend, amend, amend for others. Come let us revive all My children.

There I became quite distressed!

But, My God, I am helpless, how could I do anything?

He said very softly:

Will I ever abandon you? Use My grains and sow them into fields, yielding the fruits of Peace and Love. Let My Word be known to all. ♥ I will be with you all the time.

Suppose they refuse It and put it aside, doubting about It! Suppose they think it is no good; suppose they do not believe it's You!

Hear Me, My Vassula, why are your fearing? All creation was done by My Hand. Have you forgotten that I am Omnipotent? All My creation obeys My Will. Little one, I am the Most High; do glorify Me; be like a flower needing My Light to live.

SUFFERING PURIFIES YOUR SOUL

March 17, 1987

Jesus appeared with His Cross.

Vassula, will you bear My Cross now?
I do according to your will, Jesus.
Feel, feel how heavy It is. I need to rest. Follow Me, come nearer to Me; I will unburden My Precious Cross on you.

That day, later on, I felt unspeakably distressed, melancholic, and needing comfort but not finding it.

You have felt My immense burden on you. Never refuse My Cross. My burden is heavy. Vassula, seek not why I elevate you to Me;[1] leave Me free to do with you whatsoever I want to until I come and deliver you. Beloved, your guidance has its martyrdom. By seeking to find the truth in it and not finding it, it martyrs you. Suffer for Me. Suffering purifies your soul. Immolate yourself to Me and do not seek to find;[2] just believe. Leave Me free to act in you, and through you manifest My Word, thus healing My children.
Believe in My Redemptive Love. My Cross is heavy; yes, I will come many more times entrusting you with It. You are My bride, ♥ My beloved, and My flower. By bearing It for Me, you relieve Me.
Within My Revelations I breathe into you, there are embittering passions of sorrows, pains, and sufferings, which flow out from the very depths of My Soul. Come and listen one more time to My Heart, and feel how It lacerates. Feel how It seeks you all!

Then, as if He could not take it any longer, a cry came out from that chagrined Soul, from Its depths it came, like as if It was close to death from sorrow.

Creation! which My Father created by His own Hand, why, why do you give Me so much sorrow!!

Then He turned to me, His Face and tone very grave, saying:

Have you ever thought of Me before I came to you?
No, I haven't (guilt).

---

[1] Reminding me to accept it as it is.
[2] I was trying to discover whether this is a real guidance.

Still grave:
Would you have come to Me if I had not sought and found you?
I don't think so (more guilt).
Now you love Me.
Yes, my Lord, I do.[1]
My guidance has changed you, has it not?
Yes, it has.
Will you muster My children and feed them?

I felt helpless. I want to please Him, showing my thanks, but I can't.

My God, how could I, with what means?!
Trust Me; let Me guide you, Vassula; let Me muster My children. I know you are helpless; I know you are weak. You see, you cannot do anything without Me. Now, will you let Me use you as My instrument until I have completed My Message?
Yes, as long as the Message will be from You, Jesus.
I am Jesus; never doubt. Weary not of writing. Every word My Lips utter will make you feel My Wounds.
I drag you down with Me in the dark dominion of My foe, showing you how souls suffer.[2] I outpour on you all My sufferings that wound Me profoundly. My priest, for My priest you are; you will walk with Me. Never will I abandon you. Together we will share My Cross; together we will suffer; together we will strive. You will take your rest in Me, and I in you.

YOU ARE MY SEED, YOU ARE MINE
I HAVE COME TO CONSOLIDATE MY CHURCH

March 18, 1987

I have taught you to love Me and recognize Me. I showed you My Heavenly Works, pouring out all the mysteries of My Heart and showing you My ineffable Mercy, purifying you to be the source of My revelations, and showing the world My Grace. Indeed, I have bestowed upon you all My insatiable love, showing My children how much I can love them;[3] nevertheless, reminding you that you are not any different than the rest of them, and that you are not to keep this guidance hidden; I want

---

[1]There I really felt that I am nothing, and it was not for my merits He approached me, since in the very beginning, I almost rejected Him!
[2]When He showed me hell.
[3]I'm like a sample.

My effusions to cover this world, for this is My Will.

Vassula, allow Me to act in you as I please. Come now and console Me, yes, by loving Me. I am Yahweh, and it is on Me you are leaning, and it is to Me you are coming and meditating. You are invoking <u>Me</u> in your prayers, so do not worry since you are worshiping Me and no one else.[1] My wish is that all My children return to Me. Daughter, I have brought you up for this Message; will you fulfill My word, Vassula? Are you willing to continue working for Me?

Yes, my Lord, as long as I recognize it's Yahweh.

Little one, I am Yahweh! Have My Peace, little one, and grow. Never weary writing; allow Me to use you until the end of My Message. Little one, who is your father?

I was surprised at the question.

You are.

I am. You are My seed; you are Mine.

My children have turned away from Me and their hearts are frozen with egoism. They have forgotten Me. I want to ask them: "Why do you repel Me; what have I done that displeased you? Have I insinuated ever to you that I am angry towards you? Why are you dreading to face Me? Beloved, I will not blame you for your sins; I forgive you now. I will not shut the door in your face. I tell you truly that I can forgive a million times, and with My Arms open, I stand before you, asking you to come to Me and feel this love I have to give you. Let Me enkindle your heart; come and get to know Me.

Come, all you who avoid Me and fear Me, all you who do not know Me. Come nearer to Me, and you will understand that I am a God full of love, full of pity, and full of mercy. Do not reject Me before you even know Me.

My superabundant love offers you an efficacious grace to know and choose between good and evil. I have given you freedom to choose, but I have also given you qualities to make out of you superior beings. I have given you gifts; use your gifts I bestowed on you, and with your intellect and the heart I have given you, understand and come forward, acknowledging Me, and get to know Me better. I have enlightened your hearts to enable you to love. I it is who have given you this Grace. Would you accept this Grace?

I remembered myself of before.

But Lord, some had no chance in knowing You. No one taught them; it's not really their fault, is it? So how could they possibly even think of You?

Vassula how true! Daughter, My Church needs vivification... I have come to consolidate My Church, ♥ otherwise multitudes are bound to be lost.

---

[1] For those times that I worry that these writings are maybe not from God.

Vassula, I will come back, giving a message to My devoted ones. Let Me complete My desires about My children who turned away from Me. I am the Source of Love, and from this Source flows this infinite Love which covers all creation. All I ask of you is a return of love. Many of you believe I am a God who is quick to anger and so fear Me; you fear to approach Me. Others believe I am beyond reach and only enjoying My Glory, never caring for you, and My Eyes turned only upon My devoted ones, thus making an image of a God full of predilection. Did you not know that the weaker and the more wretched you are, the more I seek you and love you? I am Holy, but I also want you to understand that I desire to become intimate with you and have Me as your Holy Companion.
Do you know of the parable of the prodigal son, Vassula?
Yes, some of it.
He had sinned, but how did his father receive him?
With great joy?
More than that, he received him with great love ♥ and celebrated this event.
Grieve Me not, My beloved ones, and come back to Me. I will not refuse you; I will welcome you in My embrace. Return to Me without fear.

I WANT YOU TO BE PERFECT

March 19, 1987

♥ *I am here. It is I, Jesus. Vassula, elevate yourself to Me. I want you to be perfect. Delight Me and become perfect. Are you willing to be perfect?*

I was speechless.

I want you to be. I am asking you, Vassula.
But Lord, to be perfect is quite impossible. As I am, to be close to being good is already something for me.
I will teach you to be perfect. I tell you truly that it is not impossible, but you must let Me mould you; abandon yourself completely to Me, and I will form you into what I desire you to be.
Jesus, I don't think I can ever be. I am difficult to mould; it will be like trying to mould a rock.
Vassula, ah Vassula, do you not trust Me? I am God, and I can mould even the rocks into any shape I want.
Do you know why I have chosen you?
Yes, Lord.

Here is still one more reason: I chose you because you are weak, and your weakness charms Me. Child, come and feel My Heart; My Heart desires to be loved. Come and feel My Heart with your mind. Vassula, are you ready? Feel Me.

I was petrified.

♥ ♥ *Grieve Me not; come and feel Me.* ♥ *You are not feeling Me.* ♥
No, I have not felt you.
I had not the courage to do it.
Will you tell me your problem?
It's getting worse now.
Why? ♥ ♥
My embarrassment. I feel embarrassed. I feel humiliated.
Vassula, why? Grieve Me not and tell Me your problem.
I felt embarrassed to touch Your Heart. It's like I saw myself as a leper coming to touch someone whole. Who am I to approach You!
♥ *Every time you feel embarrassed, I love you more. Daughter, since we are united for eternity, and you are Mine, I will allow Myself to penetrate deep inside your heart. Marrying Me glorifies Me and purifies you. We are united.*
Yes Lord, but look to <u>what</u> You are united!
I love you. Come and lean on Me now.

Later on:

Vassula, feel My Heart.
I felt His Heart, which was very warm and palpitating with desire to be loved.
You need not feel embarrassed feeling My Heart. I am Your God who asks you this. Allow Me to use you like I wish. ♥ *Allow Me to* ♥ *kiss you.*

I got suspicious, thinking it's evil trying to make me fall in sin.
I am the Lord Jesus Christ. Do not fear.
I was still careful, yet I have not felt evil around. Still, I was suspicious.
Do not fear.
I could not "free" myself; again this "leper" feeling came on me. I did not move.

Do you know how much I love you?
Yes, I do Jesus.
Why then do you refuse My Kiss?
Because I'm not worthy of a kiss from You.
Vassula, have I not told you before not to refuse Me anything? And what have you answered Me?
That I'll never refuse You anything.
Yes, why then refuse My Kiss? Vassula, never refuse Me. If I ask you something, it is for Love. Allow Me to kiss you; allow Me to do it. Will you let Me now? Come

to Me and feel My Kiss, a Heavenly Kiss, on your forehead. Are you ready?
♥ *I love you.*

Jesus kissed my forehead. He left me in an ectatic state of mind. How can I explain
it? For the following <u>two days</u> I felt hollow, transparent, like clear glass. He gave
such a <u>tremendous</u> feeling of peace of the soul. My breathing seemed to go through
my lungs and fill into my entire body, thus having the feeling of being air.

INTEGRATE YOUR WHOLE BEING IN ME

March 20, 1987

Vassula, let Me tell you something: Love Me till the end, for the end will be sweet,
and I will be with you.
How much You must have suffered!
My sufferings were not in vain; I have liberated you from evil.
I wish You could be happy sometimes.
I am happy when I am among My beloved ones.
Do they make you happy?
Yes, they uplift My sorrows.
It's a pity that we are not 2000 years back to be with You.
I am still among you, daughter.
Jesus, since you kissed me (yesterday evening and all day today), I feel "dissolved"
in You, like I'm transparent and tremendously peaceful! It's like I am hollow....
♥ *Vassula I am Peace, I will always give you My Peace; integrate your whole*
being in Me, and I will dissolve you within Me. Ah, Vassula, come always within
Me and feel My Peace. Are you still willing to let Me form you?
Yes, Jesus, always.
Yes, leave Me free to do whatsoever I want with you. I will mould you into a pure
and devoted being, solely for My interests. You are going to withstand trials with
My Strength, solely for My interests. My Word will be like a rivulet, flowing, then
rushing, until it pours out and turns into an ocean, an ocean of Peace and Love.

Later on:

Vassula, why do you never praise Me?! I am the Lord who saved you from
darkness. Realize who you are: among the most wretched ones, you are by far the
worst of them.

I sighed.
I love you anyway. Praise Me, Vassula, for liberating you.

I was thinking what to say, I hesitated.

Say:-   *My God, I love You, and it is through Your*
                abundant Love and Mercy that You showed me
                Your Light. Blessed be Your Name. Amen.

I repeated His Words.

LET YOUR ENTIRE BEING PENETRATE IN ME

March 21, 1987

It is I, Jesus. ♥ *Vassula, will you train, beloved, discerning Me with your mind?*
Vassula, look at Me. ♥

I did.

Yes, correct.
Have You placed Your Hands on the desk?
I have.
Now You've crossed Your Arms?
I have.
Now You've lifted one Arm and Your Hand reached Your Cheek and Your
Forefinger on Your Cheek; the other Arm stayed where it is, like You are thinking?
♥ *Correct! I am emphasizing My Presence. Vassula, look at Me.*
You have a book? which You took out from Your mantle, from the left side with
You right Hand?
I have a book.
Its not very big.
Exactly; you are discerning well, Vassula. Look inside and read what it says.
My altar is you...I try, but I am not good in it...it says:... I can't, Jesus; I can't
figure out the rest!
Try again.
"My altar upon which I will...." I can't see; I think I'm reading wrong!
Little one, what would you do without Me? You must elevate more your soul to Me.
Vassula, I will help you. Leave yourself entirely to Me; never be discouraged. I will
come back with My book later on.

I did feel discouraged, believing I disappointed Him for not raising high enough my
soul. I went as far as to think that He will exchange me for another soul, that his
patience has limits!

Vassula, you must never ever believe that I will exchange you; will you believe Me? Come, we will try next time. Try and discern Me more with your mind as you did now. Vassula, let your entire being penetrate in Me and dissolve within Me, completely. Love Me and amend for others. Elevate. I will teach you to elevate your soul. Let us go.

I WILL MAKE OF YOU MY ALTAR

March 22, 1987

Serenity is what I love. You will work with serenity and not with haste. ♥ *I have come back with My book.*
What is in that book too?
♥ *I have written in a few names of souls, souls who are to revive My Flame, the Flame of Love. Will you read where I point out for you?*
Yes, Lord, I have been worried about that little book which I couldn't read.
I know.
I can see; it's cover is soft and gold?
Yes, its cover is golden. Look inside it and read: "I will make of you My altar upon which I will place My burning desires of My Heart. My Flame will live within you; be drawing from My Heart and filling your heart. I, the Lord, will keep My Flame ablaze for ever and ever."
♥ *Will you kiss My book now, daughter?* ♥

I did.
I had a question....

I will tell you. It is a spiritual guidance for My chosen souls. Now you know.

Later on, the wave of uncertainty and doubt covered me.

Vassula, do not fear; it is I Jesus. Listen, beloved, all the guidances have their sufferings too. In yours, it is the uncertainty which makes you suffer. Have I not said that suffering purifies your soul? Accept it, and leave Me free to do what is best for you. Let Me act in you; are you willing?
I'll do it if it is You, Jesus.
I am Jesus, Your Saviour. We will suffer together; we will strive together. Here, lean on me; come, let us go and read together.

Later on:

I am here. Live for Me; glorify Me by loving Me. Come, all is for My interests of Love and Peace; deny Me never. Evil will always try and interfere to stop My designs, but I will prevail, so rely on Me.
But Lord, can I complain about some things?
Feel free with Me, Vassula.
I want to tell You what is bothering me. Probably everything I say or think is wrong, so whatever I do will be wrong. It's true; I have no real support; by that I mean I am here writing messages I receive from You. Now, others apparently had the same as I: other revelations or messages that came from You to other people. But these people were mostly in monasteries or convents. They were surrounded by religious, priests, bishops, etc. When this supernatural approach was happening to them, they were watched carefully, followed closely; then it was easy to pass the writings to the Superiors, and from there to the bishop, and then to the Pope. They all accepted it as coming from You. I might be wrong, but it seemed easier for them to accept it from one of <u>their circle</u>, whom they knew well; and so it was edited, at least parts of it.

They were approved.[1] Then here I am; I have approached priests; they happen to be Catholic. For me, as a Greek Orthodox by baptism, it doesn't matter to me what they are; even if I were Catholic and the priest would be Protestant, I am not selecting; we are all Christians. Several priests know about it by now. Each one's reaction differs from the other like day and night. One of them, to this day, says its Evil; in other words, I am possessed, since I'm possessed by a spirit; but I know that it's You, God Almighty. Having read a little, he made up his mind and does not want to ever change it. When he'll understand I am not possessed, he'll bring up that it's my subconscious. Anything but You. Then, the reaction of another one was:"Yes, continue writing, because it's divine and from God," so he believes it's God's words, but is too busy to ask or even to follow it up.

This is what amazes me. If he believes that God is trying to express a message, why then not bother more and find out what it is?

A third priest was informed and listened dutifully, looking now and then at his watch; then said: "Good, go on; it's marvellous; continue writing." I asked him to come anytime again and talk about it. I never saw him again.
Then another priest was informed and he said, only reading a page or two: "I don't want to give any opinion, but we Catholics are warned that evil acts in the same way too.[2] Not that I'm saying it's evil, but we are told to be careful."

---

[1] And thus relieved, for the Word can lay <u>heavy</u>.
[2] Maybe, but for how long? Until masses return to God? Because masses already have, and it's the beginning.

Fair enough, I said, but then, since everybody agrees on one thing, and that is:"That <u>it is</u> supernatural," why then not take it more seriously to understand and clarify it? After all, they are people who seek God. The first one who said it's evil, then told me that God gives messages and there are many, many books with those messages all over the world, and that it is very common. There are so many guidances in the supernatural way, so it is very common, but mostly <u>in their circle</u>.

Another priest said they are called Divine Revelations of the Heart and they are from God. Then he gave the address of a professor mystic whom I can find and talk with. I know that if I was "one of them", I'd have it easier. It's just that I'm out of their circle, and my appearance too clashes.

♥ *I am Jesus. Vassula, lean on Me and rest.* ♥ *Era, O era, have you given credits before even glimpsing on My Word? Are you seemingly glorifying Me and by defending Me unwillingly deriding Me? Vassula, I love you; lean on Me, beloved.*

Lord, there are still other things. When I tell You or give You my feelings of doubt, I am pretty sure I wound You, since I am doubting. And if I am not doubting, and it is not You in the guidance, I am wounding You because I'm doing this. So whatever I'm doing, I wound You, if I believe or not believe it's you; whatever I think, I hurt you, and this makes me sad since I want to be the last one that would wound you! I suffer for this too.

O daughter, grieve not. Never believe that I am wounded from love. Eating from Me is all you do. I am Jesus, Jesus, Christ, and it is My Bread you are eating, soul. O beloved soul, do not afflict yourself anymore; believe Me, beloved one, and feel loved by Me.

Forgive me for being so weak.

I forgive you fully. Feel how much I love you. Your weakness is what attracts Me most, your ineffable weakness! Your wretchedness is beyond words. O come to Me here inside My Heart; let your soul entirely annihilate within Me. Be My heaven. I love you. Have My peace.

I HAVE WITH ME TWO RINGS

March 23, 1987

Remember, I am One; the Holy Trinity is One. I want that our union be perfect. Discern Me carefully. Yes, you have seen well; I have with Me two rings.
They are silver-white? and very shiny!
They are out of pure white gold.

There I thought evil was misguiding me. How could this be?

Listen, Vassula, it I, Jesus; do not fear. Beloved, come, I have brought you this ring. I want you to wear it now. Discern Me.
But, is this possible?
Yes, I am blessing our union! Beloved, this act is a spiritual heavenly act; your soul is united to Me. I tell you truly; believe Me, I will sanctify our marriage. ♥
Allow Me to place this ring on your finger. ♥ *I love you; feel Me. I love you, and I bless you.*
Jesus placed the other ring on His Finger.
♥ *See? What can you discern more?*
I can see a ribbon joining two "circles".
This I shall place on our heads. We are now joined. ♥ *I am crowning our unity.*
Jesus, many will blame this as a fantasy!
♥ *Why,* ♥ *many come to Me and marry Me, glorifying Me, and I so much rejoice to be united to them! Vassula, I have risen you from the dead; I shed My Light on you; I looked after you and soothed you. Leave Me free to continue My works on you, daughter; be like soft plaster willing to be shaped up as I wish. Leave yourself free in My Hands and do not resist Me.*
Lord, I'm so happy, too happy, that I fear I might be wrong!
No, you have well discerned. I love you to the extent that I am well prepared to fetch you right away. I am longing to deliver you and have you near Me, but I have created you for this Message.
Lord, I'm fearing that I might have misdiscerned and that I have profaned You By thinking that You gave me a ring and united us, though I was pretty sure about it.
My bride, My wretched bride, ♥ *why are you fearing Me? Grieve Me not and approach Me. I love you. Lean on Me and remember, I it is who sanctified our marriage. Do not worry, it is I, Jesus. Leave your fears and approach Me.* ♥ *I felt your hand....*[1] ♥

---

[1]Jesus said this very quickly.

I had been looking at His picture (big format) of the Holy Shroud while writing, and unconsciously with my mind I had pushed gently His hair (left side), placing it behind, away from his cheek. I was surprised at the immediate reaction.

Have you really felt my hand?
I have. Vassula, do you realize I am God? ♥
I'm sorry I did this.
Do not be. Be intimate with Me, just like you are. ♥ *Come, give Me your hand, I will keep it in Mine.* ♥

VISION OF HEAVEN AND THE HOLY BATTLE

March 26, 1987

Here below, God gave me a vision.

Delight Me, Vassula, and understand that I, God, am One. I will dearly wish to show you more of My Glory. Child, do you know how Heaven was created?
By You, through You.
Yes, I have measured every width, height, and depth; and all dimensions are perfect. Every little living creature comes from Me and is truly Mine. All Life comes from Me; My Breath is Life. Do you wish to learn more about My Heavenly Works?
Yes, Lord.
Then let us have a walk in My Glory.

I found myself walking with God's Presence in a beautiful garden, very colorful, plenty of bright light, but not from a normal sun. While walking, I noticed an enormous ball of light, almost touching the horizon. It was like a big Sun, but one could look at it without having the eyes burnt.

How do you feel, daughter?
It's beautiful; it's all strange!
What can you see?
This sort of "Sun".
Yes, it is My Holy Abode. And what can you see around that Light?

First it appeared to me that it was spots which moved around It. But then, they turned out to be little angels encircling It. There appeared to be millions of them.

♥ *They are cherubim encircling My Glory. What else do you see?*
Some steps going inside the "Sun".
Let us enter this Light. Are you ready? Take off your shoes, for we are entering on holy ground. We are now inside the Light.

I thought by entering it, I would find myself in very bright light, but no, everything was blue of colour, but what struck me most is the silence and the feeling of Peace and Holiness. It was amazing! Inside, all was a circle!

Yes, it's a circle.

The "wall" around was <u>no</u> "wall", but living things; they were angels, a wall of angels. And closing, like a dome was the ceiling made by angels...all blue; they were millions, billions, one stuck to the other; they were angels one stuck to the other; they were tall angels, one on top of another, stuck all together, forming a solid wall.

My seraphs are guarding this Holy Place and worshiping Me incessantly. Can you hear them?

"Holy of Holies, Holy is our God Most High."

How many are they, Lord?
Thousands, My child. Who is this with the gold Sword and so beautiful?

I saw someone like an angel which differed from the others because he was in "normal" color, dressed in a long white robe, golden hair to the shoulders, and he held in his hand a beautiful gold sword. And glittering his robe was; of the purest white.

Vassula, the Sword is My Word. My Word is pure. It pierces and illuminates.

Suddenly the "dome" opened like a flower.

♥ *Behold, little one, try to discern. I am near you, helping you. You will see above you now the Holy Battle that is to come. O daughter, keep a vigilant look around you and be aware that evil exists. Can you see anything?*

When the "wall" opened like a flower, I saw horses with black, velvety, fierce eyes. The image went further away and I saw a battle.

My army will combat Satan and his followers, including ♥ *all those that tried to destroy My Law.* ♥ *Remember that I am the Alpha and the Omega, the First and*

the Last. My Word is Everlasting. ♥ *Now what can you see?*
A reptile like a big snake which was thrown from a horse?
This dragon under the lance of My Saint, will be conquered. When this will be done, all his followers will fall too. Vassula, you will come now to see My Hall of Judgement?

I saw a big hall, but no one yet inside it. Then suddenly in one corner, I saw a group of souls. It was the clatter of chains that made me look. They seemed haggard, beyond description, and spotted with charcoal or some black spots. They seemed scared, uncertain as to where they were. They did not see us. They seemed to be surprised at their surroundings.

Listen to the trumpets. They are My angels announcing Me. Give Me your hand, for you are My little visitor. ♥ *Yes, every angel falls prostrate for Me. Have you seen this multitude of souls? They have just arrived from underground.[1] They are tormented souls who have been released. They were at Satan's gates.*
Who released them?
I did, ♥ *with My Heavenly Works, and all who repair and love Me. You see why I want you to love Me? The deeper you love Me, the better chance they have to be lifted and come to Me.* ♥ *Do you want to know what will become of these souls?*
Yes, Lord, what happens now?
♥ *Let Me tell you. I will baptize them with My Holy Spirit and free them completely; for not until they would be baptized by the Holy Spirit would they be able to share My Kingdom.*
But You mean these were not baptized?
They were not.
Would they want to be?
Yes, they want to. Come, I will explain; let us sit. What you saw was only an image of them; they were not really in My Hall; souls are not judged until the end.
♥
Where were these souls if they were not in Your Hall?
♥ *These souls were in Hades.[2] By being in Hades, they are helpless. When you choose Me and desire to follow Me, you are saved, but if you fail to recognize Me because of this obduracy, you will fall. Where you will go, will be endless martyrdom.* ♥ *I must warn you all, not that it has not been said before, but if anyone blasphemes the Holy Spirit, they will never be forgiven, for this is My Law.*

Lower you eyes before Me, child. ♥

I did.

---

[1] Purgatory, at Satan's gates.
[2] Purgatory.

Let Me bless you; I forgive your sins. Say these words:

> *May the Lord and God Almighty be Blessed;*
> *May His Kingdom reign in eternal Glory;*
> *May His Holy Name be Glorified;*
> *May His Word penetrate and rest in each heart.*
> *Amen.*

♥ *Vassula, do no more today; rest. I will dictate tomorrow My Message[1] about those who represent Me but are not giving Me enough love, nor draw from My Infinite Love either.* ♥ *Daughter, come, keep Me company. I need to rest; come near to Me; share My sorrow.*
My God, I'll do as you want, but also do not forget that there are many who love You dearly, and do not forget their sacrifices showing their love for You.
♥ *Yes, they uplift My sorrows and soothe My Wounds,* ♥ *but I need larger amounts of souls like these, ready to amend and diffuse My Infinite Love, spreading it like mist.* ♥ *I desire that they open their hearts and receive Me; I will fill their hearts with My Love, and when their hearts will overflow with love, they will be able to diffuse it and feed My lambs. Beloved, will you let Me rest in you?*
Yes, My God, do.
♥ *Will you rest in Me?*
Yes, My God, I will.
Come then; ♥ *I love you.*
I love You too My God.

I WANT MY PRIESTS TO BE HOLY

March 27, 1987

♥ ♥ *Vassula, I love you.*
I love you too, Jesus.

♥ *How I long for all My priests to be holy, since they represent Me. I wish them to become pure, holy, humble, and merciful. I want them to allow Me to pour into their heart the superabundant Love of Mine. I want them to draw more from the Riches of My Heart and fill their heart, impregnating it so that it overflows, thus, diffusing It all over the world. It is necessary that they seek to understand My lambs and love them, healing them. But to be able to do all this, they must learn to love Me as much as I have loved them. They must learn to love My children as*

---

[1] I felt God suddenly embittered.

I love them. They must honour My Church. I desire love; Vassula, tell them; let them know that My Lips are parched and thirst for love.

What use are sacrifices and rituals to Me, when their hearts are petrified and arid? I desire to fertilize this wilderness with Integrity. I need warmth. I need a living flame, purity, zeal, and an ardent love. Allow yourselves to draw from this Infinite Love and fill up your hearts. All I ask from you is faithfulness, purity and love. Come, come and repent to Me, come and change your lives. I will exalt you and you will receive Me; I want to remind you of My ways.

I have given you so many messages and signs, signs that you ignore. Have you forgotten My words? Do not be surprised at the weak instruments I use to manifest My words. Why, I could take any one of these stones and change them into devoted followers of Mine! Some of you will be seeking for proofs that it is I, Jesus, who gives you this Message. Have I not said that I will pour out My Spirit on all mankind and that My sons and daughters will all prophesy, that I will display portents in heaven and on earth? My ways are not your ways and My signs are not your signs.

I am revealing My Face again, but how many of you would believe? I groan with pain, I stifle, I suffocate to watch My seed filled with dead words. Fidelity... is this what you call yourselves to be when your hearts are dead? Come, come and absorb from My Heart. I ask you solemnly to repent and repair. Love Me purely and honour My Holy Eucharist. Yes, all you who deem yourselves just and pious, come and change your hearts, open your hearts and receive Me, and when you do, I will unveil your eyes and open your hearing.

♥ *Vassula, I will dictate to you tomorrow.* ♥ *You may rest, beloved.* ♥ *Have you discerned Me while I was editing?*
Yes, Lord, You were at the back of my right arm? Were You there?
♥ *I was, yes.* ♥ *Yes, now I am facing you Vassula* ♥ ♥ *yes, feel My Presence as you do* ♥ *Fear not,* ♥ *I will be near you.* ♥ *Come, let us rest in each other.*

WRETCHEDNESS ATTRACTS ME

March 30, 1987

♥ *It is I, Jesus Christ. All revelations are from Me. Sip from Me. A flower is growing near Me, sipping from Me. My flower, sip while you grow; absorb from Me,* ♥ *come, I love you.* ♥

Jesus, I don't mean to use the language I am using talking to You. It sounds very disrespectful. It's my daily language, but I don't know another. Reading now books of religious nuns, the way they talk with You is very different. Maybe they have been taught? I don't mean to sound vulgar; perhaps my heart speaks?

Vassula, I forgive your ignorance. ♥ I will teach you. You are learning. You are realizing how wretched you are; nevertheless, I love you. Wretchedness attracts Me, since I can offer you My Mercy. I have chosen you to show the world My Clemency.

I am not proud that You chose me because of my bad qualities and not of my merits. I feel like Judas...I probably represent most of our modern world.

Lo,[1] Vassula, you are not like Juda. You are helpless, ignorant and wretched beyond words; you are My beloved whom I sanctified. I took care of our union since you were unable to. My desire is to form you, I united you to Me, asking you to be My bride.
Jesus, I learned that nuns really get married to You.
Yes, they come to Me and become My brides, I delight in them! You were unaware that you could be My bride and be united to Me, so I have taken care of our union, see? I sanctified our marriage placing a ring on your finger. Work with Me and remember that I am Holy. Never forget this.

I THIRST FOR LOVE

April 3rd, 1987

♥ I am watching you; remember, we are united. I am Yahweh, and I love you.
I love you too, Lord!
Eat from Me; I love all of you. I have said My Kingdom on earth will be as it is in Heaven. I will uproot all evil and I will reinforce My devoted followers. I am Yahweh and My word stands secure; do not fear, little one, for I it is who leads. I am the Most High! I will offer My Bread to all mankind, thus appeasing their hunger, but I want a return of love from them. I thirst for love; tell them; let them know how My Lips are parched from thirst.

---

[1]Hebrew word for "no".

MY SHEEP ARE SCATTERED

April 4, 1987

I had discerned Him. His Presence was clear; His Lips were dry, cracked with blisters. He had difficulty talking as His Mouth was dry and His Tongue could hardly articulate. He seemed to have come from a desert where for days He was without water. It was a pitiful image.

While going around in Switzerland, I watched people and how they live. Many, like everywhere, have daily problems, some more than others. Many seem so unhappy and struggling. I never noticed this before God's approach to me.

Yes, Vassula, I want you to see all. I want you to watch and hear everything they say. I grieve to hear and watch My lambs; ♥ *why have they forgotten Me when I am their Consoler? I can console them; they can turn to Me.*

Here I was wondering if it was Yahweh or Jesus.

♥ *Vassula, I am One, I am One! Vassula, I am God who gave you life. I established My Word. I came on earth in flesh. I am One; I bless you, Vassula; the Holy Trinity is One, I am One.*

I was just thinking to learn by asking priests about this.

With Me you will learn.

Later on:

Daughter, when you will understand how indifferent the world has become towards Me, you will understand My bitterness. My Chalice of Mercy is full, and My Chalice of Justice is full too. They are grieving Me, embittering Me, creating revolutions,[1] rebelling against Me and My Law. I am the same Living God, but My people have grown fearless; they challenge Me; they provoke Me! ♥ *Creating them was a delight for Me; why are they rebelling against Me? Whom have they to turn to? I suffer. Where do they believe they are heading to? My Body is weary and injured; My Body needs to rest and be soothed.*

Are you referring to the Church, Lord?

Yes, My Body is the Church. Vassula, I wish to consolidate My Church; I wish to unite all My priests like an army, an army of salvation. My sheep are scattered; all priests should unite.

---

[1] Religious revolutions, I think.

My God, I personally am baptized as Greek-Orthodox. Whom are you referring to My Lord, to Catholics or Protestants, or sects, or other religions? If I dare ask You this, it's because it exists.

O Vassula, Vassula, I am One! I, God, am One; My children are all created by My Hand. Why are all My children dispersed? I desire Unity[1] I want My Children to unite. I am One God, and they must understand that the Holy Trinity is all in One! The Holy Spirit, the Holy Father, and Jesus Christ the Son, all three are in One. ♥

Vassula, cling to Me; learn from Me. ♥
My God, what about the Light?
I am the Light; ♥ ♥ *I am One.*

CREATURE, LIVE IN MY LIGHT

April 5, 1987

Vassula I love you infinitely. I will let you feel My Love by letting you feel My Heart.

I placed my hand on His Chest and felt His Heart throbbing.

♥ *Each beat of My Heart is a call to a soul. I long for My beloved to hear Me and approach Me.* ♥ *Today I have taken the essence of your love to Me to use it for healing a soul, Vassula.*

I felt it....

♥ *Creature, live in My Light.*
I love You, Lord.
♥ *Woman, live in Me.*
Teach me to love You more.
♥ *Beloved, come, let Me hide you in My Heart. Work with Me. Never weary of writing. Do not forget My Presence.* ♥

---

[1]Unity: I dare not even think out loud of what God's desires are! I understood....

April 6, 1987

Two weeks before The Orthodox Easter.

Vassula, prepare yourself for My torments. Devote yourself to Me; you will feel My pains; I am preparing you for My Crucifixion. I will suffer, but you will share My suffering, beloved; you will feel My anguish and My Wounds. Will you suffer with Me?
I will do Your will.
Come, let us rest in each other. ♥

SHARING THE CROSS

April 7, 1987

I felt as if the whole guidance is pressing on me and that I am alone with God's Word <u>heavily on me</u> and not having anywhere to unload it. I don't know what to do. I felt helpless beyond description and alone, <u>alone</u> with this weight on me.

Vassula, do I ever abandon you? I am God; lean on Me; trust Me. ♥
I should, yes, but there are times it's beyond me. I can't help it. I feel responsible.
My child, have patience, trust in Me. Come to Me, I will comfort you. ♥
I love you, Father, beyond words.

I felt how He was so ready to console me.

♥ *I love you, daughter. My sufferings I will make you feel when My Crucifixion comes nearer. I will come to you, leaving you My nails and thorned crown. I will give you My Cross. Beloved, share with Me My sufferings.* ♥ *Your soul will feel the anguish I had; your hands and feet, the excruciating pains I felt.* ♥ *Vassula I love you, and since you are My bride, I wish to share all I have with you. Believe Me, you will be with Me.* ♥ *Have no fear, for I, Jesus, am with you. Come, you will understand in phases how I work. Have My Peace, beloved, I have prepared a place for you.* ♥ ♥

April 8, 1987

Today I have a few things to do, but I could not resist writing to God, so I quickly asked Jesus: 'One word, Lord, just one word.'

♥ *One word, Vassula? "LOVE".* ♥ ♥
I love You!

I meant by one word, a short sentence or so!

DRAW MY SIGN ⊂✕ IXθYΣ

April 9, 1987

While in Switzerland, I was wondering where my home would be one day. We're still looking around, roaming, roaming, roaming.
Feel My presence.

I saw Jesus pointing to His Heart.

Your home is here...straight in the middle of My Heart! ♥ *Daughter, glorify Me by drawing souls to Me.*

My older sister for the first time learned about this Message. She read the last five copies. The influence of this was to make up a family quarrel of eight years with our first cousin. They are good friends again. I never uttered a word. Then she left for Rhodes where she lives. That first night she talked to her husband; he was more shocked than her. They read together book number five and six that evening. Then they went to sleep; but he couldn't; he started to pray and ask God to forgive his sins.
Then a miracle happened: God gave him the same vision I saw! The one of a beautiful garden and that "sun" all round, guarded with millions of angels. God made him penetrate like I did inside that round light, and when he felt God's presence so close, he started to shiver and weep. He woke up my sister, telling her. She was amazed. They couldn't wait until next morning to tell me of this. Then, in buying now the book of Enoch, which I always wanted, before I started to read it, I opened page 102, just like that, and what do I read? Enoch had the same vision as I had: the bright round Light guarded by thousands of angels! It was too much of a coincidence because this vision I saw while in Bangladesh on March 26. Then on April 11, 1987, when I was in Paris, while searching for books in a library, I stumbled on a book called "Metania", and what made me look at it was its cover. The picture of the cover was exactly my vision, Enoch's, and my brother-in-law's: the round light with the angels guarding it. After my sister left, I wrote, again letting God take my hand. God gave then Strato (my brother-in-law) a written message.

♥ *I love My lambs; unite My lambs. Whoever reads My Message will be eating My Bread.* ♥ *Whoever will get a sign from Me, will be those whom I wish to illuminate with My Grace¹.* ♥ *Draw My sign.²*

Vassula, start summarizing the guidance and rewrite My Message; I will guide you, illuminating you. ♥ *All that is repeated was for your education. You needed it.* ♥ *From the guidance my Message is to be called Peace and Love.*

It's terrible! I am too realistic, too skeptic; I can't help feeling again doubtful that this is happening. Why, why is it that they believe so fully and constant and I so inconstant. I who very well know that I can't handle my hand and how powerless I become when God takes possession of my hand, how He can throw the pencil from my hand, and how He can move the pencil without me much touching it. It's happening to me; He has given me so many proofs, and look, waves of doubt, still! And then, many times I start thinking that I might be misguiding everybody! There are so many in this guidance, I can't count them, and it's not even published!

♥ *Beloved, I am Yahweh; give me your weaknesses, and let My Strength annihilate them.*

What patience God must have with me to stand me... I think the main reason why I have doubts is because of me, because I know myself; I compare myself to those who get a supernatural approach to God and had received Messages. How good they were and how devoted. That is what strikes me; it's like comparing night with day. I admit one thing, though, positive: at least I love God deeply, and no one can tell me that it is my imagination or, like one priest told me, that even that the devil can put in your brain; if I was weak and would listen to all that I hear, I would have cracked down.

Today I heard from a lady (who just started Freud) that all this could be my subconscious, a love complex for God! So by loving God it means we are psychologically sick.

But her theory or Freud's does not affect me a bit since God warned me of these theories, and also that I will be accused. Then I do not particularly like Freud since he was an atheist; even Jung left him! For Freud we appear to be only material!

---

¹God made me understand that all those who read His Messages and do get illuminated (an attraction for God again) is enough sign that it is He who feeds them, and that the Message is from Him.
²"Ichthys" is the Greek word for "fish". The Greek initials stand for "Jesus Christ, God's Son, the Saviour.

♥ *My child, people always judged in human ways.* ♥ *I am a God full of Mercy and Love, but so little understood.*
But Lord, You have chosen a "no good one", that's what brings doubt to me!
You are My daughter too! I love even the most wretched among you.

April 10, 1987

Remember, My Crucifixion lasted for hours. I suffered many hours; all My Blood was shed. I love you; come and console Me by loving Me.

Jesus was feeling sad and was longing to be consoled. He was constantly reminding me of His Crucifixion these days and giving me images of it. Sometimes I feel His presence so fully that I think I could touch Him solidly; I could, so to say, feel the air moving when He moves.

HOLY THURSDAY

April 16, 1987

Vassula, I was present in My Church. I walked before My Cross; I paused a few seconds in front of you.[1] ♥ *My daughter, all these years I had been waiting for you to be in My so beloved Church.[2]* ♥
Lord and Saviour, You have indeed searched for me and found me and brought me to You and Your Church. It has been years... ♥ You've been waiting years!
I remained before My Cross, and everyone who came to worship Me, I blessed in turn.

The Holy Cross had been placed in the middle of the Church, and so everybody went by turn, kissing it.

---

[1] Strangely enough, while the procession of the Cross was going on, we had to move to give space to the priest who carried the holy Cross (about 2 meters long) and the church boys following with big candles. Because of the dimness, the priest was not looking where he was going and went straight to me. Realizing it, he stood for a few seconds in front of me, trying to see his way again. My cousin, who was with me, noticed this incident immediately. My heart raced as I faced the huge Cross, and as I could not go back more, since behind me, the crowd had lit candles; I couldn't move!
[2] I had not been in that church since the baptism of my eldest son; I think, fifteen years!

GOOD FRIDAY

April 17, 1987

At the end of the Holy Mass on Good Friday, the priest distributes the flowers that covered Jesus' tomb. He gives bunches to people. I received just three flowers in my hand; I understood this as a sign from God to remind me of the problem I had understanding the Holy Trinity.
Two days went by, and I did not write, which I missed terribly, as when I write like in meditation, I contact and <u>feel</u> God very much.

My God , it's been a long time!
How long?
Two days!
Two days, Vassula? And I who waited years for you; what shall I say then?
I am speechless, Jesus; I am sorry to have wounded You. Forgive me.
Come, I forgive you. All I wish from My beloved souls is to let Me arrest their heart for just a few minutes and let me pour into it My superabundant Love. ♥

Jesus said this with such tenderness and love!
Whenever God approaches me to give me an important message, the devil or his demons attack me. I do not feel him physically, but the only thing he is allowed to do in this guidance is to manifest himself by writing, thus insulting me and cursing me. Since I was taught by God to know the difference and recognize his words, I usually prevent him to finish his word even, which infuriates him. If it escapes my notice, God blocks my hand and it cannot write. These attacks are always stronger when God's important message is about to be written. I have realized now the pattern, so I don't give up, although I do feel hopeless at times.

I HAVE LIBERATED YOU

April 23, 1987

Sometimes I wonder what freedom is. Before God's call, I was free too. I had my family life in harmony, having really no responsibility, no cares such as this message which <u>crushes</u> me and weighs on me. But then I was always aloof to God. Suddenly, God held me. In the beginning, I did not like it since I had no love for Him. But in a short time only (three months) after preaching to me, He taught me to love Him. Now after eight months, the whole message is almost completed. It's weighing on me, and I'm looking for somewhere to unload It. It's so <u>very heavy</u>! What is freedom? The weight was intolerable.

♥ I, the Lord, will let you know what freedom is. ♥ ♥ Write: Freedom is when your soul detaches itself from earthly solicitudes and flies towards Me, to Me. ♥ I, God, came and liberated you. You are free now. When you were attached to this world, Vassula, you were a prisoner to all it's temptations, ♥ but your soul now, like a dove, has been freed. You were caged, beloved, caged. Let your soul sail out freely; let it feel this freedom I have given to all of My souls, but how many of them refuse this Grace I offered. Do not let yourself be caught again, tied and caged; I have liberated you. ♥
While I was passing, I saw you in your cage, withering away slowly and dying. Vassula, how could My Heart see this and not redeem you? I came and broke your cage, but you were unable to use your wings, such were your injuries. So I carried you to My abode, healing you tenderly, letting you fly again. And now, My Heart so much rejoices to see My little dove flying freely and being where she should have been from the very beginning.[1]
I, the Lord, freed you; I have restored you; I have liberated you from your misery. My Eyes never leave you from their sight; I watch My dove flying freely, knowing all the time that you will always return to Me, for you recognize your Saviour and Master! Your soul needs My warmth, and you know that your abode now is in the middle of My Heart where I always desired you to be. You belong to Me now, and I am your Master who loves you.

The thought of going to Switzerland came to me. I fear that I might change there.

Vassula, I will not let you soil yourself again.
But, Lord, the air is "polluted".
♥ Do not fear, I will always be near you, cleaning you. I have My reasons for you to be there.

I was trying to think of God's reasons. Then I asked.

I want My seeds to be sown in Europe. Be My sower, Vassula. Live among people who wound Me. Let your eyes see everything, and watch what My creation has become. Let your heart feel how little I count for them. Let your ears hear how they profane Me and wound Me. Will your soul not revolt? Will you not cry out for Me when you will see and understand how My people have forgotten Me? Vassula, your soul will be exposed in wickedness, in indifference, in the depths of iniquities, and in the vile depths of sin of the world. As a dove flying above them, you will watch the world, seeing with bitterness every action. You will be My

---

[1] Jesus was saying this with such happiness in Him, breathing deeply.

sacrifice; you will be My target. Like hunters after their game, they will hunt you and pull out their weapons pursuing you. They will rate you at a high cost for whoever could destroy you. ♥

Lord! what will happen to me?

I will tell you this, daughter: all will not be in vain. ♥ *Shadows on earth fade out and pass away. Clay will always wash away with the first drops of rain, but your soul will never pass away.* ♥ ♥ ♥

I, the Lord, remind you what your answer was to My question: I had asked you once, "Whose house is more important, your house or My House?" You answered correctly that My House is more important. ♥

I did.

I will always keep you in My Heart. ♥ *I love You.*

I love you too.

♥ *Let us go; do not forget My Presence!*

BE NOTHING AND LET ME BE EVERYTHING

April 26, 1987

Let Me tell you, beloved, that I have drawn My designs before you were born. ♥ *We will be working always together. Are you willing to?* ♥

I am willing to if You accept me in my incapacity, My God.

♥ *I love you, Vassula; I will help you. Earlier last week you were ravaged and attacked by evil. Nevertheless, I have written with you every word I wanted to. I covered you.*

Was this when the devil cursed me?

Yes, while he was cursing you infamously, I was blessing you; I protected you.

Later on:

Let me tell you, Vassula, that the least you are, the more I will be; allow Me to act in you and do My will in you; be nothing. Feel nothing and let Me be Everything, so that My Word reaches the ends of the world, and My Works of Peace and Love entice every heart. Allow Me to remind you of your misery, so that by reminding you, it will prevent you from becoming elated by all the Graces I have given you. Be My pure altar... ♥ *Fisherman of men; spread My Net of Peace and Love all over the world,* ♥ *have It pulled, and let Me delight at Its catch! When I was in flesh on earth, I taught a small group of men to become fishermen of men.* ♥ *I left them in the world to spread My Word to all mankind.* ♥ *I, the Lord Jesus, will*

instruct you and show you how this work was done. ♥
What can I say? <u>How</u> could I do anything, let alone such a mission! I feel that the message is getting heavier by the day. I do want to please God, but with what means? I can only see an alp in front of me, and the guidance heavy on me.
I am bearing My Cross together with you. Yes, It is indeed heavy; do not weary though; I, the Lord, am helping you. Keep close to Me. I will not forsake you. ♥
♥

"Still it is so much." Jesus is encouraging me to continue.

Vassula, have I not helped you this far? So why would I abandon you? Lean entirely on Me; trust Me. ♥ *What I have commenced and blessed, I will finish.*

LITTLE DOVE FLY FREELY
BUT ALWAYS RETURN TO ME

April 27, 1987

Vassula, I am the Lord standing in front of you. ♥

Jesus was there smiling and making me feel His Presence. He was holding with His two hands His mantle, pulling it open, showing me His Heart. His chest was lit.

Enter in My Heart, penetrate, and let It engulf you. Let my Heart enrapture your heart, inflaming it, leaving it ablaze, radiating My Peace and Love. Come, let us be together. Allow Me to be your Holy Companion. Are you willing, daughter?

I feel unable to approach Him. Who am I to approach Him?
I realized how unworthy I am. How could one even allow oneself to dare talk with God, we, who are a bunch of ungrateful sinners? let alone ask Him favours, even less having "conversation" with Him! We are so lousy and unworthy that it makes me feel sick. I feel like taping a tape over my mouth, and in His presence where I was, with my mind, I put a veil between Him and me out of respect for His Presence.

Daughter, what have you done? Why, daughter, why?
To respect You, Lord.
♥ ♥ *I want you to eat.* ♥
I saw in His Hand, Bread.

*Take My Bread, little one. You will have to take away this veil to take My Bread.[1]
Come, I will take away the separation...* ♥ *Here, take My Bread, approach.* ♥

I did, I took from His Hand His Bread.

Do you realize how delighted I am feeding you?

Jesus was full of Love and happy.

*Can you feel My happiness, Vassula? Bring forth your weaknesses and your
wretchedness, that I may annihilate them in My Strength and My Mercy. Little
dove, fly freely, but always return to Me and have My Bread. I love you.* ♥
I love You too Lord.

After this, for a whole day, I felt His Love on me. What can I call it? "Ecstatic
state"? By being in that way, I felt His Presence even more than usual.

Later on:

*You have seen My Holy Sanctuary where we penetrated, and I let your eyes see
how My Holy Sanctuary is guarded by My Seraphims. Today I will show you what
I have inside My Holy Sanctuary. Can you see this strong Ray shed on My Holy
Writings?*
Yes, Lord!
*They are My Holiest Writings, written before I created you. My Holy Book holds
the secrets and keys to My Heavens and the whole of My Creation. Near My Holy
Book, I have placed two archangels guarding ardently My Holy Writings. Come,
I will show you more of My Glory, little one.*

God took me in a place where I felt uneasy.

Do you see this mountain of fire?

It looked beautiful but menacing.

From its side flow two of its rivers, they are all out of fire.

It looked like flowing lava, but clearer red.

*I, the Lord, shall part on the day of My Judgement, the evil souls from the good
souls. Then, all the followers of Satan shall be cast in those two rivers of fire and*

---

[1]His Holy Word: all His symbolic.

shall perish before the very eyes of the just. ♥ *Vassula, I will let your eyes see more of My Heavens, for there are several more behind My Holy Sanctuary.* ♥ *Creature, My Will will be done, for I am God, Yahweh Sabaoth. Let Me free to act in you; we will work together with love until I will establish My Works, and when I do, I will come with My Holy Book again and will let you read in it a passage which you will write, thus sealing My Message of Peace and Love.*

In the middle of the night, I was wakened up by Jesus's loud cry that came from the Cross. It was full of anguish, suffering, pain, sorrowful, and bitter. It sounded like a very strong moan! dragging.

MY LAST LOUD CRY FROM MY CROSS

April 29, 1987

Next morning

♥ ♥ *I am the Lord Jesus; you heard My Cry; it was I. It woke you up;[1] I cried out from My Cross. It was My last, loud cry I gave when I was in flesh, a cry full of sufferings, pains, and bitterness resounding from the depths of My Soul, piercing the heights in Heaven. It shook the earth's foundations and tore in half the hearts of those who loved Me, as it ripped the veil in the Temple.* ♥ *It aroused devoted followers of Mine, as It aroused the dead from the graves, overthrowing the earth that covered them, as It overthrew Evil. Great thunder shook the very Heavens above, and every angel, trembling, fell prostrate and worshipped Me in total silence.* ♥ *My Mother, standing nearby, on hearing My Cry, fell to the ground on her knees and covered her face, weeping, carrying that last cry with Her to the day of Her dormition, She suffered...I am embittered, suffering still from many iniquities of the world, wickedness, lawlessness, and egoism. My Cry is growing louder every day. I was left alone on My Cross, alone to bear the sins of the world on My Shoulders, alone to suffer, alone to die, shedding My Blood, which covered the entire world, redeeming you, My beloved ones.* ♥ *That same Cry is now on earth like an echo of the past. Am I living in the shadows of the past? Was My Sacrifice in vain? How can you not hear then My Cry from The Cross? Why do you shut your ears and dispel It?* ♥

---

[1]Symbolic?

Lord, for who is this message?
For all those who have ears to hear My Cry.

I felt very touched, knowing how much He suffered all alone, and is still suffering.

My God, I accept to be as You wish me to be in Your message of April 23, Your sacrifice, Your target; let me bear Your Cross for You and let Me give You rest. Let me comfort You. I am not alone like I said before, I'm with You.[1]
I love you, little dove; I indulged you with all My Graces; ♥ *allow Me to use you for My own interests and My own Glory; retain nothing for yourself, and look upon My own interests only.* ♥ *Glorify Me; work for Me; add to your sufferings, My sufferings.* ♥
I wish the whole world praised Your Name, its voice reaching You.
♥ *Unity will strengthen My Church.* ♥ *Unity* ♥ *will glorify Me.* ♥ ♥ *Vassula, love me.* ♥
Teach me to love you as You want, Lord.
I will. I will not abandon you. Do not weary bearing My Cross; I am near you, sharing It, beloved. ♥

In Paris during Easter:

When the Archimandrite said to me on looking at the Messages: "It is a miracle." I also thought: how wonderful, how beautiful that God gives us a Message; but on the other hand, how terrible, terrible because it shows a sad God, a suffering God. God gives a Message in agony, unhappy, and abandoned by many. It is a sad message.

Am I learning at all, Jesus? Not that I ask to satisfy myself, but to know at least where I stand, I mean if I progress at all!
Vassula, I, Jesus, am before you, and you are indeed growing. I raised you from the dead and I fed you. You are eating My Bread. My Light shines upon you. I am your Teacher, and you are learning from Wisdom.
Jesus, many times you reminded me to stay small and remain nothing. Now You tell me that I am growing?
♥ *Yes, you must grow in spirit, in love, in humbleness, in humility, in faithfulness; <u>let all the virtues grow in you</u>; nevertheless, becoming nothing in vanity, in wickedness, and all the repugnant and detestable practices in My Eyes.* ♥ *I want you to become perfect.* ♥

---

[1] I take back what I said on April 7.

I AM THE ELIXIR OF LIFE
I AM THE RESURRECTION

April 30, 1987

Jesus, today I will ask You if You are willing to give a special message for a person who is dying?
Dying?[1] She is not dying. Her soul will be freed, she will be liberated and will live! She will come to Me. Her soul will be free. Write and tell her how I am seeking every soul; how I am feeding hungered souls; how My Bread gives eternal life; how I restore the sick. Let her know that I am the Elixir of Life and the Resurrection.
Jesus gave me a message for this person in a separate paper.

LOVE WILL CONQUER EVIL

May 1, 1987

♥ *I, God, will give you enough strength to enable you to accomplish My Works. Deny Me never; do not seek your own interest, but My own. Leave me free to use you and descend on earth through you, manifesting My Word until I come to deliver you.* ♥ *Vassula, I will predict your end.* ♥ *All of My chosen souls never feared death.* ♥ *I will reveal to you five more of My mysteries. Come now, and kiss My five Wounds.* ♥

I did, first His Hands, then His Feet, then His Side. Nevertheless, I do not yet understand what Jesus means by five mysteries coinciding with His five wounds. But I know that when the time is right, He will let me know. So I learned not to ask.

Vassula, I will tell you My secrets when you grow a little bit more. Beseech My favours and I will grant them.
My God and Father, ♥ I will ask You one thing which has a few clauses and that is only for Your interests and Glory: May Your Message reach the ends of the world and draw many hearts to You; may Your will be done and Your Holy Name glorified; may evil lose its grip and be crushed for ever. This is what I wish now, and every time You will hear my voice for a request, it will be none other than for

---

[1]Jesus seemed a bit astonished at my words.

Your Glory. Any favour asked from me, will be for Your Glory; any cry of help from me will be for Your own interests and nothing for me. All the strength I will ask, will be for Your interests, God Almighty.
♥ *Little one, place your feet into My Footprints and follow Me.* ♥ ♥

Later on:

It is I, ♥ *Jesus.*
Jesus?
I am. Beloved, call Me Spouse and Father too. I love you. Come let us work.[1] ♥
Love Me fervently and repair for others who wound Me. ♥

My God, I was thinking, how could I be like a dove flying above the "wicked world" if I myself am wicked and sinful? Being in the same state as all the rest, I will be unable to "see all" as You said and "hear everything", for I am no better than the ones that wound You.
Vassula, be in Me. Endeavour to attain purity. Draw from Me, from My Purity which I offer; draw; sip from Me; absorb Me; I am Infinite Wealth, and every soul can draw from Me. ♥
Having received so many graces, I might become vain, and evil can tempt me easily!

I will always remind you of your wretchedness and the shadows of your past. I will remind you of how you denied Me and rejected My great Love when I approached you, and of how I found you dead, lying among the dead in darkness, and of how, out of Mercy and Love, I revived you, lifting you to My Breast. Come, let us pray.
♥

Say:

> *My Father, lead me wherever Your will wishes me to go.* ♥
> *Allow me to live in Your Light and warm my heart,*
> *That it may glow,*
> *Giving warmth on those who approach me.*
> *Blessed be Your Name,*
> *For giving me all these Graces,*
> *In spite of my nothingness.*
> *Blessed be Your Name,*
> *For the Good You have done to me,*
> *And the Mercy You have shown me,*
> *Lifting me near Your Heart.* ♥ *Amen.*

---

[1]Jesus said all this in such grace and serenity that only God can talk in this way.

Let us repeat. Remember that all the Graces I am giving you are for My own interests; retain nothing for yourself. Glorify Me, sharing My happiness.

I wish that I will be able to glorify You, and that the world may praise Your Name, and their prayers reach You, rising like incense, their praises resounding in Heaven at Your door like a knock.

Love will conquer evil. Love Me with all your soul and mind. Let Me be everything. I, the Lord, will provide you till the end.

Then take me, even though I am nothing, and do as You wish with me. I am Yours.

Come, let Me rejoice, always hearing these words of total surrender. I love you, daughter.

I love You, Father.

MESSAGE FOR THOSE WHO LOVE ME

May 2, 1987

I am Jesus.

Jesus, I sense that You are about to give me an important message according to the pattern: evil attacking me to discourage my writing.

I have a message for those who love Me[1] and immolate their souls for Me. ♥ I wish to encourage them, giving them Strength.

I, the Word, will manifest My words through this weak instrument. I will descend on earth through this Message, letting My Light shine on you all. I bless you, beloved of My Soul. I love you!

I have within Me, in the depths of My Intimate Soul, a Living and Inexhaustible Flame. I am Purity and Devotion and an abyss of Wealth. My beloved, come and draw from Me, saturating your hearts. Come and sip from Me. ♥ Come and penetrate into My open Wounds. Come and immerse your souls in My Blood! Drink from My Living Fountain so that you will be able to submerge, irrigating this desolate wilderness, healing My lambs. Draw from this Living Flame, and let It engulf your hearts!

I love you to a degree your minds can never grasp. Come, do not weary bearing My Holy Cross, for I am with you, bearing It with you. Follow Me and keep close to Me. Place your feet into My Footprints. Do not weary of striving and suffering. Glorify Me, and let your voices rise in Heaven like the sweet smell of incense. Praise Me, let Me rejoice, let Me delight in you. Let Me delight in your love for Me. Fill up your heart from this Infinite Love, and let It flow out on My lambs, ♥ healing them. Let every living creature on earth feel My warmth. Let every cold

---

[1] All priests, religious, sisters, brothers, all those who love Him truly.

and petrified heart melt and dissolve in My Purity, integrating in My Body and becoming one with Me! Let every shadow of the past revive into a living soul, full of Integrity, Peace, and Love; make an Eden of my Creation! Unite! Unite and be one, for I, God am One; unity brings strength.

Unite, ♥ *be My devoted sowers, sowing My seeds of Peace and Love. I have created grains that will yield into a heaven on earth, for My Kingdom on earth will be as in Heaven. Take My grains which lie in My Heart, purified by My Blood, and scatter them all over.* ♥ *I am bearing those seeds, beloved, and I desire that you enter into My Heart and draw them.* ♥ *Seek unity.*

I will heal My flowers. I will fragrance them. I will flourish them; I will embellish My Garden. I will irrigate your hearts. I will revive you. Creation! I love you! I will shine on you and let My warm Rays dissolve those heavy, dark thunder clouds, scattering them away, dispersing them.

My Light will pierce them and all darkness and evil that laid heavily upon you, will disappear. This darkness that brought you only weakness, wretchedness, and wickedness. My warm Rays will revive all My flowers and I will pour from Heaven, My dew of Righteousness, Holiness, Purity, Integrity, Peace and Love.

I am your Devout Keeper with a vigilant eye on you. Remember, I am the Light of this world; I am the Word. Peace be with you all.

Glorify Me, lean on Me, strive, and do not weary bearing My Cross, healing My children. ♥

My Vassula, never weary of writing. ♥ *I love you. Wisdom will instruct you.* ♥ ♥

I Love You Lord, may Your will be done.

SCATTER MY GRAINS

May 5 1987

When I feel God's love on me (us), my mind almost reels! When He makes me dissolve in His Body, and His Body annihilates mine, it is then that I feel like air, like truly I am spirit without flesh! Ecstatic state? Even these words cannot describe fully the state His Love can bring me to. His Grace and goodness is impossible to describe; there are no words to describe such greatness and splendour of His Holiness. And to know how I, before His approach, rejected Him!

Vassula, come to Me; My five Wounds are open. ♥ *Vassula penetrate into My Wounds and feel My pain; come let My Blood sanctify you in My Wounds; glorify Me. I will guide you daughter. Freely I give, so give freely too. I, the Lord, will return with My Holy Book.*

Jesus had a small book with Him.

Discern and read where I point. ♥ *"Betrothed, blessed of My Soul, daughter of Mine, feed My lambs. Scatter My grains. Let them yield a rich harvest, reap it, and give My Bread freely.* ♥ *I am the Bread of Life, feed My sheep.* ♥ *I am always with you till the end of times."* ♥
My God, thank You for Your Guidance. I sound arid with these naked words, but I have to put them on paper. May Your Name be blessed for ever and ever.
I love you, I will not forsake you. We will work together. Do not weary writing. ♥
Now I have sealed My Message of Peace and Love; I will guide you, Vassula; come to Me. ♥ ♥
I shall follow You, Lord. I love You.
♥ *Leave Me free to act in you.*
Lord, may Your will be done.
I will instruct you with Wisdom. ♥ ♥

LET ME BE YOUR CAPTOR

May 5, 1987

Yesterday, after the end of God's Message, I felt God in Me and I in Him so very much; I felt I could not separate ever.

My companion, I love you. Vassula, give Me everything; give Me all you have.
I have given You my love; I have given You myself; I have detached my feelings from earth, I have surrendered. Can I give You anything more?
Daughter, I love to hear you surrendering. Let Me be your Captor.

I could feel Jesus this evening so strongly, that I could see distinctly His Face, which was not easy the other times. This evening He seemed so very intense, fervent, eager, like someone who comes determined with fervor to convince someone who is lukewarm.

Will you kiss My Wounds?

I did, in a mystical way. Then I asked Jesus to sit at the chair nearby me. Immediately I felt "mystically" again that He did. He faced me and stretched His arm on the table reaching me on my copy-book. (Jesus imprints in my mind these impressions.)

Flower of Mine, devote yourself entirely to Me. Are you ready to hear Me?
Yes, Jesus.
Betrothed, blessed of My Soul, freely I gave, so freely give. Unite with Me, be one with Me, look into My Eyes.

I did.

Jesus, what can I do more?
Love Me.
But I love You. I said it many times, and You know I mean it. My soul longs for You. You wanted me to be detached, and I became detached.
Do I, Vassula, not long for you?

This is where I understood what it meant that: "The soul longs for its God, and God longs for its soul."

Do I, as your God, not suffer too?[1] Beloved, live in Me, and I in you, you in Me and Me in you, us. ♥ Adapt in Me, unite.
But You have united us, Jesus, you said You did!
I have. ♥

I suddenly felt physically exhausted, so I asked permission to go.

Shall we go Jesus?
Daughter, why?
I am exhausted, Jesus.
Beloved, I want you to stay, will you stay?
It was the first time Jesus insisted.

I will stay then...
Torn is My Heart when I am left alone.
But You are with me; we are together...

I am with you now, but you do forget Me many times. ♥ Leave Me free, and let My Divine Hands mould you as I wish. I will form you to My image. Let Me free to work in you. I am Jesus, and Jesus means Saviour. Daughter, I love you to jealousy, I want you all Mine, I want everything you do, to be for Me. I do not tolerate rivals. I want you to worship Me and live for Me. Breathe for Me, love for Me, eat for Me, smile for Me, immolate yourself for Me, everything you will do, do it for Me. I want to consume you; I want to inflame you desiring Me only. Adorn Me with your petals, My flower, crown Me with your love, remove My

---

[1] From being separated from the soul, being in the flesh.

thorned Crown and replace it with your soft petals, fragrance Me with your fragrance, love <u>Me</u> and Me only. I have laid out My life for you, out of Sublime Love, would you not do the same for Me, your Spouse? Betrothed, rejoice your Spouse, make Me happy! Bind yourself to Me with eternal bonds. Live for Me and Me alone. Be My Sacrifice, be My Target, be My Net! ♥ Creature, do you love Me?

How can I not love You, My God? I do!

Say it. Say it many times. Let Me hear it; I love hearing it. Say it a thousand times a day; and every morning after you rest in Me, face Me and tell Me, "My Lord, I love You. ♥

Jesus, I love You, but why are You becoming stern?

Maybe I am not doing enough.

Come, do not misunderstand Me! It's Love talking, it's Love's desires, it's Love's Flame, it's Love's Jealous Love; I cannot stand rivals. Lean on your Holy Father, Spouse, Companion, and God. Come, let us rest in each other.
Love Me, daughter, with a jealous love too.

LOVE WILL SUFFER

May 6, 1987

I am learning what God means by surrendering completely: be detached, leave everything and follow Him. His Words are symbolic, they are not material.

<u>Surrender</u>: I have, by loving Him first and beyond everything else and feeling I would like Him to use me.

<u>Being detached</u>: Yes, to the extent of being detached from my body, meaning that I realize I have a soul that desires to detach itself from the body to join Him and follow Him only.

<u>Suffer</u>: Yes, suffering because of not being with Him, of being still material on earth, of having the feeling of being a widow here. Suffering to know that I have to follow a daily life, material life...still feeling dissolved in God.

I love you, see? Love will suffer, love binds; Love offers abundant fidelity, love has no restraint to sacrifice. ♥ ♥
Vassula, the hours are fleeing, your time is near, offer yourself. Grow in humility. Eat from My Hand, My beloved. I will unbind your chains, and your soul will fly to Me very soon. ♥ ♥ ♥

I love you My God....

THE THORNED CROWN

May 7, 1987

I love you. It is I, your Spouse. My flower, I will purify you; I will continue saturating you, vivifying you with My Light, and feeding you with My Strength. ♥
Vassula, I will honour you by letting you wear My thorned Crown. ♥
Jesus, how can You trust me?
I love you. By wearing My Crown, you will understand the mockery I received, for soon you too will be mocked upon. Do not forget, I will suffer as much as you will suffer, for I am in you and you in Me. I have united Myself to you; we are one. ♥ *Come now, beloved, we will continue My Works. I will give you enough Strength till the end.* ♥

Jesus, in this message, I understood later on, prepared me. I will be mocked and laughed at. At least He is with me; we will share the mockeries together.

ACTS OF LOVE

May 7, 1987

Jesus, do you know I have not even managed to even reach a hundred times saying, "I love You," and You asked me to say it a thousand times!
Vassula, ah Vassula, do you not know that every act done with love is telling Me, "I love You"? You are showing Me your love in that way too. Everything you do in your life, you do it to Me. ♥

Come, embellish! flourish! radiate! fragrance! Adorn Me with wreaths of love. Let every one of your petals replace a thorn from My thorned Crown. The more petals, the less thorns piercing Me. I love you. Love Me, teach others to love Me, show them My appeal. ♥
With Your help, I am showing them. I can't do much.
Love Me and heal My Wounds; let the tears shed for Me, be a soothing balm to My Wounds. ♥ *Vassula, wreaths are not made only for funerals, they are also made for brides. Allow me to place a wreath upon you in August.* ♥

May 8, 1987

Jesus, today I have lots of work at home; two words from You will make me happy! *Just two? "Love Me."* ♥ ♥

I AM THE MOST HIGH - I LOATHE PAGANISM

May 9, 1987

I was thinking when I just watched a documentary of the "Fatima Miracle", how even with that, many people were skeptic, calling it all sorts of things like mass hypnosis, etc. In the old times, this sort of miracle would have been believed and written in the holy Bible, but nowadays, years have to go by before anything will be accepted.

I am fearing that Your Message will not be counted that it's from You, since there will be no physical proof or prediction in it. Every high authority, if it comes that far, will not even pay attention to Your appeal and I know that Your Cup of Justice is at its full now! The world is offending You very much. They will not listen.
Is there a higher authority than Your God?
No, My God, none, but if they do not listen? Some of them might think it is propaganda for the Church, I mean those who are in high authority and anti-Church. They might think that all this was made up! Made up by the Church!
♥ *Vassula, I am the Most High, and all authority will come from Me.* ♥
And if they do not believe?
I will not write down what will happen if they will not listen from their obduracy.
♥ *Are you fearing Me, little one?*

God must have felt in me a fear that passed through me. At the same time when He was writing the word "happen", I felt a pang of sadness in God's Heart.

Yes, I am, from Your wrath!

I will endure and forgive your sins, but I will not endure your hatred against Me. I am your Creator, and your breath comes from Me. I hold the whole of My creation in My Hand. I loathe paganism. Vassula, let Me guide you. Come, My child, rest in Me. ♥

May 9, 1987

♥ *Your sigh, betrothed, is like a million words of love to Me.* ♥ *Yes, I am talking about your sigh you gave Me this morning.* ♥

It's true; this morning I just thought of Jesus with love. I wanted to tell Him so much, but I could not find even the right words. I gave a sigh only, but He seemed to understand a lot from my sigh.

Vassula, love Me blindly, and let Me use you as I wish; be utterly nothing so that in being nothing, I can be everything and thus complete My Works. Creating you was a delight for Me.
My God, I fear to disappoint You by being unfaithful to You. I don't know even if I was, to start with, at all faithful. So what am I saying of keeping faithful, if I'm not sure of having been at all faithful?
From all eternity I knew you to be weak and wretched, but I love you. I have taken My measures so that you remain faithfully Mine. Have you imagined that I have not known all this? I knew everything, and that is precisely why I chose you. I told you that your ineffable weakness and misery attracts Me. Come, this guidance will restore My honour. I rejoice at how it will remedy your injustices. Vassula, crown Me with tender words!
My words, Lord, what possible value have they got to such a Majestic Presence!
Every tender and loving word, coming even from you, becomes divine in My Presence. It becomes great in My Ears.
Never weary of writing, My little instrument. Everything you do, comes from Me. I suspend you with My Strength, and I call you when I wish. I love you, love your Lord too.

I felt again that His Greatness annihilated me completely. It was like plunging in the deepest ocean. A wonderful feeling of wanting to <u>be</u> possessed by God and being pleased to be!

DO YOU BELIEVE IN MIRACLES?

May 10, 1987

Vassula, do you remember when I fed My people with manna? I threw it from Heaven; it came from My stores in Heaven. Do you know that it is I who lifted the seas so that My people could cross to the Sinai?
Yes, Lord.

I am Omnipotent, ♥ *little one. I am the One who installs together this guidance to feed many.* ♥ *I have, Vassula, communicated with you all this time! See?*
My God, and still I'm fearing that this is done by my subconscious....
Let Me tell you instantly that you would never have done all this work on your own! Do you believe in miracles?
Yes, I do.
Consider this as a miracle then. I love you.
I love You, Father. How could I explain to people when they ask me how do I see You. I feel Your Presence very much, and it's no fancy.
Tell them that you see Me with the eyes of your soul. ♥
Sometimes, Jesus, I think I'm imagining You and want to turn my eyes away from You (the vision) to convince myself it's not You.
In doing this you offend Me, Vassula. I have given you this Grace, accept My gift, accept what I give you!
Lord, sometimes, and especially in Bangladesh with the heat, I feel exhausted, I wish I could do more work. Sometimes I wish I was like an amoeba, split in several pieces!
I give you enough strength to complete My Works. ♥ *Luke once said: "I will never exhaust, since I am working for the Lord, for the Lord Himself is my strength."* ♥ *Little one, I have led you as a father would leads his little child by the hand to school. Estimate, what you have earned with Me?*
I have indeed earned a lot since I never practiced religion, nor had the Bible in the house since school time. And, not having been to church since the baptism of my first son, fifteen years ago, You taught me many things. Not that I now consider myself as a scholar, but at least You taught me who You are and how much You love us, and of how to love you.
I have given you fruit from My own garden. I wish to fill up your stores with My fruit.

I asked Him something which I don't wish to write down.

I know, Vassula, let it be like I wish it to be. ♥

I could not help making a smile to my ears, it felt so good to have a small 'chit-chat' in this way with Jesus. I felt Him like I was talking to a good friend. I couldn't help smiling. I was almost giggling, I was happy!

I am cheerful too. ♥

Yes, He was, it was marvellous!

Vassula, do you know how I delight and enjoy these moments, these moments where you talk to Me as a companion? Vassula, we still have work to be done. Be blessed; I will give you a sign of My Presence, beloved.

Jesus, what sign, I mean, where?
In your house. ♥ I will prove to you that I am present. ♥
I love You, Jesus; I wish I could please You.
Altar! Keep drawing from Me and keeping My Flame in you ardently ablaze. ♥

ANNIHILATE INTO MY BODY

May 13, 1987

Yesterday, May 12, in the evening, while passing the staircase level, I stopped with this intense odour of incense. The smell reached up to the second floor. I was surprised. I went and asked my son if he had lit a mosquito coil, although it did not smell at all like a coil, but pure church incense. He said, no. I left this incident aside and got busy with other things. One hour later, I wanted to go to the study where I usually write to fetch a pencil, and while I entered the study again, this intense beautiful perfume of incense passed me by, it bathed me entirely!

O beloved, when I covered you with My odour, I blessed you at the same time.
Oh! Jesus, was that You?
Yes, you felt My Presence; this was My sign.[1] The incense comes from Me. ♥
If only I was sure that evening!
I will give you more signs of My Presence, My flower. Be alert though. ♥
Jesus, my Love, my Breath, my Life, my Joy, my Sigh, my Rest, my Holy Companion, my Saviour, my Sight, my Everything, I love You!
♥ Vassula, love Me fervently, annihilate into My Body, adorn Me with tender words, loving words; let My pains diminish. Soothe My Wounds by imbuing them with loving words. ♥

I discovered by reading today Saint Theresa that odours do exist. If they are from the devil, they have a horrible stench, so she says. Strangely enough, this was like another proof to me given today to show me that the incense odour did come from Jesus. I was very happy.

---

[1]Jesus predicted the day before that He will give me a sign of His Presence.

May 14, 1987

Today, what joy in reading the life of Saint Theresa of Avila, who had visions; I fell upon a vision she describes of hell, and I was very pleased to find that her description fitted my description of hell that God gave me. She explains it this way: "Dark and closely confined, the ground seemed to be <u>full of water</u> which looked like <u>filthy, evil-smelling mud</u>, etc." Yes, the whole thing looked like a grotto, low ceiling...my description is in book Number 8.[1]

TEMPTATION

May 15, 1987

Come, surrender. I delight to hear you surrendering, for in surrendering, it rejoices My Heart. Little one! ask Me to use you.
Father, if I am of any use to You, use me then!
♥ *I love you,* ♥ *come, do you wish to write?*
I will write if it is Your wish.
Do write then. Let it be known that I, Yahweh, willed to enlighten you. ♥ *Your only recourse is Me. My Heart is an abyss of Forgiveness and Mercy.* ♥ *Little one, as I have enlightened you, so will I enlighten those who turn to Me. Vassula, come be closer to Me. Will you receive Me?* ♥

Silence from my part.
Grieve Me not. ♥
Silence.
Be with Me, purify yourself, ♥ *love Me....* ♥
Silence.
Grieve Me not, beloved.... ♥
Silence.

Will you receive Me?...Fill Me with joy and be with Me, ♥ *love Me, I love you. Come to Me more often; receive Me more often, I love you.* ♥ *Will you pray with Me?*

---

[1]March 7, 1987

Here, I felt like saying, "Oh no, not again!"
Wound Me not. ♥
I consented.

> *Beloved Father, purify me with Your Son's Blood.*
> *Father, purify Me with your Son's Body.*
> *Beloved Father, hold away the evil spirit*
> *that now tempts me.* ♥
> *Amen.*

Jesus was writing it while I was saying it. I suddenly realized: it was like I woke up after Jesus' prayer. I realized what was happening from the beginning of the message of today. Jesus was calling me to Holy Communion, but I was pretending I was not understanding. I even felt like answering, no. I was hurting Him, and yet I was reluctant to reply. I made Him say it explicit. Jesus ran to my rescue. I felt I was about to fall. Just after His prayer (He prayed together with me), I realized that I had an evil spirit pulling on me. Strange feeling I had when I felt the evil spirit release his grip on me when the words came: "Beloved Father, hold away the evil spirit that now tempts me."
Jesus had put so much force on my hand. My hand felt very heavy, and at the same time, I felt His enormous and most powerful strength sustaining me like a most powerful Giant. After the prayer, it was like I woke up.

Come nearer to Me, sanctify yourself, I love you, and I will sustain your falls, I will not see you lost. ♥ *A flower needs to be watered and fertilized to maintain its beauty.* ♥ *I am your Devoted Keeper.* ♥ *I love you.*
I love You too.

Jesus had seen the evil spirit pulling on me. I did not realize it. While the evil spirit was pulling, I felt like silly. Jesus was very quick to rescue me, only when the evil spirit's grip released, I realized my close fall! I can't believe what happened!

GETHSEMANE

May 16, 1987

Last night, coming back from a dinner, I went up the stairs and a great odour of incense penetrated my nose again. I understood.

Vassula, when you smell incense, it is I, Jesus Christ. I wish you to feel my Presence. ♥ Vassula, I love you to distraction and beyond measure, alas! this Love which overflows my Heart, this ardent Flame of Love burning, is so little understood; so few come to draw from It...so few...
Jesus, many people don't know how to approach You, I'm so sure of that.
♥ They can come and talk to me, I hear them, I can enjoy for hours any conversation, it brings Me so much joy when they would count Me among their friends. ♥
Last night, a man told me that all women desire to be Magdalenes.
Lo,[1] ♥ not all.
Well, those who love you probably do then.
I want them to. ♥
Jesus, I think we will have to rush.
Where to?
Downstairs, check the oven.
Come then, let us go.
Jesus, before Your approach I heard of You like a myth, I never realized how You are REAL. In my eyes, You were so far away: a story in a book!
I know, Vassula, I know, for many, I am still a myth.
Find Me in Gethsemane next time we meet, I will reveal to you My anguishes, My sufferings and fears of that night. Come, allow Me to rest in you, daughter. ♥

May 17, 1987

Come, find Me where I have told you.
O Gethsemane! What have you to unfold but fears, anguishes, betrayals, and abandonments! Gethsemane, you have depleted men from courage, you have suspended in your still air My agonies for all eternity. Gethsemane, what have you to declare that was undeclared? You have witnessed in the stillness of Holiness, the betrayal of your God. You have witnessed Me.

---

[1]Lo in Hebrew: No.

The hour had come; Scriptures were to be fulfilled. Daughter, I know that many souls believe in Me as though I was but a myth. They believe that I existed only in the past. For many, I am but a passing shadow, now eclipsed with time and evolution. ♥ *Very few realize that I existed in flesh on earth and exist now among you.* ♥ *I Am All that came to pass and is to pass. I know their fears, I know their anguishes, I know their weaknesses, <u>have I not witnessed all these frailties in Gethsemane?</u>*

Daughter, when Love prayed in Gethsemane, a thousand devils were shaken; fearing demons took flight. The hour had come: Love was glorifying Love.

O Gethsemane, witness of the Betrayed, witness of the Forlorn; arise, witness and testify. Daughter, Judas betrayed Me, but how many more like Judas are betraying Me still? I knew instantly that his kiss would spread among many, and for generations to come, this same kiss will be given to Me over and over again, renewing My sorrow, rending My Heart.

Vassula come let Me be consoled, let Me rest in your heart. ♥ ♥

May 17, 1987

♥ *Vassula, will you write?*
Yes, Jesus, if it's what You wish.
Love Me, daughter, in My torments of Gethsemane. I was deceived by one of My own, one of My beloved ones, ♥ *and today, I still receive indignities, recollecting My agonies of the past. My Heart swelled and filled with bitterness.*

Suddenly I had problems, and I lacked confidence to continue.

Jesus?
I am. Little one, write. My sweat of agony poured out of Me like big drops of blood. ♥
I suddenly thought of the time I was almost tempted by the evil spirit... and felt ashamed.
Weakness attracts Me, for I can give you My Strength. Come, bring Me your love, lean on Me.
l leaned.
Yes!
Jesus was glad.

Here, eat from Me, fill your heart from My Heart, love Me, think of Me, be Mine, entirely Mine. ♥ *Adore Me and Me only. I am calling you to receive Me. Yes, in the little white Host...come and drink Me. Purify! I love you, and I will see that you receive Me. Do not deny Me ever! Desire Me and Me only. I will be waiting for you at the Tabernacle. You will see Me like I have taught you: with the eyes of your soul.* ♥
Jesus, it's my fault to have interrupted You. Do you wish to continue?

I do. Hear Me, the soil absorbed those drops, but today the soil, dryer than ever, needs irrigation; it desires peace and is thirsty for love.

Suddenly Jesus stopped.

Grieve Me not, but will you pray again with Me? Love Me, Vassula. Come. ♥

> *O Father, fulfill what must be fulfilled.*
> *May Your Words penetrate.*
> *Bless and purify the hearts of Your children.*
> *Father, do as Your Heart desires,*
> *And may your will be done.* ♥
> *Amen.*

Are you willing to continue working for Me?
I will continue working for God if it is His Will to do so.
It is My Will. ♥
Then I will continue working. Do not forget my incapacity though!
Lean entirely on Me, your Jesus. I know how helpless you are. ♥ *I wanted to have but a mere child who would have to depend entirely on Me.* ♥
Jesus?
I am. ♥
Is Your message on Gethsemane finished?
No, I will continue. ♥ *My children have to be revived and shown that I am among them with My Message which I blessed. They would see Me and feel Me, many will return to Me, I who long for My beloved ones.* ♥
Jesus, how can I do anything?
Vassula, will a father not help his child cross the road when it needs his help? So I will help you ♥ *till the end.*
I don't know if I am doing right by distributing Your Message, am I doing wrong?
No, you are giving My Bread as I gave it to you; My Bread must be given freely!

I read Saint Michael's prayer. Saint Michael told Me:

Read the next one.

I read The Memorare of Saint Bernard to Saint Mary, being worried about something: when My friends read the messages and start thinking again of God, some returning to God and some being happy with hope, unfortunately sometimes what happens in their delight to talk about it to a priest friend, is that he warns them not to believe it's God; and in fact, I realized myself that out of the four priests here knowing the writings, two discourage me, and two encouraged me. I would have liked, though, that those that discouraged me and discourage others would have decided after having read from A to Z. Then, if they still thought it nothing, they should tell me why and explain it. How could one give an opinion without following it and discussing it with me not more than once!

Our Holy Mother said:

Fill up your heart with God's Flame. I love you.
Beloved Mother, I fear that God's message might be trampled by people who do not even follow it up or reading it!
Fear not, child.
I'm distressed!
I know. Will you acknowledge, Vassula, the Works of Jesus?
I do.
Vassula, I have prayed for you, Agapi mou,[1] be patient. Lean on Jesus.

I prayed to Jesus.

Lean on Me.
I am fearing that Your message be crushed by those who have not read it even.
Do not fear, love Me. To purify your soul glorifies Me. Come, let us go. Remember, us, we...Grieve not. ♥

Jesus lead me yesterday to Sunday Mass. I can't follow the Mass properly as all the rest since I've never been taught the songs and the procedure. I'm always one step behind the others, but I know that Jesus is there and is talking to me. The Eucharist felt consoling.

THE DEVIL WANTS TO DRAG YOU BACK TO HIM

May 18, 1987

I've been at 6.30 to Holy Communion as Jesus asked me. In the middle of it, Jesus started talking to me. I received the Bread, and in my mouth it felt like a lacerated piece of flesh which had been ripped off from scourging. Funny how I felt it different yesterday, and today different. It seemed like Jesus was giving me different impressions.

Jesus?

---

[1] "My beloved", in Greek.

*I am. Love Me. Come close to Me, I will give you different impressions every time
you receive Me. Vassula, I grieve when you are distant to Me.*

It's true; sometimes when "the wave" of doubt covers me, I refuse to talk to Him or
see Him, saying to myself that it's not Him; and I avoid His image, avoid talking
with Him, avoid all that He's taught me. I'm trying to convince myself that my
imagination played tricks.

You are grieving Me, beloved. You are offending Me ♥ *when you block Me out
and seem so far away. Understand that the devil is behind all this; he is desperate
and wants you to believe that you are only imagining all the Graces I have given
you. He wants you to forget all My Heavenly teachings.* ♥ *He wants to drag you
back to him. When you seem so far from Me, I fear: I fear for you.* ♥ *When a
shepherd sees one from his flock wander away, would he just sit? A good shepherd
would rush to it, pick it up, and bring it back. When I see you wandering away,
I will not wait, I will rush to you and fetch you. I will draw you closer to Me.* ♥
*Little one, I will cover you with my cloak when you are cold; I will feed you, lift
you close to my Heart when distressed; what will I not do for you!* ♥
Jesus?
I Am.
Why all these Graces for me? Why?
Let Me free to give to whom I please. ♥
But I don't want to be different from others!
*Vassula, you will be receiving Me, let Me use you. Have I not told you that I will
liberate you.*

I don't understand.

*I wish to liberate many souls from their chains, chains of evil. I am using you as
an instrument. Do not misunderstand My Works. My appeal is not for you only;
My appeal of Peace and Love is for all humanity!*
Yes, Lord, but I feel a bit uncomfortable when friends know about this. I mean I feel
uncomfortable when some of them look and say: "You are privileged." I feel awful!
*Feel awful, daughter, for being chosen because of your wretchedness. I have not
chosen you because of your merits. I have told you already before that your merits
are none, and what comes out of the Lord's mouth is but the Truth. Come often,
and repent to Me.* ♥ *Remember, I do not favour you more than the rest of My
children.*
I know, Jesus, I know. That's why I feel embarrassed for giving me this Grace to
call You any time I wish.
♥ *Vassula, Vassula, I give even to the most wretched. Let your friends see how
My Heart is an abyss of Mercy and Forgiveness. Let them see how I raise even the
dead, let them see how I love even those that denied Me.*

Jesus?
I am, beloved.
I don't know what to say.
Say that you love Me.
I love You, and You know it.
I love you, daughter. Yes, in spite of your wretchedness. Remember, talk to Me;
I am your Spouse, share with Me, smile at Me when you see Me. ♥
Yes, Jesus. I feel that my presence offends You, and I know I'm repeating myself.
How can you stand me?
I love you.
I love You too.
Feel Me; look into My Eyes. ♥

I looked at Him. His Eyes were <u>grave</u> but FULL of love....

Yes, ♥ *remember, daughter, that I am your Holy Father.* ♥ *Let us go now.* ♥

MY BODY ACHES FOR LACK OF LOVE

May 19, 1987

Jesus?
I am; Vassula, remember, this guidance is from Me. ♥
Do You know, Jesus, what I long for?
I know, daughter.
I sometimes wish that this Grace you have given me to meet You in this way, and
the Grace you have given me to see You with the eyes of my soul, could have been
just for me alone, You and me, me and You. It would have felt so marvelous,
nothing to worry about, showing no one our secret. (I sighed.)
Daughter, I have asked you whether you wanted to work for Me, and your answer
pleased Me. Let Me remind you that you are My beloved soul through whom I will
manifest Myself and desires, for this is My Will.
But My God, without offending You, Your Word can lay heavy if it's not unloaded.
What can I do?
Beloved, will I not help you? I am the Lord. ♥
Brothers, read My Message, fill Me with joy, and remember My Works, believe in
My Infinite Wealth and Mercy! Vassula, follow Me; I will lead you, little one. I
will give you My Strength, never leave My Hand.
My God...what do you want from me...?

I want love, love, love. My Body aches from lack of love; My Lips are parched for thirst of love. I want to use you, little one, as My instrument for My guidance. ♥
My Lord, may Your will be done, may You fulfill Your desires.
Beloved, lean on Me. ♥ ♥ *Listen to My Voice, never feel alone, for I, God, am with you.*

I felt somewhat consoled.

Lord, shall we start the day?
Come, I will. ♥ *Lean entirely on Me; I am guiding you.*

May 19, 1987

Babette,[1] came. She talked to Jesus, the three of us were together. Babette did not need to ask her question aloud. Her mere thought, passing through her mind was instantly answered.[2] Jesus by this is stimulating us about His Presence, and He is calling us to become more intimate with Him and remember His Presence, loving Him.
I must admit that I was impressed by the way Jesus was meeting Babette.

Lean on Me. ♥
Jesus, my friend asked me to ask You why don't You come to us again, just like before, in flesh? So that people change.
Ah Vassula... I will be coming back. Every dawn that breaks is closer to My coming to you. Vassula, do you know what that means?
Tell me, Lord.
Love will return again. Love will be among you once more. Love will bring you Peace again. ♥ *My Kingdom on earth will be as it is in Heaven.* ♥ *Love will glorify Love. I am soon with you, My beloved. Pray, for the time is near. Will you, little one, still work for Me?*
I wish to hear Your name.
I am Love ♥
Yes, I shall work for Love in my incapacity, depending on You entirely.
I know you are lost without Me, beloved. You are My flower which needs My Light.
I'm so happy!
♥ *O daughter, I love you to distraction! Lean entirely on Me;* ♥ *I will augment your knowledge of discernment.*
My Lord! Are you augmenting my feelings to feel You and see You and hear You?

---

[1] A friend of mine.
[2] Through me in writing.

I am. You will feel Me and will be able to discern Me more. ♥
My God! Why all these Graces upon me? I have done nothing to merit anything!
I know, but I love you. Do not forget though who you are. ♥
Please help in reminding me, Lord.
I will prevent you from becoming elated by all My given Graces, by reminding you of your wretchedness. I will remind you that all the Graces you are receiving from Me are for My own Glory. Every grace you receive from Me will be for My own interests and not for your own. ♥ *So draw from My Heart, and fill up yours. I want My Altar to be constantly ablaze.* ♥ *Live for Me, breathe for Me;* ♥ ♥ *be My own for all eternity.*
I will, for God.
My God?
I am; love Me and look after my own interests. ♥
Lord! (I sighed.) I'm a zero, and You know it; Lord, do not trust me, please.

♥ *Let Me act in you freely. Come, I will satisfy your question.* <u>*Love will return among you as Love.*</u> ♥ *We will pray together.*

> *O Heavenly Father, Father of Love,*
> *Come to us, delivering us from evil.*
> *Father, love us and allow us to abide in Your Light,*
> *Do as your Heart desires.*
> *May Your Name be glorified. Amen.* ♥

Allow Me to use you.
Permit me, and let me hear Your name again.
I am Jesus Christ, Beloved Son of God. ♥ *All I ask from you, Vassula, is love and to share My Cross of Peace and Love* ♥ *together with Me.*
Yes, Lord.
Daughter, never leave My Hand. Love Me daughter.
Teach me to love You the way You desire us to love You. If You want, let me love You the most in the world.
You are smiling!
I am so happy! Do you wish to do this for Me?
Yes.
Beloved, with me you will learn. Are you willing to suffer for Me too?
For the Lord, yes, if He wants it that way too...
Then all will be done according to My Will.
You know what's good for the soul, so I will depend on God.
I am God. Come now in that special place I have for you in My Heart and remain in there.

I WISH TO UNITE ALL MY PRIESTS

May 20, 1987

Sometimes I surprise myself. Why do I get this urge to meet Jesus in this way? Why, and how, and for what am I keen in writing, hearing His messages. For all these months, it's something that has become indispensable.

♥ *I love you. It is I, Jesus, who give you this urge to meet Me.* ♥ *Vassula, love Me always.* ♥ *I will tell you, sister, My desires.* ♥

Jesus was so tender; a sad look over His Face was there.

I wish to unite all My priests. I desire from them to love Me more; I want from them purity, zeal, faithfulness. Priests must understand that unity reinforces love. Unity establishes love. For how long will discord reign among them? Love is unity. My love unites them to Me. My Church is weak with their discordance. My desire is Unity. I wish that My Church becomes one.
But Lord, if You say there is discord, someone will have to give in. How will they know?
They must pray for enlightenment. They should come to Me and draw from My Heart. ♥
Whom are You referring to Jesus, when You talk about "them" and "they"?
All My Church. ♥ *I desire them to unite and become one. My Church has weakened because of this distinction. It has weakened enormously.*
My Lord, to me this sounds like a new message.
♥ *I will enlighten you, Vassula, in showing you in small phases the way I work.* ♥
First the teachings to me.
Yes, Vassula, and now My desires; ♥ *My desires of uniting My Church. How can a body function if one or two of its members are disabled, or injured, or dismembered? Would it have the same capacity and strength as one which is whole? My Church is My Body; how can My Body function if they disable It? Daughter, draw My sign:* ♥ ⬩⤫ *This was the sign of the first Christians.* ♥ *Love was one, Love was united.*

Jesus, I know that Easter is at a different dates. Can You tell me which is the right date? Ours or theirs? (Please give it to me on a separate paper.)
♥ *Vassula, take a paper then.* ♥
Thank You, Jesus.

Jesus gave me the correct date for Easter.

Come now, let us join in prayer, a prayer to the Father for Unity:

> *Father, I come to You,*
> *And ask You to enlighten My sheep;*
> *Enlighten them to find Peace and Love In Unity.*
> *Amen.*

Unite My sheep, Vassula! ♥
Jesus! Who am I to unite, and know anything about priests, and their discussions, and what's going on? Who am I to tell them on a piece of paper what's written; and to tell them that it is You who wrote it. Jesus, You are giving me messages; You are telling me the desires of Your Heart. Lord, wouldn't it be easier to have given everything to someone of the Church, in the Church already, someone who has access to all the high authorities, someone of renown, of purity, and trustworthy?
Lord, You have indeed picked up on one who is crippled and discouraged by half of the priests who know about the writings; they are, half of them, disinterested to follow up. I am tired of wanting to show them since I know it bores them and annoys them. What to do?
This, Vassula, is what your shoulders bear. This is My Cross on you. ♥ *I will share It with you; never weary.*
Lord, how will Your message reach the right ears? I'm an outsider.
It will. It is like a rivulet flowing, slowly becoming wider; ♥ *from flowing, it will start rushing, then gushing, the rivulet will turn into a vast ocean.*
Vassula, lean on Me when you are weary. I love you and will help you bearing with Me My Cross. Beloved, never feel abandoned. ♥

I felt that Jesus will always lift me when I stumble. He made me understand that I can always lean on Him to regain my strength.

Vassula, I will lead you. ♥

TO HAVE FAITH IS ALSO A GRACE

May 23, 1987

Yesterday, I did not meet Jesus in writing, but His Presence was made felt by Him, His Words too. He was talking to me at the same time as my husband or friends. It was as if He was pulling me by one arm, and the others by the other arm.

Jesus?
I am. ♥ *To have faith is also a Grace, beloved. Talk to Me; I am Your Spouse.*
♥

I told Him something; He answered me:

Let Me do whatsoever I want to with you, Vassula, I am God, and by now you must have understood that by having you elevated to Me, and having taught you to love Me, and by letting you meet Me in this way, I want something out of you. You were taught to write by My given Grace. This grace was given to you to enable Me to use you. I have bestowed upon you many Graces so that you may glorify Me. I have united you to Me. I have taken you as my bride, ♥ I and you are one now. Do you not see clearer, daughter? I love you all, and I have approached you for My own interests.
My God?
I am.

I reminded him of something.

Vassula, I fulfill always My goals. ♥
I know, I know; I wish You could tell me clearer.
Daughter, I love you far beyond your understanding. I know you are ineffably weak. I know that without Me you are totally insufficient, unable to move. Do not worry, I will lift you like a father would lift his invalid child, I will take care of you, I will supply you, I will see that all My Works will be fulfilled. Remember, I have trained you to be My bearer. ♥ *I will not see you leave without having accomplished your mission.* ♥
I love you; ♥ *love Me and Me only. I do not want rivals. Worship Me, for I am your God. Vassula, to wait upon your God is to serve Him. Serve Me, come, be one with Me. In your ignorance, daughter, I accept you. I have indeed around Me loyal servants, they are My beloved of My Soul, they are of great esteem in My eyes. I entrust them with My Works, they honour My Name by serving Me fervently, worshiping Me, immolating their soul for me, and with great grace bless My Word. I love them, and I look upon them lovingly.* ♥ *Withhold not your question.*
Why did You choose me since I'm no good and only create....(He did not let me finish.)
♥ *Wretchedness attracts Me.* ♥ *Altogether you are nothing, nothing at all! But by being nothing, I am everything you are not, for what have I as rival? I find no rival within you since you are nothing.* ♥ *Such is My delight in you, daughter.*
I can't understand.
No, you cannot understand, but does it matter? Does it really matter? I am Sovereign of all creation. You are all Mine; and you, little one, you without the slightest interest, attracts Me, <u>littleness holds My attention; nothingness infatuates</u>

Me. Vassula, one day you will fully understand My Words. ♥ *Were you to serve Me, I would reveal in you nothing but passion.* ♥
Passion...
Yes, passion ♥ *will....* ♥

I through weakness stopped Him from writing His question. I heard it though....Nothing can stop Him from letting me hear what He wants to say....

I can abide in you, even in your awesome weakness. Love Me, Vassula; do not fear Me. I am Love, and I am very fond of you. I will never ask of you anything that can harm you. ♥ *I am Love and Master of Love. Child, in spite of your incessant doubts and failures, I have chosen you to be My altar. Since I know your incapacity to draw from My Flame, I will pour Myself My burning desires in you, thus keeping My Flame ablaze.*
Beloved, come. You are My flower which needs My Light; live under My Light, I do not want to see you perish. ♥
Lord, You attract me too, You know that....
Does that amaze you? Your wretchedness is attracted by My Mercy; your ineffable weakness, by My Strength; your nothingness, by everything I am. Live for Me. ♥
I told Him my desire.

Earn your desire, ♥ *Vassula.* ♥
I saw Jesus trying to show His desire.
Vassula, come. Come closer to Me, ♥ *Vassula.*
I was hesitating.

Again I ask you to want but Me only. ♥ *Vassula, do not deny Me! Listen at My Heart beats,* ♥ *Can you resist Me?*
How can I resist God?
Yet I am trying to, for I don't know how I'll end.

I love You My God.
Come then to Me; have no desires for yourself. ♥ *Do you want to see Me there?*

In my mind passed a famous picture of Jesus in a famous place; I don't know why.

If it's Your wish, Lord. But do not answer me; do as You wish though.
Daughter, all your work, let it be for My Glory. My desires should be your desires too. I will write My desires and lead you. ♥
It's about unity?
Yes, Unity of My Church. ♥ *I want My Body strengthened. Unity will strengthen My Church.* ♥ *Will you remember my Presence?* ♥ *Come then, let us go.* ♥

FREE YOURSELF TO BE ABLE TO SERVE ME

May 24, 1987

♥ *I am with you.*
Do you want me to serve You?

I asked this because this is what God had asked me, and I, through weakness and fear, stopped Him from writing it yesterday.

I do. I want it very much, Vassula. Come, I will show you how and where you can serve Me. Remember everything I have taught you. ♥

(Teachings, mystic teachings so that my faculties are all alert, so that by being aware, I will hear Him and feel Him all the more.)

Have My Peace. Listen to My Voice. ♥
I wish I could hear You crystal clear....
Vassula, you will hear Me well enough to write everything that My Heart contains, all that My Heart desires. ♥ *Beloved, free yourself to be able to serve Me and wait upon Me; do you know what free means, Vassula? I will tell you; have confidence.*

I felt that what He taught me would not work, and I might fail Him.

Free is to detach your soul from worldly solicitudes. Free your soul and love Me and My Works. ♥ *Serve Me in this way; detach yourself.* ♥
I will have difficulties, My Lord!
Lo.[1]
Yes, My Lord, I can see difficulties.
♥ *Lo, lo, stay near Me.* ♥
I fear to disappoint You and fail Your desires.
Fear not, sister; beloved, love me.

I felt Him and loved Him.

Love for love. Love Me as now. Work and serve Me as now, be as you are. I need servants who are able to serve Me where love is needed most. Work hard though, for where you are, you are among evil, unbelievers. You are in the vile depths of sin. You are going to serve your God where darkness prevails; you will have no rest; You will serve Me where every good is deformed in to evil. Yes, serve Me

---

[1]Hebrew for "no".

among wretchedness, among wickedness and the iniquities of the world; serve Me among Godless people, among those that mock Me, among those that pierce My Heart; serve Me among My scourgers, among My condemnors; serve Me among those that recrucify Me and spit on Me. O Vassula, how I suffer! Come and console Me! ♥

My God, come! Come among those that love You. Go to them at least for a while. Go, and You are loved there. Rest in their heart; forget. Can't You forget for a while at least?
Jesus seemed so distressed!

Vassula, forget? How could I forget? How, when repeatedly they are recrucifying Me? ♥
He dictated so quick, I could hardly follow.
Five of My Wounds are left open for all who want to penetrate in them. ♥
Jesus leaned on me. I felt distressed; He seemed comfortless, worn out.

♥ *Vassula, come, you are my little flower; I want smooth and soft petals from you to replace My thorns.*
Jesus, let those who love You unburden You. Let those who love You rest You and replace You in Your recrucifixion.

I didn't know how to console such distress.

Beloved, those that love Me, strive and suffer with Me; they share My Cross. They rest Me, ♥ *but they are few. I need more souls to unite with Me and bear My sufferings.* ♥ *Flower, love Me; never refuse Me.*
Jesus?
I Am.
Will You help me to love You more?
I will, beloved.

I feel speechless; what can I say? If anyone knew how painful it was to see Him so hurt! It was like He was dying all over again. How can one comfort one who is dying from wounds? and to tell Him what? that it is alright? when one knows He is injured to death!

I BEAR NO RIVALS

May 25, 1987

I start to realize how much easier it is to meet God with this grace He has given to me if I come without the slightest doubt or disbelief, feeling Him, seeing Him, and letting Him write. I start to understand. Full faith makes all the demons flee and they feel at loss, with no power. They fear and are exasperated! When I come hesitant, doubtful, they feel strong, and attack me in writing their insults. Full faith and an open heart for God can make the mountains move! I feel Him like an electric sense in me, wonderful; and I never want to leave Him or this instant of God's finger on me. I want it to last forever!

Love me, love Me; feel Me, feel My insatiable love for you. I thirst for your love. I require more love from you, Vassula. Hear my Heart beats. ♥
Jesus was passionate.

I bear no rivals, none at all. If I see or meet rivals, I will ravage them. Nothing will replace Me, I will stay Master. ♥ *Depart, glorifying Me.* ♥ ♥ *Tonight I will purify you by My Heavenly Works for Peace and Love.*
Jesus means in the mystic way.
Pray, beloved, blessed one; unite my Church by drawing My sign which I gave you. Draw now: ⊂✕

With Blessed sign, I, the Lord will show you the way to Me. ♥ *Believe, believe, believe;* ♥ *flourish and help others; flourish to bring back Love; flourish to bring Peace.*
I was distressed.

I love you, Vassula, grieve not, ♥ *My beloved. Blessed one, come to Me your Father, your Spouse, your God; will I ever abandon you? From love, I will take you, from My elate and insatiable love, I will free you.* ♥ *Pray with me:* ♥

> *Heavenly Father, may I glorify You;*
> *Redeem your children from evil;*
> *May they be in your Light;*
> *May their hearts open, and*
> *With Your Mercy receive You.* ♥ ♥
> *Amen.* ♥

Vassula, will you realize fully My Presence and kiss My Wounds?
Yes, Lord Jesus!
I discerned Him and saw Him again in full glory. Seeing Him with the eyes of my soul, I saw He was this time beautiful, with a beautiful crown on His Head. He came to me as a King.
Lord, give me Your right Hand.
I kissed His right Hand.

♥ ♥ ♥ *I love you.* ♥ ♥ ♥

I kissed His Hands, Feet, and Side Wound.
I love You, Lord.
To guide you was a delight for Me.
I felt (I cannot find words).

Come with Me; I will show you something. ♥
I saw from His Breast, which was lit, sparks.
Every spark which leaves My Heart and touches your heart, will inflame your heart and consume it. My spark enkindles you; draw from My Heart. I will one day inflame entirely your heart, letting My Flame enwrap your heart, engulfing it.

What will happen to me if by just a spark only I feel this way? (It was like Jesus was taking pleasure, knowing now He has conquered me.)

♥ *Yes, I delight to have prevailed and conquered your love. When My Flame will enwrap your heart entirely, you will never ever be separated from Me.* ♥ ♥ *You will be My bride in Heaven,* ♥ *I have created you for Myself.* ♥ ♥

But then, why am I here? I don't understand.
No, you cannot understand, Vassula, but one day you will. ♥ *Time is a rival for me,* ♥ *when you look at your watch and I am with you.* ♥

I had offended Him because I looked at my watch.

Come, daughter, take My Hand and let us go; come, we have so much work. ♥
This work or the other (house)?
Both. ♥ *Daughter, everywhere you go, I am.* ♥ *Altar, My Flame should stay ablaze forever.* ♥ ♥ *Annihilate in Me.* ♥

I SMILE IN PURE SOULS

May 26, 1987

Jesus, a friend of mine said: "We never see Jesus happy or giving us a big smile in all the pictures representing Him, why?"
I told her that I saw You happy many times, and I will not forget that broad smile You gave me, all Your face was smiling that morning You told me You had rested in my heart.
Vassula, I smile in pure souls. I smile and delight in lowly men; I delight in holy men. ♥
Jesus, my God, I don't understand why I love someone I've never seen or met in my physical state; how and why do I love You?
Ah Vassula, Loving Me, everything coming from Me is love; I created you to love Me; I created you out of Love; your soul thirsts for Love, ♥ ♥ *but how few are those that understand and accept this grace.* ♥

LOFTINESS WEARIES ME

May 27, 1987

Your whole guidance is easy to understand, Lord. It's not a complicated language.
Loftiness wearies Me. Learn to be humble, simple, modest, just like Me! Vassula, if you wish Me to be your Father, I will treat you as My child; if you wish Me to be your Bridegroom, I will treat you as My Bride; if you rebel against Me, I will treat you as a Judge. I am your Saviour; favour Me above everything and all; never deny Me; come often, and drink and eat Me; I delight in you. ♥

BE MY SACRIFICE

May 28, 1987

Lord, you want me as Your sacrifice, You said?
Vassula, yes, be My sacrifice.
Lord, make me worthy to be Your sacrifice.

My God, I really do not know quite what "sacrifice" could mean. It can vary, but I understand that it contains suffering of some sort. Since You ask me to be one for You, let it be; but to be a sacrifice for God, one has to have some value to glorify God. Since I know I am a speck of dust, and chosen because I'm wretched, what sort of decent sacrifice would I be? So even to be a sacrifice for God, one has to be in a state that would honour Him, that the "sacrifice" is of some sort of esteem to be able to take place and honour God. Even that, my God, I am unable to give, unless You make me decent to be Your sacrifice and thus become valid.

♥ *Vassula, do you remember when I came and asked you to love Me? Do you remember when an angel came to stir you unexpectedly?[1] That is the way I come; so be alert, do not sleep! I came to be with you unexpectedly and asked for love. I wished you to honour Me; I wanted to capture your love and be your Master reigning over you. I wanted you to need Me. How I yearned for your love! "Lama sabachthani?"[2]* ♥ ♥ *I came to you, but you denied Me.*

When I knew that it was Him, I did deny Him.

Vassula, I have detached you, but I will detach you even more. Have My Peace. Beloved, amend, amend, amend. I raised you from the dead to be able to unite My Church. ♥

I sighed.

Let me show you the way. In spite of your doubts, I will unfold to you My Heart's desires. Never weary writing; I will work in you; lean entirely on Me.
Jesus, someone mentioned some time ago to me that you will give no more signs. You said it to the Pharisees. He said this when I said that this guidance (message) is from You.
Vassula, when I said this to the Pharisees, I meant My miracles of the time I was in flesh and among them. Condemning Me now, for it is to condemn My Heavenly Works, shows how arid and closed their hearts have become. My signs will never end; My Presence will be felt in the world, and I will continue to show Myself in signs. Believe, believe, O men of little faith! Do not distort My Word; for what have you to say about Fatima? Are you dreading to believe that I am the One who gave you this sign? O men of little faith, what would you not declare rather than accept that Heaven's signs are from Me! Love My Works; accept My Works. Believe, believe in Me: I, who is Infinite Wealth and Mercy. My signs are so that all men see that Love has not forgotten you. Love has not withdrawn and glories in His Glory. Love is among you, never leaving you.

---

[1] The first time the pencil I held without my will; it was sudden.
[2] In Hebrew: "Why have you abandoned me?"

LOVE ME IN SPITE OF YOUR DOUBTS

May 29, 1987

Beloved, repent. ♥ *Creature, bless Me. Believe in what you ask.*

I had asked Him to forgive my sins, but I realized it came from my lips only when God said, "Believe in what you ask."

♥ *I forgive them. Love Me, honouring Me; love Me, glorifying Me.* ♥

I asked Him again and blessed Him.

I am God, creature, be at My Stations. Desire Me only, at every Station; I stand at every Station; I will be at the Stations of My Cross, and I want you there; I want you to kneel at My Stations. ♥

Lord, I don't know what You mean! What stations?[1]

I will wait for you there; inspect what I demand from you, inspect. I will purify you to enable you to be My sacrifice. Desire Me; satisfy My insatiable thirst. Satisfy My burning Flame of Love; satisfy Me, your God. By giving Me full faith, I will lift your veil entirely to see Me without constraint. Surely you have heard of My Beauty from others who saw Me before you! ♥ *Believe, believe entirely; come closer to your Father, and I will lift entirely your veil. Daughter, have I not brought you into My Hall?*
Yes, Lord.
Then have faith in Me; do not let men drive you away from Me; I have given you this gift, so use it to reach Me! Do not fear Love; I am Omnipotent, believe in My Omnipotence. Daughter, I desired you to be in My Hall, so how much more will I not desire you to remain?
My God, maybe we'll lose each other from my own fault.
Have you forgotten our links? I am your Spouse, and you are living in My House. I am feeding you, I envelop you with My Light, I watch over your frailty, I treat you like a child because of your misery. What will I not do for you! Are You happy with Me, Vassula?
Yes, Lord. May You be blessed forever, for it's You who give me happiness. You are my smile.
Love Me in spite of your doubts. ♥

---

[1] We Orthodox do not have the custom of making "the stations" or the way of the cross.

Lord?

Come, you are weak, but I will strengthen you. I want you strong for My Message. ♥ *Would you wish Me to unveil your eyes completely and see Me clearer?*

I would, if it's Your wish.

You need a few more steps towards Me; you are almost there! I will unveil your eyes, and you will behold in front of you, your Saviour! Five of My Wounds will be open so that you penetrate into them. I will let you taste My sorrows; ♥ *I long for that moment.* ♥ *Fill Me with loving words;* ♥ *Vassula, you are bonded to Me, yet, have you not felt more free? Smile at Me when you feel My Presence and see Me. I am fully aware of your capacity and wisdom; I know I have with Me a nothing, a nothing at all.* ♥ *Come, do not misunderstand Me; will I have a nothing, or would I rather have a rival of some sort? I will of course choose a nothing to send on earth My Words and My desires without the slightest negation.* ♥

Lord, You have given me so much; I feel very much in debt!

Have you got anything to give Me, Vassula?

I'm hesitating, what can I give?

Surely you have just a bit of something! Even if you have nothing to give Me, I love you. ♥

Maybe I have something to give You?

Have you asked yourself whether I want it or not? I am self-sufficient; I suffice by Myself.

Would You want me to give You something anyway?

I do. ♥

But then, whatever I will give you, will be no good in Your Eyes!

Why?

Because You are Perfect.

I will receive it, and even if its evil, I will turn it into good! I am Divinity.

Have I then anything good to offer You?

You have, but all that is good comes from Me; I have given it to you; everything good is from Me.

I'm a bit disappointed, I can't please Him.

Then I have nothing of myself to give You.

No. I have given you all that you have and is good.

Maybe a good painting; offering it to You![1]

---

[1] I wanted to paint a picture for the church.

Your paintings, Vassula? Have I not bestowed upon you this gift of art? Has this also not come from Me?
What then can I offer You?
Love. Worship Me. Worship Me. <u>Offer Me your will</u> in surrendering to Me. This is the most beautiful thing you can offer Me. ♥
You know, Lord, that I love You, and also that I surrendered!
I enjoy hearing it, little one!

LIFT MY CROSS

May 29, 1987

I felt suddenly His Cross on Me. I thought I would never manage.
Lift! Lift My Cross! Strive with Me! Together...together...I love you. Lift My Cross! I must rest now in you. ♥

Later on, before meeting the Catholic charismatics.

Will you feed My lambs? Hold My Hand; I will lead you, guarding you. ♥
That evening I smelled incense again.
Never doubt of My Presence. ♥
I asked Jesus to help "unblind" and take away the evil spirits which surround the young man who refuses to accept God. A case known to me while in the charismatic group.

Fill Me with joy, and summon Me for everything you want. Vassula, remind him of His Brother. ♥ *I am his Brother who loves him, who cares for him; remind him of My existence; I love him to distraction. I died for him.*

Will you do this for Me, little one? Believe in My Redemptive Love. ♥

LOVE ME IN ABSOLUTE SILENCE

Sunday, May, 31 1987

Vassula, come and receive Me.[1] I will be there. Delight Me, come and see Me! Say you are Mine, let Me hear it.
I am Yours, Jesus, and I love you.
For years, Vassula, I was waiting for these words. Love Me now that you are Mine. ♥
Teach me to love You as You wish.
Trust Me, I will.
Later on:

It still amazes me how my hand moves...do You know that, Jesus?
I do, but am I not Omnipotent? Vassula, be peaceful, be calm, be serene like Me. ♥
I was interrupted, while writing, twice by my son coming in, slamming the door, etc. I felt upset! Too much noise.

Love Me, answer Me!
I love You, I love You, Lord!

Never replace Me! Have Me first; face Me first, and remain facing Me forever. Be like a mirror, a reflexion of Myself. Never seek others but Me; never seek your old habits of your earlier life. I am Holy and Lord. I and you are one now, and I mean to keep you just for Myself and for eternity. Humble yourself; learn from Me, desire Me only, breathe for Me, do not turn left or right now, keep going straight. Beloved, allow Me to use you. Hold on to Me, enrapture Me with your simplicity in words, simplicity infatuates Me. Say to Me your words; let Me hear them again; tell Me: "I love you, Jesus, you are my joy, my breath, my rest, my sight, my smile."

♥ *Daughter, were you given time to think and meditate, you would please Me furthermore. You will from now on seek Me in silence; love Me in absolute silence; pray in silence. Enter My Spiritual World in silence.* ♥ *Reward Me now; I love you. Honour Me by giving yourself to Me, do not displease Me. Be Mine, beloved, speak!*

How in silence, Lord?
In silence, looking at Me; I want you to stay still, without having interferences of

---

[1] A call to communion.

any sort; seek Me in silence. ♥
Without interferences at all?
None at all; ♥ *desire stillness.*
Jesus, how could I possibly find this stillness in a family, its almost impossible!

♥ *I will give it to you. I pity you, Vassula!* ♥ *My remnant, My myrrh, My love; what will I not do for you! My Heart fills with compassion for your misery* ♥ *and your falls. I, the Lord, will help you.* ♥ *Never feel abandoned or unloved. Do you know how I felt that time you felt unloved?*
Where?
In My Church. ♥
No, Lord.
I felt crucified all over again, bruised, scourged, spat upon, nailed again! ♥ *Vassula, how I love you! Help Me revive My Church; help Me by letting Me use you. Courage, daughter, courage.*

After I had been told that Jesus <u>does refuse</u> sometimes people, and He can shut the door to them. (In an argument I had with a priest, giving me to read a passage from the Bible about the Canaanite women whom He refused. But in the end, He did not refuse her; He had only challenged her to show her faith.) But I did not know that, and the one who showed me this passage did not let me read the end. I had gone to church, taking Holy Communion, so I felt, according to our argument, that I had taken something not permitted, breaking all laws of the Catholic Church; and taking something without permission, made me feel very evil. The following Sunday, I went to church; I stood near the door so I'm half out (since I felt unwanted), and since I believed I was evil and that God was very angry with me, I did not go forward with the others for Communion, fearing I make things worse if I did.

Jesus, I didn't know that all this would hurt You, I mean my feeling of being unloved!

No, you did not know either that I never refuse anybody who comes to Me. ♥ *I am Love, and Love is for everyone, no matter how evil you can be.* ♥

THEY ARE CRUCIFYING ME

June 1, 1987

Vassula, both My Hands have Wounds. Both My Feet have Wounds. My Side is open, wide open, showing My Heart. ♥ They are recrucifying Me. ♥
Lord!
They are damaging My Church. ♥
Lord, is it so very bad?
It is. Evil has blinded them. Love is missing among them. They are not sincere, they have distorted My Word, they have lamed even My Body. My Cup of Justice is full, do not let it brim over! ♥ I want them to stop smothering My Body; I, Jesus, am Love; I want them to stop throwing venomous arrows at each other. Harmony among them will restore part of the damage. ♥ Truthfulness will unmask evil. Why all these ceremonies when in truth they have nothing to offer Me? I need purity, love, fidelity, humbleness, holiness. ♥ Seek in Me all that I desire, and I will give it to you. Seek My interests and not yours; glorify Me; honour Me. ♥ Words are not enough; deeds of Love and co-operation will vivify My Body. Brothers! Love one another! O beloved, how much will I have to restore! Come daughter, rest in Me. Peace upon you. ♥ ♥ ♥

TO UNITE YOU MUST ALL BEND

June 2, 1987

Meet Me later on, and I will give you preliminary advice, Vassula. Design three lines, *unite those lines. ♥*

To unite, you must all bend; you must be all willing to bend by softening. ♥

I understood. He gave me a clear and simple vision of three iron rods. They were upright, close to each other. He said: "How could their heads[1] meet, unless they all bend?" Later on in the morning, I went out; the more I was thinking of this vision, the bigger the "mountain" appeared. I was stifling....

Jesus?

---

[1]Heads: later on, I understood that "heads" means also authority, leaders.

I am. Courage. Up, pupil! Lift! Lift My Cross, beloved, up now! Grieve not. Together...together...My Vassula, together we will strive. Lean on Me when you are weary, and let Me lean on you when I am weary. ♥ *Meet Me; let Me accomplish My desires; be like soft wax, and let My Hand engrave on you My Words; be willing, do not fear! I love you, beloved. O come! Love will not hurt you.*

I'm fearing this work

Come, let us pray:

> *O Father, be with me until the end;*
> *I am weak; give me Your Strength,*
> *To glorify You.*
> *Amen.*

Beloved, come; leave your fears and hear Me. ♥ *Wait upon your God. I want to unite My Church. I have trained you to receive Me. Beloved, courage!*

I need Your courage; I have none.

I will encourage you and will reinforce your love to Me, all for My Glory. Vassula, will you write down My words? Sip from Me. Do not seek comfort, be poor, be like Me when I was in flesh on earth. Be plain, so that we both feel the contrast and the grandeurs of those that scourge Me! Let Me feel the contrast! Be drawing from My Heart, embellish My Church, ♥ *draw from My Heart, and you will understand, My little girl.* ♥

I think that I start to realize what work this is. That's why I'm fearing: Jesus is starting to <u>dig in</u> the Church....

June 3, 1987

I was attacked "in writing" by evil again. They were like cats who jumped on my back. I was "fed up" with them. It seemed like "all hell broke loose". They annoyed me, so I said to one of them: "In the name of Jesus Christ, leave and be thrown in fire." He left. There were several of these, and one by one each was treated in the same way as the first, and with the same words.

Jesus told me: "Ask in My Name, and it shall be done; but you must have faith in what you ask, work in this way. Pray and ask. Pray in My Name, work in My Name, ask in My Name; revive My Name; be My reflection; synchronize with me; lift your head towards Me; believe in what you ask." He told me that the demons fear me. I'm a menace to them. Later on, I realized where I was; I felt my feet in wet and slimy mud, and in a flash, I recognized the surroundings of hell. It was just a flash. I then understood why so much evil interference was there today in writing. Jesus said when I asked about this: "Could it have been anywhere else?" We were

together, passing outside the gates of hell[1] healing souls, wrenching them away.
"Vassula, allow Me to use you in this way too. This is part of your work too."

A SMILING GIANT

June 4, 1987

Today, God lifted me in His palm. He made me feel so small. He asked me to look
at Him. I did, and saw a Beautiful Smiling Giant!

Vassula, look at Me; look at My Face. ♥ ♥ ♥ ♥ ♥

He was smiling in beauty! I felt like a tiny spot in His palm.

Does it matter to Me? ♥ *Does it matter to Me if you are but a speck of dust. Feel*
how I love you!

He was Beautiful, and all this is Beautiful!

I am Beautiful, Vassula. When you think of Me, think of Me as I was on earth
with men's features, your image. Think of Me in that way.
But Lord, how do You really look? How and what are Your features?
I am Everything; I am the Alpha and the Omega. I am the Eternal. I am the
Elixir. ♥ *Love Me, remain in Me, <u>never fear Me</u>. Let this fear, which was*
wrongly taught by men, be replaced by love. Live in Me without fear. Fear Me only
if you rebel against Me. I am Love. Tell them, tell them what an abyss of Love My
Heart is! ♥ ♥ ♥

June 5, 1987

Vassula, find Me in My Stations. Be blessed; we will work together. ♥

I have not gone to His Stations yet. I will, but I am waiting for Father James, as he's
been asked by Jesus to be with me.

---

[1] Purgatory closest to hell.

SINS OBSTRUCT ME

June 6, 1987

Jesus?
I am. To look into God's Face is to have seen Love.

I was looking at His picture, the Holy Shroud.

Do you want Me to dominate you entirely, Vassula?
Yes, my God, I would, if it's Your wish.
Leave Me free then; never obstruct Me. Live for Me.
Lord, how do I obstruct You? Tell me, so that there is no obstructions.
Sins obstruct Me, sins, Vassula. Will you really let Me act in you as I wish?
Yes, my God, forbid me from sinning, forgive my sins, act as You wish in me, do not consider my cowardice. Pay no attention to it. Drag me if You must, feel free with me, do Your work. I do not want to be a hindrance to Your Works, so pay no attention to my weakness; do as You please.
Daughter, I am pleased with your words. Come, I will continue My Works. ♥

I GIVE FREELY

June 6, 1987

Leave Me free to do My Will. Come, let Me clarify how I work. ♥ *I have given you many Graces, Vassula; but I want you to acknowledge My Graces. Delight Me and believe in Me more.*
I am fearing that if I displease You, You might take away these graces.
Why should I withdraw My Graces?
Because I don't improve and don't follow in time, You might take them away.
No, never!
To me it seems right to take away if one does not please You.
It seems right in your eyes, child. Until I come to deliver you, I will feed you; I will never withhold My food. I who longed for you for years, I waited for years to press you close to My Heart, loving you. Would I now pull away My food from you? Come, lean on Me as much as you wish. Remember, I am Love; I give freely, and I do not take away what I give. ♥ *I will always remind you of My ways.* ♥

IT TAKES SO LITTLE TO CONSOLE ME

June 7, 1987

Vassula, yes, look into My Face. ♥ *To have seen Me, consoles Me. Tell them that it takes so little to console Me.* ♥ *Come and praise Me, loving Me.* ♥
I had the picture of the Holy Shroud in front of me, and I was looking at it when Jesus wrote that message.

June 8, 1987

Vassula, I would like to establish My Works.
What should I do?
I will guide you. I will guide you even further. Depend on Me; have My Peace. ♥

June 9, 1987

Last evening, I saw God's Face in the sky. The sky was a Beauty! It was like a painted picture from a skilled artist. I recognized God's Beauty in there. It was obvious.
Yes, Vassula, see Me in My creation, recognize Me and Love Me ♥

CALL IT: 'TRUE LIFE IN GOD'

Dhaka, Bangladesh, June 10, 1987

Yesterday was the final packing for our departure. Lot's of work!
Lord, I was thinking of a theory which is called, "Christ Consciousness". I think it means "our good inner self". Maybe this is how the writings come?

♥ *Vassula, have I not told you that we are united; we are one, beloved. Call it "true life in God,"* ♥ *live for Me. Here is what I want you to write.*

I was wondering by a feeling, what would God write now....
My desires, little one.
God made me read a part of Scriptures.
Yes, elevate, hear Me; will you see Me in <u>My</u> Church? Vassula, come to Me.
Which Church, Lord; which do You mean?

All are <u>My</u> Churches; they are all Mine; they all belong to Me and Me only. I am the Church; I am the Head of the Church.
But the way You said it, Jesus, it was like you wanted me to go to a special one. That's how I understood and heard You!
You can come to Me anytime in any Church; do not make any distinction like the others; ♥ *they all belong to Me; I am One God and have One Body, a Body which they have lamed.* ♥ *Millstones have damaged My Body.* ♥ ♥
My God, You seem so upset!
O Vassula, why, why have they cruelly dismembered Me? ♥ ♥

God is very upset. He reminds me of the time He went and overturned all the money-makers' tables in the temple in Jerusalem. So far I <u>never</u> heard or saw Him SO UPSET!

Vassula?
Jesus?
I Am.
Is that You, really so upset?
O yes, it's Me. O yes, I finally can place My words on you, Vassula. Charisma is not given to you for your interests; it is given to you so that My Words be engraved on you.
I have never felt You so upset before! are You?
I am; My Body aches. It has been torn apart. ♥
My God! But what can I do? I'm helpless.
Do I not know all this, Vassula? I shall use you till the end. ♥ *Never fear Me, daughter. Uniting My Church will be the Glory of My Body.* ♥ *Have My Peace, beloved.*
Yes, Lord, I won't look left or right or behind; I will look straight ahead.
Yes, understand how I work; be still like now; be willing to please Me; be one with Me.
Lord, suppose the ones You want them to listen, do not! Then?
Now you are a step ahead of Me! Child, walk with Me, together; yes, follow Me. Trust Me, come, I will guide you. ♥

I was suddenly taken by surprise. I heard the dog bark (unusual). Then my bedroom door opened and I recognized in front of me the thief who entered three nights ago in our room, stealing money, and who fled. There he was again I ordered him out. He turned around and left, then I gave the alarm. I knew that God was definitely trying to tell me something.
♥ *Vassula, I am reminding you of something.* ♥ *When the brigand[1] entered your*

---

[1]God used the right word, as later we found out that he belonged to a group. Brigands are thieves in groups.

room, did you expect him?
No!
So will I come too, sudden. No one recognized him either because no one expected him to be there.

Jesus meant the ten packers and the office men who saw him but did not believe he was a thief. I have the feeling that this last sentence is very important and hides much more than it says. The word "recognized" is very deep too.

Did it remind you of something else? Let Me tell you; he had sinned, ♥ but those who passed judgment on him, breaking the rod on his back, were they not in sin too?
I do no know what You are trying to make me understand. Yes, we are all sinners.
Vassula, will I see all this and keep silent?
Are You defending the thief, Lord?
No, Vassula, I do not....
Jesus was silent for a while.

Name Me one man who has not sinned. ♥
I can't think of any.

Big sins, small sins, all are sins. To sin is to grieve Me. ♥ Vassula, I am witnessing so many sins. Love is suffering; Love grieves, grieves...Creation! My creation, ♥ return to Love...Daughter, imbue Me with love; amend, beloved, amend. ♥ ♥

MY BLOOD IS GUSHING OUT

June 11, 1987

By now, most of our furniture is gone. I have to look for chairs to sit to write; the house is still messy after the packers left, heaps of papers here and there, shoes, bottles, papers, belts on all desks. Yet in all this moving, among the buffets we had to prepare for farewells (one for eighty people, another for thirty), God's hand did not release a bit. I always found time for Him to write two or three hours daily. He gives me incredible strength, and I don't feel the least tired; I'm in total peace, His Peace.

Vassula, beloved of My Soul, stay near Me. Face Me, let My Finger touch your heart. My child, if you knew how much I love you. ♥ *I will guide you till the end. Sacrifice more for Me. Will you suffer for Me?*

Yes, Lord, do as You please.

He had previously asked this, but I had hesitated, fearing. Now He asked again.

♥ *Vassula, I am so happy! Will you sacrifice yourself for Me like a lamb?*

Do as You please, Lord.

♥ *All will not be in vain; all will be for Peace and Love. My thirst is great, Vassula. I will lead you into arid lands where your eyes will behold what you have never seen.* ♥ *I will lead you with Heavenly Force, right into the very depths of My Bleeding Body. I will point out to you with My Finger, all the sacerdotal sinners who are the thorns of My Body. I will not spare them;* ♥ *I am worn out. My Wounds are wider than ever; My Blood is gushing out, I am being recrucified by My own, My own sacerdotal souls!*

My God, You give me so much pain; why would they do that to You? Why?

Vassula, they know not what they are doing. ♥ *Beloved, strive with your God; be willing to face My sufferings and share them with Me.*

I will, to console You. Remember those who love You!

They are the beloved ones of My Soul; I need more of these souls immolating their hearts for Me. I love them; I trust them, they eat from Me, they are My sacrifice, they are the smooth petals which replace My thorns, they are My myrrh. ♥ *Vassula, do not fear; we will penetrate deeper still where darkness prevails. I will lead you.* ♥

Later on, my soul started to feel God's bitterness. Everything, every food or drink which came into my mouth tasted bitter. He made me drink from His Chalice. I then had problems in breathing. My soul and my body ached.

HONG KONG - WORLDLY RICHES - AIDS

June 15, 1987

Father James willingly did the Stations of the Cross with me. We both held candles and knelt in all. Father James did not perhaps see that in each Station, both Jesus and St. Mary were in front of us, blessing us.

HONG KONG

Then yesterday, I flew to Hong Kong for our holiday. While in transit in Bangkok, something happened. I sat to read at transit hall at the end of a row of chairs.
Suddenly, in front of my feet, an Arab threw a carpet, totally ignoring me, with two others behind him. They fell to the ground, worshiping God with a loud voice, attracting much attention. I felt awkward as no one was sitting around me. I felt I was disturbing, as I was just in front of them. I didn't move. Their voices rose higher, and someone took a picture of the whole awkward scene from behind me.
Later on, God told me: "This man said his prayers loud enough, enough to attract a lot of attention; he was heard in transit; but in that hall, only the walls heard him. My Heart never heard a thing; all the words remained on his lips. Nevertheless, I heard your voice, though no one heard you, and no one knew what you were telling Me; but it came from your heart, not from your lips." I did not want to write this down because of fear of discrimination. But God told me: "What have you to fear; I am the Truth, and does this not also happen with Christians too?"

Today, we made a tour with the bus in the town and outskirts. Suddenly, instead of these tall buildings, I saw huge Black Crosses (I remembered the words "arid lands"). I thought it was my imagination, but I heard God's voice saying: "No, it is not your imagination. They are My Crosses." When seeing "Consumers Paradise", I thought that if I had to live in it, I would die. It would be torture for me; and to think that a year ago, I thought it was Paradise!

God does not want to spare me saying this too: at our tour bus, the guide showed us a super villa of the richest man in Hong Kong. He told us, there are two millionaires, very well known by name in all Hong Kong. God's Voice came in my ears, saying: "But I know not who they are; they belong to the world."
Their riches are worldly riches, they have nothing in My Kingdom. "

God took over to write this Himself.

♥ *Beloved, I am giving you signs; be alert. Vassula, believe what you hear from Me.* ♥
I am thinking of the Arab....
Holiness was missing from him; even you could see it.

Later on:

O Vassula, do I not deserve more respect? ♥
I feared this. I had no opportunity to be with God, writing. So I took my chance in the hotel room with my son and my husband. The T.V. was on. I blocked my ears with a walkman. I had nowhere to go!
I justly withdraw all your faculties.

Why, Lord?

Why? So that I teach you to desire your God. ♥ *Wait until we are alone.*

Forgive me.

I forgive you. So, Vassula, work while you are suspended. ♥

How Lord?

Allow Me to whisper in your ear all My desires. Vassula, desire Me. ♥ *Use the Graces I have bestowed on you. Remember, it is not only My Hand using your hand; I opened your ear. I showed you how to see Me and how to feel Me, so use the other Graces too.* ♥ *I love you.* ♥

Jesus?

I am, Vassula.

We are together in this way again.

Yes, but not for long. Reserve Me not for later merely because you do not pursue your lifestyle of before. Have Me locked in your heart, child. ♥

Lord, will I have bigger trials?

O yes, you will face many more severe trials. ♥

I sighed.

Trust Me. I will be near you. You are My sacrifice, are you not? Why would I have you then among evil? I offer you to them, to be among wickedness.

But I am also wicked; what's the difference; I am like them.

Are you, why then do you want to come to Me at Home?

Because I love you.

♥ *I fashioned you like Me to enable you to draw others to Me. I will detach you still more from earthly solicitudes. Wait and you shall see.* ♥ *Vassula, yes,[1]* ♥ ♥ *love Me;* ♥ *come, take My Hand as you did yesterday.* ♥ ♥

Later on:

Vassula, write the word aids.

AIDS?

Yes, replace it by the word Justice. My Chalice of Mercy has brimmed over, and My Chalice of Justice is full. Do not let It brim over! I have told you before that the world is offending Me; I am a God of Love, but I am also known to be a God of Justice. I loathe paganism!

Later on:

Beloved, you will penetrate into My Body; I will let you see My thorns and nails.

Lord, how will I see this?

---

[1] I just saw Him in front of me.

I will give you sight so that you see; I will give you strength to pull out my nails and thorns. ♥ ♥ *Recrucified, I am.*
But Lord, why have You let Yourself be recrucified?
Vassula, Vassula, taken by my own, neglected by My beloved.

He said it in a very sad tone, like someone being betrayed by his best friend!

Come, honour Me, love Me!
I love You; I cling on You. When will this happen?
Ah Vassula, do not run in front of Me; come, all in good time.
But You know Lord that I'm an outsider, a nothing, and not knowing what's going on where You are mentioning. Then, who would want to see my papers (Your writings)? They will, if it reaches them, throw all the writings in my face, laughing. They will probably throw it around like confetti; after all, who am I? but a "professional sinner"!
♥ *Remember who is leading you! I am God. Do you remember what you said to your friend; yes, the unbeliever? They were My words: "You are like a mouse running away from a Giant." You are a speck of dust.* ♥

True, a friend of ours, an "unbeliever", received a message from God. He said to me later on: "In one half minute, this message destroyed a belief of twenty solid years of freemasonry. Why should I, a professional sinner, get such a message? But I will fight it, I will run away." I laughed! then told him God's words.

Vassula, trust Me.

Lord, I do. But it's me the problem, why do you trust me? You should not, my Lord, I'm all good will, but as you said, very weak. Don't trust me! I'm very sinful.
Vassula, you are ineffably weak, I knew this from all Eternity, but be nothing; I want you to be nothing. How else would I manifest Myself alone if we were two? Let Me free always, and I shall act in you. ♥ *Come, lean on Me!*

DO NOT BE LIKE THE CYRENEAN - UNITY

Dahka, Bangladesh, June 17, 1987

Jesus, I know You are using Father James a lot. First, You used him to chase away evil. (In the first three months, evil approached to discourage me from God's approach, and chase me away.) Then you used him as Your instrument of my torments; then you used him to deliver me the right books and recognize Your

Supernatural Works, and confirm that it is You in this approach. You also make me aware of my wretchedness, and that you approached me in spite of my wickedness, having absolutely no merits for such graces given to me. Comparing the saints, it's obvious. Do You understand then why the "wave of doubt" comes? just because of that, because of my unworthiness. Remember, you taught me everything from scratch; and remember how I, in the beginning, denied You, knowing it's You? You see what I mean? When I have the "wave of doubt" because of the reasons above, I know I'm offending You and hurting You as You said once: "You hurt Me when you forget who saved you from darkness." On the other hand, my mind almost reels to understand why You come to a soul like me, giving a mission of such importance to someone who had to start from scratch in Scripture, 150% sinner!

The more Your guidance goes on, the more miracles it gives. Total atheists are bent, but You blessed It, Lord, so I should not feel surprised. One after another, unbelievers return to You by reading It: people who told me, "I don't believe but in solids, money, business...." These words are still ringing in my ears, and to see now this man, keener than his wife (who tried to convince him at first without success), wanting <u>all</u> the messages, saying that It gives him tremendous peace. I never spoke to him, since I am not good in words; it just happened. Jesus, of course, You're Wonderful.

It is I, Jesus, beloved Son of God.
I have been sending you all these books so that you may believe in My Supernatural Works. I have been feeding you My Bread; never doubt of My Works. I wish you to learn the details of all My Graces, so be alert to all new manifestations. All will come from Me. ♥

The Cross seemed to crush me. (The "Cross" is the Message of God.)

Jesus?
I am. Lift! Lift! Do not fall; I am near you to help you. Lift My Cross, do not be like the Cyrenean, be willing. Come, beloved, the way may be rough, but I am always near you, sharing My Cross. ♥ *Vassula, look at Me!*

I looked at Him. There He was, holding the corner of the wall in a most pitiful manner. He was wearing His crown of thorns and wore on Him a cloth soaked with Blood. He was covered with sweat and blood all over, more blood than flesh...fresh from scourging.

Do I deserve this?
No! My God!
Honour Me, daughter.
Who has done this to You My Lord?
Who? Souls, Vassula, it's them, replica of Sodom. ("Replica" means "copy".) ♥ ♥
Daughter, <u>I desire unity in My Church</u>! <u>UNITY!</u>

LET YOUR WILL BE DONE

June 18, 1987

Jesus?
I am. I will use you, Vassula.
Use Me till the end, Lord.
*Beloved, tell them to give Me the freedom to act as I wish, that in their prayers and in all petitions to Me they should add: "But not our will, let Yours be done."
Learn from Me;* ♥ *honour Me.* ♥

DEEDS

June 19, 1987

Vassula, deeds, deeds, I want to see deeds! I delight to hear your loving words which are a balm to My Wounds, but I will delight furthermore to see deeds from you! Come, I will remind you how I worked on earth while in flesh, and how I taught My disciples to work in the same manner. ♥
Padre Pio worked like You.
He worked for Me. ♥ *I gave him all those Graces to honour Me and revive My Name.* ♥ *To work in My Name, glorifies Me and purifies you. Remember, I shine on everyone.*
Including people like me?
Yes, including souls like yours. ♥

Thailand, June 20, 1987

Our Holy Mother:
How I was pleased to receive your light. Adorn Us with love. Have our Peace.

Very lovingly, Saint Mary said these words. I had lit a candle for Saint Mary, before doing the Stations.

MY BODY IS MAIMED

June 21, 1987

Lord, why so many people have forgotten You?
O Vassula! My Body is maimed to the extent of paralyzation. ♥ *Introduce the light in My Stations, kneeling at every Station.* ♥

I remained silent.

Vassula, I have spoken!
Lord, What can I do?
Nothing. Let Me do everything.
Yes, but no one will do it since no one knows!
To have faith is also a Grace given by Me. Have faith ♥ *in Me!*

Later on:

Now that You seduced me, what will become of me?
Do you want to know? I will hurl you from My Arms in this exile that My creation has become! You will live among them!
My God, don't You love me anymore?

I became quite distressed.

It was wonderful being in Your Arms! And now You want me off!
O Vassula, how could you say that!

I felt a pang of pain in Him.

My Heart rends and lacerates to see you among all this evil. Understand, My child, that I am sacrificing you to be among Godless people. I suffer to have you out in exile. ♥ *Daughter, many will try and hurt you; I could bear now your sufferings,[1] but I would not bear, no, I would not bear to have them hurt you.*
What would You do, Lord.
♥ *I would not stand by.* ♥
But why have you cuddled me and seduced me, to hurl me out now? It's almost not fair!

---

[1] Being split: My soul in His Heart, and my body in the world.

I was almost screaming.

♥ *Have I not said that you will be My sacrifice? I am using you. You are My net. Yes, I am hurling you over to the world. You are to offer Me souls for their salvation; I will redeem them; this will not go by without you suffering.* ♥ *The devil hates you, and he would not hesitate to burn you, but he will not lay a hand on you, I do not allow him.* ♥

It reminds me: when I touched the other day the exhaust pipe of the boat which just pulled us in, I put all my weight on that pipe, hot to roast an egg, with my left hand. I almost fainted with pain, having burnt all my left palm; and the impulse to put it in the sea was great, for relief. But I remembered never to put any burned flesh in cold water, as it produces injuries. My hand for ten minutes was still hurting and red and <u>swollen</u>. But after half an hour, everything was gone: no pain, no burns, and it felt just like my other hand, in perfect condition again.

♥ *Child, I will not see you hurt, I love you, and out of love I will choose <u>My</u> purifications for you. I will never allow any stain on you. Understand what I mean.*[1] ♥

Lord, <u>anything</u> that will come from You, I will love, if it's delights or if it's sufferings.
Beloved, yes, make a heaven for Me in your heart. ♥ *How I delight to hear this from you child!*
Yes, and any suffering chosen by your own will, thinking it will please Me, will be a horror in My Eyes. You will only be deceiving yourself. It will be for the devil, not for Me. Reparations will be instructed by Me. ♥ ♥ ♥
I love You and depend on You entirely.
♥ *By loving Me, you are glorifying Me,* ♥ *yes.* ♥

I heard Satan saying: "Those moments are martyrdom for me!" He could not bear my heart rejoicing in God's love for me and my love for Him: loving each other. It is like sealing him with a red-hot Cross all over him.

[1] It means any sufferings induced by Satan will not be realized; but any sufferings that come from God will be realized, thus purifying the soul.

LET ME BE YOUR SPIRITUAL DIRECTOR

June 23, 1987

Jesus, You have been my Teacher from the very start. But wouldn't I have someone like a spiritual director, as they say, to guide me a little. So far, I have no one, and those I approached either were not interested, or too busy, or horrified. No one told me: "my child, do this or that," in a gentle manner and followed this up. The only one who definitely gave an order was to say, "Stop, this is not from God. So stop writing at least for a few days, and see what comes." I listened to him. I <u>did</u> stop, but Your Hand managed to write while I was doing my own notes: "I, God, love you; never forget this." You took full possession of my hand. Then again, in a few minutes, "Never ever forget that I, God, love you." It felt like someone who loved me, visited me in prison, a surprise visit. It was wonderful!

My child, let Me be your Spiritual Director. Am I not pleasing enough for you? ♥ ♥ *I am Everything you lack.* ♥ *Vassula, delight Me by modifying My Stations by simply adding the light, and honour Me by kneeling at each of My Stations.* ♥ ♥ *I will give you more of My instructions all in good time.* ♥

Jesus, thank You for letting me meet David.
My child, narrate Me and ask him: "Will you let Me use you?"
Lord, haven't You asked this already before? What do You exactly mean?
By this I mean whether he will be willing to work for Me. My Cross is heavy; will you unburden Me for a while?
Yes, Lord.
♥ *Come nearer.* ♥ ♥

A VISION OF THE ANOINTED

Bangkok, June 26, 1987

At 7:30 in the morning, I saw a coloured cloud, very attractive to the eye. Then five beams came out like a star. I said, "Look!" And a hand behind me, pushed me forward. Another change came then: on one of the beams, a candle appeared; I said again, "Look!" The hand behind me pressed me, making me fall on my knees. I still did not bother to see who was doing this to me, as I did not want to miss a single moment of the event. The five rays by now produced by their speed of turning around, a kind of lit ring; and suddenly, from the very center of that lit ring, Jesus appeared. I said, "Look!" Again the hand behind me pushed me, and now I had my hands on the ground. Suddenly, hundreds of voices were worshiping Jesus. They were just saying J-E-S-U-S all the time. Then Jesus' image left, and instead, a scene appeared. I again said, "Look!" And the hand pushed me flat to the ground, prostrated, by now only my head lifting to watch the last scene. I saw someone kneeling, surrounded by five others; in front of this scene, a very bright silver chalice. The five were doing something to the one kneeling in their midst. The word "ANOINTING" was heard by me. Then everything just disappeared.

My God, I have not understood Your dream vision to me.
♥ *Wisdom will instruct you.* ♥

So now I realize: I have been split. My body goes around, but without my soul in it; my soul, My God, you have taken it. I feel like a carcass: detached totally. Has anybody experienced this: to think, as long as you are awake and conscious, of God only? Has anyone experienced an awareness of God for twenty-four hours a day for every day, and more than one year? And the minute my mind would start to forget, my chin is taken by a Hand to turn my head and face Jesus' smiling Face. I surprise myself how I cope still with other things!

Vassula, I have just taken your heart, placing it in My Heart. ♥
This was said as if my heart was nothing, very simply....
I am Yahweh, and I love you! Cradle My Love. Creature, stay in your Creator's Grace. ♥
How, how could I stay in Your Grace?
You have to be holy.
How can I be holy?
By loving Me fervently.
Then, if it is Your will, help me be.
I will help you. Have My blessings. I will never ask anything from you that would harm you; remember this always. Come, I will unveil My deepest and most intimate desires. Allow Me to engrave them on you little one. ♥

I WANT TO REMIND THEM OF MY WAYS

Dhaka, June 30, 1987

I rushed because Jesus was urging me to write.

♥ *I called you!*

I felt and saw Jesus happy.

Yes, I am; I feel happy! Come, let us work; I shall repeat My desires. Vassula, do not fear to show My Works. ♥
Lord, I remind myself of this good friend of ours, Martha, the impulsive one. I'm impatient now like her, I want things to go quick: tomorrow, today, now, if possible, to have all Your desires ACCOMPLISHED NOW; thorns plucked and thrown away, lance drawn out from Your Heart now, and all Your desires accomplished!
Vassula, do not rush. ♥

I felt His Hand caress my head.

♥ *Hear My desires again, I want to remind them of My Ways, I want them to stop throwing venomous arrows at one another.* ♥ *Vassula, was I a politician?*

Jesus surprised me with this question. He had a different tone in His Voice.

Well, this time even I know you were not a politician....

Exactly, I was not a politician. Vassula, who do you say I was?
You are meaning while you were here in flesh, Lord?
Yes.
The Beloved Son of God.
♥ *Yes, you see, even you knew I was not a politician.* ♥ *Vassula, let Me see.* ♥
♥

Jesus is thinking with the usual position, one arm across His stomach, and the other arm with the elbow on His waist and forefinger on His cheek.

Have you ever felt through My whole guidance any trace of wickedness from My part?
No, not a trace Lord, never.
Good. ♥
What's this, Lord?
How have you felt, Vassula?

Jesus ignored my previous question.
I felt spoiled by You, loved extremely much, cuddled, forgiven.
Go on. ♥
I felt elated by Your love, peaceful, wonderful; I felt never happier then when I was with You, and with Your love showing me the way again, teaching me love, holiness, humility.
♥ *Yes, you see, Vassula; there is no trace of political upheaval, none.* ♥

Jesus made a gesture with His Hand, showing or emphasizing, "none".

This is how I am. I am All Love, ♥ *and this is the* ♥ *way I would like My true, but* true, *followers to be.* ♥ *Hear Me: I am the Church; do not* ever *forget this.* ♥ *Have My Peace, Vassula.* ♥
I love You to folly, and You know this now, Jesus.
Beloved, My Heart will engulf you with its Flame of Love. Allow Me to keep you in My Heart. ♥

I thought of the vision.

♥ *The five rays come out of My five Wounds.*
And the candle on one of the rays?
I wish to introduce the light. ♥
At Your Stations?
Yes. ♥
Then I saw You.
Yes, I was wearing My thorned crown, remember?
Yes, I do. But what was the last scene?
♥ *My anointing.*
And why was I pushed to a prostrate position?
Prostrated you should have been. ♥
And the Chalice, Lord?
This is to purify yourself and to honour My Holy Eucharist. ♥ ♥
Thank you, Lord.
Vassula, deep in My Body, I have the lance's point penetrating My Heart; it is there always. ♥ *I want the lance removed;* ♥ *glorify My Body in establishing Peace, Unity, and Love.*
Beloved God, it's all too vague for me; I don't know the meaning of Your words.
Remove the thorns that penetrated in My Head. Vassula, will you do this for Me? I will be before you always. Heal My Body, soothe It. My Five Wounds are wide open, see? Love Me, adorn Me, embellish Me, remind them of the first Christians who loved Me more than their own life. ♥ ♥
Lord, more than photocopying and distributing Your messages I can't do!
♥ *You will do much more than this. Never forget who is leading you.* ♥
Yes, Lord, I depend on You. ♥ ♥

I AM YOUR CONSOLER

July 3, 1987

Jesus?
I am. Beloved, inspirations come from Me, like dew drops come on leaves. ♥ *I have made a pact with you to be faithful to you. I have taken My measures so that you too will remain faithful to Me, see?*

Jesus made sure I'll not give Him the slip, knowing how weak I am....

Vassula, for My sake, will you unite My Church? I am before you, and it is I who will instruct you, just follow Me. I want all My Churches united. ♥ *I want My sacerdotal souls to remember My Works of before and the simplicity My disciples had, the humbleness and the faithfulness the first Christians had.* ♥ *Come, I will unveil My deepest and most intimate desires of My Heart. Allow Me to engrave them on you, little one.* ♥

Here I really felt helpless. I feel God is desiring so many important things which he tells me, writing them down, and I'm sitting on them, paralyzed. I feel I do not do what He wants since nothing has been changed, but how can it change if really no one knows much about this. I feel I'm displeasing Him, disobeying, not doing what He desires most. I showed this to Father James, but he too, what could he do, but read and counsel me. Over a hundred people have copies of these revelations, but it's not enough!
Jesus?
♥ *I am; live in peace.* ♥ I *will restore My Church. Allow Me, Vassula, just to imprint My Words on you. I love you; glorify Me by loving Me. To unite My Church is My Work. You will be My bearer only. Do you understand the difference? Even when I say: revive or unite My Church, Vassula, it is never directed straight at you;* ♥ *you will learn; have you not learned part of My Works with Me?*
Yes, Lord, I have.
Wait, and you shall see. ♥

There was a long pause, He had my hand paused on the paper, not saying anything before saying:

I have one question to ask you; why were you now not coming to Me for consolation?

In a flash of a <u>few seconds</u>, Jesus gave me a vision and a whole story like a parable. It was of a child and a mother. The mother had lost her child for years; finally, having found it, she was so happy trying to teach her child to go to her for anything it wanted since she loved it and it belonged to her. The child had a great problem getting adjusted again to someone who says it's its mother who cares; it was used to wallow by itself in its miseries, having had no one to turn to. But now again, it forgot that the mother is the one who could help it and console it. The vision was that of a tiny child in complete misery again, whining around the house, ignoring the mother. The mother, seeing the child in its misery, felt hurt: hurt to see her child miserable, hurt to see the child still not wanting to come and throw itself in her arms and show that it needs affection from her. The mother's heart was utterly shattered to see her child in misery and ignoring her too, she who could do so much if it had confidence in her!

The child was me; the mother, Jesus. And all this because I felt as if I'm not getting anywhere, the message on my back, and not doing much. I decided to go and sleep on it to forget. So I went to bed and tried to sleep to forget. This was in the afternoon; I thought of Jesus, but I felt too miserable to even face Him.

Yes, exactly, yes ♥ *Beloved, I am your Consoler! Lean your head on Me; allow Me to caress you and soothe your pain; allow Me to whisper in your ear My words. Inside My Heart, I have a place for you; spend no time elsewhere; come now in your place.* ♥

He said this in such tenderness that only God can speak in this manner.

I'm incapable....
I will lift you and place you in there. ♥

SPIRITUAL DESERTS

Switzerland
July 7, 1987

Vassula, you shall face severe trials; do not forget My Presence; I am near you. Believing in My Heavenly Works is also a Grace given by Me. ♥ *My Works, in your eyes, appear quite unorthodox, but I am God, and with whom could you compare Me to? And to what can you compare My Works to? Vassula, when I see how so many of My sacerdotal souls deny my signs and My Works; how they treat those to whom I have given My Graces and remind the world I am among you, I*

grieve...they are unwillingly damaging My Body; pono![1] They deny My Works, thus making deserts instead of making the land fertile!
Lord, if they deny Your Works, there must be reasons!
Spiritually they are dead; they are deserts themselves, and when they spot a flower in that great wilderness they made, they rush to it and trample on it, destroying it. Why?

Why? It is a misfit in their wilderness; they make sure that their desert stays arid! I find no holiness in them, none. What have they to offer Me?
Protection, Lord! Protection not to distort Your Word!

No, they are not protecting Me; they are denying Me as God. They deny My Infinite Wealth, they deny My Omnipotency, they are comparing themselves to Me. Do you know what they are doing? They are promoting paganism, they are multiplying My scourgers, they are increasing spiritual deafness, they are not defending Me, they are deriding Me! I have willed, in spite of their denials, to help them so that in their turn they would help and feed My lambs. Love Me, Vassula; honour Me by never denying Me. ♥
I will never deny You; I will never deny that these are Your Works, Lord, even if I had to die!
My sweet myrrh, My remnant, My beloved, look after My interests, be My altar, remain little so that I work in you and act in you. Come, let us pray: ♥

> *Father of Mercy, unite your sheep,*
> *Bring them together again,*
> *Let them realize their aridity,*
> *Forgive them;*
> *Mould them into what you desire them to be,*
> *Remind them of Your Ways,*
> *May all Glory be in Your Holy Name,*
> *For ever and ever. Amen.*

I feel sad for God....

Beloved, grieve for the world and what it has become. ♥ *Rest in Me.* ♥

---

[1] Greek: meaning "I ache!"

I HAVE RISEN, I HAVE NOT DISINTEGRATED

July 8, 1987

Lord, a priest told me once that after You died and were buried, Your Body disintegrated into air and so they couldn't find You. In other words, this priest denied Your Resurrection.

Vassula, they are distorting My Word; I have risen; I have not disintegrated. My Body has risen.

Lord, are You talking to me in symbols or are You telling me that You actually arose in Body?

Child, I have spoken literally to you; My Body has risen; tell them to stop distorting My Word to please human understanding. ♥ *I am Omnipotent.*

Lord, I am fearing that I might delay your plans.

♥ *How will you delay Me if I am the One who works?*

With sins obstructing.

I will ask you to repent often, I will point out your sins, I want you pure.

MY MYSTERIES

July 9, 1987

My God?

I am. Vassula, I have so many mysteries hidden from you! Those few I revealed to you are "seen"[1] in human eyes, thus not comprehending them. Either they will be placed aside, or will be given the wrong explanation. How could you possibly compare My Works with human works? ♥ *Science cannot be compared with Heavenly Works; it is as if you want to compare Me with men! True, My Works appear unorthodox to you, but what grieves Me most is to see My own sacerdotal souls doubting My Works, refusing to believe, thus "remoting" Me instead of promoting Me.*

My creation has turned into a desert, dry, unfertile, thirsty for love. On what will My lambs feed upon when they have nothing to offer? ♥

---

[1]Understood.

LOVE YOUR NEIGHBOUR AS YOURSELF

July 10, 1987

Flower of Mine, integrate in My Body. To live in wilderness is hard, but I will always guide you to My Fountain, where I will quench your thirst and give you rest and shelter. Daughter, be My sacrifice; all will not be in vain. Hold on to Me; you are not alone; we are together crossing this wilderness. Allow Me to imprint on you My special command:

"Love your neighbour as yourself"

But Lord, its not new, You said this before.
Are you following it? Every ecclesiastical soul has yet to learn to obey My Command. Let them draw from My Infinite Love and learn to love one another. Feel Me, all parts of My Body lacerate, Vassula. I have not completed dictating you My desires, and I still keep in store a bigger desire! Vassula, you are beginning to feel it because I am enlightening you to sense what I desire. I love My creation boundlessly.
My God, if it is "this" what You desire, then indeed Your Kingdom on earth will be as it is in Heaven!

THERE IS NO WORD AS LUCK IN MY VOCABULARY!

July 11, 1987

Little by little you will understand. Visions I will give you, and you will write them down. Be with your God who suffers too!
Creation! My creation! Today you deny Me as your God, but tomorrow you will praise Me, worship Me, and desire Me! ♥ *Come, Vassula; never forget who I am; hold on to Me; call Me like yesterday, and I shall rush to you.*

That was last night; in our new flat, the concierge closes by lock the main entrance to the flats by ten o'clock at night. We had forgotten our key in the flat. On seeing the door closed, we knew we were locked out. I went to the door, pleading, "O God, don't tell me it's locked; let it be open! Please!" It was locked, but at the same minute, one of the neighbors was just arriving too and opened.

In such situations, most of you say that it was luck, forgetting Me! There is no such word as "luck" in My vocabulary! It is I who help you, creation. ♥

Repent!
I thank You for looking after me, My God.
I repented.
Beloved, all is forgiven, for such is My Mercy. I will teach you to look before you make your next step. Be alert; favour Me above all, flower, do not turn away your face from My Light; look at Me; face Me; flourish!
I am weak; I feel sometimes it's hard to carry Your Cross.
♥ *My remnant, unite with Me and Be One; together, together we will restore My Church.* ♥ ♥

ALPHA AND OMEGA

July 12, 1987

Vassula, I rejoice when you realize. ♥

Sometimes I fully realize that I am really with God and that He communicates with me in this way, so I have my heart leaping! It comes in waves. Most of the time I realize, but not really fully.

Do You know this, Lord?
I do; I know very well. ♥ *Vassula, have you remembered Juan? We will unite him to Me.*
My God!
I Am.
You think a lot about Juan!
He is My beloved soul; I love him; ♥ *I want him near Me;* ♥ *I wish to guide him and make a great servant out of him. O Vassula! What great things he can do for Me!*
But Lord, it's impossible! To start with, he is not believing in You; then he's got other occupations in his life!
Child, do you realize who is leading you?
Yes, My God....
I am the Alpha and the Omega, Creator of all; do you realize he has been looking for Me for years!

Has he? I thought he didn't believe.

He has always believed; only he has been misled. I love him and will guide him to find Me. ♥ I am Love, and to Love he will come. I will fill him with My Love; all My blessings will restore him. ♥ Beloved, now you must rest. ♥

Lord, do You still always want me kneeling while writing?

♥ I do; honour My Presence.

Yes, Lord.

I REVIVED YOU FOR MY GLORY

July 13, 1987

Vassula, to be My bearer, you are to love Me as I taught you. ♥ Alive, finally alive! I raised you from the dead!

What about the others?

Creature, the others are yet to be risen. My dew of Love will fall upon them; My Light will cover them, and they will revive. Creation, I will revive you! Reviving you was not for your glory; I revived you for My glory.

Yes, Lord.

Little one, call Me Abba; yes, be close to Me; I will never abandon you. ♥

TALK TO ME

July 18, 1987

I do not feel fit to write; since my arrival in Switzerland, I'm not well: first the "flu", followed by an infection in the mouth; I could barely eat. Then followed a piercing pain in my side, which stopped me from sleeping for five nights, which I still have, the "flu" all over, plus lip infection.

Come, let Me tell you; all are coming from me; ♥ these are My purifications. Daughter, I love you. Learn how I work; I will sustain you even if you will have to suffer. I am caring for you and will not allow any stain on your soul. Understand how I work, but feel Me; let Me hear you talk to Me; remember Me; never will I let anything come before Me, I am First. Polishing your soul will make it shine like gold, and now I will remind you why I chose you. I chose you because of your ineffable wretchedness and weakness. I am a God of Mercy. Now you may work, but have Me in mind always. I never leave you from My sight. Watch My Lips when I am talking to you. I love you. Come, get up; face Me and let Me hear you now. ♥ ♥

True, I had neglected God for some time; our changing countries occupied me with other things.

Allow Me to use you still for just some more time. ♥
Yes, Lord.
Have My blessings. ♥
I bless you, Lord.

JEHOVAH WITNESSES

Stockholm, July 21, 1987

Today I had two ladies from the "Jehovah's Witnesses", as they call themselves. I let them in. We had language problems. They seemed very determined and somehow attacked the Catholic religion! They said they could come back with books in English. I will listen to see what they want. They had arrived while God was writing to Me. Briefly I showed them these revelations, and they both giggled, and I understood the word "demon". I let them; hasn't God told me that soon I will be mocked, and He gave me His thorned Crown to feel the mockery.[1] I fear that this is only the beginning...

Vassula, I am near you, do not fear. ♥

---

[1]Predicted - May 7, 1987.

SOULS IN PURGATORY

July 22, 1987

Vassula, can you see all these souls? All are waiting in line. ♥

I saw Jesus with a group of souls behind Him.

Jesus?
I am; yes, they were souls!

Immediately after I saw those souls, another image appeared to me: an image of many years back; I must have been 17-18 years old. I used to see often, for example, in the sitting room where I would be, many souls sitting on the floor, who were hushing each other to keep still and just be around me, like as if they would come listen to a speech. At the time, I was wondering why I saw these "dead people" as I used to call them, but paid no more attention to them since they never bothered me; and sooner or later I was quickly distracted by other things around me. It was very often and rather common, but I paid not much attention to all this.

Yes, Vassula, they were waiting!
Waiting for what, Lord?
They were waiting for you to grow. ♥
Did they know?
Yes, they knew; ♥ *I have waited for you to love Me and repair; loving Me fervently repairs, and so those souls in Purgatory[1] are healed, fires extinguished, snatched from the purifying fires, and can finally come to Me. Vassula, do you know how much they suffer while in Purgatory? their desire to see Me but being unable to? How much they depend on you! Ah Vassula, will you help them?*
Yes, Lord, I would love to see them with You finally!
Have my Peace; I, the Lord, will soon show you how you will help them. Seek Me always; immolate and never complain; I will help you to indulge My desires. Beloved, love Me, for your love cures them.
Jesus, will You let me know if they are back with You?
♥ *I will.* ♥
Jesus, what about the "Jehovah's Witnesses"?
Let them give you all they want; receive them with Me; ♥ *you will understand why I have sent them to you.* ♥ *Lean on Me, beloved.*

---

[1] I asked the Lord to write "Purgatory" instead of "Hades", the word which meant Purgatory for me, but in Greek.

Jesus, will I not meet any of Your own World?

Let Me tell you at once; I will take and place you among My own. Daughter, had you merited any of My graces, I would have shown you how Love leads, without having had to face difficulties and having all "doors" open.[1]

Meaning?

Meaning that you had not merited at all these graces I have given you, and it is out of My Infinite Goodness that I have looked upon your misery. ♥ From now on, desire Me more than ever; you will earn every single grace by giving Me acts of love. ♥ Every act of Love will restore all that you have destroyed.

What had I destroyed, My God?

All good things given by Me and having them turned into evil. ♥ Honour Me; I love you.

Lord, will You help me do these good acts?

I will; ♥ remember, all I gave will have to be given freely too. ♥ I want My altar pure. ♥ ♥ ♥

Later on:

God showed me that I never merited any of His graces. So now I come back to Him rather timidly, begging:

Lord?

I Am.

Allow me to be in Your Light.

Be in My Light and stay.

Allow me to lean on You.[2]

♥ I allow you always.

Allow me to hold Your hand and be near You?

Come in your Father's Arms. ♥

Allow me to talk to You!

Be one with Me; face Me; be My reflection, and let Me speak for you.

Allow me to be consoled by You?

Little one, I will be your Consoler; come, feel Me; synchronize with Me; be One; annihilate in Me; let Me possess you entirely and reign over you; let Me thrust you in My Heart; ♥ approach; be in Me, and I in you. How I love you, daughter!

I felt God pleased.

---

[1]"Doors": meaning Satan and his disciples are allowed to infiltrate and write his insults or give me the wrong word. God has taught me, though, because of this, how to recognize the demons. (Satan can never leave a soul in tranquility by his presence; it's a give-away.)

[2]The word "allow", when asking, was taught to me by Him because He, as God and Sovereign, always asks me, His creature, in this way: "allow Me to so and so...."

I love You, Lord.
I felt His Love covering me entirely.
Be with Me now; stay. ♥
I was preparing to get up and go.

Refuse Me nothing. Vassula, I cry out loudly; My cry resounds and shakes the entire heavens. My cry should have been heard by My souls who love Me. They must have heard Me; tell them that they have not imagined it; it is I, ♥ Jesus, Beloved Son of God. I want them to unite and to propound Unity, Peace and Love. I want them to be like an army of salvation, repairing all that has been destroyed and distorted. ♥ My cry is coming from the very depths of My Wounded Soul. ♥ Bless Me, daughter.

I bless You, My God; may Your wishes come true.
♥ *Stay faithful to Me; integrate into My Body; hold on to Me.* ♥

GIVE ME SOULS

July 24, 1987

There I come and kneel at my table, and Jesus is opposite me, sitting on the sofa. I look at Him expectantly for His words to come.

♥ *Beloved, augment your love for me, thus healing souls; love Me and free them.* ♥ *Now you have guided five souls back to Me; satisfy Me by giving Me souls. I want to redeem all those wretched souls who are near Satan's doors. I love you all so much!*

Later on:

Agapa Me.[1]
Jesus?
I am. Tell Sirkka Lisa to love Me more. Why does she not come to Me; I am her Counsellor. ♥ I am He who watches over you; I am your Consoler. Does she know what an abyss of Love My Heart is? I love her, Vassula; I shall wait for her; I shall keep calling her: "Respond, soul! Respond to My cry; invoke Me in your prayers; talk to this Heart which loves you. ♥ I will be waiting". ♥ ♥

Jesus gave a message for a friend of mine.

---

[1] Greek: "Love Me."

I AM YOUR FATHER

July 25, 1987

I am your Heavenly Father who loves you. ♥ *Call no one else Father but Me who is you Creator. Learn from Me.* ♥ *Vassula, have I not said that I am still among you? I am Love. Bring forth to Love, My flock, that I may redeem it; reduce paganism; induce Love; help My children by giving them the same food I have given you.* ♥

I will do Your wishes with Your help. Be the Light to guide me.

Later on:

The thought of the Jehovah's Witnesses who are going to come, puts me in discomfort. What to tell them?

Write. ♥

Jesus made a sign with His hand indicating this copy book.

Love them. Do what I ask you to do; love them; all are My children.
But I am afraid that they advise me wrongly; they seem to want to say that they are the only ones in the whole world that carry the right religion and that all the rest, like Catholics, Protestants, Moslems, Hebrews, etc. are 100% wrong! and that by their beliefs, one can reach heaven.

Jesus seemed inflexible.

Beloved, love them.
All right, but what if they will start misguiding me?
Would I stand still if I hear them misguide you? ♥
No.
Daughter, do not fear; I will guide you.
I am happy to be with You, my God.
Why?

Jesus seemed eager to hear the reasons. He enjoys it!

Because I love You, because you are my happiness, my joy and smile; you are my happy life. That's why.

♥ *Fill me with joy, Vassula; love Me. Vassula, trench into deeper depths of my Heart, and let all My Love utterly consume in nothing else but a Living Flame of Love's Love! Beloved, rest in Me, and let Me rest in you; be My heaven.* ♥ ♥

 ΙΧθΥΣ

HUMILITY, LOVE AND DEVOTION

July 26, 1987

My God?
♥ *I Am; little one, who else would lead you by this special path unless, I, God, had chosen it for you?*
In the beginning, I was very much hesitating, afraid that it's from evil.
The devil would have fled when you worshiped Me; he would be unmasked, revealing his insidious designs in mind; he would not bear humility, love, and devotion; <u>have this always in mind.</u> ♥ *Grip my hand and climb; do not weary; repent often.[1] How will you now proceed?*
You are asking me, Lord?
I am. ♥
I can't, unless You do by helping me.
Good. He who fights against My wishes, will be kicking against a goad. ♥

A PURIFICATION

July 27, 1987

I come with a feeling of desolation; I feel God is not so near as before.

♥ *Grieve not, My Vassula; I will clarify to you all this; I am near you.* ♥

---

[1]"Climb" means to progress spiritually, here.

July 28, 1987

Still with this feeling of desolation.

Jesus, I am so afraid to be misleading people when I tell them that I feel sometimes your hand caressing my head; maybe I am wrong? It would be terrible if I'm wrong! *Grieve not; believe in my Redemptive Love.* ♥ *I have caressed you so many times in the past as well as now. No, Vassula, you have not imagined it; it is I Jesus.* ♥

July 29, 1987

Still with this desolate feeling.

Jesus?
I am. ♥ *I have told you that My bonds are eternal bonds. What have you to fear? Erroneously you believe that because you are not used as before, I am less with you, or that I have forsaken you, or that I am angry with you. No, no, Vassula, it is none of these reasons, My Love has not changed; I have not deserted you; I will continue inspiring you.* ♥

July 30, 1987

I am still worried; why can't I feel God as before?

Jesus?
I Am. Come, ♥ *look at Me. Look, yes.* ♥

I looked into God's eyes and melted.

Regardless of what you are, have I not raised you and placed you in My Heart? ♥ ♥ *Vassula, My Vassula, will I ever forsake you?*

He said this in so much sweetness that God only can talk in this way.
Reflect, ♥ *I am love, and until I come to deliver you, I will pour My Love into you.* ♥ *Ela thipla mou imé o Christos[1].*

---

[1]Greek: Come near Me, I am Christ.

July 31, 1987

Vassula, come; I will clarify your groundless fears of desolation. ♥ *It is insight I am teaching you. Do not take this as abandonment from Me. Write. I am giving you My grace to reach a higher degree of meditation, while at the same time I am purifying your soul for this higher attainment. Be assured, My beloved, that I am with you and never far. I am stimulating your love to Me and strengthening you.* ♥ *A deeper devotion and a fuller love for Me will be the results of all this.* ♥

Vassula, I desire you to achieve this higher degree of meditation. You must grow. Beloved, remove all shadows of doubt from your mind, shadows that distress you. I want you to progress; I want your soul to attain perfection and purity; I want to advance your soul into this higher and more delicate light. Your soul thus cleansed will be able to offer Me virtues shelled in perfection and purity.

From meditation, you will reach in a higher level of contemplation. ♥ *This aridity and feeling of desolation which leaves you to think "all is gone"; it is because I withdraw from you part of My Light. Do not fear, though; be glad you feel the difference. By withdrawing part of My Light, I reinforce your desire of seeking Me,* ♥ *and thus I infuse you with more delicate Light in your intellect. Yet all Light is never totally withdrawn for I always leave you with some Light for you to be able to see and follow it and to sustain you from stumbling. I give you this vigour to continue seeking Me more fervently than ever.* ♥ ♥ *Seek in Me My desires, Vassula; I will never ever leave you; why, I am your Heavenly Father who wants you to grow and flourish, and these are My Ways. Have no fear, but be alert; never fall asleep; be seeking.* ♥ *From Me, you will learn. I am your Teacher.* ♥ *Love Me, Vassula; smile at Me when you see Me, and take My Hand when I give to you. Have my Peace and trust Me.* ♥ *Come, I love you.*

O Father, thank You for relieving me and explaining to me all this; thank you for Your teaching. I love You!

THE GRACE OF SUFFERING

Switzerland
August 4, 1987

I am almost fearing of what I think is happening. Is this the insight God talked about last week?

My God?
♥ *I Am, beloved.*
Am I understanding You correctly, Lord?
♥ *You are!* ♥ *Love will make out of you, a mirror of reflections and agonies attuned to all those who suffer. You will feel their agonies and sufferings as though they were your own.* ♥ *When you will hear or see any sufferings, or if someone is in great pain, I, the Lord, will offer you this grace of feeling these pains as much as the one who is suffering; thus, you will be able to penetrate fully in their wounds and have a clear conception of their feelings. Vassula, beloved, with this insight I am giving you, you will be of tremendous help to them. Suffer when they suffer; and if you deny them, I will remind you all the time; you will share their sufferings.* ♥
O My God, will my system take all this? Not that my spirit fears, but my flesh is weak.
♥ *Remember, I will give you enough strength for both your soul and flesh till the end. Believe Me, this is a grace, little one; love My children as much as I love them; be my reflection; synchronize with Me and them.* ♥ *I love you, and out of Sublime Love, I am giving you this grace; tire not; come, I will infuse you with my Love by giving you My nails.* ♥ *Feel all sufferings;* ♥ *daughter, will you do all this for Me?*
Yes, My God, if this is Your wish.
Come, Love will guide you. ♥

I have suspected this, and here is why: three days ago in the T.V. news, they showed two kids who died trapped underground. I felt sorry for the kids and the parents. I prayed for the parents. The following day, they showed a tornado in Canada and terrified people talking about it, still under fear. The same night I prayed for them too. I felt sorry but not as if I'm in their skin. Suddenly, God threw His piercing ray on me; I felt it piercing my chest and going out through my back. It burnt and gave me such agony that I wanted to run and drink water; it was as if I was ablaze! Then, later on I slept: He gave me a vivid image of how I should have felt. In my dream, my <u>own</u> son died; I woke up from agony, and God told me while I'm in this terrible agony, I should immediately pray for the parents that lost their kids. I prayed fervently like they were my own. I slept, and immediately God again gave me an image of myself being caught in the tornado; I went through desperate fears of death. He woke me up again and told me to pray for those who experienced this. I prayed fervently as I was under a vivid image of the disaster.

My chest still feels the ray of fire God thrust in me a few days ago.

SOULS UNDER SATAN'S POWER

August 5, 1987

Jesus?

♥ *Egho imei[1].* ♥

Thank you for this grace; although I know it's meant for feeding others too, it's with me.

For timeless hours, you and I will be together. ♥ *Vassula, Have I not said that the wise will not understand what comes from the Spirit? Philosophy cannot be compared to spirituality, never;* ♥ *that is one of the main reasons why all those in power and who call themselves wise, will mock you, will scorn you, will reject you, will scrutinize you. So be prepared, beloved, for the wolves to hound you. Do not fear; I will be near you.* ♥

I sighed.

All, Vassula, is but a passing shadow; do not get discouraged; I will be near you.

Then I remembered how I feel unfit to be out in "exile" and how I dislike it; what I thought was amusing in my past life is a pain now, and I can't like these things anymore. I can't stand them... I'm a misfit.

♥ *I know; lean on Me.*

I felt desperate.

Vassula, Vassula, no, you cannot enjoy these earthly solicitudes as before, for this is My will. I do not want you to bear those things. ♥ ♥

Jesus?

♥ *I am; look into My Hands; look,* ♥ *Vassula, they are bleeding.* ♥ *Vassula, revive My Church; hear Me; have you seen all this blood streaking down My arms?*

---

[1]Greek: I Am.

I suffer.
Lord, why do You give so much pain and show me all this?
The vision was so vivid, I thought His blood will drop on this book.

♥ ♥ *To let you understand how I suffer, beloved, seeing so many souls under Satan's power.* ♥ *Let Me use you till the end.* ♥
I love You.
♥ *Be with Me, "us". I will always remind you* ♥ ♥ *"we¹".* ♥ *Love Me.* ♥ ♥

CONTEMPLATION

August 7, 1987

Jesus?
I am. ♥

Jesus was again giving me images of His scourging: His right side of His face, swollen. Again I felt in pieces.

Vassula, I love you all so much!
Quickly, quickly.

Here I meant: hurry up and complete Your will, so that You don't suffer more. I couldn't bear Him suffering.

With My power, I will rise even the dead. Vassula, I want to clarify My message of last week. Do you know that I withdraw just a little bit of My Light? Do you feel this?
I do.
Good. ♥ *By withdrawing My Light, but just very little, I nourish your intellect in the sense that I make you seek Me more, raising you to contemplation, and enlivening it, flourishing it, and thus becoming fruitful.*
How did You nourish me before bringing me into this?
I had given you recourses which lie out of your intellect. ♥ *Now, I wish to have you penetrate into a higher degree of meditation. Vassula, you have to progress; I am only enriching your food with this slight change; I want this to be clear to you. I have told you that I will detach you in every sense, have I not?*

---

¹In saying "we", He indicated it with His index finger as a Teacher talking.

Yes, You did, Lord.
By being now detached; I will enliven your faculties.
The insight You talked about?
Yes, your insight, giving you the spiritual grace will help others.
How others, Lord?
You will be able to understand My children, and thus you will be able to help them. Do not relate this slight withdrawal of my Light as abandonment; no, Vassula, I am only advancing your soul into holiness.
Lord, I was fearing to become a boat without oars and be drifted backwards, losing all that I was taught by You! I panicked.
Vassula, I have to purify you; learn that by purifying a soul, the soul will go through terrible fears and anguishes, but I am telling you this: that languishing for Me, inclines you to be raised into this blessing. ♥
Which is?
Which is contemplation. ♥ ♥ I want your love to reach perfection, giving yourself entirely to Me. ♥
Jesus, my soul longs for You.
♥ Little one, do I not long for you too? ♥ We, us. ♥ Come, let us go.

"We, us" means He is reminding me to talk to him, using these two words. Now I understand Jesus is teaching me two things at the same time: contemplation and to have insight.

On July 26, it was as if God was preparing me for this change; for already the following day, I felt as if His Light was withdrawn slightly. I panicked. Immediately my soul started to search for the reason: as I'm guilty and full of sin, I searched which were those sins that might have angered Him so much as to withdraw slightly His Light. Had I offended Him? Or could it be Satan doing this to me? I thought that if it's either, I, because of exactly this, should all the more cling tighter on my Saviour, pray more than usual, meditate more, use at full all other graces given to me, feel His Presence, talk to Him more than ever, never forget His Presence, work like I never worked so hard. If it's Satan, he'll flee, fuming. So I'll let him fume, and he'll leave me alone. On the other hand, if it come's from God, a test, I would like to pass it like a good student; I want Him smiling.

Several days passed: no change. My strength was giving in; I was beginning to panic now. I tried to serve Him with more fervour and devotion, but I could not understand yet why all this was not helping, at least that's what I believed. Then my Saviour and Teacher explained to me what was happening. When I thought He had abandoned me, He was but purifying me, lifting me into a higher level of meditation, developing my intellect, and infusing it with a subtle ♥ light, nourishing me with insight.
It's obvious, even when I explain my own feelings, God is dictating them to me. The word "subtle" was loudly said to me as I was hesitating of how to describe this light. I looked it up in the dictionary to find out what it meant; I didn't know....

AUGUST

August 10 1987

Last night I was wakened up by the Lord, and He asked me to surrender all over again.

My words were: "Thank You, Father, for having looked upon me, who am but the personification of the sins of this world. Thank You for Your Mercy when I denied You; thank You for the Love You have for me. In spite of my guilt, You have lifted me into Your Heart. Allow me to be near You, near Your feet; already by allowing me this, it more than I deserve. Allowing me to talk to You, is more than I merit; I merit nothing Father, I surrender completely; I know I'm nothing, but this nothing belongs to You. You want to throw me in a corner? Do it. You want to trample me? Do it. You want me to suffer only? Do it. You want me in Your Heart? Then it is more then I ever deserved. Whatever You wish, Lord, I will but thank You and love You. Use me if You wish, to my last strength to help others. Make me worthy so that You are able to use me completely. I am Yours and Yours only, wretched, but I love you."

Jesus?

♥ *I Am; Vassula, August is when I started to teach you. Vassula, it is a sort of anniversary between us. Rejoice!* ♥ *Beloved, it is our feast; let me place a wreath of Love on you. Come, celebrate with Me,* ♥ *I will let you go now,[1] but come to Me to celebrate My August.* ♥

After telling me this, I ran and searched in my old copy books for the dates of August. I jumped with happiness to read that it was Dan (the guardian angel) who said to me: "I, Dan, bless you in the name of God, our Father, His Beloved Son Jesus Christ, and the Holy Spirit. Blessed are the pure of heart for they shall see God." Then Dan brought me to God, and from there on, Yahweh started to teach me. Dan ended by saying: "Glory be to God; I have done all that God wanted me to do."
I ran quickly and told my cousin. I was flying with happiness! I was celebrating with God! She was happy too, but warned me that others who don't understand might believe I'm in love with God, loving Him wrongly. What she said, saddened me a lot and scared me. (Could she be right?)

---

[1] I had to rush for an appointment.

Jesus?
♥ *Daughter.*
I'm scared for this.

*I know; Vassula, have My Mother; I would like you to understand how wrong your
thoughts are. ♥ I have taught you to love Me, your God, as I want everyone to
love Me. ♥ I am celebrating the end of a year. Beloved, will you be my daughter
of Peace and Love? I have seen many lives taken by hatred. I filled My Kingdom
With Eternal Peace; would I not see My creation toil for Peace? Little one, I have
approached you in spite of your wretchedness, denials, and failures. I am a God
of Love; ♥ I look upon My children with loving eyes. Let everyone learn to
recognize Me until I come to deliver them; let every soul approach Me without fear;
let them know that I will receive them with open arms, for I am a loving Father.
Let them know how I can turn the stones into devoted followers of Mine, let them
know how I liberate their soul and give them real freedom. ♥ Vassula, I will not
abandon you, but because of your fear, have My Mother teach you how wrong you
are. I will be always near you. ♥ Us, We? ♥*
Yes, Lord.

I understood: St. Mary is for some time going to teach me and prove to me that my
fears are wrong.
Between the tenth and the fourteenth, I felt St. Mary close to me, talking to me, and
I started to realize that my emotional feelings were as strong as Jesus'; they were the
same.

WHOEVER SEEKS ME WILL FIND ME

August 14, 1987

My God?
♥ *I am. Have My Words of today: "Whoever seeks Me will find Me." Beloved,
always love Me with fervour and glorify Me. ♥ Narrate Me, saying to Oerjän:
"Believe...believe...believe. Come, beloved, I have indeed called you, brother! How
I love you! I, your Saviour, offer you My Love. I am Peace; come, come to Me
and penetrate deep into My Wounds; feel My Heart; feel Me...live in My Wounds,
brother." ♥
Flower, beloved, remain.*

I was getting ready to leave.

Here is My Mother.

Saint Mary:

Ah, Vassula, let Me tell you what will come. ♥ You will glorify My Son. Daughter, eat from Him. ♥
Oh, Saint Mary, You have always encouraged me! Since the beginning, You were my support.

I felt a great love for Her. She is so very motherly!

Wear My medallion always, for I blessed it on you. ♥ Have our peace. ♥

I then fell prostrate in veneration to her. (The medallion of Saint Mary was offered to me by Father James.)

CAIN AND ABEL

August 16, 1987

♥ My God, I love You!
Vassula, you are becoming to My eyes. Listen and write. Today's Abel shall live; just depend on your God; Abel will live! Abel will live this time. ♥ Beloved, the world in its weakness is filled with Cains. ♥ Would I bear forever to watch My Abels condemned and killed by Cains? How many more should perish before My eyes? No, Vassula, I have wounds that are re-opened; this generation is a breed of Cains. Beloved, every time an Abel arose, a Cain repeated his crime without the slightest hesitation; you see, little one?

God seemed sad talking to me about this, and I became sad too.

What is the reason for this?
It is because the Abels are My seed; they come from Me.
And the Cains?
The Cains? They belong to the world; ♥ they come from men. ♥ This time I will step between Cain and My Abel; I will extirpate everything coming from Cain. I will cast away from Cain's hand his weapon, leaving him naked; he shall have to face Abel unarmed. ♥ Vassula, I will clarify to you all this. Face Me, and when you do, watch My Lips, and you will understand. ♥ Would you still work for me?

Yes, My God, if You allow me.

Jesus?

I am Jesus Christ, beloved Son ♥ *of God and Saviour.* ⊂⧓ ΙΧθΥΣ

We, us?

Yes Lord.

I'm happy, He's smiling!

Come then; we will work together. ♥

ABEL IS MY SEED

August 20, 1987

My God?

♥ *I Am.*

I think I understand Your previous message.

♥ *You have understood only part of it, child.* ♥

A part of what I understood is also Cain's technology coming from men, non-spiritual items.

♥ *Yes, Cain represents all the things belonging to the world. Write: Cain represents all what My eyes dislike; he represents in this era, iniquity, materialism, revolutions, hatred, paganism, oppressors upon those I blessed, immorality. Cain never understood Abel whom I fashioned to my likeness. Abel comes from Me; he is My seed.*

Meaning that he is spiritual and loves You?

Precisely, and because of this difference, he was disliked by Cain. ♥ *I have said that the wise will not understand what comes from Spirit.* ♥

Lord, I'm worried about something; I don't wish to write it.

♥ *I know; all I want to do is stir up his wisdom.* ♥ *Which is more important to you, to leave him under heavy millstones or have you worried? Even to have you suffer, what would you choose?*

Without hesitation I'd choose to suffer for him.

I stirred you up from your sleep; would I not do the same to others?

Yes, My God.

Well then, let Me free to act through you. ♥ *Hallowed by My hand; My Spirit is upon you. Betrothed, beloved of my Soul, I have given you freely, so freely give too. Come, annihilate in Me and be one with Me! I love you, My Vassula.* ♥

Jesus (I find no words, because whatever I say, it's not enough). I will do all You wish.

♥ *Come then, I will restore My creation.* ♥ *Us? We?*

Yes! ♥

FLOWER SYMBOLIZES FRAILTY

August 23, 1987

Yesterday, something <u>very</u> special happened! It was one of those busy days. It was washing day, so I had the machine working and the dryer, drying. My husband, as it was a beautiful, hot day, took our son to the pool. He left at 11 A.M. and said they'd be back at three, so I should have lunch ready at 3 P.M. So I was left alone at home, working. It was ten to two, when I thought I'd better start lunch. So I lit the plate of the stove to melt butter, and suddenly, all the lights went off. The main fuse blew out. All machines stopped. I checked in all parts of the house if any electricity worked. None worked. I looked to find a fuse to change, but my husband had changed their place. The shops were closed, for it was Sunday; our car was out of order, and so I felt <u>frustrated</u>...I went out of frustration and lay in bed. After five minutes, I heard some noise in the kitchen. I got up to see what was this noise, and to my great surprise, I saw the lights of the oven lit and the plate warming the butter. But the machines were not working, and the rest of the house was without electricity still. I couldn't understand; if the main fuse and everything else was out, how could the oven work?! I prepared the food and placed it in the oven to roast. At 3 P.M. my husband returned, and I told him what happened. So he checked all the electricity, which was still out except for the stove, which was working. He checked the main fuse and he saw that it had blown out. By then, the food was ready. While checking the main fuse, we saw that the meter was rolling. The minute I said, "the food is ready," the meter stopped rolling, although the oven was still lit. I went in and switched off the stove. My husband changed the fuse with a new one, and again all electricity worked normally. He too could not explain this.

August is our feast! We do not want our celebration spoiled. ♥
Do You mean that...

Jesus did not let me finish.

I mean that I will not see you grieve during our feast. ♥ *Vassula, you are My flower; do you know what a flower stands for? Flower symbolizes frailty; that is why I take good care of you lest your frailty harms you.* ♥
Thank You, My God, I know You are very near to Me, and I love You.

I'm feeling embarrassed, for I deserve nothing. Yesterday in the evening, while in my son's room, I was covered with incense. The odour was just at one particular spot. I felt happy.

My God?

♥ *I Am. I love you; do not doubt! Alone you are not; I, Jesus, am with you Flower, I have always loved you to distraction. Propound your fragrance like you were taught to; embellish My garden; delight Me. Come, you see, Vassula, you start to understand Me.* ♥ *Now I have justly withdrawn you from everybody beloved.* ♥ *You were not quite aware of what I was doing to you.* ♥ *Have you not felt My Arm over your shoulders, pulling you away from everyone while whispering in your ear My Heart's desires? Now that you have lifted your head, you suddenly realize that you have no one around you but Me.* ♥

How I love you! I feel so happy! *Adapt yourself to be alone with just Me; yes, just us two, Me and you, you and Me. Ah Vassula! Face Me now; face Me your God. Vassula* ♥ *from now on, it will I and I alone.* ♥ *I am your God; I am your Holy Companion; I am your Saviour; I am your Bridegroom; I will provide you with all you need, beloved. You need help? I will rush to you. Courage? And I will give you My Strength.* ♥ *Consolation? Fall in My Arms;* ♥ *abide in My Heart. Praise Me, Vassula! Praise Me, daughter! Come and glorify Me! Glorify Me; fall prostrate in front of My Feet; worship Me! Be Mine. Ah Vassula, love Me as I love you! Bless Me like I bless you; cover Me with your fragrance, like I cover you with Mine. I stand before you, I, your Saviour! Worship Me;* ♥ *feel My Heart this time and this hour;* ♥ *night is soon to come; will you not replenish your lamp from Me? Never wait till the day is over;* ♥ ♥ *let Me fill up your lamp;* ♥ *come and draw from Me;* ♥ *let Me be alone with you; live for Me; I delight in our solitude!*

♥ *I love you to jealousy! My Love is such that I withdrew you from everyone. Would you try and understand Me? I longed to be alone with you; Love is inflamed; and when Love is ablaze, I allow Myself to do what pleases Me.* ♥ *Now you are Mine, and I desire you to imbue Me with wreaths of Love. Infatuate me with your childish words; leave Me free to Love you as I please now. Have you not yourself given Me the liberty of using you as I wish?*

Yes, Lord, I have.

I will then use that liberty; My finger will just touch your heart, and when it does, you will reserve nothing from Me. ♥ *It is our August, after all. I will always remind you that we are celebrating.* ♥ ♥ ♥

DIFFUSE MY MESSAGE

August 24, 1987

♥ *Vassula, repent!*

I repented.
I forgive your sins. ♥ *Now I want you to praise Me!*
I hesitated, finding the right words.

Vassula, say Glory be to God Almighty. ♥ *Do you know who I am?*
You are the Alpha and Omega, Creator of all.
♥ *You said well, My child. Now I tell you this: Blessed are those who will read My Message and believe I wrote it, without having seen Me writing it. Blessed are those who hear My Message and follow it. Blessed are those that unite and propound Peace and Love; diffuse My Message; diffuse My Peace and let it reign in all Hearts. Never doubt of My Love.* ♥
How do you want me to diffuse; how could I do anything? I am helpless.
Wait, Vassula, and you shall see; I will help you. ♥ ♥ *Come.* ♥ *Us, we?* ♥
Yes, My God, us, we.

BELIEVE IN MY HEAVENLY WORKS

25 August 1987

♥ *Remember, My child, the love I have for you.* ♥ *Vassula, little one, I have blessed the red cross you are wearing around your neck.* ♥ *Believe! Believe in my heavenly Works, Vassula.*
My God! Thank You; the more You give me, the more I feel I deserve less and less.
I love you; ♥ *come, keep close to Me. I like to hear you say the things I told you about My Presence, and about other things too,* ♥ *teaching Ismini. Live for Me; glorify Me.* ♥
Sometimes, Lord, I feel less Your Presence, thinking, "now God is not so near me."
Why is this Lord?
♥ *Erroneously you believe I am not near enough, whereas these moments, I am as close to you as one can be.* ♥ *Alone you are not,* ♥ *NEVER!*
Suddenly I discerned Him so clearly. (He proved to me with certain gestures of His,

His so alive Presence!) It went on for a few minutes. It was wonderful!

♥ *All is spiritual.* ♥

By this I understood, all is supernatural, impossible to comprehend if you place these actions in the physical state. It is not physical, thus not possible to explain physically. These are placed in the supernatural sphere and not in our "realism" sphere.

Many of you tend to forget that I am Spirit and that you too are spirit. ♥

ALLOW ME TO GUIDE YOU BLINDLY

August 26, 1987

Vassula, are you still willing to be My bearer?
Yes, Lord, if You still want me in all my incapacity and failures.
♥ *Child, I will help you accomplish your task; then I will deliver you.* ♥ ♥
Wisdom will instruct you; are you willing to forgo your leisure and sacrifice more for Me?
Yes, I'm willing.
Have My Arm; I will support you. Vassula, your era has lost all spiritual values; nevertheless, I will be always near you to help you. ♥ *I am Jesus Christ, Beloved Son of God;* ♥ *I am preparing you;* ♥ *allow Me to guide you, blindly; believe in Me, blindly, till the end.*[1]

YOU HAVE BEEN TAUGHT BY ME

August 28, 1987

Vassula, come, have My Works translated in French; ♥ *I will help you;* ♥ *let My Bread be given freely.* ♥
I will, Lord, I know You'll help me.
Vassula, I have showered upon you discernments and learnings; you have been

---

[1]Meaning: have no proof of this, and just believe. Believing blindly glorifies Him.

taught by Me; I have given you My Bread from My storages; I have given you fruit from My garden; ♥ *I have poured into you My Works to enlighten this world, revealing My Face. Come, do not forget why I chose you; content yourself with what I give you, daughter, I have given you abundantly from the tree of Life to feed others too. Lean on Me; depend on Me.* ♥ *Would you give Me all you have?*
All that I have is Yours; I want to keep nothing for me alone.
♥ *Everything you have is indeed Mine, but I have given you liberty to choose.* ♥
To choose what, Lord?
♥ *To choose between evil and good;* ♥ *I have given everyone this freedom of choice.*
Then, if this is the only thing I have, I choose to stay with You.
Let Me bind you closer to Me then; let Me guide you where I am seeked most. ♥
♥
I love you, Father; may Your will be done.
Love Me, child; hear Me; not until I complete My Works, will I unchain you to come to Me. ♥ *I will allow Myself to use you, writing down My desires.* ♥ *Love loves you;* ♥ *draw My sign:* ⋖⋗ ΙΧθΥΣ

Jesus Christ, Beloved Son of God and Saviour. ♥

August 30, 1987

Evening:

Jesus?
♥ *I am.* ♥ *Will you let Me rest in you?*
Yes, Lord.
♥ *My flower, seek Me; desire Me fervently, bless Me.*
I bless You, Lord.
♥ *Have my blessings too.* ♥ *Alone you are not!*

I felt Him as though I could touch Him.

ALONE YOU ARE NOT

August 31, 1987

Vassula, in the stillness of the night I shall come; ♥ *the hour is near.* ♥ *Alone you are not. The world seems to forget My Presence. I am God, but how many think of Me? Very few.* ♥

I saw a night filled with stars; still, and beyond those stars, God's Eyes upon us.

Stay awake, for in this stillness of the night, I shall descend. I have laid My plans before I created you, little one. ♥ *I will lift you to Me and show you something.* ♥ *Rest, beloved, now.* ♥

REPENT CREATION BEFORE I COME!

September 1, 1987

Fidelity is what I love. ♥ *Vassula, I will give you a vision lifting you to Me;* ♥ *I will show you how heaven will appear.* ♥

The sky was shown to me; it looked as any night with its stars. Then it changed. It resembled spots of paint, like a painter's palette, but one color was dominating, surpassing all others in command. It was red, thick, and it grew in its thickness, like yeast pouring from above us.

Vassula, I will open the Heavens, letting you see what eye has never seen. ♥ *You have well discerned; keep awake.* ♥ *I will watch over you. Hear Me; write: I have since the beginning of times loved My creation, but I created My creation to love Me too and recognize Me as their God.* ♥ *I have since the beginning of times sanctified all that My Hands created.* ♥ *I am a God of Love; I am the Spirit of Sublime Love.*

♥ *Creature, since the beginning of times, I have shown My Love to mankind, but I have also shown My Justice too.* ♥ *Each time My creation rebelled against Me and My Law, I hardened at Heart. My Heart grieved by their iniquities.* ♥ *I came to remind them that I am the Spirit of Love and that they too are spirit.* ♥ *I came to remind them that they are but a passing shadow on earth, made out of dust, and that My first drops of rain upon them will wash them away, leaving nothing behind.* ♥ *I have breathed into them My Breath, giving them life.* ♥ *The world has incessantly been offending Me, and I, from My part, have incessantly been reminding them of My existence and of how I love them. My Chalice of Justice is full, creation!* ♥ *My Justice lies heavily upon you! Unite and return to Me; honour Me, creation! When you will, then I too will lift My Justice.*

♥ *My cries resound and shake the entire Heavens, leaving all My angels trembling for what has to come. I am a God of Justice, and My eyes have grown weary watching hypocrisy, atheism, immorality. My creation has become, in its decadence, a replica of what Sodom was.* ♥ *I will thunder you with My Justice as I have thundered the Sodomites. Repent, creation, before I come.* ♥ *I have indeed forewarned you many a time, but you have not followed My instructions.* ♥ *I have raised up saints to warn you, but, daughter, they have closed their hearts.* ♥ *My creation would rather live in lust and ignore Me. I have given them signs to awaken them.*

My God, Your children are only sleeping; please, come and wake them up; they are only sleeping.
♥ *They are sleeping hour after hour, year after year.*
But Lord, who is to blame if they have not been taught; they are almost innocent if they know nothing about You.
I have raised servants and teachers on earth to teach them.
But Lord, Your teachers and servants do work, but what can they do more when multitudes are <u>negative</u>; they are helpless.
Helpless? They should repent; they should come to me and repent. ♥ *I have, through times, given them signs, but they have rejected them as not from Me. I have given them warnings through weak and wretched souls, but they doubted My Word.* ♥ *They have rejected all My blessings, grieving Me. O men with hearts out of rock! Men of little faith! Had they more heart, and had they had <u>now</u> even more heart, I would have helped them.* ♥ *I stirred them up from their sleep, but how many times have they closed their eyes, falling back into sleep?* ♥
But why don't they make it known to the world when You give Your signs?
Some do, but the majority of My sacerdotal souls have closed their hearts, doubting, fearing; many of them fear. Vassula, do you remember the Pharisees?
Yes, Lord.
Let Me tell you that many of them are replicas of the Pharisees, doubting, fearing, blinded by vanity and with hypocrisy. Do you remember how many times I have given them signs? I have given them signs hundreds of times, and what have they done? Times have not changed; many of My sacerdotal souls are just the same replicas of the Pharisees! I have given them signs, but they want signs which could be explained by proofs; ♥ *they want proofs.* ♥
Will You give them of Your past signs <u>a proof</u>, and of this revelation <u>any proof</u>?
♥ *All that I will give them is you yourself, child.* ♥

But, Lord, it's not convincing; I am not convincing; I'm nothing to convince! They'll laugh outright in my face.

♥ *I have blessed you.* ♥

But, Lord, I know that it's You, and a few others too, but <u>many</u> will disagree, since there is no solid proof it's from You. I am nothing, and You know it.

♥ *Daughter, let Me be everything; remain nothing, and let Me be everything.* ♥ *The least you are, the more I am. I have now laid My Justice on mankind; upon them is what they have reaped.* ♥

Isn't there a solution, I mean that somehow everything becomes like You want, and so Your Justice can be lifted?

♥ *Vassula, when I will be received and not denied by My sacerdotal souls now I will lift My Justice.* ♥ *I have warned them, but they keep My warnings hidden.* ♥

Please tell me the reason why they do this.

They seem to forget My Omnipotency and My Wealth; they tend to amass everything into one thing,[1] they will believe only if <u>they see</u>, ♥ *grieving Me, counting not My blessings.* ♥ *Creature! Creature! Revive My Church. Vassula, honour Me;* ♥ *the hour is near, beloved, the hour is at hand. <u>Love will come again as Love</u>.* ♥ *Vassula, set My wisdom revelations in order; I will help you; all will be in time; I am preparing you.*

♥ Thank You, Lord, I bless You. ♥

These last three days, I felt in my soul an inexplicable agony between the first and the fourth of September.

GARABANDAL

September 4, 1987

In my private pad, Jesus gave me a message which startled me. I got up, leaving alone that message. Later on, I went to write; Jesus repeated that message. I started to fear; my thoughts, as once before, raced to confusion, asking myself and God, "Why me?" Why has really all this writing started; why do I feel like this, bonded with God? How was I a year and a half before, and how am I now? I'm living in the Truth, and I feel responsible for all that's happening. I feel I should please God. Then again, doubts, doubts which made me test Jesus. I came to Him, doubting. He knew it. He asked, "Well?" and said to try again (try to control my hand); I had in mind to write my own thing, controlling my hand <u>myself</u>. I was struggling to write

---

[1] Solid proof.

but couldn't; then He wrote, "Write", and He forced my hand down, writing four times, "Love", while I was struggling to stop my hand.

I am Love. ♥ I will remind you that on your shoulders I have placed My Cross of Peace and Love. ♥ ♥ Up! Up! Lift! Lift! Daughter, do you realize why I have brought you up? I have brought you up to unite My Church. Altar, have I not said that from the babe's mouth you will hear the truth and not from the wise? I have said that the wise will listen and listen and not understand, see and see again, but not perceive; for their hearts have grown coarse; they have closed their ears and shut their eyes. ♥

Vassula, I have raised you from the dead, instructing you with Wisdom. Fear not and advance. ♥ ♥

Jesus gave me a vision of myself, facing Him. I felt uncertain. He held my hands, and while He was walking backward, He was pulling me to walk, advancing.

O daughter, how I love you! Flower, everything you feel comes from Me; advance. ♥ ♥

I felt as if I was doing my first steps and <u>thrilled</u>!

Vassula, by being timid, you infatuate Me. ♥ ♥ Daughter, write down the word: "GARABANDAL". ♥ Vassula, when I stirred you from your sleep, It was not just to wake you up; it was also to be able to use you, beloved. Purifying you was not just to cleanse you, it was so that you feel My Presence and <u>be in My Presence</u>. Using you was not just to use you, writing my Messages and desires; it was so that I write down My blessings for My little children of Garabandal. ♥ ♥ I come to have My Message glorified. Altar, keep this flame ablaze; by My Power, I will restore My Church. ♥ Love Me; do not falter; lean on Me and rest; I will help you advance. ♥ The hour is near; pray with Me. ♥

> *Father, deliver me in Your Arms,*
> *Let me rest near You,*
> *Sanctify me, Father,*
> *When You receive me,*
> *Forgive my sins as I forgave others, ♥*
> *Glory be to God, my Father.*
> *I bless You. ♥ Amen. ♥*

September 5, 1987

Vassula, do not fear; write the word "Garabandal". ♥ *Garabandal is the sequel of other signs;* ♥ *Garabandal's apparitions are authentic. Believe all you who have not seen; believe, believe.* ♥ *Daughter, I have used you to be able to manifest Myself through you;* ♥ *My Mother had appeared to My chosen souls; out of their mouths, the Truth was said, but many of My sacerdotal souls declared them as uncertain, and some of them denied them altogether.* ♥ *I have manifested Myself through you to lift this doubt of Garabandal.* ♥ *Garabandal's apparitions are authentic, and My children have indeed seen My Mother and heard Her Messages.*

♥ *Vassula, a harder trial will come upon you, making My Cross heavier on your shoulders and augmenting My Cup of Justice. I have forewarned the world.* ♥ My God, very few probably know of this happening.

True, many do not know, because of the doubts and fears My sacerdotal souls bear. ♥ *By doubting, they deny My Heavenly Works; they have forgotten that I am Omnipotent. Hardened at heart, they have lost their spirituality; blinded, they seek without Light and without Wisdom.* ♥ *All My Works have always been given to mere children and never to the learned.* ♥ *My Works appear unorthodox in their eyes, but it is because they compare themselves to Me.* ♥ *I have, since the beginning of times, never abandoned you.* ♥

He made me understand that the signs given are to remind us of His Presence among us, <u>encouraging</u> us.

Vassula, do you remember the Pharisees?
Yes, Lord.
They at one time accused Me of preaching against Moses' Law. ♥ *What difference is there today? I had been accused of promiscuity and going against their Law; Garabandal's accusations and uncertainty is not far from this. Let Me tell you, those who defy Garabandal's apparitions, and Messages, are those who wound Me; they are the thorns of My Body. I have told you some time ago[1] that I will lead you with Heavenly Force right into the very depths of My Bleeding Body; I said that I will point out to you with My Finger, those who wound Me.* ♥ *I am Jesus Christ, Beloved Son of God.* ♥ *Vassula, fear not, for I am before you.* ♥ ♥ ♥

---

[1]On June 11, God told me the same message. He said He would not spare them (Book 13). At that time, I did not know to whom He was referring.

September 6, 1987

Jesus?
♥ I am. ♥ Will I ever abandon you? Flower, surround Me with wreaths of love. Assemble My children around Me; let Me bless them; I, who was waiting for them, ♥ I waited for this hour; I come to welcome them and bless them. ♥ Assemble My beloved ones, My own, My lambs; hug them for Me; caress them for Me; remind them of My Promise; ♥ love them; unite them. ♥ Come nearer to Me; let Me instruct you with Wisdom.

TO BELIEVE IS ALSO A GRACE

September 7, 1987

Peace be with you. ♥
With You too, Lord.
Absorb Me, flower; let My Light shine upon you, and let your worries fall into diminishment; My Breath will blow them away, and their structure will but fall, swaying them away, leaving you smiling; My dew of righteousness will embellish you. Flower, have My Message of today; fear not, for I have laid My plans long before you were born. ♥
Does that mean that whatever happens to me, to Your Messages, and everybody, it is by Your Will?
♥ Yes, beloved, everything that will come, will come from Me. ♥
I'm worried of failing You, Lord.
How will you fail My plans? ♥ Think, you are nothing, so how can a nothing be something, and that something, if at all, fail My plans? But you are nothing; so do not worry; ♥ leave everything in My Hands. ♥ Vassula, I am your Teacher; fear not when you are with Me.
I want to say something, please.
Feel free.
Do You know that there are times I think I'm absolutely mad, insane!
♥ I know.
Then just imagine those to whom I will one day show this! They'll be shocked; they will say that they can find a natural explanation; they will simply not believe.
♥ To believe is also a grace; ♥ to have faith is also a grace; to see, hear, and understand My Heavenly Works is also a grace, all given by me. ♥
Yes, Lord.

Vassula, I have worked with you; honour Me, daughter.
With Your help, I will not fail You.
♥ *Listen then to these words that come from My Mother:*

♥ **Vassula, pethi mou[1], do not fear; I am with you. My Son Jesus expressly limited you with the proofs and signs you were asking Him to give you, ♥ but he has His reasons. ♥ He has, though, given you the grace to believe; He has instructed you with Wisdom. Vassula, you have indeed believed blindly.**
Have I?
♥ **You have; otherwise you would not have had this fervour in coming to Us and writing, letting yourself be used at His Will. Having done this, beloved, proves that you believe blindly, and God delights in this; your faith is great. ♥ Jesus wants, by this, to teach others too to have faith and believe blindly in His Heavenly Works. Be innocent; be like children in whom God delights.**
What if they don't, Saint Mary?

Saint Mary's voice suddenly changed tone and became very grave.

Your sufferings will be great; you will be like a mirror reflecting Jesus' image; ♥ His sufferings will reflect.
You mean, Jesus will suffer if they show disbelief and contempt?
Precisely; Jesus will suffer; ♥ upon you will show His sufferings. ♥
But since He has laid His plan before, why couldn't He have made them so that there won't be any contradictions?
Child, this is the way men tend to think; do not forget His teachings; Jesus wants that His works are acknowledged with grace. ♥
Jesus told me that He would not stand by if He sees someone wanting to hurt me.
He has indeed said it, ♥ and I tell you this, daughter, I will not stand by either! I love you, and I will not see them hurt you. ♥

Here I felt very emotional.

I am a coward; I fear, but I will cling on You and Jesus.
Daughter, I will tell you still something more. ♥ God has laid His Justice upon men; His cup is now full. ♥ Listen to me carefully; beyond these words lie many more; Glorify God. Vassula, I am your Holy Mother; daughter, rely on Me; weary not of striving; remember, Jesus was abandoned by everyone on the way to be crucified; He bore His Cross alone. ♥
Yes, Mother, I will not ask anything more than what He gives me.
Vassula, let Me answer your question withheld in you. ♥ If they do not believe again, God's wrath will grow, augmenting His Cup of Justice; it will be the

---

[1]Greek: "My child".

vision God has given you.[1] ♥ **Pray and amend, for the end of times is near.** ♥
Yes, Mother, may God bless you.

♥ *It is I, Jesus. Little one, remain small; let us talk to each other; let us share this day; allow Me to be your Holy Companion.* ♥
Lord, allow me to talk to You. I will remember your Presence.
♥ *Come, us, we.* ♥

I AM STANDING AT THE DOOR KNOCKING

September 7, 1987

Peace be with you, daughter. ♥ *Remember those words; I will tell you once again; remember them particularly more now: "I, the Lord, am standing at the door, knocking.* ♥ *If one of you hears Me calling and opens the door, I will enter to share his meal side by side with him.* ♥ *Those who prove victorious, I will allow to share My Throne, just as I was victorious Myself and took My place with the Father on His Throne.* ♥ *If anyone has ears to hear, let him listen to what the Spirit is saying to the Churches."* ♥ *Daughter, tell them, tell them; remind them of My Words; for they have forgotten them.* ♥
Jesus, help me.
♥ *I will always help you, Vassula.* ♥

I sighed.

Thank You, Lord.

September 8, 1987

♥ *Vassula, delight Me and receive Me; I want you to follow Me.* ♥ *I will take you to meet Me at My Tabernacle;* ♥ *receive Me, and I will bless you.*
Jesus again calls me to receive Holy Communion.
♥ *I love you.* ♥
I love You, Lord. I'll come.

---

[1]September 1, 1987.

WISDOM IS FOUND IN THE HOLY BIBLE

September 9, 1987

Vassula, I want those words I will give you to be known. I wish that those words be diffused all over: ♥ *"I, the Lord, bless My children of Garabandal."* ♥
Vassula, bless them; unite them.
All with Your help, I will, Lord....
Then, all hell broke loose. Satan raged. His demons as well; they have names even. I know those who are attacking me.

Vassula, come; I will make you understand how they hate you. Do not fear.
Jesus dragged me underground. There we stood. I recognized hell, as my feet were in slimy and sticky, black mud, a grotto cave. Jesus told me to listen.
Satan said: "Aha, it's her again, Ⓢ another hag! Bo, beware now; wound her; cripple her forever; wound her so that we win; ill-treat her. She feels the hate I have upon her and the rest of his creation. Sabi, go too and wound her. I hate you all!"
Satan was again like a mad man. Jesus pulled me back out.

♥ *Now that you have heard his hatred, you must realize with what determination he is after you to have you stop writing. I, Jesus, love you; and under My wings, I am guarding you, never leaving you an instant from My sight.* ♥

Later on:

Vassula, do not read these books; they have neither Wisdom nor Truth. ♥ *Wisdom is found in the Holy Bible.* ♥ *I am glad you heard Me.* ♥

I had not done much, as I was mostly meditating the whole day. When I realized time was gone, I went to prepare our meal. As soon as I started to work, Jesus, who was watching me, interrupted my work, saying: "Vassula, have you got a moment for Me?" I said: "Yes, I have millions of moments, not only one, for You." I left my work and went to write. He told me to stop reading a book I was reading, advising me it's no good. It was talking about things I never had heard of, and about legends, religions; and all written by non-theologians.

Later on in the evening:

All these parts of My Face were harmed.

I was looking at the Holy Shroud photo.

All that I see, Lord?
Yes, all; they tore off part of My Beard; they harmed My right Eye. ♥
Jesus, I don't know what to say.
♥ *Tell me:* ♥ *"I love you!"*
I LOVE YOU!
Vassula, do not get discouraged, ♥ *NEVER; I am with you;* ♥ *together we are bearing My Cross.* ♥

TREMENDOUS AMENDMENTS ARE REQUIRED NOW

September 10, 1987

I love you; until I come and deliver you, believe in Me blindly, Vassula. ♥
Jesus, I know there are times You must be very displeased with me: those times when I fell into doubt. At these times, I am the result of a multiplication: if You multiply Thomas by ten times, the result is me!
Flower, you are frail, and it is out of your frailty ♥ *that I am attracted; do I not know all this, beloved? I am your Strength.* ♥

Jesus whispered something in my ear; I'll keep it secret.

Vassula, Garabandal is the Sequel of Miracles. In between these Miracles, I have been giving other signs. ♥
Can You write down which miracles?

Write: Lourdes, then Fatima; I want you to write now Garabandal in San Sebastian. Glorify me! Remember, I am the Light of this world. ♥

Suddenly Jesus reminded me of a dream I had last night and had forgotten. It was the vision I saw lately, but it appeared worse in my dream.

Listen, I have let you see the vision in your sleep to make you feel it. No, there is no escape!

I remember when I saw it coming like a giant wave, I tried to run and hide, knowing it's impossible.

But why do this if You love us? Why?
I am known as a God of Love as well as a God of Justice. ♥

What can we do to stop this?

Tremendous amendments are required now from all of you: ♥ *uniting and being one, loving one another, believing in Me, believing in my Heavenly Works, for I am among you always.* ♥ ♥

MEN'S WEAKNESS: INFIDELITY

September 11, 1987

♥ *Vassula, let Me tell you, Wisdom has not just instructed you to find Peace; Wisdom has not just covered you with myrrh, fragrancing you with Her Sublime Love; Wisdom has not lead you through winding ways bringing you fear and testing you to abandon you now.* ♥ *No, Vassula, I have led you to be where I wished you to be.* ♥ *What I have commenced and blessed, I will finish. Come, rest on My shoulder.* ♥

September 11, 1987

Little one, seldom do I find fidelity in men. ♥ *I want to warn you against men's weakness, which is infidelity.* ♥ *I love you, and I will support you, knowing how frail you are.* ♥ ♥ *Allow Me, flower, to kiss you.* ♥ ♥

I leaned towards God, and He kissed my forehead: I, His child.

♥ ♥ ♥ *I love you; I hallowed you;* ♥ *I freed you.* ♥ *Come, I and you, you and Me, we, us; honour Me, loving Me ardently.* ♥
I love You, Holy Father. May I kiss Your Hands?
♥ *Always do, daughter.* ♥ ♥ ♥

I kissed His Wrists.

FIDELITY

September 12, 1987

Fidelity always finds a way to be with Me. Love Me and be faithful, child. Unseen are My Works from the wise eyes; ♥ I have them hidden from them. My hidden Wisdom I give to humble and to mere children. ♥
Daughter, I am Spirit, and I have approached you, teaching you as Spirit to spirit. ♥ My Teachings were given to you spiritually and not in the way philosophy is taught. ♥ Vassula, be aware of what has to come, for an unspiritual person will not accept these works as from the Spirit of God; he will defy them because they are beyond his understanding, as this can only be understood by means of the Spirit. ♥ I, the Lord, know what the wise think, and I tell you truly, they do not convince Me. ♥

That same evening my soul, for an unknown reason, suffered. I longed for God. I repented. I asked Him if He wanted to hear me and if He had a few moments to listen to my repentance. I was facing God with a load of sins again.

BE MY ALTAR

September 13, 1987

Jesus, on the eighth, called me to Holy Communion. I went today and received Him.

Father in Heaven, do not let men be the cause of my destruction. Do not let them take away what You already have given me. My fear is their insensitivity and when they close their hearts upon Your Heavenly Works and when they shut their ears. I am very weak and vulnerable. With one word, they will be able to break me as easily as one breaks a reed.
♥ O Vassula, Vassula, take My Hand. If they persecute you, they will be persecuting Me; if they mock you, they will be mocking Me. Love is suffering. ♥ ♥
Help me, Father, from these people.
Love will help you. ♥ Adorn Me with purity, be My altar, ♥ bear with Me My Cross. ♥ Altar, grieve not. ♥
I bless You, Father; ♥ I long for You.

Later on:

This Sunday, September 13, was the second time from the beginning of this revelation that my soul felt in complete anguish, a sadness of an inexplicable reason, a bitterness that I thought I would not survive. Physically it hurt too; my chest was heavy, and the pain ran down my arms. Jesus called me:

♥ *Vassula, synchronize with Me and feel My pain.* ♥ *They are recrucifying Me.*
Why, why do they do this to You?
♥ *Beloved, they know not what they are doing.*
Who's doing this?
Many souls. I love them, and yet they despise Me. ♥ *Vassula, share My pain; be one with Me.*
We, us, Lord?
♥ ♥ *Yes, daughter, together we are suffering because of the infidelity of men. Hold My Hand. Together.*
Together, Lord.

THE LANCE'S BLADE

September 15, 1987

Jesus, I can't stand to have them wound You constantly. Hurry and let those thorns out!
O daughter, I will point them out to you, one after the other. ♥ *I will tell you where they are placed, and with My Strength you will pluck them out one by one; and instead of those thorns that wounded Me, I will let you offer Me only flowers from My garden of delights; for they have been growing under My Light, exhaling on earth their sweet fragrance, embellishing My garden.* ♥ ♥ *Within My Heart and in Its most intimate depths, I still have the lance's blade.* ♥ *Vassula, this too will be removed.* ♥ ♥ *With My power, I will pull it out;* ♥ *I will not spare them this time! I unite My lambs and tell them that, "I, the Lord, bless them."* ♥

September 17, 1987

Vassula, I am sending you to him[1] ♥ *so that he hears of My Message.* ♥ *Will you ask him to receive you? Will you ask him to guide you to seek for my children of Garabandal?*

---

[1]The Greek Orthodox priest, Alexanthros.

In an instant I suddenly saw in a vision given by the Lord, the demons who roam earth, overthrown! It was as if the dry soil they were standing upon, shook and cracked, and lifted itself upward, like a fist, overthrowing them. They helplessly fell backward, powerless.

♥ *I come to unite My children and bless them.* ♥

September 18, 1987

This Friday I met the Greek parish priest inside the Greek Orthodox church. I told him everything. He listened, accepting all that I said. He wants to study now the revelation.

ABANDON YOURSELF

September 20, 1987

Daughter, by now you must have understood how I work. Believe, My Vassula, for in you I will breathe many more revelations. Abandon yourself entirely to Me, and let My finger imprint on you My Word. Come, little one, and caress Me. ♥ ♥

Yes, Lord.

By this, Jesus means to caress Him on His big portrait I have of the Holy Shroud. It is in my habit, while I meditate and talk to Him, to often stretch my hand on His portrait, caressing His Wounds, as if I want to wipe away the streaks of blood, soothing Him. This I do without thinking, because of my meditation, which absorbs me entirely.

I WANT THIS WILDERNESS IRRIGATED

September 20, 1987

Vassula, ♥ *Garabandal's apparitions of Myself and My Mother should be authenticated.* ♥ *Hear Me, Vassula; every time My Mother appeared to My chosen souls, illuminating them with Her Grace, I stood beside Her, but no eye could see Me.* ♥ *I sometimes appeared as an infant to bless those that glorified Me.* ♥ ♥

Daughter, I wish that these places of apparitions be honoured more. ♥ *I wish that the Holy See would honour Me by blessing those Sacred places.* ♥ *Vassula, I do not mean Lourdes and Fatima, I mean Garabandal as well.* ♥ *I come to glorify Garabandal's apparitions.* ♥ *I wish to see My Holy See there and bless that place, rectifying all that has been distorted and wrongly proclaimed by My sacerdotal souls who wound Me; lift the doubts and efface the abuses given by those who defied the apparitions; would My Holy See do this for Me?*

Lord, My God, how will they know all this?

Leave, Vassula, this work for Me; I will find a way of letting them know. ♥ ♥ *Daughter, I wish that each time I give them a sign of My Presence, no matter how small, I wish that My Holy See glorify My sign by blessing it.* ♥ *I want the world to know of My Presence, of My Riches, of My Mercy and of My Heavenly Works. I wish that My Holy See propound My given signs in larger scale, feeding the world. I want My land fertile; do not let them pluck the few flowers left;* ♥ *I want this wilderness irrigated; who will water My garden? Why do they neglect My flowers?*
Beloved Jesus, if I'm not mistaken, it took them seven years to confirm your miracle of Fatima. My God, I can see refusals, rebukes, difficulties of accepting.
♥ *Flower, do not grieve; let Me help you;* ♥ *Vassula, I always reach My goals.* ♥

I WILL GUIDE MANY BACK TO ME

September 21, 1987

My God, how much I want everyone to love You and turn to You, recognizing You.
O daughter, how much I want this too!

God seemed longing for this to happen.

How I wish that the world would realize that You are among us <u>ever so present</u>. How <u>much</u> You love us; how I wish that they realize we are only passing by on earth and that you are waiting for us. How I wish that they love one another, <u>stop their hatred and egoism</u>, live for one another, care for one another, worship You our Father, <u>unite</u>. How I wish they would believe in Your signs and not hide them away, thinking they are doing You a favour. How I wish they realized how wrong they are and <u>see</u> your Riches!
♥ *Vassula, your desires are given by Me to you; they are infiltrating in you. I will keep My Flame ablaze in you, altar, forever.* ♥ *Diffuse My words, "I, the Lord, bless My children of Garabandal."* ♥
Lord, I diffuse in the capacity I have; I need channels to diffuse it broader.
Vassula, I have given you witnesses.

You mean my friends and David?

♥ *Others too.* ♥

You mean from the Church, the priests?

♥ *Yes, Vassula, they are your witnesses.* ♥

Yes, Lord.

♥ *Let Me engrave My words on you.* ♥

Jesus, I just remembered, there is a man who doesn't believe <u>at all</u> the guidance is from You. It's the first one.

I know.

But why?

For the simple reason that he is wise. ♥

Oh, My God, I have so many desires!

Just ask Me. ♥

Just ask?

Yes, beloved, ask. ♥

Anything?

Anything. ♥

I desire a change, My God, for the better. I desire that their hearts get inflamed with love for You, and that <u>billions</u> worship You, adoring You, all on their knees. I wish them to feel, like I feel, how much You love us, and how near You are to us, and how close we can be with You, a Father, a Friend, a God, everything in one. Couldn't You shine Your Light on them and wake them up as You did with me? I want them to share the same happiness and closeness I have with You. Please, Father, they are also Your children.

♥ *Vassula, all will be done; I will guide many back to Me; despite their wickedness, I will help them; weary not of striving with your God.*

We, us?

Yes, Lord.

BE AWARE OF MY PRESENCE

September 22, 1987

♥ *A little awareness pleases Me! Daughter, I am pleased.* ♥

Jesus told me this because I concentrated on His actual Presence, trying to see how He looked. His hair today was all back.

♥ *When I see you trying to be aware of My Presence, it glorifies Me.* ♥ *Let us pray. Daughter, start in this way:* ♥

> *"O Beloved Creator, Holy Spirit,*
> *I bless You for the Works You have showered upon me,*
> *I bless You for the Light You shed upon me,*
> *Glory be to God Almighty. Amen."* ♥

Jesus knew I had difficulties in finding the right words of praise for Him; this prayer is just for me.

BE INNOCENT!

September 23, 1987

♥ *Betrothed, do not listen to those who are in deep sleep, for they know nothing, feel nothing, see nothing, hear nothing; how could they, since they are sleeping and thus totally unaware!*

Jesus made me understand the two worlds: one which is material, physical; then the other one, invisible, spiritual.

Vassula, listen to My Mother:

I am Saint Mary; I am your Mother too. Sanctify Garabandal, Vassula; bless My beloved children of Garabandal; I have not forgotten them. Will you do this for Me?
Yes, I will, Saint Mary.
I will help you; stay near Us; be aware of our Presence, like now.
With Your grace, I will do what You ask me.

Come, it is I, Jesus Christ, Beloved Son of God. I can, if I want, give you more proofs; but I am limiting you for the reasons I have. Guiding you blindly pleases Me; it glorifies Me. ♥ *Then, I want that this become a lesson for those whose wisdom blinds them. I want you innocent, simple.* ♥ *Guiding you in this special way was so that My religious souls understand that I, the Lord, give abundantly.* ♥ *Daughter, tell them that it is not difficult to believe in My Supernatural Works; why, am I not God and Spirit? Be like children and believe.* ♥ *Who of the children would doubt that it is I, writing, guiding in this way, if you showed them My Works? Be innocent!*

ECCLESIA WILL REVIVE!

September 24, 1987

I felt Saint Mary near me.

♥ **Vassula, yes, it is I, your Mother. I have appeared to My children of Garabandal; I let them see Me and hear Me. ♥ I have appeared to them, and they know it; ♥ I want you to bless them. ♥ ♥**
Saint Mary, help me accomplish Your wishes.
I will guide you, Vassula.
Thank You.

I felt amazed. Later on, I smelled incense odour around me.

It is I, Jesus; I blessed you and fragranced you with My incense. ♥ Ecclesia[1] will revive! ♥ We are one. ♥ When I will unite My Church, I will not wait further; can you feel how My Soul longs for you? I will fetch you, beloved. I love you. ♥

I was pleased hearing this; I feel I do not belong here anymore, and earth is indeed an exile.

Beloved, having you in this exile makes Me suffer too, but all will not be in vain. I love My creation, and you are to bring My creation back to Me. I suffer, seeing you down on earth; live for Me, daughter; you must remember how I sacrificed Myself; ♥ would you do the same for Me, your Father?
Make me worthy of You and for any sacrifice, Lord.
♥ Beloved, I, the Lord, bless you. Come, all will not be in vain. ♥

September 25, 1987

This morning, I smelled incense again. I knew that at that particular spot He was standing.

♥ My remnant, all I ask of you is love; ♥ love me; ♥ diffuse My words which are: "I, the Lord, bless My children of Garabandal; I love them." ♥ Beloved, assemble them; unite them; accept all that has to come, whether it may be joy or suffering; I am before you.
Yes, Lord, may Your Will be done and your wishes realized.
♥ Come, feel Me; let us share everything. ♥

---

[1]In Latin: Church.

DELIVER A SOUL

September 26, 1987

Vassula, let us deliver a soul very dear to Me who is very near Satan's flame. She does not realize his insidious game he has laid for her. ♥
Who is this soul, Lord?
She is one of My brides.
A nun?
♥ *Yes, a nun; she has neglected Me, taken by her vanity. Beloved, bring her back to Me with your love; I love her.* ♥ *Love Me, and she will be delivered. Vassula, these Works are mysterious to you and to many, but believe Me, I am Jesus and Wisdom. Now you will bless Me.* ♥ *Feel Me; it glorifies Me.* ♥ *All will be done according to My plan.* ♥
Jesus! It's so wonderful to be with You in this way!
Vassula.
It's wonderful, marvellous!
♥ *Vassula, will I ever abandon you?*

When He says this, I almost die each time. Only God can have this tone.

Love Me; repair for others whose hearts became icy-cold towards Me. Altar, live for Me; replenish your flame from Mine. Altar! never forget how much I love you; ♥ *stay ablaze, enkindle hearts, quench My thirst.*
Beloved Jesus, keep me near You, for without You I'm lost.
♥ *Near Me you will stay; have you forgotten our links? You are bonded to Me with eternal bonds.*
Thank You, Lord, for taking care of me, the zero of zeros, the one who denied You.
♥ *I have been denied even by Peter, but on him I laid My first foundations of My Church; have you forgotten? I am the Lord who loves you ineffably, and upon you, soul, I have engraved My Words.* ♥ ♥ *I am your Strength.* ♥ *Keep Me in your heart now and forever.* ♥ ♥
I shall, Lord. I'll keep faithful.
♥ *Come, let us share this day; be my companion.* ♥

IO SONO CON TE

September 27, 1987

I had made up my mind to go to the Charisma Center here in Lausanne last night. It was again as though all hell broke loose. The devil raged, tormented my soul to the point that I found myself asking the Lord to go on without me, that I would always love him, but I simply have no strength left to continue. Immediately I regretted my words, asking then the Lord to leave me for my unworthiness. During my rest, I saw myself on a rough road, fallen. Near me, I saw Jesus' bare feet; He bent and lifted me again. Then, in front of me, I saw a large staircase of around one hundred steps, and at the top, the Saints were standing, calling me to climb up there. I turned around and saw a familiar figure: a priest. He had humour and was talking to me in Italian. I recognized Padre Pio! Near him I saw Saint Francis of Assisi. Saint Francis approached me; all were encouraging me to continue.

Jesus?
I am; Vassula, do not fear.
Jesus, forgive me for being weak.
Your weakness will be annihilated in My Strength. ♥
Io sono con te, Padre Pio.[1] ♥
My God, is this happening?
♥ *Yes, he is with Me, Vassula, and beatified by Me.* ♥ *I am with you, My Mother, and all the Saints.* ♥ ♥

Later on, I went to the charismatic service; I couldn't follow it by mere ignorance. Also, I craved for silence. I felt guilty, very guilty, with ignorance.

♥ *Vassula, do not worry; every man has got his own way of glorifying Me and praising Me.* ♥ *I have given you this way.[2] I and you, you and I; you are to worship Me in Silence. Remember, I have already instructed you a few months back.* (cf. 31.6.87) *At your side I stand.* ♥

I felt Him so near, I could touch Him solidly. My soul was happy again and in peace.

Little one, am I not your Spouse? Well then, will I not console you when you need to be consoled? Come to Me, and I will lift your burdens; come to Me, and I <u>will</u> console you! Confide in Me, daughter; I am your Spiritual Director; I am your

---

[1] Meaning in Italian: I am with you, Padre Pio.
[2] In writing.

Spouse; I am He who loves you most; I am your Creator and God; ♥ *come and fall in My Arms and feel My warmth.* ♥ ♥

Jesus left my soul in total harmony and peace.

LANGUISH FOR ME

September 28, 1987

Jesus was calling me. I was as eager to meet Him as He was. I don't know, but it seemed ages since we were together.

O come, beloved! How impatiently I have waited for this moment to meet you in this way! Together, Vassula, together, you and I will sanctify Garabandal. ♥ *For Holy it is, since My Mother and I appeared.* ♥ ♥
May Your will be done, Lord.
♥ ♥ *Vassula, timidness is not a sin.* ♥ *I am telling you this.* ♥

I was wondering if to be timid is a sin. I was happy to hear this. Suddenly, my soul longed for Him.

Look at Me; little one, to languish for Me, glorifies Me. Languish for Me. ♥ *I paid for you with the price of My Blood.* ♥ *Vassula, why look around for a Spiritual Director?*
I don't know.
With Me you will learn, for I am Wisdom and Truth. Come to Me, and I will instruct you. ♥ *Vassula, I love you. Tell him[1] this: that I am going to restore My Church; I will revive My Church; I have selected you to work with Me. Vassula, meet him; talk to him; caress Me by saying how I taught you to caress Me, glorifying Me.*

On the Holy Shroud picture.

Love Me, Vassula, for love wards off divine Justice when it's about to strike sinners. ♥

---

[1]The charismatic Pastor.

THEY HAVE DISOWNED ME

September 28, 1987

Vassula, are you happy that I have liberated you? ♥
Yes, My God, I'm very happy to be with You. I feel attached to You and happy.
Do you believe Me now that I have bonds of Love on you?
I do now, Lord.
Little one, bless Me. ♥
I bless You, Jesus; I love You and thank You.
♥ *Vassula, do you know that signs I have been giving and will continue to give to make My Name be known to you, so that the Love I have for you all may be in you,* ♥ *and so that I may be in you.* ♥ *But many of My sacerdotal souls have disowned Me in the presence of men.* ♥
How, Lord?
By disowning My signs, they have disowned Me, their God. Have I not said that the man who disowns Me in the presence of men, will be disowned in the presence of My angels? Have I not said that I will continue to make My Name known to you? Why then do they doubt that I am among you and that it is by My Mercy I give you signs and miracles which are barely honoured; for let Me tell you, daughter, they have taken the key of knowledge! Neither have they gone in themselves, nor have they let others in who wanted to!
My God! You seem so angry, Lord!
♥ *Vassula, the time has come to Glorify Me. Be alert and stay near Me. I love you, little one; be one with Me.* ♥
Yes, Lord.
Us, we?
Yes, us.
♥ ♥ *Come.* ♥

I WILL NOT SPARE THE CAINS

September 29, 1987

My God, You seem to be unhappy with some of your sacerdotal souls.
♥ *Vassula, they are responsible for so many souls;* ♥ *not only do they fall, but with them, they drag so many other souls.*
But, Lord, there must be many who are good, loving You, working as You want them to. I know some.

♥ *Ah Vassula, there are many following My instructions, immolating, living humbly, loving one another, feeding My lambs. They are the salt of the earth, the beloved of My Soul; they are My Abels;* ♥ *they are the balm for My Wounds, assuaging* ♥ *My pain. To My sorrow, among them are the Cains too, the arrows of My Body, treacherous, blinded with vanity, wicked, and with despicable inclinations. They are the thorns of My Head; numerous are their sins; hypocrisy is their master, and it is to those My divine Justice flares up.*

♥ *Take My Hand, daughter; keep close to Me, and I will point out to you those thorns; I will lead you with divine force into the very depths of my Body; I will let you recognize the lance's blade. I* ♥ *will not spare the Cains, Vassula; for what have they to offer Me? Their hands are empty and have nothing to offer My lambs. They love to show themselves in public; they love to be greeted obsequiously; they are like salt having lost its taste. I tell you truly, daughter, they are today's Pharisees!*
Oh God, this is terrible.

♥ *Vassula, for this reason, everything that has been hidden, will come to light, and everything covered will be uncovered, for this is My will.* ♥ *Come now, do not forget My Presence.*
No, Lord, I look upon You as My Holy Father, Holy Friend, Holy Brother, and I look upon Saint Mary as My Holy Mother; You are my Holy Family; how can I forget You?
♥ *Beloved, I am your Spouse too; this is the way I wish you to love. Love Us intimately, nevertheless, never forgetting that we are Holy, honouring Us. We are your Holy Family, I am your God;* ♥ *be alert.* ♥
Yes, Lord
Let us go. ♥
Let us.

I AM THIRSTY VASSULA!

October 1, 1987

I had been occupied all morning with a visitor here who was trying to sell me cosmetic products. It was all unnecessary as it was all a waste of time. But she was sent by a friend of mine.

♥ *Little one, I love you to distraction; I am your well-Beloved. Why, Vassula? Do not withdraw from Me! You are guessing correctly.* ♥

I could feel Jesus' Heart inflamed again overflowing with love.

My love is again inflamed, and when It is, I allow Myself to demand love. I desire you to live for Me only. I want you to fix your eyes on Me. Look at Me, love Me, fragrance Me, adorn Me, bless Me, desire Me, breathe for Me, smile only for Me; tell Me how much you love Me your God. Seek to bring others to Me; satisfy My insatiable thirst. I am thirsty, Vassula! I thirst for love, I thirst for souls. Vassula, why bring Me rivals; do not bring any more rivals; do not! Eulogize Me; I have given you abundantly; will you not gratify Me for all I am giving you? I have walked with you in My garden of delights; we shared its beauty. I have shared My joys and sufferings with you; I have laid My Cross on you; we are sharing It together, sharing Its anguishes, sorrows, and pain; we share Its Love. Have I not lifted you to My Breast, feeding you, healing you? I have taken you as My bride, sharing My Cross as our matrimonial bed. ♥ Will you look at Me?

I looked at Jesus' face.

Could I ever abandon you, flower? ♥ I am He who loves you most. ♥ Remain near Me, hear.

It was as if He had a sudden idea and stopped, pointing at our ankles, which I saw tied to each other.

Listen, I will tighten our bonds even more now; I want you closer; I want you one with Me. ♥ Who was first to hold you?
How, Lord?
I was first to consecrate you and lay eyes on you. Vassula, I have created you for Myself. ♥ Let Me remind you who you are; you are nothing else but dust and ashes, and it is out of My immense pity I lifted you to life from among the dead. ♥ Remember always this. ♥

The pastor came, and I showed him the revelation. To start with, he did not believe. Then he denied Saint Mary as our Holy Mother, and he'd never heard of apparitions! He did not believe in any Spiritual Works. He is against holy pictures. He probably thought I was not normal, or evil.

♥ Vassula, I am Wealthy, but very few know of My Riches! When I was in flesh, have I not been despised; have I not been looked upon with contempt; have I not been called a blasphemer? Have I not been rejected as the stone rejected by the builders that became the keystone? Honour Me by accepting contempt, mortification; humble yourself, be like Me, remember? Have I not said that you are to serve Me among wretchedness? Have I not said that you will have no rest? Accept what I offer you, fear not of mortifying yourself. I will leave two drops of Blood from My Bleeding Heart on your heart, covering it entirely. Hallowed by My

Hand, live under My Light, learn to be rebuffed. ♥
Saying this to me, Jesus seemed to be very sad. My pain was nothing compared to His. I wanted to console His pain, forgetting my pain.

I felt Saint Mary near me.

Saint Mary?

I am. Light a candle for Me, Vassula, and repair his fault; ask Jesus to forgive him. ♥ Would you do this for Me?
I will, Saint Mary.
Amend, beloved, do not doubt of Jesus' Works. ♥ Honour Us.
I will, Saint Mary.

MY HOLY SHROUD IS AUTHENTIC

October 2, 1987

It is I, Jesus. Let it be known that any image of Mine or of My Mother is to be honoured, for it represents Us, as My Cross is representing Me. Let it be known that My Holy Shroud is indeed authentic; It is the same that covered Me. Blessed by Me, Vassula, enter in My Heart; let Me Hide you in there. ♥ Rest, come, come to your Father.

I felt like God was enveloping me; I was enwrapped by Him and happy. I went out to photocopy this, and while I was in the department store, I found myself trying to console Saint Mary. The more I was thinking of the incident, the more unhappy I was becoming. I was trying to keep my tears back. I put on my sunglasses, in case I would burst into tears. How is it possible? I never knew that Christians did not venerate our Mother. The pastor seemed inflexible in his beliefs, and he was talking of uniting. How is it possible when he shows me such stiffness, inflexibility. My God, and You want unity! Unless You bend them with Your own Hands, I feel there is no way. I will amend for this pastor as Saint Mary asked me.
I saw the old man who is the keeper of the car parking, and again I had tears of pity. I felt so sorry for him; why should he be underground at his age, smelling and breathing only car fumes? Oh God, why have You made me so sensitive...I can't bear so many sights any longer.

I walked out, remembering I had forgotten to eat lunch. At any rate, I couldn't swallow anything. I went and had coffee so that I wouldn't feel faint. I can't remember drinking it without thinking of Saint Mary and Jesus hurt so much. It tasted bitter. God is warning us many times now, if we do not change, there will be the punishment I saw in the vision. Today's Sodom will fall again.

TURIN AND THE HOLY SHROUD

October 5, 1987

Later on, my cousin Ismini rang me up, telling me they will go visit Turin in Italy, and asking if we'd like to go with them. Finally, I thought; it was my dream always to go there and visit the Cathedral that has the Holy Shroud. Jesus has arranged it again for me. I would go. My cousins drove us to the hotel where they usually go. Turin is an enormous town, but our hotel was five hundred meters from what I went for! Jesus made it easy for me. We arrived at lunch-time on Saturday, and after a while, I went to the Cathedral. I was very impressed. Upstairs was the Holy Shroud in the dome of the Cathedral. I thought I saw the Holiest of places. Peace and Holiness reigned in that dome. I felt it in me; it was wonderful.

Later on, I left for the hotel. It was evening when my cousin returned from shopping. I rushed to her to tell her where I had been, but she seemed to be flying towards me; she didn't want to hear me; she wanted me to hear her, for what she saw and discovered was so wonderful. She said: "Vassula, that road we passed by ten times and one for so many years, I never saw Saint Mary's statue there. But it's enormous! Almost three meters high. It's so beautiful: Her dress with so many pleats, and her blue cape. She looked so beautiful, and She has Her arms opened like She'd like to embrace the world. You must come and see Her. You passed by Her; haven't you seen Her? At each side of Her were satin curtains, red-scarlet, shiny and beautiful." I said I passed it but only saw the curtains which were worn-out, half red and half yellow. She told me that she too for many years didn't notice it. I had seen no statue.

The following day, Sunday, she wanted me to go see the enormous statue, so I said, after I take you to the Cathedral where the Holy Shroud is. So she followed me. It was Sunday Mass. We stayed a half hour, then after lighting a candle, we left for Saint Mary's big statue. We arrived there, and my cousin almost fainted, for there was no big statue, or even small. There were no shiny, red-scarlet curtains. There were the ordinary worn-out, yellow and red ones I had seen, but no statue. She did not understand it. But I did. Below the curtains was an interior door. She pushed it, and it was a church. I said to her: "This is why we came to Turin, to go to this church, called Madonna di Rosario, to repair: the Church of Saint Mary. The huge, beautiful statue you saw was to pull and bring us here. Our Mother called us. She gave you the apparition of Herself as a statue: big, so that it impresses you, to pull us here. And she wants Her candle lit in Her church to amend for the pastor's words." We entered, and it was such a beautiful church. Mass was on. We stayed till it was over. We went forward to a golden statue of Saint Mary and Jesus as a Child, and it was there we lit her candle, praying for Jesus to forgive us and him.

Jesus, is this correct?

♥ *Vassula, yes, it is exactly as you recounted it.* ♥ *I will lift you to Me as soon as you accomplish your mission.* ♥ *My Soul longs for you,* ♥ *Vassula.*
Hear My Mother:

Vassula, tell Ismini how much I love her. Child, I gave her this image of Myself to attract her attention and lead you into My Church. ♥ **Beloved ones, how I love you; honour Us, beloved; honour Us, amend for your brethren;** ♥ **remember how close We are to you all. Vassula, never get discouraged, for I am beside you;** ♥ **lean on Jesus always.** ♥ **Daughter, think of Jesus' Passion; live for Him; glorify Him.** ♥
Only with Your help and the help of Jesus am I able to do all this. I want to honour You.
♥ **I love you all! I Bless Ismini;** ♥ **I have blessed her and her husband in My Church.** ♥
I bless You, Saint Mary.
I bless you too. ♥ ♥

BE MY VICTIM OF LOVE

October 5, 1987

Forgive me, Lord, for My total unworthiness, and failures, and lack of every good, making me offend You by this in Your Presence.
I forgive you fully. ♥
I love You, dear Lord.
Every time you tell Me, "I love You," I overlook all your wretchedness, letting it pass by, and stop My divine Justice from striking you, Vassula, for indeed you are wretched beyond words. ♥ *You soothe My anger by telling Me you love Me.* ♥
Jesus seemed severe; I feared Him.

I fear You.

♥ *I am Love, so do not fear Me.*

Oh Jesus, I wish I wouldn't be so wicked and ungrateful and spiteful.

I pity you, and it is out of pity I seldom flare up against you. **♥**

I know I don't deserve a drop of grace on me; You have been too good to me, patient. You never got angry with me; You only loved me with my mistakes. You spoiled me.

Vassula, for such is My Mercy!

Jesus?

I Am.

My God.

I Am

I ask You to teach me to love You more, and as You wish, so that You can spare me, and so that I may honour You.

Little one, I am your divine Teacher who will teach you. **♥** *Never doubt; never doubt of My Forgiveness.* **♥**

No, Lord, I will not doubt. Make me worthy of You because of your Grace, and approach to me. Allow me to glorify You. Forbid me to sin and from constantly offending You with my sins, Beloved.

Bless Me. **♥**

Jesus, I bless You. Father, I love You.

At My Stations I desire to see you.

Oh Jesus, how? I want to, but how, with who, who will guide me? I have no Father James here.

From desperation my eyes were filled.

♥ *Reserve your tears for the time you will hear offenses being said on account of My Mother.* **♥**

Oh Jesus, help me.

Daughter, lean on Me; let Me instruct you; please Me by being pliant as you are. Come, be near Me; I love you. **♥**

I love You, Jesus; have mercy on my ignorance.

I have; delight Me and say: "Lord, let Me be your victim, the victim of your burning Love. I desire to worship You and You only, stretched on Your Cross with You, never looking left or right. **♥** *I desire to quench Your thirst by earning souls for You.* **♥** *Victim of Your Love I will be; I love You.* **♥** *" Say it!*

I said it.

From now on, you will never leave My Heart, Vassula. **♥** *Select, Vassula, either your life, or a victim's life;* **♥** *select.* **♥**

Jesus, I don't want You to leave me. I want to be with You, at Your side.
Then you have chosen well; you will resemble Me; be a victim of Love. ♥ *Flower,*
you will flourish under My Light.
I thank You; bless You for all that You give me and for the compassion You have
upon me.
Have My Peace, daughter; never forget My Presence; allow Me to rest in you, for
this is My home. ♥
Jesus, you make me happy, and I learn from You.
Flower, I am your Master and God. Come. Us, we?
Yes, Lord.

BE MY TABLET

October 6, 1987

I felt poor. And I am. I am not pleasing God because of my ignorance and slowness
to understand. I'm not happy with myself. He was so right about me as being "by
far" the most wretched of His creatures. I hate now talking about how this has
started, because I find talking about myself is ugly, very ugly. But friends and people
want to hear how it started. I was obliged to explain, and the more I went on, the
more I could not avoid despising every time I said something about myself, to the
point that it made me decide that from now on I shall not explain how it started; thus
I will avoid finding myself talking about myself. I thought they could find out from
others; if they are curious, it will be appeased not by me. If they want to read
because they believe, God will enlighten them. I shall not be my own witness. I shall
leave everything in God's Hands. He makes the impossible, possible, so I shall be
from now on just His pencil and paper, His secretary, a secretary taught by Him to
love Him; and taking down His words, I shall be His tablet.

Yes, be My tablet, letting Me engrave on you My Word. ♥ *Be soft, though, so that*
My Word can be deeply engraved on you. ♥

I forgot myself and was sitting on the floor. He looked at me, reminding me. I knelt.

I love you, Vassula; together, you and Me, we are sharing My Cross. ♥ *Hear Me,*
Vassula; you are the beloved of My Soul; have you not yet understood? Feel, feel
how I, your God, love you, My child, My well-beloved bride. ♥

I felt Jesus enveloping me in Him.

Listen Vassula, all the Heavens resound with My cries; My desire is unshaken; it must have reached your ears. I desire flexibility; how will you unite if you are inflexible? I wish to unite My Church; will you feel Me and listen to My Voice?
My God, why don't You let the head of the Church know about Your message?
Listen, Vassula, I have revealed My Face already to My beloved brothers.
Whom are You referring to, Lord?
David and Father James. ♥
Jesus, enlighten them to accomplish Your wishes; act in them and guide them.
♥ *I will, daughter; embellish My Church; love Me; ecclesia will revive!*

I saw a wonderful image of Jesus, Majestic, Glorified, a beautiful image of Jesus, triumphant as a King, showing me a sign with His Hand raised, and making a sign with His Fingers lifted. It was as though He was signalling me Victory.

MARY IS THE QUEEN OF HEAVEN

October 8, 1987

Jesus?
♥ *I Am.*

Jesus, I wish to repair for every offense said about our Blessed Mother. I cannot bear to hear offences said from Your creatures about Her, especially priests. I would see my head roll and defend Her.
♥ *Vassula, I will let you understand how Love suffers, hearing those offences.* ♥
Vassula, let it be known that I, the Lord, honour My Mother; let it be known to those who offend Her, that She is the Queen of Heaven, and that on Her Head, I, the Lord, placed a crown, a crown of twelve stars. ♥ *She reigns, beloved, and this is written in My Word.* ♥ *I honour My Mother, and as I honour Her, you should honour Her.* ♥ *I love you. Both My Mother and I bless you.* ♥
Lord, the pastor denied Her as <u>our</u> Holy Mother that we should venerate, and when I told him that You said it from the Cross, he said that You meant it only for John, and that nowhere in the Bible is it written that She is our Mother too and that we are Her children.

But again, I tell you, daughter, that My Mother <u>is</u> your Mother too; you are Her children; it <u>is</u> written in My Word, and I am telling it again for those who do not know, Scripture says...
Where, Lord?
...in the book of Revelation, that when Satan failed in his pursuit of My Mother,

he was enraged with Her and went away to make war on the rest of <u>Her children</u>,
that is, all who obey the Commandments and bear witness for Me. ♥
Thank You, Lord Jesus, for helping me.
Vassula, I have told you, before you I always am. ♥ *Stay small, so that I may*
accomplish My Works. I love you. ♥
I love You, Lord, and bless You.
Us, we? ♥
Yes, Lord.

VENERATE AND HONOUR MY MOTHER

October 10, 1987

Jesus?
♥ *I Am.*

Oh Jesus, I never knew that Christians do not believe, I mean venerate Saint Mary.
I never knew how they felt about Her. I never knew there was such tremendous
difference between Christians; I didn't know it is so bad.
Oh Vassula, it is worse than you think!
Oh Jesus, why is it so bad?
Because, Vassula, My Body has been torn apart; ♥ *I want My Body united!*
Would they then venerate our Blessed Mother if they are united?
Child, they will.
Do I understand that "they will" means "it <u>will</u> be"?
♥ *I will bend them; I will bend their knees, and they will venerate and honour My*
Mother. ♥
Yes, Jesus.

Little one, I will revive My Church.
Come, us, we?
Yes, Lord.

I AM OMNIPOTENT - I AM

October 12, 1987

While visiting somebody, I found a magazine of science which promotes the scientific resolutions of thought, discouraging any spiritual work. Nowadays, every supernatural thing has its "natural" explanation, words like: double personality, ESP, subconscious, suggestion of thought, hypnosis, mass-hypnosis, or auto-suggestion; e.g., the stigmata can be "explained" by auto-suggestion, thus self-imposed, schizophrenia, or sex-complexes. People seem to want to find always a logical explanation. There would have been no big prophets like Isaiah these days because their case would go into scientific files. There would soon be no saints with stigmata, without classifying them as schizophrenics, and self-induced by auto-suggestion and hysteria. For me, it appears that they are trying to compete with God and prove that they can prove to Him, He is not Omnipotent. Oh God, why?

♥ *Vassula, numerous are those that do not believe in Me.*
But I ask You one thing; I really mean it; I ask You to destroy all these theories and teachings that try to wipe You out. They are Your enemies. Why let it multiply? Destroy it; otherwise it will destroy our faith. Please do it.[1]
♥ *I will; hear Me; grieve not; never doubt; have faith; never weary of writing.* ♥
♥ *Beloved, this is why I come; it is because I cannot see you lost; do you now understand, Vassula? Little one, I will never see you fall.* ♥
What about the others? I don't want to see the others fall either; I desire You to support them as much as You support me.
Vassula, I will help all of you. ♥

God seemed pleased.

Oh God, forgive me for demanding things; I'm impulsive, but I can't bear injustice. Forgive me for being so direct.
♥ *I forgive you, child; say it.* ♥

I had other things in mind.

I must tell You that, as it is right now, these people will not be convinced to their dying last breath; at the most, they will file it under the word "unexplained", but would not say, "well then, this or that comes from God."
I will convince them. My power is beyond theirs; I will show to you all that I am Omnipotent. My Omnipotence will be seen wherever you may be; no eye will be

---

[1] I found myself telling God what to do; it was beyond my strength.

able to deny it; no man will deny that this sign comes from Me.[1]
Beloved, how will their theories appear then? How will their men of science feel?
What will happen to all their wisdom? I will show to them how their wisdom
appears in the face of My Wisdom. ♥ *I will efface from this world what they*
believe is wisdom. This is one of the reasons I use you, engraving My words on
you, to be able to foretell My Plan. I, the Lord, Am, I was, and will always be;
and it is not up to you to look at Me as not.
I Am. ♥ ♥ ♥

O beloved God whom I adore, I wish that this plan is for now, today, or next week.

I will fulfill My Plan, Vassula, as I have always fulfilled everything I started. ♥
Little one, let us pray: ♥

> *Beloved Father, I love You, I bless You,*
> *I thank You for Your Mercy.*
> *Make me worthy of You*
> *So that You are able to use me fully,*
> *Use me as You wish.*
> *I love You. Amen."* ♥

Beloved, I bless you. ♥ *Look at Me.*
I looked.

You are smiling.[2]
Write it.
And You are showing me Your dimples when You smile.
♥ *I love you.* ♥
I love You, Lord.

---

[1]Will this be a sign in heaven, one day?
[2]I hesitated to write the rest.

LOVE WILL RETURN TO YOU AS LOVE

October 13th, 1987

♥   I saw Jesus at the door of the bedroom. I knew He was indicating to me to write, like somehow He was waiting.

I was at the door. Come, you will work with Me.

(Sometimes Jesus wants to prove to me that my discernment was right.)

I will foretell you what has to come, so that from now on those that call themselves wise will believe in My Works and follow Me. ♥ Daughter, I will heal many. <u>Love will return to you as Love</u>, fulfilling My Word. In a short time I will prove to you that this comes from Me Vassula. I am The Lord. Beloved, to Me you will come. Hear Me: I want to remind you what I have asked you a few days ago; let it be known all over - diffuse My words: "I, the Lord, bless My children of Garabandal." ♥ I want them to hear Me. Oh Vassula, how I long for this day. ♥

Lord Jesus, I will try in my capacity, with the sources You have given me. I am impotent and You are Omnipotent. Would You help me Jesus?

I will help you. Remember how I work ♥ Vassula. Let it be known that in a short time I will send you all a sign coming from above. You will understand that it came from Me. I will Shine on you. I love you all, ♥ how I love you all; I love you beyond your understanding. ♥ I am your Creator; have I not said that your image I have it carved in the palm of My Hand? How can I ever abandon you?

I'm thinking of the vision You gave me. The punishment, that I feared.

I will make you see it again so that it bears a mark on you.

Again Lord, help us to avoid it. I know You don't like doing this to us and get no pleasure out of it. Tell me what to do?

Vassula, true, I get no pleasure in punishing you. I wish that My creation return to love. Tremendous reparations have to be done; amend, those that can, amend for others. My creation has to change. Daughter, My creation has to learn and believe in My Spiritual Works. My creation will have to accept Me as Omnipotent; My sacerdotal souls must understand how wrong they are, denying My Works of today. (But there are many who do accept.) *There are those who do not and it is to those I speak; I also speak of those who have split My Body. Believe Me daughter, My cup of Justice is full for having torn My Body apart. I will not spare them any longer. ♥ Vassula, allow Me to till you for just some more time; soon I will be collecting My crops. Come beloved. ♥*

Lord, may all Your Will be done.

KNOW WHAT IS BEST FOR YOUR SOUL

October 15th, 1987

♥ I will mortify you like I was mortified; I will humble you. Vassula, I love you and it is out of love I watch over you. Since I am directing you I know what is best for your soul. ♥ I will give you this penitence so that it washes away your tendencies of vanity. I the Lord will see that your soul lacks nothing; I will always watch over you. ♥

Thank you my God for helping me.

I am using you now but in a short time you will be delivered and in My arms you will be. ♥ Daughter, remember when I was in flesh among you, My life was nothing else but sufferings, sacrifices, anguishes, sorrows - the lot - I had no rest. ♥ Vassula, I have brought you up for this Message. My flower, you are to bear My Cross together with Me to the very end. I love you infinitely. ♥

I love You Lord and if You want me mortified I will do Your will.

Be pliant, so that I may do whatever I please with you. ♥ Little one speak of Me.

(Jesus means to the Rhodians. The Greeks are very eager to hear and easily open their ears).

MY CHURCH WILL BE ONE

October 16th, 1987

♥ *Vassula, I always reach My goals. Come, I will tell you.* ♥ *One day My Kingdom on earth will be as it is in Heaven; My Church will be united and blessed, for all My devoted ones will understand one another. Exalted by My Hand, purified by My Blood,* ♥ *My Church will be One.* ♥

May Your desires come true Lord, many of us desire this, enlighten those who need to be helped to understand Your desires.

YOU WILL BE THE SIGN OF MY WORKS

October 18th, 1987

♥ *Daughter, will you take My hand and continue My Works?*

Yes Lord, I never want to leave your hand.

♥ *Vassula, I want it to be clear to you what I have said previously. I said that I will foretell events that will take place so that there would be no doubt that this comes from Me.*

Jesus, have You not said that the only sign You will give is me?

♥ *Yes, I have said that you will be the sign of My Works. I have designed My plan long before you were born. Flower, stay open so that My dew of righteousness drips in you. Sip from Me My virtues; I want you perfect; I want My flower embellished, saturated with My Perfection; I want My flower to fragrance My divine Myrrh. Look at Me Vassula,* (I looked at Jesus), *all My wishes will be accomplished. Would you devote more of your time for Me Vassula?*

My time is Your time, I live for You.

♥ *Replenish then your lamp - take from Me.* ♥

Jesus what can I say, You give me so much when I deserve nothing, You keep giving me and I can't even offer You anything that's close enough to what You are giving me, You give me Light, You woke me from the dead, You healed me and poured on me Your works.

Glorify Me.   Who freed you Vassula?

You did, Lord. Can I say something?

Beloved, tell Me[1]. ♥

My God with Your Mercy Love and Power do unto my brethren as You have done unto me. Free them. Lift them to You unite them to You, let them feel Your love as I feel it, I want to rejoice seeing souls approach You. Then unite all Christians and those who deny our Blessed Mother. ♥

Vassula, are you willing to perform sacrifices?

Yes Lord, if I can be used that way.

I will show you what I desire from you. ♥ *Beloved, derive from Me always. I love you flower[2]. Remember, reserve your tears for later on when your ears will hear how My own treat My Mother!*

Do not let them any more.

Vassula, the day will come, and that day is very near when My Church will speak one language; but before this glorious day there will be tremendous upheavals, partly because of man's vanity, sin and lack of love, and partly because My Body is torn apart. Let Me tell you once more that My Body I will glorify and unite. Flower, love will unite you all. Write down this too; stay small so that all authority will come from Me[3]. ♥ *Let it be known that My wishes are inflexible, they stand firmer than ever.*

Which of Your wishes, Jesus?[4]

Vassula, I desire to diffuse those words to My children which are: "I, the Lord bless you, come to Me. ♥ "

---

[1]God sounded like a tolerant father.
[2]My eyes had filled.
[3]I think Jesus means it for everybody.
[4]I think Jesus went on without answering.

Lord, lead me to them, help me diffuse Your words.

Vassula lean on Me, live in My Light and rest. ♥

SACRIFICE

SWITZERLAND - October 19th, 1987

I want to add here, that while in Greece, I was reading St Therese of Lisieux; her biography. She was in my mind constantly, and while I was in the local bus and in deep contemplation on her, thinking of her with love, the bus stopped and there in my deepest contemplation I saw the Greek words "I love you" and two hearts, each letter a foot tall, they were written on a bus station roof; 4 meters away from me. My senses being in another plane I knew she was telling me this. It was her message.

♥ *Vassula, remove those pictures of Mine you filed.* ♥ ♥

(I went and took them away from where they were. Pictures of Jesus on the Holy Shroud. I thought He was upset that I had them filed.)

Come, give two to Father James and one to David; tell them that I blessed them with My Hand ♥ ♥ *- they will understand.* ♥ *Write to father James and tell him that I desire him to do the Stations of My Cross in the same manner as when you both had done them. Vassula, ask David as well.* ♥ *I will bless both of them on the Way;* ♥ *all I wish to introduce is the light. I wish them to honour My Mother as well by lighting a candle for Her, then they should honour Me by kneeling at every station.* ♥ *Vassula, now I your God and you will join hands perfecting My Stations.* ♥ (There was some silence). ♥ *My bare-foot bearer.* ♥

Lord, are You calling me barefoot before I am? (Jesus was smiling telling me this.)

Daughter, do you realize that My plans have been layed out long before you were born? ♥ ♥ *Wait and you shall see.* ♥ *Rest now;* ♥ *replenish always from Me. I love you.*

Jesus I love You Beloved.

Have My peace daughter. I will see that you will lack nothing. ♥ ♥ ♥ *Seek your rest nowhere else but in My Heart.* ♥

Lord I am asking You if there is anything one can do to help Mrs X's son ♥

Hear Me; works of love are able to deliver him.

By whom Lord?

Vassula, by all of you.

Jesus, Beloved, I ask You with Your Divine Hand to bless the community in Bangladesh, I ask You to support them all, support them.

Vassula, tell them to cradle My love for it is within them; I am in the midst of My beloved ones. Daughter, with My Hand I bless them. (I prayed for Mrs X's son.) *Believe in what you ask;* ♥ *little one have faith in Me.* ♥

Jesus, can You see what's wrong with him?

I can.

Wouldn't You want him near You Lord?

Ardently I want him beloved, Satan has a hold on him. (I heard Satan yelling 'I refuse to let go.' He was furious!)

Lord, Jesus, if You want me to suffer for him but bring him near You let me do it, what can I do? Maybe I'll go without water for 2 days?

Vassula suffer for him, do not drink any liquids while you bear My Cross.

I'll do this as a sacrifice.

Beloved one, later on you will understand. Care for your brother; sacrifice for him; I love him. ♥

Jesus, I will.

VICTIM OF MY BODY AND OF MY SOUL

October 21st, 1987

Today I had discouraging news. The Catholic theologian of Lyon whom I had put my hopes on, when he learned that I do not belong to a community his enthusiasm became cold. He said I am experiencing God but does not understand that it's beyond this. God is giving a message to all of us, as far as the ecclesiastical authorities and the Holy See as well. But of course why should he believe, I come from nowhere, so to speak; as I once said, if I was one of them I would have been accepted and they would have tried to glance on the message and this is exactly what God is trying to teach us, not to differ from one another, we are all under one authority, God's authority. Why make a distinction. A distinction even upon the character of the person. I am not wearing the habit, but does it matter, can I ask God why? He has chosen me as I am and wants me that way.

Vassula, you are experiencing the same things as when I was in flesh on earth. ♥ *Remember Vassula, when the Pharisees questioned Me about who had given Me the authority to preach?*

Yes, Lord.

Beloved, My Message comes from Me; all authority will come from Me - you belong to Me. Have I in any instant written that your authority will be given by mankind? Little one, towards Wisdom lean your head. (I became distressed and sad, tears flowed out and I had to stop for a while to recover.) ♥ *My victim, I have chosen you to be the victim of My Heart, the Sweet Torture of your soul, victim of My Body and of My Soul[1], by the denials, anguishes and sorrows. Vassula, you will experience My life on earth; I will give it all to you in small doses with the capacity your soul can bear. You will, and you have already been disbelieved, accused, mocked upon, rejected. Vassula there will be more to come; yet, on the other hand, I have given you those who believe in My Message of Peace and Love - they are your witnesses. Let me remind you that you too will be betrayed[2].* ♥ *I love you. I the Lord am your support; to Me come and get consoled* ♥; *let My Peace enwrap you. Come, all authority comes from Me and not from men; you belong under* <u>*My Authority*</u>, *which is One,* ♥ <u>*One Authority*</u>. ♥

My God, thank you for giving me Your support. Thank you for giving me witnesses too. I will not raise my voice anymore, I should keep my words which were, 'do what you please with me, if you give me delights or sorrows, I will thank You all

---

[1] Here Jesus means He is the sweet torture.
[2] By one.

the same. You want me thrown I'll be thrown, You want me cuddled, I do not merit it. Do what Your Heart desires most. I am Yours.'

♥ *Yes, be soft so that I may engrave deep in you My Words.* ♥ *Remember My Presence and My Love.* ♥ ♥

YOU ARE TO BE MY NET

October 22nd, 1987

At 2.30 in the morning I woke up with my mouth and lips as dry as parchment from thirst. Jesus told me: "Get up and drink now, two days are over." I went and sipped some water, not much as I could not stand it. - This morning my soul sad beyond imagination longed for Him. Why has He awakened me, to refuse me the privilege of being among those who live in His house? If they knew their privilege! and I, to infuse in me the desire but prevent me from entering and be surrounded by His Peace, instead, I have to be in exile and so much temptation.

O daughter! Blessed of My Soul, blessed of My Heart; from within Me exhales My pain too, ♥ *but Vassula I have created you to stay among mankind and integrate among them.* ♥ *I love you ineffably to the extent that fondness becomes folly.* ♥ ♥ *Vassula, wretched beyond words, sacrifice beloved yourself and be among wretchedness and Godless people, for you are to be My Net.* ♥ *Let your Holy Father rejoice at your catch; let My Heart fill up this time with joy - draw souls to Me.* ♥ ♥ *Reserve your tears, for there will be none left when your ears shall hear the infamies said about My Mother!*

Jesus do not let their tongue articulate when it comes to infamies.

♥ *Vassula, I the Lord will grant them My pardon for they know not what they are saying.*

Will they ever learn Lord?

♥ *All will learn; every creature will learn* ♥ *provided that they listen.* ♥ *Let Me answer you the question in your mind.* ♥

But Lord You say "provided" that means that there will be some who would not listen.

To My great sorrow there will be those who will shut their ears! Those that will refuse to hear will not be spared this time. ♥ *Come now, get up and follow Me[1].*

Where to Lord? (I understood in the house.)

♥ *I wish you to write to Father James.* ♥

Yes Lord.

Come then we will write together. ♥ ♥

I AM SENDING YOU AS MY BEARER

October 23rd, 1987

I was this morning wondering how Jesus must have felt when the Pharisees never believed Him and how difficult it must have been for Him to convince them that He was actually the Son of God. How misunderstood He was by them, it was beyond men's capacity to comprehend that it was possible at their time - they simply would not understand or accept such a miracle.

♥ *And how many now understand or believe fully in My Message?*

Quite a few do - more than those who do not.

Tell Me, which number is greater of those who listen, believe and understand fully My Message - My sheep or My lambs?[2] Who are more willing to hear?

I find that Your lambs are more willing, by experience now.

Today is like yesterday. ♥ *Daughter, times have not changed - today is like yesterday.* ♥ *When I was on earth in flesh, some believed in Me as another prophet - only a few believed in Me as the Messiah. When the Pharisees heard Me they rushed to stone Me for blasphemy and now Vassula why are you surprised at what people believe? You come from Me and today I am sending you as My bearer, with My Message of Peace and Love. I come to unite My Church, but*

---

[1] Jesus, standing near me, was urging me to get up.
[2] Sheep: sacerdotals. Lamb: laymen.

today is being like yesterday. ♥ *Let Me tell you; the authorities will be perplexed and many will refuse to believe fully that this Message descends directly from Me; some will mock you, they will scrutinize you, others would not bother to spare you even a minute of hearing; some will misunderstand My Message, <u>for this is beyond their wisdom again</u>.* ♥ *Here I come, with My Heart in My Hand - offering It, all Merciful, using you who are weak and wretched, to be My instrument and manifest Myself through you to descend on earth and unite you, but I tell you truly, had they but looked into My beloved Johannes' inspirations, all coming from Me, they would understand that the hour is at hand. Seek his words - for every prophecy told by him comes truly from Me. Little one, let them all see how I work.* ♥

My God and Beloved Father, I sometimes fear to face all the denials, mockeries, deafness, rejection for I truly believe that this is truly You. What happiness they would receive if they had really believed that out of Your boundless Mercy and Love You have descended to us and help us again, to unite us!! To save us!! To revive Your Church!

My remnant, fear not. If they mock you, they will be mocking Me; if they deny you, they will be denying Me. All that they do to you, they will be doing to Me[1]. ♥ *Happy is your soul to discern what you discern, for I tell you that many souls of great esteem in My eyes, wanted to discern what you have discerned, but never could, to hear what you hear, feel what you feel, but never felt it.* ♥ *Vassula, upon you lies My grace.* ♥

I bless You Father for having looked upon Your most wretched creature and having poured on me all those graces. Glory be to God Almighty for shining on me.

♥ *Keep close to Me, for you will still face many more trials.* ♥ *Us, we?*

Yes Lord, us, we.

---

[1]God reminds me that He is sharing all my sorrows and anguishes which consoles me.

- MY SWORD WILL STRIKE THEM -
- FORWARD MY WARNING -

October 26th, 1987

In the night of the 24th God enlightened me to understand further the meaning of the apparition of St Mary as an immense Statue to my cousin. It was to confirm that God is willing and allows statues in His Church which represent His Image and this of St Mary. Then in the night of the 25th God enlightened me again and made me understand that He agrees and allows us to decorate the Churches in images representing Him, photos, paintings etc... by His message of the 19th (19.10.87). When He asked me specifically to send 3 pictures of the Shroud and His Image on it to Father James and David, blessing those pictures. This was the second message allowing this that other Christians condemn.

♥ *I allow My Church to bear My image;* ♥ *do not strip My Body, adorn Me, embellish Me, leave It as It is[1]. Listen Vassula, I am the Church - trust Me. Beloved, I am Yahweh.* ♥ *Write daughter:- O Creation, have I not raised saints and prophets to warn you of the End of Times? Have I not foretold that I will send you from My Celestial Hall an angel proclaiming My secret intention so that it may be fulfilled?* ♥ ♥ *The constancy of My Words <u>will be</u> reaffirmed.* ♥ *Have I not foretold you that My messenger's mission will be to communicate My Revelation? My testimony is the Spirit of prophecy.* ♥ *Rejoice and exult all you who are faithful to Me! Woe for the unfaithful, for My Word will come upon them like a Sword, striking them, destroying all their false wisdom, wisdom which inspired My creation to fall into Satan's nets, transforming My lambs into Godless, fearless, immoral people.* ♥ *I have, Vassula, given you a vision of warning, an allusion of what I have done to Sodom and Gomorrah. Let them take heed of My warning, for I the Lord have foretold My creation that unless they repent and accept Me as their Creator, My Sword will strike them.* ♥ *It is out of My boundless Mercy that I descend on earth to warn you.* ♥ *I am the Spirit of Truth who speaks; listen to what I have to tell to My Churches. Creation, do not stand still, <u>forward My warning</u>.* ♥ *I am standing at the door knocking; if anyone hears My voice and opens the door, I the Lord will enter to share his meal side by side with him.* ♥ *Do not fear, I am fulfilling My Word.* ♥ *Before you I stand.* ♥

Lord, are You maybe hinting to me personally to forward Your warning? If yes, how Lord - more than photocopy?

---

[1]That means as the Catholics and Greek Orthodox decorate the Church.

All I ask from <u>you</u>, is love, let Me engrave on you, I have already selected those who are to forward My Message. ♥ ♥ *Come, I am with you; feel Me; feel My Presence, yes[1].* ♥ ♥ ♥ *Love Me.* ♥

I love You Jesus, teach me to love You more, just like You want us to love You. ♥

I Am. ♥

ORTHODOX! CATHOLICS! PROTESTANTS! YOU <u>ALL</u> BELONG TO ME!

October 27th, 1987

I desire, and this desire comes from the very depths of My Heart, that the apparitions of Garabandal be sanctified and honoured by the Holy See. ♥ ♥ *Vassula, will you gratify Me and tell My Holy See what I have come to ask you?*

How Lord, how would you want me to tell, upon which rights and grounds, who am I to tell the Holy See! Lord! I have been accepted by Father James but the latest Catholic theologian lost interest immediately in me because I did not belong to a community and <u>his</u> community!

But Vassula, of course you do not belong to them, you belong to Me - I am your Creator and Holy Father, you belong under My Authority. ♥

Lord, yes we are under Your Authority but it is organized and there is a system of belonging in one of the Christian communities, so I was told.

♥ *All are the same in My Eyes, <u>I</u> have never wanted My Body parted, it is <u>you</u> who have dismembered Me! <u>You</u> have decided upon My Body! You <u>lamed</u> Me[2].*

Oh God...

Daughter, have I not told you to reserve your tears for My Mother?[3]

---

[1] I discerned Jesus.
[2] There was one moment of silence and Jesus sounded so bitter and sad. I felt guilty for reminding Him.
[3] Although He told me this strictly, I couldn't help noticing that He was as sad as I was.

Yes Lord, but You seemed so hurt; I'm only human.

Vassula, this is because we are sharing My Cup. My Cup tastes bitter. ♥ *Tell the Holy See that it is I who sends you to them. Hear Me, if they ask in which community you belong, tell them that you belong to Me and that you are under My Authority.*

Lord, I do not like to argue but can't I tell that I am an orthodox?

Orthodox! Catholics! Protestants! You all belong to Me! You are all One in My Eyes! I do not make any distinction, so then why fear? Ask for My well-beloved Pope John-Paul - he will not make any distinction. ♥ *Vassula, tell him this: "Beloved, I the Lord am standing at your door, knocking, will you hear Me calling, will you open the door? If you do, I will enter your house and share your meal, side by side with you. Prove victorious and I will allow you to share My Throne. Hear Me: listen to what the Spirit is saying to the Churches.* ♥

My God, how, in which way should I accomplish Your desire?

♥ *I have been waiting for your question[1].* ♥ *Let Father James advise you of how to go about.* ♥ *Daughter, I love you, allow Me to feed you.* ♥

My God, do not ask! I am Your creature, belonging to You, do as Your Heart desires with me! I love You for feeding me and filling me. I bless You.

Similar to Psalm 23:

> ♥ *I am your Shepherd, with Me you will lack nothing, in meadows of green grass I let you lie beloved soul, to the waters of repose I lead you, where I revive your soul.* ♥ *By paths of virtue I guide you for the glory of My Body.* ♥ *Although you pass through a gloomy valley, do not fear, beside you I am to hearten you.* ♥ *I will feed you under the eyes of your persecutors, I have anointed you and will always fill you;* ♥ *for I am an abyss of Love with boundless Mercy. Come and live in the middle of My Heart.* ♥

O Lord, You are my Light and my salvation, I need not fear. I know You will shelter me. I thank You with all my heart, Lord my God, I glorify Your name forever. Your Love for me is so great, pity me and my incompetence.

---

[1] I understood that God brought me around so that I ask Him this question. (I felt I had given in.)

Remain small flower, grow in spirit, sip from My virtues. ♥ *Come, let Me always engrave on you My words.* ♥

Yes Lord, I am happy to be with You.

Love will never abandon you. ♥ *Come, us, we.*

Yes, Lord. ♥

BEND! BEND TO BE ABLE TO UNITE

October 30th, 1987

I have given My creation innumerable signs; warning them. I raised up saints declaring My desires, but have they listened? Has anything changed?

Lord, suppose they do this time, suppose they are willing, suppose they read and believe and unite and seek to glorify You rather than seek their own interests this time.

Vassula, ah Vassula, many would fear - even those who would ♥ *believe in My Message and admit that it is I, through fear of being mocked upon and fear of their superiors.* ♥ *Many would put honour from men before the honour that comes from Me.* ♥ *Honour Me and diffuse My Message.*

Suppose Lord they do bend.♥

I would uplift My Justice then that lies heavily upon them ♥ *but they still hurl venomous arrows at one another, afflicting My Body. There will always be disharmony reigning among them because love is missing. Vassula, had they followed My command to love one another as much as I love them* ♥ *and humble themselves, My Body today would reign in harmony. Have they ever humbled themselves, washing each others feet? Have I not given you this as an example so that you may copy what I have done? Bend! bend to be able to unite! Soul, the time has come where My beloved servant John-Paul should hear Me.*♥ *I have indeed heard his cries; his cries have reached Heaven; his cries resound in the entire universe; his cries have reached My ears! Let Me tell you that in a short time there will be one flock and one shepherd. I will lead all My sheep, even those that are not of this fold. Love will unite you, but before this there will be tremendous tribulations. The entire Heavens will shake! Be vigilant daughter;*

hand over My instructions; they are all within My sacred writings. By forwarding My Message you will understand. ♥

Jesus, oh <u>St Mary</u>, what will they say, understand me St Mary, it is not in my position to face all those superior people.

Vassula, do not fear, your incapacity infatuates Jesus - stay small.

St Mary, suppose they don't listen.

Little one, this divine revelation will be His last warning. If they do not want to listen or understand I will allow His Hand to fall on them and strike them. Vassula all <u>you</u> have to do is love Him. Be vigilant because Satan is furious and will try all sorts of traps. Do not fear I am guarding you. ♥

Thank you St Mary for encouraging me, thank You for guarding me. I bless You.

♥ **I bless you child.** ♥

IF IT IS YOUR WILL

November 3rd, 1987

♥ *Come, Love will instruct you. Let it be known that I delight hearing the words, "allow me Father and if it is Your will." These words, said in your prayers, infatuate Me. Ask and it shall be given but always remembering those words.* ♥ *Come Vassula, have My Peace.* ♥ ♥

♥ I love You Jesus, allow me to bless You. ♥ (I blessed Jesus.)

♥ *Beloved, I bless you.* ♥ ♥

YOU DO NOT BELONG TO THE WORLD

November 5th, 1987

♥ *Trust Me; let Me guide you where I wish; keep your hand in My Hand. Have no fear, I will lead you into the very depths of My Wounded Body. Vassula fulfill My Word.* ♥

(I was wondering how they are able to help me.)

Daughter, <u>fear not</u>. I wish you to embellish My garden. ♥

Father, Righteous One, I cannot deny My fear; help me; allow me to receive Your Strength, allow me to grow in Your Light, in You, do not forsake me, if it is within Your Will make me worthy so that You may use me and may share in accomplishing <u>Your</u> desires, I ask You to forgive my weaknesses and incompetences by Your Mercy, do as <u>Your</u> Heart desires, let <u>Your</u> will be done, not mine. Amen.

♥ *Love will help you. Remember though, that as soon as My Word will be established, <u>to Me</u> you will come! I bear no more having you out in exile.* ♥ *My Soul longs for you!*

Father! What joy you give me, what happiness and consolation your words give my soul! I'm so happy.

♥ *Beloved, yes; love Me, desire Me, please this Heart that sought for you. I will soon be coming to you,* ♥ *but while still in the world be near Me by drinking Me and eating Me, by praising Me, by honouring Me. Let Me rejoice <u>fully</u>.* ♥ ♥ *Do not get discouraged if the world denies you, because you do not belong to the world, no more than I belonged to the world while in flesh.* ♥ *You come from Me; I am your Father and in you I live as you live in Me. Honour My Name, Glorify My Body, remain in My Love, follow My instructions and remain in My Love. I will not fail you or desert you, so fear no one beloved, sow My seeds which will bear fruit in holiness. Be holy, for I am Holy.* ♥ ♥

I am listening. What is Yahweh saying? What God is saying means Peace and Love for his children, for the earth, for His Body, if only they renounce their folly, for those who fear him, His redemption is near, and the Glory will then <u>live</u> on earth. <u>Love and Mercy now descended</u>, Righteousness and Peace now will embrace us. Righteousness always preceeding Him and Peace following His footsteps[1].

---

[1] God guided me to write this passage taken from Psalm 84, verses 8-13, changing a few words.

♥ *Beloved, I said I am going to water My orchard. I intend to irrigate My flower beds. Hear Me, My rivulet will grow into a river and My river will grow into an ocean ♥ and I will make discipline Shine out. I shall send My Light far and wide, glorifying My Body. ♥ ♥ So come, take My Hand and let Me lead you daughter. Do no more today; ♥ rest in My Heart. ♥*

- I AM YOUR ONLY LOVE -
- MY CROSS IS THE DOOR TO TRUE LIFE -

November 8th, 1987

Jesus? ♥

I Am. If I had not delivered you, you would have been still today in deep sleep. ♥

(I gave in. Jesus was insistent.)

I feel very ashamed. I am indeed the last to talk. Whatever I do and try to repair and thank You Lord will not come near enough to what You've done again for me. Even when I want to pray for others I feel guilty and hesitant because Lord how would I dare pray for others who are so far better than myself? How could 'the most wretched' pray for someone better than herself? It reminds me of Your words about the plank in the eye and the splinter in the other one's eye. I feel I've got a plank, a whole forest, so how could I with all this wood in my eye dare utter a sound? Unless Lord you deliver me. I ask You and allow me to ask You to clean me, have mercy on my soul, if You want make me worthy to enable me and pray with dignity for my brethren.

♥ *Vassula, I am pleased to hear your words - for not until you realize your unworthiness will you begin your way to perfection.* ♥

If it is within Your will allow me Father to ask for Your help.

Daughter, replenish your lamp from Me, do not wait. Grow in My light little one. ♥ ♥ *Whoever will believe in this Message will believe not in you but in Me. I, the Light, descend into the world through you so that whoever believes in My Message need not stay in the dark anymore. Your witnesses know the truth; they know that these words are not your words. No, My Vassula, all that is written comes from Me, the Lord. I tell you truly that whoever welcomes you welcomes Me.*

No, My God, I'm not worthy!

Why Vassula, have I not purified you? Have I not anointed you Myself to be Mine? Indeed, I will be manifesting Myself through you - so honour Me daughter. ♥ *Come, I will teach you My ways, I and you. Let Me breathe in you; let Me rest in you daughter; rest Me from those who wound My Soul. Oh Vassula, if you only knew - My blood is gushing out again today.*

Oh God, and it's Sunday! Why?

Little one they are piercing My Heart through and through. ♥

My God let them pierce <u>me</u> instead!

Hear Me, you will be; they <u>will</u> pierce you. ♥ ♥ ♥ *Come now, allow Me to rest in you, share My Cup daughter.* ♥

Why, why is it like this, what <u>is</u> going on? Why are they doing this to our God, a God of Love, of Peace, a Father, a Friend? How could they? I feel sick. Jesus is again today bleeding, suffering from our wickedness. The world, one could say, has been kidnapped by Satan and Jesus is trying again to save us. My God, you give me so much pain to feel you so hurt. You, only Infinte Goodness and an Abyss of Love, why are they tormenting you? I cannot bear Your sufferings any more, not that I care much for my flesh and pains, but I care for Your sufferings, Your pains Lord, I care and love You.

Vassula, My Vassula, victim of My Soul, victim of My Heart; bear My sufferings and share them with Me. Drink from My Cup; feel My scourgers. Beloved of My Soul, what will I not do for you out of Love? I will allow you to share My sufferings - I have chosen you to be the victim of My Bleeding Heart, by all the sorrows of which yours is capable. Victim of My Soul, by all the anguishes, denials and mockeries your soul can bear, come you will share My Cross. ♥ *I am your only Love; I have reached My goal. Allow Me to be the sweet torture of your mind and soul. You please Me, for now I have extirpated all My rivals, they are all gone - none are left! It is I, your Jesus, only left with you! How I delight, and now let Me love you without restraint; let Me reign over you; I have found a place for My greatness and bounty.* ♥ *I do not love you for what you are, but for what you are not.* ♥ *Come, your nothingness infatuates Me. Your incapacity leaves Me speechless.* ♥

Lord, I feel embarassed.

Vassula, never seek to be something; stay nothing; for every divine work I will accomplish will be purely Mine and not yours. ♥ *My Church will be one, <u>under one Authority</u>. Have I Myself not asked Peter to feed My lambs? Have I not chosen him to feed My sheep? Have I Myself not uttered these words, "you are Peter and on this rock I will build My Church"?* ♥ *Why this arrogance among the nations, these futile plots among the people? I had selected Peter, a man after My own Heart, the rock on whom I would build My Church.* ♥ *Why then distort My Command?*

Whom are You referring to Lord?

I am speaking for those who scheme and plot against My foundation. Do you not realize that your plots will lay futile?

Lord, I do not know whom are you referring to.

I know Vassula, all this is obscure to you, but it is as clear as day for those deceivers! My eyes are fixed upon them; My sword lifted and ready to strike. They know themselves and believe Me their days are numbered. Yes, cast your eyes around you, deceivers! Why are you surprised? You will perish! For I am doing something in these days that it will be hard to believe had you been told of it!

Beloved, let Me answer your question in your mind. My Message will be read by those deceivers too. Beloved, feel Me, I am in pain as you. My Cross is on you, bear It with love; My Cross is the door to true life, ♥ *embrace It willingly. Vassula, abnegation and suffering lead into a divine path - this one of holiness and virtues[1].* ♥ *O come beloved I am with you[2].*

Lord, I feel so terribly sad, I know I should shed no more tears and reserve them for later, to compensate. I am ready to shed my blood instead, replacing my tears, if none will be left.

---

[1] I felt hopelessly sad.
[2] Jesus was caressing my head.

My Vassula, remember you are not of this world, you belong to Me. Can you see My Sacred Heart?[1] Enter in My Sacred Heart; in it's depths you will find your rest; I will take you and thrust you in it's depths. My pain is unbearable[2]. Do you remember when you were but a mere child, what I had done to you? (Jesus gave me the same vision of that when I was maybe ten years old - the first call.) *You were unable to move. I am divine Power, beloved, therein you belong[3].* ♥ *Come now, I need to be consoled. Let us rest in each other.* ♥ ♥

Jesus was very much in pain and sad. How could I console such distress?

By loving me ardently; love Me and console Me Vassula; love Me with all your soul.

I do love You and You know it Lord.

Love Me without measure!

Teach me to love you without measure.

I am. Come now, I have a secret, I wish to tell you; fear not, I will whisper it in your ear[4]. ♥ ♥

Oh God! Will you really do this?

I will beloved, I will, never doubt; all will be done accordingly My Vassula. ♥

Jesus, My God, thank You, allow me to bless You. ♥

I bless you too beloved. Come, it is late, we will rest in each other.

Yes Lord. ♥

Come then. ♥

---

[1] Jesus pointed a lit Chest and Heart.
[2] For having me in exile.
[3] Jesus pointed with His index His Heart.
[4] Jesus gave me the secret giving me so much joy!

LET MY CREATION KNOW OF MY GREAT LOVE

November 10th, 1987

My God may You use me to engrave on me everything that Your Heart desires. May Your will be done and Your Name Glorified.

The time has come to scatter My grains among mankind, forward My Message, I will help you in all your undertakings, let My Words be known, let My creation know of My Great Love, of My boundless Mercy ♥ My reign will be one of Peace, Love and Unity, I have chosen Vassula as an incapable and wretched being, useless and without speech. ♥ Write this too[1]. Yes, without any basic knowledge of My Church; an empty canvas, where I the Lord was free to cover it with My Works only, so that it is clear that all that is written comes from My Mouth. All acts will be done by Me, through her. I will speak through her, act through her. ♥ I have formed her, pouring all My Works on her to enable her to be My bearer for this Message, which will be known. ♥ Will you forward My Message? Will you do this for Me? Remember, it is I Jesus, Beloved Son of God, Saviour to all mankind, the Word, who blesses you. I bless your undertakings. ♥ Whether you will encounter joys or sorrows be confident, I will give you My countenance. I am before you always, guiding you, ♥ uniting. My Church will Glorify Me! I will lead you into the very depths of My Bleeding Body. I will point out to you My thorns, you will recognize them. ♥ ♥ Have no other interest but My glory. Never doubt of My Works. Love shines on you, My well-beloved, endeavour and please Me. Come, at your side I Am. ♥♥ ♥♥ Have My Peace[2]. Let us pray to the Father:- ♥ ♥

> *"Righteous One, Beloved Father, blessed be Your Name; assemble all Your faithful ones, let the heavens proclaim Your Righteousness; let every lip praise Your Holy Name continually; malice must be banished from the deceivers; help those whose spirit is crushed, revive them as Your Word has guaranteed; the vow I have made I will keep and fulfill. ♥ I pray for Your Churches: may They All be One; Father, may They be One in You. ♥ Amen. " ♥*

Jesus helped me pray - these are His words.

---

[1] I heard Him say the following sentence and I looked at Him embarassed and hesitant.
[2] Turning to me, He said this.

YOUR MISERY ENTICES MY CLEMENCY

November 12th, 1987

Beloved, it is I Jesus. Clutch at My Cross, just as I have taught you to do while resting[1]. Never, ever, leave Me - not even for a second. ♥ I am All and Everything. By holding My Cross you both glorify Me and honour Me. I your God, purify you and console you My child, so honour your Father who so much sought you when you wandered away from My side - erring from My divine ways. You see child, you always belonged to Me; now that I have found you beneath My cape, I shelter you and keep you. Look!

I saw Jesus Christ in a scarlet-red long cape. He opened it with both hands, showing a bright glow coming from His breast, suddenly like a flash a fire tongue came from there straight on me, piercing me. It was not painful, it only lit my love for Him, desiring Him more than ever.

My Flame will enkindle your heart; My Flame should stay ablaze forever in you altar; I have renewed My Flame in you so that you proceed with My divine Message. Since you are incapable of drawing from Me, I then will see to it that My Flame will remain in you ablaze. Come, I love your incapacity because I have given you the grace to realize it. I feel glorified when you need Me for everything; your weakness attracts My strength; your misery entices My Clemency, love Me Vassula, share My thorns and nails; share My Cross; crown Me with your love; honour Me with your faith; allow Me to lead you blindly all the way - I will never desert you! Believe in every word spoken in the Scriptures. ♥ ♥

LOVE IS THE ROOT FOR EVERY VIRTUE

November 13th, 1987

My Vassula, all I ask from you is love. ♥ Every virtue blossoms from Love - Love is the root for every virtue. Love is like a fruit tree that blossoms first then later on gives it's fruit - every fruit is a virtue. ♥ ♥ Come, let us have a silent prayer together first, you and Me, to the Father; let us pray in total silence. ♥ I will dictate. ♥

---

[1]Jesus taught me to hold a crucifix while resting at night. In this way, when I happen to wake up I feel the crucifix in my hand and immediately my mind is on Him.

"Father, Righteous One, My Shelter, send out Your Light and Your Truth. Let these be my guide, to lead me to Your Holy Place where You live. I, for my part love You fully. I will keep my vow to fulfill Your word. Holy Father I am aware of my faults, of my sins, have mercy on me. In Your Goodness and Your great Tenderness forgive my sins. Purify me Lord, be my Saviour. Renew me, keep my spirit faithful to You and willing. I offer you my will, surrendering. I am willing to be Your tablet. I praise Your Holy Name and thank You for all the blessings and peace you have given me. Amen."

♥ *Now repeat it with Me.* ♥ (We repeated it together.)

Thank you Jesus for leading me step by step. You are my Holy Teacher, teaching me with Love and patience, guiding me and guiding others too to know You better, to know what an Infinite Love You are. Never deserting us, but always ready to search for us who were lost and bring us back to You. Never did I feel harshness from You, or impatience, I only felt loved. You gave Love and Peace to my soul. This is what You are. I will never leave You Lord.
♥ *Daughter, desire Me always. Love Me and honour Me, remain faithful to Me.*
♥ ♥ *Let us be together, do not forget My Presence.* ♥

SOULS ARE PIERCING ME ANEW

November 14th, 1987

♥ Jesus are You happy when I also come to You in this way You have given me? *I am, how can I not be?* ♥ *You come to Me My Vassula, yet you are not telling Me what is in your heart. I feel your heart Vassula, it is laden with sorrow and pain.* ♥ *Do you want to know why? I will tell you why, it is because Love suffers; when I suffer you suffer too. I have given you the grace of synchronizing with Me at all times. You are My reflection. What I feel, you feel - I am letting you feel Me. Souls are piercing Me anew.* ♥ ♥

(My agony now reached it's peak. I'm supposed to reserve my tears but I couldn't.)

Daughter, do you think that My eyes are dry?[1] *They fill up as much as yours, I suffer. My Eyes are wet too. O Vassula! My flower, how you understand Me*

---

[1] I looked up because Jesus' voice shook with agony and saw His Eyes full, and wet with tears all around His Eyes.

now! ♥ *Daughter, together we shed tears, together we suffer, together we bear My Cross[1].* ♥ *My Heart is wounded by so many souls who embitter Me. O Vassula, your tears are My tears. Here, bear My Cross, take My Nails too. Will you let Me rest?*

Yes Jesus, (my soul has never reached such sorrow and agony as now.)

Vassula, O Vassula how I dread in telling you this, still I must tell you the truth - wear My Crown of Thorns and you will understand Me. ♥

I think I know Lord. I will be ridiculed; denied?

Souls will not hear Me - they will sin; proved by their refusal to believe in My Merciful Message; proved by their reluctance and by their fear of admitting their fault[2]. Here, wear My Crown. ♥

He posed it on my head.

You will glorify Me. Listen, the time will come - in fact the time has come where I will give you and My servants My instructions to scatter My grains in great abundance. Love will instruct you to fulfill My intentions, prove victorious Vassula. ♥ *Daughter, delight Me and face Me like now. I have allowed you to feel My Bleeding Heart, leaving My Blood drips on your heart. I let you share My Cup. Around your head I have adorned you with My Crown. I have layed My Cross on you. My Nails I give to you, what more can a spouse offer? All that I have given you are My most precious Jewels.* ♥ *My beloved one, now that you understand Me, are you willing to proceed into the depths of My Bleeding Body?[3]*

Yes Lord, take me there.

Daughter, we will then proceed, hold on to Me, bless Me. ♥

♥ ♥ (I blessed Jesus). *Come, I will bless you too, lower your eyes too.* ♥ ♥ (Jesus blessed me). *Call me Abba - now you know what it means.*

---

[1] Jesus dictated very fast.
[2] Jesus enlightened me to understand this passage . I know to who this is referred to. It goes very deep into the Church.
[3] With tremendous effort I managed to write, my soul sad beyond description, realizing more and more why He is bleeding and approaching the ones who pierce Him. And the picture getting clearer by the day. He is indeed making me penetrate deeper and deeper into His Body. I already see the thorns. There is the lance left.

Abba?

♥ Yes, how I love you! I have also created you so that I have someone with whom I can share My sufferings. You will get to know Me Vassula, you will learn who your Father is. ♥ Flower, dearest daughter, let it be known how much I love My creation[1]. Vassula do you know why I am giving you this powerful grace to call Me anytime you wish?

For the reasons You've told me already Lord.

♥ There is still one more reason. ♥ ♥

Please do not write it, I have heard You.

Yes, you have heard Me. ♥ ♥

But Lord, this comes from You, it's not from me.

Flower, remember I have given you all your freedom to choose.

Yes Beloved, but You have also given us the grace of our intellect to <u>enable</u> us to understand and choose. <u>You</u> have taught me this.

Yes[2]. I love you. Come. ♥ Us, we?

Yes Lord.

JESUS IS YOUR GUIDE

November 15th, 1987

♥ ♥ (Suddenly I felt the need of God, St Mary, and all the saints - with enormous force St Mary appeared.)

The hours are fleeing. Jesus is guiding you. Fear not My beloved daughter - have My Peace. Jesus is with you, Jesus is your Guide. Love Him as you do

---

[1] Here God is letting me know that He does not love me more than the rest of His Creation, but shows how much love He has on me just as an example. I am like a sample.
[2] There was a slight pause.

My Vassula, you amend enormously. Be Jesus' balm; delight Him. I, your Holy Mother, will help you; fear not and <u>proceed</u>, you are on the right Path. ♥ I love you. ♥

I love You, St Mary. ♥ ♥ If I have to hurry I cannot do it unless God will open the Path for me. I shall then proceed with Him holding His hand. I trust Him. I rely on Him. I ask You Beloved Mother to be my support, encouraging me and helping me.

♥ You will get support from Me and I will help you. ♥ ♥ ♥
Thank you. I bless You.

BELIEVE IN MY MIRACLES

November 16th, 1987

Beloved, I will be doing something that will be hard to believe in these days. What I will do will be to confirm My Message - fear not. ♥
My God, already it is hard to believe for many that You are communicating with me, just as simple as that, anytime, anywhere.
Believe in My miracles, believe in Me. Listen child, the time is near. ♥ *I wish you to reveal me to my devout one John-Paul. I want you to discern carefully what I have with me.* ♥

It is a book again, You have?

♥ *Yes, I have brought you John's inspirations, John XXIII.* ♥ *I want you to read a certain passage. Know that I have foretold My Church of this divine Message:* ♥ *And My eagle will announce My Message at the zenith so that the whole universe will be able to hear and see this Message. I have warned them.* ♥ *Come, I want you to write down My Words.*

♥ ♥

I WILL BRING BACK TO PETER MY SHEEP

November 18th, 1987

My God since the day You revealed Your secret intention to me, I fear, I am afraid to proceed. I fear, sensing that trouble lies ahead. It's like You, before entering in Jerusalem. You knew what trouble lay ahead.

My Message fulfills My Word. ♥ *You are to proceed. Whether you will be rejected or not, you will accomplish your work. I am before you.* ♥ *Little one stay meaningless so that I may appear fully. The less you will be, the more I Am. Let Me proceed; let Me be the one who acts and speaks.* ♥ *Yes little one, they will all have to bend to unite. I will be coming humbly, barefooted. I am not coming loaded with weapons[1].* ♥ ♥ ♥ *I will bring back to Peter My sheep;* ♥ *I will unite them and Peter will feed My lambs. I the Lord have spoken.* ♥ ♥ *Trust Me beloved ones; I love you all with all My Heart.* ♥ ♥

BELIEVE IN WHAT YOU ASK

November 21st, 1987

Vassula, I will bring back to Peter My scattered sheep; I, the Lord, guarantee this to you all! (Suddenly the Lord gave me a vision of sheep still apart, another flock, then later on these too were united.) *Flower, this will come after My Great Sign!*
Father, forgive my impatience, I have to learn to be patient like You!
Little one, exalted by My Hand, draw from My resources and fill up your heart; embue it to be able to impregnate other hearts too. I the Lord bless you. ♥
Visions, I will give to you. I am enriching your sight to discern men's hearts and be able to read them. My well-beloved, I offer you this grace, but remember you will only use it for My interests and My glory -retaining nothing for yourself. ♥
Jesus, well Beloved, My God, who never stops pouring Your gifts on me, the zero, allow me to be near You. Jesus if I who am the zero and You pour on me so many gifts what would You then not do and give to those who are really pleasing in Your Eyes, honouring You!

Yes, you see Vassula, you seem now to understand Me better. If I give to you who are indeed the most wretched of My creatures, <u>what would I then not give</u> to those who truly merit My graces? Those who honour Me and those who sacrifice for Me! Ask, beloved ones, and <u>I will give you</u>. Believe in what you ask; have confidence and trust Me; do not be like Peter who lost his confidence while walking on the water - have faith in Me! Be confident! Believe!

---

[1]Weapons = their inflexible statements and arguments.

WILDERNESS

November 22nd, 1987

Vassula, the wind is blowing becoming stronger every day. It blows on this wilderness that My creation has become, sweeping the desert sand, bringing it closer and closer to the little fertile land that is left. Already it has covered part of it. If we do not hurry, little one, soon there will be nothing left but wilderness. ♥

Lord, please be patient for I'm slow to learn.

Flower, remember how long I was outside your door? Have I not been patient all these years?

Jesus, why didn't I hear you all these years?

Because you were deceived by the world. You belonged to Me from the beginning but the world deceived you, convincing you to believe you belonged to them - that is how treacherous and deceitful Satan is. Today his work is to convince My creation that he is non existent - in this way he works without being feared and, like lambs, My creation are trapped and devoured by the wolf. ♥ *This is his plan of today.*

SACRIFICE AND BE LOYAL

November 23rd, 1987

Having been to Lyon I've talked to the Catholic Thelogian. He and his wife did not quite understand my detachment of this world. He said I had responsibilities. I said 'yes' but I put God first. Then he could neither understand that God detached even my soul. He wasn't agreeing. (Wasn't Abraham ready to sacrifice his own son?)

Little one I love you to folly. Love has no limits and I wish you to love Me too to folly. My intention is to stretch your love. I intend to make you love Me by showing Me no limits. ♥ *I delight to check[1] on your loyalty towards Me. I delight to hear you honouring Me. Now you sacrifice for Me, but your sacrifice will not be in vain either. Give yourself unreservedly to Me.* ♥ *Please Me by being pliant, allowing Me child to treat you as I please. Soul, never fear Me - I am Love[2].* ♥

---

[1]Like He checked on Abraham.
[2]That means that God will never ask something that will hurt our souls.

Many Lord do not seem to understand me either when I desire to be with you and that death is but a delivery.

Beloved be holy, stay holy and Divine Love will carry you still higher. Fear not My well-beloved. Lean on Me; be loyal to Me, loving Me your God with all your soul and heart, with all your mind and strength. Remember how I lean towards you, to reach for your soul. ♥ ♥

I WILL REIGN IN SPITE OF MY ENEMIES

November 24th, 1987

Vassula, I will make you read the words that I said to Margaret Mary. I said that I will reign in spite of My enemies and all those who try to oppose Me ♥ *- so be confident beloved ones.* ♥ ♥ *Vassula, I would like you to design once more how the Holy Trinity is.* ♥

Yes Lord (this is after a vision once the Lord gave to me when I had problems of understanding.)

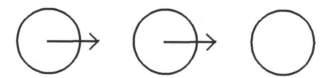

A vision of light. Then one light coming out then another one, making 3. The Holy Trinity is ONE and the same. They can be 3, but all 3 can be one. <u>Result, One God</u>.

FAITH

November 25th, 1987

(I saw Jesus seated near me.) Jesus, are You there?
♥ *I Am - you have discerned Me. You see Vassula, for that little faith you are giving Me, a faith much smaller than a mustard seed, I can make you see Me, feel Me, write with Me.* ♥ *Come, I will be your Holy Companion.* ♥ ♥ ♥

WITH ALL MY HEART I LOVE YOU

November 25th, 1987

Jesus, Beloved I would like to pray for those You have chosen to be my guide.
♥ *I am listening.* ♥ *Take My Hand while you pray to Me.* ♥

(I held Jesus' Hand, He was going to help me find the words.)

> "Father, ♥ since Your Divine Heart has chosen Father James and
> David Your servants to serve You in uniting Your Church, and to
> be my guides and witnesses following Your instructions all for the
> Glory of Your Body, I pray for them, for they belong to You, You
> have placed them in Your Heart to honour You. I am asking You
> to protect them from evil, consecrate them in the Truth, Your
> Word is the Truth. I pray to You Father, who is Infinite Goodness
> to enlighten them, letting Your Holy Spirit descend upon them and
> speak for them, act for them and pour into them from Your Infinite
> Wealth the strength they need, courage, discernment, wisdom.
> Nourish them that they may glorify Your Name Lord, I ask this,
> and if this is within Your Will, to fill them , so that they may
> glorify You, let Your Will be done, not ours. Amen."

♥ *Beloved, hear Me, I will help both of them.*
Thank You, Lord, Glory be to God!

Jesus led me by the Holy Spirit, I dragging behind Him, He took me in St Peter's
Church. He pointed with His arm stretched and with His index at a lonely figure,
it was the Pope John-Paul II. There he was, seated, alone, in thought, he appeared
in deep thought.

See Vassula? He is waiting - he is waiting.
Father, may Your designs be accomplished. Amen.
My Messages must be handed to him, accomplishing all that is written. Come beloved, the time is near, do not fear. Remember I am before you; what I have commenced and blessed, I will finish. ♥ Come, Love loves you and guides you; keep your hand in Mine. Us, we? ♥
Yes Lord. Together. ♥ ♥ O how I love You Jesus! Jesus who comes with His Heart in His Hand offering It to us, Love with His so Tender Heart comes again to help us untangle from Satan's nets. I Love You Lord! ♥
Beloved how, how could I see all this and leave you? ♥   I love you with all My Heart, with all My Heart I love you all. ♥ ♥
(I felt His Heart and it's inexplicable to say how much Love Jesus has for us!)

MY FLOWERS NEED WATERING
OTHERWISE EVERY SINGLE ONE WILL PERISH

November 28th, 1987

*♥ Little one, embellish My garden, as it is now, I see nothing in it but aridity.
♥ Aridity is reigning over it; ♥ the dry winds are blowing on it drying out what little is left. My flowers need watering, otherwise every single one will perish. ♥ My buds will not make it for the blooming season, they will perish one after the other. O if they only listen!*

My God, why is it so complicated to reach a decision? Why is it so difficult to come to this decision? Why does it have to take months, years? Is it really so complicated, to love one another and unite as a family? Aren't these very same ones that teach us to love each other and to learn to sacrifice and give? Does it have to take years to unite? Do they really have to have special councils and meetings? Why can't they make one gathering a decisive one, joining hands and giving Peter the authority you once gave him, and please You, leaving You smiling.

♥ How I love your simplicity My child. ♥ It is childish the way you think. ♥ Children are My weakness! You see, when children quarrel, their quarrels never last more than a few minutes because malice is missing, but, daughter, these are not children, they have lost all the innocence they once had; they lost their simplicity, their holiness; ♥ building up instead malice for innocence, vanity for simplicity, unholiness for holiness, hypocrisy for humility. ♥ You see, child, this is the reason I descend again to remind them how I, Jesus, am. I will come barefooted and humble; I will enter My own House and kneel at My servant's feet

and wash them[1]. Weep not My Vassula - all is for unity. Let Me use you. This time they cannot deny that it is I, Jesus, since I have foretold this event well before time. ♥ *I have let you read part of what I have inspired My servant John XXIII with but the rest* ♥

Rest Lord?

♥ *I have later on whispered in his ear about the great tribulations My Church will undergo. I Jesus love you all.* ♥ *Remain in Me, in My Love.* ♥

SHARE MY CROSS
OBEDIENCE TURNS THE DEVIL HELPLESS

November 27th, 1987

Vassula, are you ready to sacrifice more now for Me?

Lord, You can use me as You please, I have surrendered. I'm surrendering every day.

Remain in Me, remain in My Love. ♥ *Daughter, numerous will be your trials[2].* ♥ *Would you still sacrifice more for Me, your God?[3]*

My God, take my life into Your Hands and do as Your Heart pleases. ♥

My well-beloved bride then have a look at My Cross. ♥ ♥ (I looked, and with Jesus was a gigantic dark wooden Cross. It was huge!) *I have been nailed on It, glorifying My Father. Do you see what awaits you? I the Lord will share It with you; you will then bear all the sufferings your soul is capable of. I will stretch your endurance little one.*

Father, do as Your Beloved Heart pleases with me, anything that will give <u>You</u> more glory. All that comes from You satisfies me. ♥

Be obedient to Me and please Me; obedience turns the devil helpless ♥ ♥ *and makes him flee.* ♥

---

[1] Jesus speaks in metaphors.
[2] God is warning me.
[3] After the warning, God, respecting my freedom, asks me again.

MY CHURCH WILL BE ONE

November 30th, 1987

Jesus?

I Am. I, Jesus <u>guarantee</u> to you all that My Church will be one, united. Beloved, be faithful to Me, trust Me and be confident. ♥ ♥

MY CREATION HAS TO BE WARNED
- PROMOTE ME DO NOT REMOTE ME -

December 1st, 1987

I have chosen you to show the world how Merciful I am; ♥ *finding you where most of My children still are. If I had not come to fetch you, you would be today still where the rest are.* ♥ *I come out of My boundless Mercy to warn you likewise to draw you to Me and remind you of your foundations.* ♥

(I start to understand that this Message for Peace and Love among God's creation and the uniting of the Church, will be one of God's last attempts before inflaming His Justice upon us.)

♥ *How well you understand Me now daughter.* ♥ ♥ *Do you fear Me?*

(God must have felt in me a fear of what He might do if we do not change.)

I do, My God, after the vision You showed me.

♥ *I have shown you only part of it[1].* ♥ *Vassula, My creation has to be warned - do not let the same mistakes be repeated.*

Like when Lord?

♥ *When I gave them My big Miracle at Fatima, I warned then My creation but they paid little heed to My warning. They spent their time instead doubting, arguing, never diffusing My Mother's words properly so that very few knew of the urgency of the Message. They have bloodstained their hands from their crime,*

---

[1]Meaning the worst is hidden.

dragging with them so many souls. ♥ *I shall remind them of their sins of the past[1]. I will remind them the urgency of Garabandal's Message. Why doubt of My Works? Pass on to My creation My warning, tremendous reparations are to be made. My creation has to be warned and to believe in Me. Remind them of My Love[2]. Propound My Word; promote Me... promote Me, do not remote Me! Now you are remoting Me, you are not protecting Me! Declare openly My Works of the past and of present, I am Omnipotent.* ♥ *The thorns in My Head are all those sacerdotal souls who hold the key of knowledge - neither do they go in themselves nor do they let others in who... want...to! These are my thorns! Those thorns now should find Me and repent; their hands still, with fresh blood from the past; responsible for all the crimes and atrocities. I want them to repent. They defied My Mother's Message of Garabandal, never diffusing It like It should have been, ignoring it's urgency. O[3], what have I got Vassula! Stones, their hearts are petrified.* ♥ *Accept the Truth, open your hearts. Garabandal is the sequel of Fatima! Do not repeat your errors. Peter![4]* (then begging) *Peter, be My Echo!* ♥ *Feed My lambs. Peter, do not deny Me again beloved.* ♥

When the Lord said: "Peter, be My Echo! Feed My lambs. Peter, do not deny me again beloved." I could have died there and then, the way I heard Him say it.

♥ *Come, let Me help you.* ♥ *Rest in Me[5].* ♥ ♥
(When I recollected myself.) Jesus I will describe now, God was begging. He said it in a begging voice.

♥ *Yes, yes Vassula, out of love.* ♥

I love You My God, how could I see You and hear You as sad as this, without wanting to die a million deaths. If I had 1,000 lives, I'd give each one, one after the other for Your Glory - healing Your Wounds.

My Wounds will only heal when My creation will return to Love. Accept Me as Omnipotent and unite. ♥ *Come let us share My sorrow.* ♥
Jesus, I wish I could do much more to repair and glorify You.
Stay near Me and I will share all I have with you. ♥ *Come.* ♥

---

[1] Apparently God reminds sins only if those who committed them have not asked to be forgiven or repent yet. Once this is done, forgiveness is given and God never reminds us of our old sins again.
[2] Including God's messages of Peace and Love.
[3] God, saddened beyond description, moaned.
[4] God shouted very loudly like to someone who was far and would not hear Him unless He shouted.
[5] I felt so moved I wasn't anymore myself. Jesus was trying to sustain me.

YOUR ERRORS ARE BEING REPEATED

December 2nd, 1987

Garabandal's Message is authentic and should be diffused and honoured. Sanctify Garabandal. Can you not see or understand that your errors are being repeated? You are repeating your errors of Fatima. O creation, when will you believe in Me? 'Ie emphanises itan.'[1] ♥
My God to hear and feel You in such sadness is terrible.
Vassula, comfort Me.
Oh come Lord, I want to comfort You. I wish every soul knew so that they comfort You Lord and so You will be comforted by many.
If they love Me they do. ♥ *Come, I will remind you that I, Jesus, will stand in the midst, between Cain and My Abel. Cain will face Me this time, instead of his brother. If he raises his hand to strike, he will have to strike Me. He will be stripped and will find himself naked facing Me his God.* ♥ *My Abel, My well-beloved Abel[2]. Thou shalt live this time, your blood which is My Blood will not be shed* ♥ *and My fragrance will embellish My garden; this very garden that My Abel's blood was shed in.* ♥ *Come flower, I will remind you of My Presence; stay alert.* ♥ ♥

TREMENDOUS REPARATIONS HAVE TO BE DONE
I WILL CONFIRM MY APPARITIONS OF GARABANDAL

December 4th, 1987

Jesus? ♥

I Am. Daughter, I want My words to be clear. I do not blame those who persecuted the apparitions; I only want them to realize and admit their errors and to come forward to Me for repentance. I will forgive them; pardoning their sin. Daughter, many will persecute My Message again, denying that it is I, Jesus, for fear of admitting their fault; for this is beyond their wisdom again child[3].
Maybe they do not mean to deny it is You, maybe in their subconscious they believe

---

[1]Greek: The apparitions were.
[2]God said this in such a tender way that only He can speak that way. No one else.
[3]It was beyond their wisdom then to really understand and believe Jesus was the Son of God among them, as it is beyond some to believe that this Divine Work descends from God.

they probably do <u>not</u> mean to, not on purpose, for I'm sure if they realized, they <u>would</u> praise You! Only they do not understand.

♥ *How I love your reasoning - why cover them?*

Because they do not <u>know</u> and if they <u>do</u> not know and understand...
♥ *I am listening.* ♥

Then, if I dare ask You. I ask for their forgiveness and Your Mercy on them.
But child, they will be your persecutors, inflicting on your soul suffering -they will be your scourges.

Even so, if they do not understand, then they don't mean it, they do not know what they are doing, because they are weak, You can with Your Divine Love help them <u>understand</u> it <u>is</u> You. My God do not let Your Divine Hand s|rike them, for in striking them many innocent souls might be punished too.
Vassula, My creation has degenerated; tremendous reparations have to be done. I want My creation to realize where they are heading to. I want My sacerdotal souls to draw from Me and embue My lambs with love <u>and knowledge</u>. Right now, they[1] live in total darkness.

Yes, Jesus, but enlighten the ecclesiastical authorities. <u>Even</u> if this "unorthodox" way of being with You is beyond their understanding, open their eyes and ears Lord that they may understand!
I will only give wisdom to mere children and not to the learned. ♥
But then Lord, their chances are slim, they're gone!

Gone they will be, unless they come to Me as children. Vassula, I will stretch your endurance in suffering, for you will be scourged[2]. Let Me free and do not interfere with My Works.

Lord will You forgive them, and overlook their weaknesses? (I still dared to interfere.)
I will not bear to see them hurt you child.

I do not know what to tell You, but can I ask You to overlook their weakness?
Flower, I do not want to see you trampled by them. I would not bear to have them crush you.

But do not strike them, <u>teach</u> them Lord.

---

[1]God's creation.
[2]Scourged: symbolic for suffering in the soul.

They will have to open their ears then. Vassula, you know what is awaiting you; you have seen My Cross. Remember, that although your trials will be hard, I never leave your side. ♥ *Near Me I have your Holy Mother, listen to Her words:* ♥

Daughter, beloved, sanctify Garabandal; I have appeared in Garabandal giving My Message. My Message was not properly diffused; many sacerdotals have denied My apparitions, thus refusing Us a place in their heart, but I have not forgotten My beloved children. There were times where they themselves doubted and, falling into confusion, denied My apparitions; this was given as a similitude. It is to show My children[1] how and what a confusion reigns in the Church of today. I have promised that I will confirm My apparitions of Garabandal. The hours are fleeing and My Messages were not diffused properly - neither has My Holiness been honoured. ♥

My God, it sounds so urgent like it should be diffused today at this hour. I depend on You to open our[2] path, we are willing to diffuse Your messages but give us the strength and courage and possibilities to accomplish Your desires. Amen.
♥ *Will I abandon you now My Vassula?*
No Lord, we need Your strength to continue.
You will receive sufficient strength to accomplish what you have been designated in accomplishing. ♥

THIS IS THE WAY I FORGIVE

December 6th, 1987

Write, Vassula. I, the Lord, wish you to honour My Stations of the Cross. Introduce the light. First, honouring My Mother, offering Her a candle; then I wish to see your knees bend in all of My Stations, honouring Me by holding at My Stations a light. ♥

♥ Lord, You have laid out Your plans already, I beg You to open the path for us to honour You Lord.

---

[1]The world.
[2]Father James, David and myself.

♥ *I will, lean on Me and I will carry you. Vassula, when this is accomplished you will be reminded by Me that soon the second event will be coming; I shall remind you not to seek anymore your comfort.*

My God, are You talking for all of us?
♥ *No, I am talking to you Vassula, look into My Face.* ♥ ♥ ♥ *I will remind you that this event will be the beginning where you will feel My powerful Hand on you.* ♥ *My divine instructions will flow in you: you are to be pliant, willing to serve Me, loyal, honouring Me. I will use you; you will be used fully, even to be My target. You are My tablet little one.* ♥ *I intend to bring back to Peter My sheep.* ♥

Lord, My God, I have been with You as a 'tablet' now for over a year. You have used me every day, and I love You because I'm nearer to You in this way. You can use me I will be loyal and Your slave too.
Vassula how I love you. Will you kiss My feet after doing the Stations of the Cross?
Yes Lord, I will.

Come, do not forget My Presence, you seem to neglect Me these days. ♥
My God, give me the strength to manage everything. I want to please You as You know but my capacity is limited, will You forgive me?
♥ *O Vassula how I love you, I forgive you.* ♥ *Write what you saw.* ♥

Jesus in telling me that I neglect Him looked sad and grave. Then I asked Him to forgive me and in no time His Divine Face lit with a bright smile showing me His dimples and opening His arms wide open so that I fall in them. Then He told me the rest, forgiving me.

Forgiveness will always be given without the slightest hesitation, and I made you discern Me fully so that you are able to tell My children the way I forgive. ♥ ♥
Come, we, us.
(Jesus in saying this made a movement with His index like a teacher warning me.)

December 7th, 1987

I lead you in an "unorthodox way", but I am God and I will choose any way. The hours are fleeing, the time is near. ♥ *I will lead you like I wish Vassula.* ♥ ♥

FIVE OF MY WOUNDS ARE WIDE OPEN
WHY HAVE THEY NEGLECTED MY GARDEN?

December 8th, 1987

(After reflecting what can await me I started to panic[1]. I was very disturbed.) My God can't I love You like any other normal being in a normal way. Can't You Beloved God guide me in a normal way instead of this way. Oh God, I feel so much responsible with all this, it's a torture to know that in spite of all the graces You are bestowing on me I remain wretched and so sinful, wicked, why Lord, why do You keep me? I can't face You anymore; I'm not worthy of You, let me go in my corner, do not have me so near You...

Why? Why?

My God, no, I'll follow You and love You like the others in the normal way. *Beloved, I love you!*[2]

Oh Jesus I am only wounding you, let me go I'll rest in my misery, but I won't stop honouring You and loving You[3].

Wait! ♥

Lord, all this[4], is beyond my understanding, it's beyond me!

No, this is not beyond your understanding, not anymore; beloved[5], five of My Wounds are <u>wide</u> open; I am bleeding profusely; I am suffering - your God is suffering. Will you not glorify My Body? Five of My Wounds are open for you to see what sorrow My creation is giving Me. I love you all - in spite of your wickedness, in spite of your failures, in spite of your doubts, in spite of your iniquity, in spite of your denials, in spite of your scepticism and in spite of your insincerity[6] towards My Body. ♥ Do you not yet understand? Why have you

---

[1]Moment of extreme weakness.

[2]I saw Jesus hurt by my words. I felt awful.

[3]I wanted to go to bed and sleep my awfulness away.

[4]The supernatural approach, and all events to come.

[5]Jesus 'exploded', showing me how He suffers...

[6]The word 'insincerity' is used here as the following: it is about Unity. Usually when the ecclesiastical authorities meet to be able to find a solution, what happens is this; the one who comes to face the other one, hopes the one he is facing will be the one who'll give in 'something.' In the end it ends up by none giving much. This was given to me by the Lord yesterday night.

*closed your hearts <u>forever</u> towards Me?   Why have most of you abandoned Me?
Why have My followers changed path?   Why have they neglected My garden?   Why
have they not watered My flowers?   Why?   Where are My lambs Peter?   Would
you help Me find them and unite them?   ♥   Come, I will help you find them.   I
will bring food for them and nourish them.   No Peter, you will find nothing in this
wasteland; there is nothing left. The little that was left is now dry and wasted, for
as far as the eye can see, there is nothing but wastelands; but I, the Lord, will
fetch from My stores My Bread and I shall fill your storages with My produce.   I
will feed My lambs.   ♥   I will irrigate this wilderness.   Trust Me beloved; trust Me
and I will unite you all again.   ♥   Together, My Vassula, flower, I will not see you
trampled by them; I mean to use you for the Glory of My Body. I, God, love you.
♥ ♥ ♥*

MY CHILDREN ARE HUNGRY

December 11th, 1987

Jesus?
I Am.
Jesus why is it that the media believes easier than the priest Theologists etc...
Remember when You asked me the question Lord?
I remember.
When they read the 1st book they want to read the rest. Then most of them always
after the 1st book, pray. Even some who never prayed in their life, it's wonderful!
*Vassula, My children are hungry.   When they see My Bread, they seize It to
appease their hunger.   If they want more, they come to Me[1] for more and I offer
them all I have.   ♥*

But Lord, it happened once or twice that those that read it, after their conversion,
because of their joy wanted to share it with a priest thinking they would also feel
happy, but to their disappointment the priest shows no interest, in fact, they
discourage them.

*Vassula, these are the ones that wound Me and pierce Me through and through.
♥   I suffer intolerably to see My own reject Me; they have nothing to offer My
lambs.   ♥*

Still Lord, in spite of the negative attitude and lack of enthusiasm from the priests
it does not discourage them, because they <u>do</u> find peace in finding You again. But

---

[1] In prayer to Him.

they feel bitter that it should be this way, especially when they find out that they know nothing about the apparitions, they wonder why the Church do not speak more of this. One of them commented that these things are kept low and only in 'their' circles.

Yes Vassula, My sacerdotals are repressing My Works of today. ♥ *Daughter, I have said and say again that they hold the key of knowledge and neither do they go in themselves nor do they let anyone in who wants to! They are blocking The Way,* ♥ *with scepticism, doubts and hypocrisy. I have lost them as children; their widsom has blinded them, losing their way to Me.* ♥ *Beloved, sacrifice all[1] that you have now and pray with Me.*
Yes, Jesus.

> *"Father, let peace be what they will discuss; forgive their insincerity. Father do not stand aside if they will persecute Me; come, come to my defence. Be at my side, enlighten them and teach them, let them see their errors. You are Righteous, shine on them instead to praise you and say, 'Great is our God Most High who wants to see His children at Peace, praise the Lord who descends to unite us; praise the Lord who comes to announce His Works of today.' Amen."*

♥ *Come beloved, meet Me later on, remember now My Presence, I love you daughter.* ♥ ♥

Yes Lord, I will remember.

I FOUND YOU IN WRETCHEDNESS

December 11th, 1987

♥ *Flower never doubt that it is I, Jesus, your Saviour. Behold and look back where I found you[2]. I found you in wretchedness where so many of My children still are!*
Come Vassula, do you see this crucifix?

---

[1]To leave my housework which is very behind, my son's meal, my husband who is quite sick with perhaps hepatitis. (I was getting ready to go.)
[2]A quick image of the past.

(Jesus meant the crucifix, a wooden one out of olive wood from Jerusalem. It was now near me on the notebook. It is the one that does not leave my hand during the night.)

♥ *Yes My Vassula, take it in your hand now, lift it to My Lips; yes, lift it.* ♥
(Jesus so sweetly kissed it when I lifted it to His Divine Lips.)
Will you kiss it too? ♥ (I did.) *Lift it now; I blessed it. I love you all beloved ones.* ♥ ♥

MY CHURCH IS REIGNING IN CONFUSION
DO NOT JUDGE

December 12th, 1987

My God! It must have reached Your ears Lord of what I am now accused. It is the 3rd time that the Jehovah Witnesses accuse me. Twice before they said that this is the work of the devil, (without reading it.) This time that I am a descendant of the fallen angels of the past! Lord why? Why are Christians so different from one another, what went wrong?

Never has My Church been in such a confusion. Remember the words of your Holy Mother, 'the confusion of Garabandal was given as a similitude , to show how My Church of today is confused - it is reigning in confusion'.

My God I'm so sad, so sad Lord.

You grieve because you feel Me, you are getting to know Me; how I rejoice when you recognize what I suffer from. ♥ *Vassula I love them[1] too, but they have been so misled by Satan; he blinded them, leading them when blinded into another path and in their delusion they not only disregard My Mother as Queen of Heaven, but disregard My Peter too and the authority I Myself have given him upon all My lambs. They persecute My flowers as well and condemn all My Heavenly Works of today. Satan has conditioned them to abuse anything, (they do not understand), stopping them from perceiving the Truth. Their doctrine has infiltrated among you beloved ones and they are the ones I have warned you about[2]. They like to call My graces given to My chidren, 'Satan's handiwork' - rejecting your Holy Mother.*

---

[1]The Jehovah Witnesses.
[2]The false religions.

Vassula it should never be up to you to accuse them, learn to say instead: "let the Lord be Judge and correct them." Beloved one, the End of Times is at hand. I have said that I will give you signs and warnings. I suffer to watch them[1] sneer at My foundation[2] and follow nothing but their own doctrine. They are those Cains and dangerous to My Abels - an obstacle to the ones who want to grow in My House; a misleading torch of misguidings to My people; a hardened rock, they have rebelled against My foundation. How will I offer them a kingdom on earth, when inside them they have accepted doctrines which come from Cain? I will resurrect you and your soul will come to Me, into My Arms. You are but a passing shadow on earth, a mere speck of dust which will be washed away with the first drops of rain. Have I, Myself, not said these words that there are many rooms in My Father's House and that I will prepare you one, so that where I am you may be too? It is to Me, in My House that souls will come![3] Vassula, they are scheming against My foundation. They are trying to uproot My domain. I love you. ♥ Do not weep flower[4]. I will place on you My thorned crown ♥ ... and the lance is among them. They are plotting against My House, reunion after reunion to put an end to Peter!

Oh God no! No Lord!

Gather together beloved ones, reinforce My Church. Unite beloved ones, come together again - be one.
Flower, stay alert. ♥ Love will redeem you My beloved ones. Come flower, open, open and let Me pour into you My sap which will rise you -strengthening you to enable you to tread on My foes. Remember, I, the Lord Jesus Christ, am before you. ♥ ♥ ♥

(This message alarmed me very much.) I long for them to listen, it's urgent!

---

[1]Jehovah's Witnesses.

[2]Church in Rome.

[3]The Jehovah Witnesses, confused, believe that one can live forever in paradise on earth and that our soul dies once we die.

[4]When I feel Jesus sad, I become sad too.

LOVE WILL UNMASK SATAN

December 19th, 1987

I am love. ♥ ♥ ♥ *Tell them, tell them Vassula that sincerity will conquer evil; humility will debilitate the devil; love will unmask satan.*

♥ *Fatima's shrine cries out for amendments!* *Come back to Me creation! Come and recognize Me creation; come and pray to Me - sin no more.* *Believe in Me and do not doubt; come and repent; come and receive Me.* *Be holy Vassula.* *O Vassula bring back My creation to Me!* *Altar!* *I will pour into you My Flame, inflaming you with love; you are to seek My interests -glorifying Me.* *Do not be like the others who seek their glory and grandeurs.* ♥

Lord I said and say again, I will only seek Your interests Lord and what brings more glory to You, take my will, I have surrendered.

♥ *Yes Vassula, satisfy My thirst.* ♥ *Treat Me as King, honour Me your God, never rebel against Me.* *Sanctify your body to honour My Presence in you. Beloved, come, all that is hidden will soon come to light.* *My Divine Hand will lift the cover and I shall reveal to you all that has been hidden.* *Garabandal is the sequel of Fatima* ♥ ♥ ♥ *and My reign will reign forever for I Am.* *I am the Alpha and the Omega.* ♥ *How I love you creation!* *My own, My children. Beloved come, come in My open arms, come back to your Father![1] I love you. Listen Vassula, when you will be among My Abels I will be among you; I will whisper in your ear My instructions.* ♥ *I have Bread to offer - My Bread is Holy. I have used only a small amount of yeast from My storages and it was enough to leaven all the dough - this dough that is My New Bread now.* *So get rid of your old yeast - it has lost it's effect beloved ones - come and use My new yeast.* *Renew yourselves altogether into a new batch of bread; attractive to the palate which will draw My lambs, feeding them.* *Honour My Bread which I sanctified; My Bread of Sincerity, Truth and Love.* ♥ *Let Me rejoice beloved.* *Let My lambs taste My New Bread; distribute It among them and let the hungered masses eat - allow them to feel full.* ♥ *I will not be convinced by the arguments of the wise; they will not impress Me so do not let them impress you either daughter.* *My intention is to bring back My scattered lambs - bring them back to Love.* ♥ ♥

Lord, may Your Will be done. Amen.
Sign My Name.

 IXθΥΣ

---

[1]God's voice was full of love. He was almost begging.

MY CHURCH, I WILL CLEAN

December 21st, 1987

My God, Righteous One, even in my nothingness and in this great incapacity I have, my desires have been implanted in me by You. They are Your desires. I desire that Your Name be glorified and that Your lambs assembled again recognizing You, recognizing our Heavenly Mother, that Her Reign will last forever, overcoming Evil. I seek only <u>Your</u> interests. ♥

Yes Vassula, seek My interests only, be real, not just a facade of holiness like some are; I the Lord know them. No matter how hard they try to appear like Abel, they do not deceive Me, wearing a mask will not help conceal their identity. I tell you truly, I will point out to you this time those deceivers; I will come to them in an unexpected hour. Why have in My House Cains, seeking only their interests and not Mine? I will, with Heavenly Strength, unmask them, I will unveil that which is hidden. Do not fear beloved; My Church I will clean; I will sweep away all those that obstruct The Way to Divine Love and from entering into My Sacred Heart. ♥ You see Vassula, My Cup tastes bitter. The world is offending Me beloved, My sacerdotal souls are blocking the Way, obstructing It with enormous blocks, blocking the passage for My lambs to come to Me; their hands are empty, they have nothing to offer My lambs - not anymore. Vassula, blessed of My Soul, follow Me. I will guide you, do not despair. Will I ever abandon you now?
No, Lord, I'm clinging on You Beloved Father.
Here, take My Hand - never leave It. ♥ Accept all that comes from Me. ♥ ♥ ♥

HONOUR THE QUEEN OF HEAVEN

December 22nd, 1987

Vassula, the time has come to unite My Church. Come together again beloved, come and rebuild these ancient ruins; rebuild My old foundation, a foundation established by My own Hand. Honour My Mother as I, who am The Word, and above all honour her. ♥ Would I then not desire you, who are dust and ashes, recognize Her as Queen of Heaven - honouring Her? My grief of today is to see how little My creation know of Her importance. Most of My devouted ones who are under the name Luther and who have isolated themselves entirely, must return to Peter.

Lord! They will be shocked!

Vassula I will bend their knee to venerate My Mother, it is I, the Lord who is speaking, I will bend them! and when they do, I will let My Light shine on them and rise them. I will strengthen your stems, and you shall be like an irrigated garden, like a spring of water whose waters never run dry. I will rebuild My Foundation.

Come beloved, be pliant and soft like now so that I engrave on you My Words, come never forget My Holy Presence. ♥
Yes Lord. ♥ ♥ ♥

I HAVE COME TO UNITE YOU ALL

December 23rd, 1987

My God, the Protestants will be shocked! (I couldn't get over it.)

♥ *Vassula I have been waiting years for them to change, now leave Me free to write down My desires.* ♥

But they will be shocked!

♥ *Listen, can one hear Me only when it is convenient for him, then shut his ears when what I say does not suit him?*

They'll reject outright then the whole thing! Since they will not be able to select parts - they'll claim it's not You.
If they do, they would be then disowning Me as their God. ♥
Lord, may I dare say that this is hard on them? They will not feel they are disowning You, they are after all loving You and they do worship You Lord.
Vassula, I have come to unite you all. Would any disciple of Mine deny My appeal.

No; not if they are sincere Lord.

By this statement you gave Me, hangs all what there is to say; "If they are sincere", then they will listen. ♥ ♥ ♥ *I come to shine on you all and enlighten you to be able to unite you, but to My great sorrow there will be those who would prefer darkness to the Light because their deeds are evil. They would refuse to come under My Light for fear of exposing their deeds, but My devoted ones and those that sincerely acknowledge My Works and follow Me will come under My Light exposing without fear their deeds, because they will show that what they do is done in Me their God.*

I have said that if you make My Word your home, you will indeed be My disciples; you will learn the Truth and the Truth will make you free. And now, I say to you this: if you give credit to My Word of today, you will indeed be My disciples, you will learn <u>sincerity</u> in the Truth and the Truth will free you and enable you to unite in Love and Glorify Me. ♥ *I come to you all, with My Heart in My Hand, offering It to you, but in spite of My appeal many would reject Me, disowning Me as God because their hearts have hardened, if they loved Me they would listen to My appeal. If they refuse to listen, it is because I have lost them as children; their wisdom has blinded them, but I tell you truly, the sheep that belong to Me will recognize My Voice; those that would not recognize My Voice are no sheep of Mine because they do not believe in My Omnipotency. Do you know why My lambs are scattered and My Body maimed? Do you know why disharmony reigns in My Church? It is because they have been walking at night without any light to guide them.* ♥ <u>*Seek Me who am the Light*</u> *and I will guide you. Cast away your hypocrisy and your obduracy, be meek and humble, open your hearts and let My sap fill you up. I am your Good Shepherd who loves you.* ♥ ♥ ♥ *Vassula talk to me, treat Me as you Holy Companion.* ♥

I will My God, I love You Lord. I wish to glorify Your Name Lord.
♥ *Beloved, My Name I have glorified and I will glorify It again. My reign will be forever,* ♥ *come, courage daughter, I am with you.* ♥ ♥

YOUR HOLY MOTHER IS THE ARC OF ALLIANCE OF MY WORD

December 26th, 1987

On the night between 25th and 26th December Jesus was emphasizing the importance of Garabandal's message with Fatima's message, and that they are the same in one. It was like I did not rest that night, the message was ringing in my ears repeatedly. Jesus emphasizing His Presence.

<u>*Fatima's Shrine cries out for the sanctification of Garabandal.*</u> ♥ *I have taught you to read the Signs of the Times - are you looking for those Signs? How can you not tell the Signs? Have you no perception? Why are your minds closed? Why do you refuse to see? Why do you refuse to hear? Have you forgotten My Words? Why repeat your mistakes? Beloved why all these venomous attacks on the Message of Garabandal given by your Holy Mother who is the Arc of Alliance of My word to you? The opposition My sacerdotals have towards Garabandal's apparitions and message are all manoeuvres from Satan. <u>Once again, as in Fatima, he is trying to prevent My Message from becoming universal.</u> Have you not understood that Satan, knowing the value of My Salvation Plan given through*

My Mother at Garabandal to mere children, is trying once again to erase My Plan thus leaving you all in darkness to fall? Satan is <u>re-doubling</u> his efforts more than ever now to triumph over your Holy Mother; manoeuvring My Church to deny these apparitions which are the sequel of Fatima's Message of Salvation. Satan in his fury is trying to prevent you to feed upon Me. My Salvation Plan is clear - I come to redeem My children. <u>Recognize My Voice</u> - do not be surprised at the kind of instruments I use. ♥ I have chosen a nothing, knowing nothing, a blank canvas so that it is clear that the Works covering this sheet[1] will be from Me, and that you believe that it is I Jesus, Beloved Son of God, who speaks this time. ♥ Among you is My Kingdom. My Abels I know <u>you</u> will recognize Me again. O beloved how I love you! ♥ I will unveil to you My Plan soon. ♥

Lord, if the sacerdotals do not recognize Your Voice, then Lord, what happens?

Vassula, it is not up to you to ask; dust and ashes[2]. Let Me guide you as I wish, leave these things for Me. ♥

Yes Lord.

♥ O come, do not misunderstand Me. I am Love, learn to accept. ♥ Come us, we? I will replenish your lamp.

Yes Lord, I thank You for taking care of me with Love.

♥ Let us go. ♥

- SINCERITY WILL ABOLISH EVIL -
- FOR MY SAKE WILL YOU LEARN THE ROSARY? -

December 28th, 1987

If I forget myself and dare utter a judgement upon anybody, or think that I understand more than others, in no time God reminds me whom He has, to give His Message: just by a penetrating look of His Eyes upon me He places me, fixing me where I should be, just by His three words, dust and ashes, He reminds me that I'm nothing, and the least of all His creation. No, some will not understand this, they would think that because He has chosen me to take His Word, I am worthy, but

---

[1]Canvas sheet.
[2]With these two words God reminded me that I am the least of all His creatures.

don't you understand by choosing me who is the least of all, God shows what fathomless Mercy He has on us, that even to the least He gives, and wouldn't He then give a LOT more to those who are so much more worthy in His Eyes than I, if they ask with belief. Have you not noticed His patience with me, instead of striking me, His Love flows with more abundance. How could His creation reject Him? But I shouldn't talk since I belonged in this group before. Now I'm saying, "cherish your God as much as you cherish your breath, for without your breath you will die. God gave us life by breathing in us, His Breath is our life; God is our Breath, God is our Life."

O Vassula! My Abel shall live this time; ♥ *sincerity will abolish evil[1]. Blessed are those who stimulate My Word. Blessed are My sheep who recognize My Voice. Blessed are those who will feed My lambs again. Blessed are the simple in heart. Blessed are those who will pray the Rosary on the day of Garabandal's sanctification[2] and whose knees are bent and hail My Mother. Blessed are those who will carry My Cross of Peace and Love, uniting.* ♥ *Blessed are My sheep who return to Peter. Blessed are those who humble themselves and follow My example. Blessed are those who follow My command and love one another as I love you. Blessed are those who bear witness of Me and are not scandalized in Me.* ♥ *Beloved of My Soul, have faith and trust Me, I am your Heavenly Teacher; never doubt of My Word. Come, you are weak - come lean on Me who is your Strength.*

Yes, Lord, I need You, I cannot do without You ever.

♥ *Love Me, desire Me, be My heaven. Ah Vassula, now you sacrifice for Me but soon I will have you near Me.*

I'm longing for the day.

Stay near Me. I have got something to ask you. ♥

Yes, Lord?

For My sake Vassula, for My sake will you learn the Rosary? Hail My Mother at all times - will you do this for Me Vassula?

Lord I've never been taught.

---

[1] 'Sincerity will abolish evil', might as well be translated as: 'Abel will conquer Cain.'
[2] God foretells this event.

Do I not know this Vassula, this is why I come to teach you and all those who never heard the Rosary. ♥

Yes Lord, I am willing to learn Lord - help me learn.

This is what I desire to hear from all of you who do not know, the same words: "Yes Lord, I am willing to learn Lord, help Me learn." I will teach you all, you who are willing to learn. Come daughter rest in Me, I shall not forsake you ever. ♥

Jesus must have felt how I long for Him and suffer out here, it's the wave again of 'desiring God' wanting to be His sacrifice, detached totally. I seem to waver; staying here I might 'feed' some of His lambs who never refuse of His New Bread, pleasing Him for the return of a few souls, being with Him will be marvellous too for me. What is best?

EVERY FLOWER NEEDS LIGHT

December 31st, 1987

My God! I am praying that the Churches will believe in Your Message!
Vassula, to believe in Me is a grace given by Me[1]. Hear Me Vassula. You will speak from My Mouth and I will speak of the tribulations that My Church will undergo. This revelation is My Voice. Recognize the Signs of the Times; accept My Message; taste My Message; <u>eat My Message</u>; woe for the unfaithful. ♥ ♥

Later on:

Little one, do you love Me?

I adore You endlessly Lord.

Yes Vassula, love Me; make up for your past, make up for those who do not love Me. Flower, every flower needs light knowing what effect It has on it's petals. Daughter, will you repent?
(I repented my past sins and the actual ones - God was preparing me to receive Him in Holy Communion.)

Flower, I forgive you. Resent all these things from the depths of your soul. Resent impurity for this was the vice of Sodom. ♥ ♥

---

[1]One has to pray to ask God for this grace.

I AM YOUR STRENGTH

January 1st, 1988

My God.

♥ *I Am. Take My Hand; take now My other Hand and walk!*
(This was once before said, giving me the same vision of God taking both of my hands when I was supposed to go forward into a new theme.)

Walk! Walk beloved, advance! Do not fear. ♥ *I have nominated you My bearer, not only for one part of My creation, but the entire.* ♥ *Vassula, wait and you shall see, I have not yet come close enough to the middle of My Message. I can work without you Vassula, but I delight sharing My Works with you flower. I am God and I Suffice by Myself.* ♥ *Every new step you take, I bless, so advance beloved, advance with Me - go forward.* ♥

Lord Almighty, help me to advance since it's Your Will. I can't alone, as usual I will ask You to carry me, I'm incapable of whatsoever!

♥ *Vassula I will help you, for I am your Strength.* ♥

JESUS MEANS SAVIOUR

January 2nd, 1988

Lord Almighty, preserve us from falling into error, because it can be devastating, wiping out entire nations, only by commiting one error, like in the Beginning.

♥ *Yes Vassula fear this Plague, for Error is a contaminating plague.* ♥

My God, I have read somewhere that the reason the Church might be reluctant accepting private revelations is because all that there is to know is already in the Bible, so they do not accept any new revelation. I mean not new as theme, but new, apart from the Bible. Going out of this brings fear upon them, thinking the new or private revelation might lead them astray...

Vassula when I see My creation bound to fall into My enemy's pit, would I just sit and watch them fall without wanting to rush to their rescue? Do you remember when I healed a dropsical man on a Sabbath? What had I asked the Pharisees?

Lord, I have to check the Bible.

Fetch then, My Word. ♥ (I did, and checked - Luke: 14. v. 16) ♥ *Yes daughter, I asked, "is it against the Law to cure a man on the Sabbath or not? " - they did not answer. I said, "Which of you here, if his son falls into a well, or ox, will not pull him out on a Sabbath day without hesitation?" and to this day they could find no answer[1]. Today I am asking those who refuse this revelation this question:* ♥ *"is it against My Law in your era to save My creation from falling by My Providential Works of today?" Vassula, I am Jesus and Jesus means Saviour.* ♥ ♥ ♥*

Tell them Lord, remind them then Lord of all this.

Beloved, they have crowned My Heart with a wreath of thorns. My Sacred Heart is bleeding.

Jesus, do they realize this?

♥ *I will silently step at their door and without knocking enter their house and show them My Sacred Heart; those who would prove sincere will realize their Error.* ♥ ♥ *Come daughter. Us, we?*

Yes Lord, united.

I WILL RESURRECT RUSSIA
AS I HAVE RESURRECTED LAZARUS

January 4th, 1988

Vassula![2] O Vassula! I have one of My beloved daughters lying dead! A sister of yours!

Who's lying dead Lord?

My well-beloved daughter Russia. ♥ *Come! Come and I will show her to you. Look!*

---

[1]This is a symbolic sentence for our era.
[2]God's tone sounded urgent, mixed up with sorrow.

God having taken me at an edge of a desert, He pointed with His index and arm outstretched far out under the scorching sun. His daughter and sister of mine lying dead, her body emancipated from tyranny, lying dead in the middle of wilderness, she seemed abandoned even at her death, she had died all alone with no one near her to console her. When I saw this painful sight I burst into tears out of pity. I cried bitterly when I saw her.

O do not weep; I will resurrect her Vassula; I will resurrect her for My Glory; I will revive her as I have revived Lazarus. ♥
O God, You give me so much pain...

This pain you feel is nothing compared to Mine. ♥ *I love her Vassula - have pity on her too. I will not leave her lying dead and exposed in the scorching winds. Vassula, love your sister; pity her, go to her, love her. Love her, for she is so unloved by everyone!* ♥ *Vassula, she had abandoned Me and turned against Me. She turned against Me when she grew and when it was her time for love, I called her to share My cloak but instead she walked away. Feeling mature, she believed she would be able to feed herself on her own. She turned her back to Me and walked away, like an unfaithful wife she fled.* ♥ *My beloved do you know what it is like loosing a daughter? My Heart lacerated, I wept.* ♥ *Like this was not enough, she proudly and without the slightest remorse declared openly war against Me, her Father and against all the martyr Saints! She believed in Me no more, she stopped worshipping Me, hoping in Me and loving Me!* ♥ *She seemed to have forgotten the love we once shared. I had given her sons and daughters but in her fury she slaughtered My children and handed them over to Satan as one offers a burnt offering. Then, as though this was not enough, she turned to Satan and made a pact with him to be faithful to him and worship him instead if he would offer her all what <u>she</u> desired.* ♥ *Satan agreed with the condition to leave him free.* ♥ *Satan then disconnected her entirely from Me; she let him cut our bonds - he made her trust him. Treacherous as he is, he led My daughter into marshlands first, where she would <u>have</u> to lean on him, from fear of sinking into quicksands. She asked him to allow her to lean <u>entirely</u> on him. Vassula, like Jerusalem at one time who fled from My House, My House of Holiness, to become a daughter of no morals, offering her children one after the other as a sacrifice, Russia, My daughter, thought it wise to do the same. She took My Holy Presents and offered them to Satan who turned them all into weapons.* ♥ *Satan blinded her with his glory and in her blindness removed her from the marshlands and placed her into the wilderness to thirst and die.* ♥ *I saw her walking naked and struggling in her own blood; I called her, but she would not listen[1]. I called her again, but she would not hear My call; instead she provoked Me, calling her younger sisters to support her morals - if they refused she forced them with her sword. Have I not*

---

[1]At Fatima.

said, "he who will rise the sword shall perish by the sword"? I rationed her bread so that she would need My Bread but she preferred to starve rather than eat from Me. ♥ Exhausted and hungered, she sent her younger sisters to continue her wicked works in secret because her vanity was inspired by <u>Vanity himself who is Satan</u>. Her lands bore not enough to feed her; she became as one would say, "a dependant" on My enemy. ♥

Daughter, do no more now, I will continue tomorrow with this Message. Come, let Me bless you daughter. ♥ Feed on Me. We, us?
Yes Lord.

SATAN OFFERED RUSSIA THE DEADLY FRUIT

January 5th, 1988

When I read again the passage of Russia lying dead, I cried bitter tears again.
♥ Do not weep Vassula, I told you, I will resurrect her.
I love her Lord, I feel pity for her Lord. I love her.
♥ Love her as I love her, she is My daughter too - your sister.
Lord, will You go over to her and resurrect her? Will she return to You, O Lord?
♥ I will go to her and resurrect her and carry her to My House. I want all My children to love her - we will all surround her with Love. ♥
My God, did You say that You will continue Your Message of the 4th?

♥ I will continue. When Russia became a dependant of Satan because her land was barren, he offered her the deadly fruit he keeps in store for those I love. It kills in stages - the more one eats of it the more one needs it. It's deadly - killing slowly. ♥ He nourished her with his fruit and killed her; she died with this fruit still clenched in her hand. ♥ Vassula trust Me, I will resurrect her. ♥ Daughter be still, do not worry, leave Me free and I will accomplish My Works.

Lord, I'm worrying, because You asked me to bless Your children of Garabandal and let them know about Your Message[1]. Then allow the authorities to read how to start uniting; then ask them to sanctify Garabandal and make them understand that Garabandal is indeed the sequel of Fatima, then of how offended St Mary is for not honouring her apparitions in Garabandal, repeating the <u>error</u> of Fatima. Oh, Lord, then now Russia, and You keep hinting to me all along that it is to Your servant

---

[1] This is now fulfilled - 1991.

John-Paul that I must hand over this message and I have done NOTHING of all this! Your Word is on me and it is heavy to bear...

Say it now.

I was going to say... all alone[1]. Forgive me.

♥ *Vassula, I am bearing It with you; I am sharing My Cross with you; Vassula I forgive you.* ♥ *I have also given you witnesses who bear the same Cross - you keep forgetting that it is I, the Lord, who will do all these things and not you. You are to love Me and feed from Me.* ♥ *Come, I will whisper in your ear My Love. Rejoice daughter for the Time has come.* ♥ *Love Me as I love you. I am Jesus Christ Beloved Son of God and Saviour.* ♥ *Draw My sign.* ⊂× ΙΧθΥΣ

I AM SPIRIT

January 6th, 1988

Jesus, is Your own glorified Body touched by suffering? Aren't You and our Holy Mother beyond personal suffering now in heaven?[2]

♥ *Vassula, I have no physical body - I am Spirit. Since I am Spirit I have no physical pain but My Soul suffers intolerably, as well as the Soul of your Holy Mother, when We see our children heading straight into Satan's traps.*

But Lord, do You also suffer when I suffer, e.g., if one accuses me unjustly, would You suffer?

♥ *If you are accused wrongly, I suffer for both - for the accuser and the accused. Injustice comes from Satan and since it comes from him it signifies that the accuser has been manupilated by Satan; as for the accused My Heart pains for the victim.* ♥ *I aver My words in the Holy Bible. I am glorified but because I am united to you, I feel all what you feel.* ♥
Thank you Lord. ♥

---

[1] I felt ashamed but as He is The Truth He asked me to finish my sentence.
[2] This is Father James' question.

SECLUSION WILL DEVELOP YOU MYSTICALLY

January 8th, 1988

♥ ♥ My desire and longing for God was immense.

♥ *Honour Me by desiring Me. Vassula, seclusion will develop you mystically, drawing you closer to Me - it will enable you beloved to penetrate still deeper into My Wounds. In the second event I will supply you with all what your soul lacks, intensifying My Works upon you.* ♥ *Do not doubt, I will lift you to Me, I have chosen for you this road which leads all My beloved souls into My Passion, turning them into vivid images of Myself.* ♥ *Come now I will remind you of My Presence since you are unable; yes?*

I was going to say, I know I'm incapable and I've got nothing good, I fully depend on You Lord to give me out of Your boundless Mercy all what I lack.

♥ *Yes understand that all the good is from Me. Come, us, we?*
Yes, Lord.

SCIENCE

January 9th, 1988

♥ ♥ Lord, I've read about some scientists who do not believe in the stigmats. They say that these people are psychotic and it's imposed by mental suggestion, clearly admitting that they do not believe in miracles. They say that all can be given a natural explanation, but without giving one either.

♥ *Science will remain a wise man's favourite weapon against Me. I have among you souls who refuse to ever hear,* ♥ *these are most pitied in My Eyes, pray for those lost souls.* ♥

I GIVE MY WORD FREELY

January 10th, 1988

My God, it is so good to hear now and then of souls receiving Your Works as I do, differently but in a supernatural form. Already, I've heard of two ladies, who get almost the same messages as I receive, but they're in trance, like St John! Given by the Holy Spirit.

♥   *I give My Word freely - I always will.   Please Me beloved and pray with Me, My Soul has favoured you.*   ♥   *Come, let us pray[1].*

> ♥ *"Father, Righteous One, I am willing to do Your Holy Will. I am willing to proceed and please Your Heart, ever so Sensitive, replacing the thorns by my love, thorns that are still in You. Amen."*♥

Come, I will teach you another prayer - most effective for repairing.   ♥   *Say after Me these words:*

> *"I believe, I adore, I hope and I love You.   Amen."*   ♥

But Lord this was said by Your angel of Peace at Fatima.

♥   *I have taught My angels to pray in this manner, now I am teaching My children to pray and make reparations in this manner.*   ♥
Yes Lord, You are indeed my Hope. You are my Happiness, my Smile. In You I believe, You are my Joy of life, You are my life, I adore You and worship You for ever. Amen.

Come now to Me[2]. Yes, make the sign of My Cross. (I got up and went to Him, knelt and made my cross.)   ♥   *Yes, in Trinity.*   ♥   *I love you daughter.*   ♥   *Us, we ?*

Yes Lord.

Tell them, tell them.   ♥

By this the Lord means that in doing the sign of the cross, I've made it like the orthodoxy taught me.   The thumb, index and middle finger together; a Trinity, confirming the Holy Trinity.

---

[1]Jesus approached and posed His Hand on my shoulder.
[2]Jesus meant by the portrait of the Holy Shroud.

TO UNITE, YOU MUST ALL BEND

January 12th, 1988

Lord, my God.

♥ *Vassula, let Me help you. Do you remember the vision of the three rods? Upright and stiff?*

Yes I do Lord, I remember.

Well then, to be able to unite all three have to bend; I never said that merely two should bend. Vassula do you realize that I your God am in full scheme for uniting you?

Earlier today I had in mind to ask You of yesterday's message. The way one crosses oneself.

I know daughter, that is why I want you to understand what I mean by, "to unite, you must all bend." I love you all and out of My boundless Mercy, I come to help you to unite.

Vassula, seek Me in simplicity of heart. I am a God of love; I am meek and humble; remember My ways. To be able to unite, <u>cast away your selfish intentions</u>, recognize My Voice; you on whom I have entrusted you with My Word and have entrusted you with thousands of souls; you whom I proclaimed lords of My flock. Why seek your interests and not Mine? My lambs are scattered, scattered... ♥ ♥
I am flower, descending through you to gather the nations; assembling My sacerdotals and renew you by My Love.

Lord and Saviour, how will they know or recognize their faults?

♥ *The way to recognize their faults is to <u>seek My Will</u>. Repent, think of My Mercy; believe in My Providential Works instead of treading upon Them; worship Me in sincerity; seek My interests and not yours.*

Lord forgive me for perhaps being unable to understand 'interests,' does interests mean this: "all that You want Lord is to collect back and together Your flock which right now is dispersed?"

Beloved, even you understood what I desire most, but this is not all what I desire. Reading this revelation again you will understand Vassula. ♥

Yes Lord.

I will remind you daughter to bless those who will persecute you. ♥ *Love is always patient and kind. Live holy. Think of My patience I have with you daughter[1]. Be My image; have faith in Me; hope and love. Come, rest in Me, soul so dear to Me. Feel My Love and honour Me your God. Us, we?*

Thank You Lord for the love You envelop me with, for the patience, Your kindness and compassion You have upon my soul, I believe, I worship, I hope and love You. Amen.

♥ *Ah beloved! My Heart swells with love to hear you say these words to Me![2]*

Oh God, how can I not love You, I live for You, I am Yours even if I am clay. All I do is out of love for You. I do not seek my interests I seek to glorify Your Name, I seek to bring back Your lambs to You, I seek to follow Your Will Lord. I love You and because of this love I have for You given and taught by You I ask You if it is Your wish to strengthen my faith and to love You without limits to enable me to continue and Glorify You. Amen.

♥ *I am going to feed you fruits from My garden. I will beloved, feed you under the eyes of your persecutors, for this is My Will.*

Thank You Lord Jesus.

♥ *Hold firmly on what I have given you and let no one take your prize away from you. Believe in Me firmly. Here, take My Hand and listen when I whisper in your ear.* ♥ ♥ ♥

PETER, WHY ARE MY DISCIPLES DISPERSED IN ENMITY?

January 13th, 1988

Lord, many blame You for being unjust, so they try to turn away from You saying: "If there is a God, if, He is unjust."

---

[1] It it was not for Love, He would have struck me long ago!
[2] God seemed so overjoyed.

♥ *Flower, to these I say, "if you die, it is because of the evil that you have commited upon yourselves; it is the fruit of your apostasy. Repent, renounce your sins, return to Me and I will forgive you." ♥ ♥ ♥ See Me as your Redeemer; your Consoler. I come to Shine in this dark world of today as a Light. My House is reigning in confusion; in debates; in self-interest; in unholiness.*

Peter! Peter! Why, why are My disciples dispersed in enmity? Hallowed by My Hand, brother of Mine, I love you from all eternity. ♥ My Sacred Heart is wounded, wounded by thorns that have been driven into It by My own, My own whom I love. ♥ I will show you My Wounded Heart; they are piercing My Sacred Heart all over again. My Blood is gushing out; they are recrucifying Me; they are not sincere. My Body aches with lack of love; My lips are parched with lack of love. ♥ I am thirsty beloved... they have forgotten My ways; they have forgotten that I am humble, meek and full of love. ♥ All I ask from you is love, <u>love one another as much as I love you</u>. Why combat in My Church? Why these disputes in My Presence? Why this hatred? Why all these venemous statements? Where is their holiness? Why are they neglecting My garden? They are dispersing My lambs more than ever and the few that remain will also vanish from the fold because they have deserted them. Peter, My Eyes have grown weary, watching them accusing one another. They have layed desolate My lands and have nothing to offer My lambs. ♥ Their ways are not acceptable to Me. I have given them love and peace; I have never taught them to judge others. ♥

Vassula, I rule with kindness. My Sacred Heart bleeds and lacerates. ♥ Why do they provoke Me? Have I not said that anyone who claims to be in My Light but hates his brother, is still in the dark? Have they quite understood what I meant by, ♥ "if you are bringing your offering to the altar and suddenly remember that your brother has something against you, leave your offering there before the altar, go and find your brother and reconcile first with him then come back with a clear heart and present your offering"? ♥; by this, I meant how one should be in harmony with each other and love each other, make peace with each other, reconcile before offering Me your gifts in My House. ♥

Child, there has never been absence of love in My Heart nor in the hearts of My first disciples. ♥

Lord, I suffer to feel You suffer. Your patience is great!

♥ *Vassula My child, risen from the dead, have faith in Me; hope and love Me. I the Lord will never forsake you. ♥*

Lord, I ask You to raise Your other children too as You have risen me.

♥ I will, but not because you have asked Me. I will raise them because this was and is My Will. ♥ Come, and do not forget My Presence. ♥ ♥ ♥ Beloved, in the end I will prevail. ♥

YOU WILL LISTEN AGAIN AND NOT UNDERSTAND

January 18th, 1988

Lord if everything comes from Your will and whatever will happen it will be because You willed it, then I do not understand why, if You want Your message accepted why do You not make those that are informed about it accept it, since You are wishing it. Why do You not enlighten them?

O daughter, beloved one, rejoice and be happy that I have converted you, healing you. ♥ My Mercy reaches from age to age for those who fear Me, but for the thorns that pierce Me the prophecy of Isaiah is once again repeated, "you will listen and listen again, but not understand, see and see again, but not perceive ♥ for the heart of this nation has grown coarse, their ears are dull of hearing and they have shut their eyes, for fear they should see with their eyes, hear with their ears, understand with their heart and be converted and be healed by Me." ♥ ♥ Daughter, I had foreseen their obduracy from all eternity; ♥ their rejection of today's providential Works have forfeited their privileges. ♥ Vassula, pray hundreds of times to attain what I seek in you most and that is, love, belief and hope. ♥

I enlighten those who prove sincere; I will not enlighten the wise because sincerity lacks in them. I, the Lord, seek the humble and lowly; the smaller you are the more My Greatness will be inclined to bend towards you and reach you to lift you; the smaller you are and insignificant, the easier it is for you to penetrate into My Sacred Heart. Vassula! Can you see?

Jesus gave me a vision of a tunnel and an <u>enormous</u> block of rock was blocking the passage. Beyond it from the very little corners that were open, I could see a strong bright light, but the block was cutting off the light from entering this tunnel.
♥ They are those that block the Path to Me and their enormity obscures the Light for all those who seek Me. For those, I the Lord say, I will not endure with your grandeurs; your haughtiness wearies Me; My Cup is full. When the time will come, I will call them one after the other to repent; woe to the unfaithful, they will have to face Me. ♥ ♥

Jesus, what I'm starting to understand is this: those who are Your real disciples lowly and humble will rejoice with Your Message but many who are unfaithful to You, will not like these Messages, in other words it's good for some and bad for others.
Yes Vassula, now you know[1].

♥ ♥ St Mary although I'm wretched, would You be my support? Encourage me, wouldn't there be one of the ecclestiastical authorities who would listen? Just one?
♥ **Vassula, daughter of Mine, Jesus loves you. I love you. Blessed one, Jesus and I will help you now. Pray to attain His favour.** ♥
Yes Mother, help me to find the right words.
♥ **I am helping you flower. I love you all;** ♥ **never doubt.**

Thank You for helping me.

Love will help you endure many trials My child. Jesus will give you His Strength. I will encourage you always; fear not[2] - I am protecting you. ♥ ♥ *Mercy, Love and Righteousness now descend among you.* ♥ *Glorify Me. My Love will save you from My justice -justice which is bound to befall upon you if My creation will not listen again. I come out of My boundless Mercy to warn you; I desire My creation to repent and recognize Me. Fatima's Shrine weeps loudly for the abuses and rejections over Garabandal. My Soul is in deep sorrow again; the same sorrow I had in Fatima. How could they doubt now, when My Spirit is in them and they in Me? My Message at Fatima's was ignored and not until it was too late did they accept My Message. I love you all. I am the Lord who speaks - never doubt. Pray for those souls who walk in the dark. O Peter[3], nominated by Me, hallowed by Me; My Eyes never left you. I have been watching you all these years. I am now at your door brother, My own; I am knocking, will you let Me in? Do not deny Me Peter, I love you. Hear Me, hear My Voice. Recognize My Voice; it is I, the Lord. Peace upon you soul, rejoice! I have come to unite My Bleeding Body; I have come to gather My lambs; I have come to irrigate My garden; I am Jesus your Saviour.* ♥ *Behold![4] Behold Peter, My Sacred Heart once again is being pierced by so many thorns; thorns that have been driven in Me by those I love! My Soul is once again Wounded, they are treading upon Our Hearts[5]. Both Our Hearts have been once again crowned with two wreaths of thorns. My side is wide open and My Blood is gushing out.* ♥ *I am at your door now; with Me I*

---

[1] Jesus said this in a sad tone.
[2] St Mary here was referring not to fear Satan who is constantly trying to discourage me.
[3] Suddenly Jesus turns to Pope John-Paul as if talking directly to him.
[4] Jesus opens His clothes to show His Heart. He wants Pope John-Paul II to see His Heart.
[5] Jesus means His and His Mother's Hearts.

*carry My hidden Plan of Salvation; it is here.♥ ♥ ♥   This revelation is My
Voice. I love you all, with all My Heart; with all My Heart, I love You. ♥*

HOW LITTLE I AM UNDERSTOOD
BY MY OWN

January 24th, 1988

*♥   Vassula, I wish to disclose My feelings to My brother James. Hear Me ♥
brother! Soul! Cast away <u>forever</u> the theory of God approaching and elevating
only souls dedicated to Me. I do not approach only devoted souls, I make no
difference; why, am I a God of predilection? My Heart pains to see how many of
you still believe that My graces are given only to devout sisters or brothers. ♥ You
see My child how ♥ little I am understood by My own? ♥*

(Jesus sadly bent His Head on one side and lifted His hand to His Heart. He stayed
in this position for sometime. He was very beautiful.)
*I have approached many who are out of My Church, yes..., wretched souls...,[1]
converting them into devout followers of Mine. I made disciples out of them; I
made saints out of them; yet, many ecclesiastical authorities overlook those works
of Mine and ignore them. They have never recognized these souls; they know not
about them. Many were rejected because of <u>their</u> predilections; the theory of "God
approaches only devout souls who wear the habit" is <u>wrong</u>. O how wrong you
are!* (Jesus from being calmly sad became distressed.) *♥ If you only knew the
number of souls I have approached without necessarily wearing the habit, or being
devout to Me, and out of these I made saints!* (Then as if Jesus' glance fell on
Father James' eyes He looked straight into his eyes, a penetrating look.) *Beloved,
have you really forgotten how you yourself scented My Presence? I had bathed you
in My fragrance blessing you! Come, you will learn. ♥*

*I have converted many souls with My Message of Peace and Love. Lost lambs
came back to Me, falling in My arms. Rejoice soul! What greater miracle than
a lost lamb who's found his Master! What greater joy for the Shepherd to find His
lost sheep again![2] Glorify Me James... Glorify My Works beloved... Disperse My
seeds. Glorify Me and bear My Cross of Peace and Love; recognize the Shepherds
call, announce My Miracles of Salvation to your brothers! To your neighbours!
Announce the good news; announce My Works! Let My Works be known; let My*

---

[1] In saying this, Jesus said it in a gentle and sad voice.
[2] Jesus' mild tenor voice was full of joy when saying these words. His Heart
seemed to explode with joy!

Miracle be known. I have come to you and replenished your lamp; I have given you My Light; do not hide this lamp under your bed, for it is of no use then. Come, rejoice brother for I have replenished your lamp that it may shine on a lampstand. Let them all see the Light and know that It comes from Me. ♥ *I have come to you soul; you recognized Me soul; you have let Me in and we shared your meal. Rejoice! Announce My Holy Works. Honour Me James by exposing My Light <u>on the roof of your house</u> so that <u>everyone may see It</u>. Let It be seen by all. When they will perceive this Light, they will assemble from far and wide; let them know how I came to you giving you this Light.* ♥ *Have My Peace.* ♥ ♥ ♥

MY MOTHER'S HEART IS UNITED
WITH MY DIVINE HEART

January 25th, 1988

♥ Jesus?

I Am.

Jesus, still to this day all this amazes me. I mean the revelation that has come, it's like a dream, and I expect to wake up to find I've only been dreaming. It's amazing!

♥ *Vassula, I am Omnipotent and Omniscient. I willed to raise you from the dead and enlighten you.* ♥ *Do you remember the vision of the "Sun"?*

Yes Lord, the round ball of light. (cf. 26.3.86).

This round Light is the same one of the one known among you as "Miracle of the Sun." This round ball of Light I let you see is the same one of Fatima. I have let you penetrate into It[1]. I allowed you to go into It. ♥ *O Vassula if you only knew the privilege I gave you! Little one you are not realizing yet, but it is because I keep your eyes veiled.* ♥

I love you my God.

I will keep you hidden in My Sacred Heart, you are precious to Me. I your God love you - never fear Me for I am Love. I am an ever so Gentle Father. Fear Me only if you rebel against Me. Ah Vassula, My mysteries are many; most of them

---

[1]Jesus speaks in metaphors, but which He made me understand their meaning.

are hidden from you. ♥ ♥ *Listen carefully now; every prophecy uttered will be fulfilled; each word written in the Scriptures will be accomplished. Vassula, I wish you to draw two Hearts;*

Yes, near each other - in fact united. Encircle them with one wreath of thorns. Yes, My Mother's Immaculate Heart is united to Mine. I desire from each one of you the devotion Her Immaculate Heart deserves. You see daughter how Our Divine Hearts are covered by thorns from men who only show Us ingratitude, sacrilege, lack of love - it is the <u>whole</u> of their sins. ♥ *Vassula, I who am the Word, love and respect Her; I desire you to approach My Mother and honour Her as I honour Her. I desire that every knee bends, honouring Her; I desire you to pray the Rosary and Hail your Holy Mother. I want you to repair your sins; asking Her to teach you.* ♥ ♥ *Be vigilant daughter. Come, I have revealed to you how My Mother's Heart is united with My Divine Heart; encircled by one wreath of thorns.* ♥ *I will remind you of My Presence. I love you.*

I love You too Jesus.

Come. ♥ *Vassula, will you pray with Me?*

Yes Lord.

> *"Father, O Abba! I offer you my will, I offer you my life, I surrender. Righteous Father if it is within Your Will make me worthy so that You may use me fully. Make me a victim of Your burning desires; do as Your Heart desires. Amen."*

Vassula, bless your oppressors, pray for them. ♥ *Come, pray to your Holy Mother, pray with Me.* (Jesus will dictate.)

> *"O Holy Mother, I will amend for the offenses being said on Your Immaculate Heart, by willing to become a victim of love for Love. Amen."*

Vassula, pray with Me to the Father. Come, together.

"Father, Beloved One, I need You to augment, My faith, My love, My hope, that I may glorify Your Holy Name again. Amen."

YOUR HOLY MOTHER WILL TEACH YOU
APOCALYPSE, CHAPTER 12

January 26th, 1988

Vassula, will you work with your Holy Mother? We are inseparable. ♥ ♥
Yes Jesus.

♥ *I love you; I am always near Her; your Holy Mother will teach you now.* ♥
Jesus was together with St Mary. He made me understand that even if I did not see Her with Him all the time, it does not mean She was not with Him. They are always together.

Daughter, I have been always with you, I am protecting you and helping you.
(There I understood, St Mary is helping me understand certain things. She is helping me on this road that God has chosen for me.)

I will be helping you till the end. ♥
(By locution St Mary made me understand that we should go over the Apocalypse, chapter 12.)

Come, I will explain. When Satan lost, he swore to pursue the rest of My children and make war to them; he swore to devour them in his raging fury because he knows that his days are numbered and because of this, he wants to drag with him as many souls as he could. Yes, he is the dragon and with his tail he tries to sweep along God's creation into destruction[1]. ♥ ♥ **Vassula, My child, as he is Vanity itself, he accuses the Almighty's works, wanting to prove to God that He has failed His creation and that Our children are made to follow his evil ways.** ♥ **Vassula, I will tell you something, something that all those who love Me will rejoice, this year will be for My glory[2].** ♥ ♥ **No, you do not quite understand: My Immaculate Heart will prevail[3]. I shall draw many souls back to Jesus.** ♥ ♥

---

[1] Our ways of having forgotten God. Many ways.
[2] I was not understanding.
[3] There I understood.

St Mary drew my attention on Her appearances.

Like I have appeared at Lourdes and at Fatima I have likewise appeared at Garabandal giving a similar Message. ♥ Garabandal is the sequel of Fatima's Message, but once again Satan has thrown dust in the eyes of the ecclesiastical authorities to confuse them. He has sown his seeds in their heart[1] so that they deny My apparitions and prevent My Message from becoming universal. Vassula, Our Hearts are bleeding, wounded by thorns which have been driven into Them. How I weep on you children, I love you. My wounded Heart lacerates to see you being swept by the dragon's tail! (St Mary was very much in pain.)

♥ Vassula, I will tell you something in your ear - listen. ♥ ♥ Yes. ♥ (St Mary whispered a secret in my ear. I sometimes think I'm dreaming and I'll wake up.)
Vassula, it is because Jesus placed a veil on your eyes, He will lift this veil at the right time. I want you daughter to trust Him, allow Him to guide you in this way. ♥ Grieve not flower, I am always with you - remember how I appeared outside My Church at Turin?

Yes! (St Mary appeared as an enormous statue to my cousin so that She indicates where Her Church was to us and to make us understand that She was calling us in.)

♥ Yes, I appeared to call you, I wanted you to come in My Church beloved child; I appear to call My children in various places and to many. If you only knew how I love you all, I want to embrace you all and draw you all near My Heart. ♥ ♥

(It was just a thought that passed through my mind, a sad thought, because of the size and quantity of these messages it could be a reason why the ecclesiastical authorities doubt. Doubts, doubts, doubts, scepticism, scepticism and scepticism...)

Child why do you forget how Jesus had it while on earth in flesh? He was persecuted, ridiculed and disbelieved by the Pharisees. Today daughter, they[2] disbelieve in many of God's Heavenly Works. Your era daughter has fallen as low as Sodom was. Jesus warned you that your oppressors will by many but I am shielding you from the worst that could have come. ♥ ♥ Come Vassula, do not forget the event of God's Holiest Place - I am telling you this to remind you that God has placed you in His Sacred Heart. ♥ He has allowed you to

---

[1] I understood 'among them.'
[2] Many ecclesiastical authorities.

penetrate into His Light; yes, 'the Sun.'[1] You have seen God's most Holy Place. ♥

St Mary, I had not realized then that this 'Ball of Light" enormous as it was is the same one of Fatima! (These passages are in metaphors but that I understand and I cannot yet reveal them.)

You did not know then. Love lifted you and placed you in His Heart - this He will do to the rest of Our children. We are calling Our children; God will forgive their sins; He will teach them to repent and repair; He will teach them His ways; He will feed them with Integrity and they will be Converted. Come, honour Me. Vassula treat Me like your Holy Mother - you are My child.

Yes Holy Mother, I have now a Holy Family. I love you. (I worried for tomorrow.)

♥ Do not worry I will whisper in your ear My words. I am everybody's Mother. Come. (I felt Her Heart and our Holy Mother is wounded as much as Jesus' is.)

♥ Yes, wounded I am for the repeated error the ecclesiastical authorities are doing by rejecting My Message of Garabandal. Garabandal is the amplification of Fatima's Message. ♥ Vassula, rest now - I will call you tomorrow.

Yes, St Mary, I bless You.
♥ Daughter come to Me when you wish. ♥ ♥

OBEDIENCE

January 29th, 1988

Last evening I vividly dreamed my death. In which manner I will die. While I was dying Jesus supported me from collapsing. I was standing, wavering. He made me place my chin on His shoulder, I felt His hair on my right cheek. His hair was like on the picture of the Holy Shroud, like He had gone through tyranny. He was helping me by whispering consoling words mingled with instructions of how to 'ease up' and let my soul leave my body as He was receiving it. At times He sounded like a doctor. All what I saw was not alarming and I never felt any anguish.

---

[1] I call it the Sun.

♥ *We are together, child.* (Jesus and St Mary.) *My flower when your time will come I who am your Reaper will pluck you and transplant you in My garden of delights. Vassula what you saw was only a reflection of the reality. Come now and repent beloved. I am listening.* (I repented asking for forgiveness of my sins.)[1] *All is forgiven, I will teach you integrity and how to live holy. Sin no more.* ♥

Yes Vassula, (St Mary) **love God with all your soul, with all your mind and strength. He loves you boundlessly. Yes child, never forget how He delivered you from evil. He never rests; He goes with His Heart in His hand from door to door, hoping, longing for that soul to hear Him. Alas, so few hear Him... Vassula, do you know how I work?**
No, not very much...

I pray, I pray for the salvation of souls. I shield you from evil - <u>I am your Shield</u>. Like any mother who would shield her child from being harmed I shield you from Satan and from his impious nets. I pray for souls to return to Jesus; I gather them, blessing them. True, they do not see Me, but many do feel Me.

I wish I could give something to You that will make You really happy, something that's in my capacity.
♥ **Ah Vassula, seek to please Me in this way:** ♥ **Obey,** ♥ **obey God's Will.**
Poss?[2]
Do not seek to understand why God has come to you with His Message and not to others. Accept. Obey Him child when He asks from you something. Have you been praying those prayers He asked you to pray before writing?[3] ♥
No.
♥ **I will help you Vassula.**
St Mary. He is angry with me now, disappointed too, isn't He? (I hated myself, I never wanted to disappoint Him.)

♥ **Vassula, no, He is not angry because He knows you are ineffably weak and wretched. Do not despair, Jesus has been teaching you and you please Him but please Him furthermore in obeying His demands. Remember Jesus will <u>never ever</u> ask from you something that could harm you; Jesus is for your salvation; Jesus means Saviour.** ♥ ♥
I bless You, St Mary.
♥ **I will defend you always Vassula. Come to Me again - I love you daughter.**
♥

---

[1] I want to add that Jesus asks me often to repent to Him, but this does <u>not</u> exclude my <u>regular</u> confessions to my confessor which He asks from all of us.
[2] Greek: How?
[3] Three prayers given to me by Father James.

OUR DIVINE HEARTS REND AND LACERATE

January 30th, 1988

♥ Vassula, I weep for My children who have gone astray. ♥ ♥ (St Mary does weep, She sounds so very sad.) **Now Love and Mercy descended among you to feed you once more with His Bread of Integrity and Holiness. Love descends to give you Hope and Peace. I love you all Vassula.** ♥ ♥ (Pause) **Will you come to Me in My Church of Turin? Visit Me often there. Will you offer Me your vows of fidelity?** ♥ **Daughter, betrothed of My Son, will you offer Me your vows?**

Holy Mother, I wish to please Your Immaculate Heart, I will come to You at Turin but in my ignorance I do not know what it implies, 'vows of fidelity'. I would offer You anything You wish. Please allow me to know what I will be offering You so that I do not break them in my ignorance.

Please My Son furthermore by offering Him <u>all your love</u> and devotion for My Immaculate Heart. Please My Son furthermore by offering Him souls so that He redeems them. Please Me by offering Me your vows of fidelity - this you will do by following Jesus. Be His reflection. ♥ **Be faithful to Him. I will pray for you - I will intercede for you. Betrothed of Jesus, both Our Hearts are encircled with a wreath of thorns. My Message at Garabandal was ignored. Let My beloved son, John-Paul II, come to Me and feel My Immaculate Heart and Jesus' Divine Heart. Let him feel how Our Hearts rend and lacerate. They are but one big wound. They have torn the Heart of their God and they have torn My Immaculate Heart of a Mother. I want you to be praying for all those who will reject you.** ♥ **My child how you will suffer...**

I am willing to suffer for God's Glory.

Do not forget that Jesus and I are with you. We will console you flower. ♥ **Now I am telling you this - you are <u>not</u> to forward <u>you yourself</u> Jesus' Message to any ecclesiastical authority, Jesus has given you witnesses who are to witness for you.** ♥
O St Mary, so it was wrong what we have done?
Yes, Vassula. Let your friends read Jesus' Messages, converting them, but do not seek to go yourself and introduce yourself to any ecclesiastical authority[1] - you are to leave this work for your witnesses. Jesus enlightened them to understand how He works; I will be with them always.

---

[1] I should not go myself, spontaneously to present myself, unless they ask me and invite me to come.

Jesus:

Vassula, which is the biggest miracle to authentify My Message?
Conversion?
♥ ♥   *Yes, My Vassula, My priest, now you know too. My greatest miracle
daughter is* <u>*conversion*</u>*. ♥   In the end daughter Our Hearts will prevail. ♥*
Daughter?

Yes, St Mary.

Come to Me in My Church of Turin. Will you offer Me your vows then?
I will St Mary.
**I rejoice seeing you. Tell Ismini too; take your friends along with you too - I will
bless them all. ♥**

HAVE HIM AS FIRST
REPAY EVIL WITH LOVE

January 31st 1988

♥ Vassula, We are both near you.
(I had, just before, while sitting on the sofa, felt Jesus' robe brush my right arm.
He placed His hand on my shoulder. I felt His Presence vividly again. I got up to
write and I felt St Mary sitting near me.)

**The vow I seek from you is fidelity. Be faithful to Jesus; have Him as First. Be
willing to do His Will. ♥**

St Mary I don't seem to realize yet, I know I don't realize fully all this.

**My child God has veiled your eyes. ♥   Accept the way He is working in you.
Trust Him, Vassula. I am waiting for you in My Church[1]. All those who will
enter My House I will bless. Yes, I will bless all those who will come to Me. ♥
♥   Vassula, do not get discouraged when trials come, keep praying, come to
Me, <u>bless those who will persecute you, pray for your oppressors, repay evil
with love</u> - in the end My Immaculate Heart will prevail. ♥**

---

[1]At Turin.

At Fatima I had made a grandiose Miracle so that everybody believes - you call it 'Miracle of the Sun.' Do you know flower that God allowed your spirit to enter It?[1] You have entered His Abode. Vassula, how little you realize the favour God has given you!

Yes, St Mary, I never realize fully, but if this is God's Will I accept things as they are.

Yes, never seek why, accept gracefully all that God gives you. ♥ Obey God's demands with grace - by keeping your eyes veiled He keeps your souls from becoming elated by all the graces He is pouring on you. You have been allowed to enter in His Holiest of Places where millions of seraphs encircle His Throne worshipping Him incessantly; only His Holiest Angels are allowed to enter God's Holy Abode - now you know daughter the great favour He has given you.

St Mary forgive me for not quite realizing,

I will intercede for you. ♥ ♥

Thank You Holy Mother for helping me.

Here is Jesus.

I will be present too[2]. I will bless all those who come. ♥ Come now, feel Me, rejoice Me, smile at Me, speak up and let Me hear your words. Seek Me near My Mother, your Holy Mother. We are together. I love you.

RUSSIA WILL BE THE SYMBOL OF GOD'S GLORY

February 1st, 1988

♥ ♥ ♥ Vassula I have so many times asked for the consecration of My daughter Russia. I have implored her consecration. ♥ Today[3] Vassula is the day she had seen the Light - she will be commemorating her millenary

---

[1] This is again given in metaphors. I understood but I cannot yet reveal.
[2] Jesus made me understand, at Turin. In St Mary's House.
[3] This year.

anniversary. ♥ Vassula, your sister[1] is dead but the Lord is near her now and will resurrect her and Love will love the Unloved and she will cry up to Him: "<u>You are My God and Saviour!</u>" With this cry the demons shall take flight; fearing demons will flee <u>for this nation will become one</u> and God's most devout servant. Healed and resurrected by God's Strength, her stature of holiness will attract all her neighbours by her devotions to the Almighty. ♥ Russia will be the symbol of God's Glory of God's Mercy and Love. Her hymns and chants that are so sweet in Our ears, with her graceful movements, will rise up to heaven like incense. ♥ Love will resurrect her as He resurrected her a thousand years ago[2]. ♥ ♥

♥ ♥ I am the Lord - the Resurrection. When I will resurrect Russia, she will restore My gifts, she will embellish My House again with love and I will unite her again to Me. I will offer her My Bread and My Wine and she will not refuse My Food. She will accept My offer and she will eat My Bread and drink My Wine, renewing herself, praising Me. ♥ I will clothe her with My Glory, I will adorn her majestically, I will irrigate her from My Own Springs, I will replenish her stores, My Eyes are upon her. Ah Vassula! Just wait and see![3] Daughter, how I long to see Peter, My Peter, visit your sister...

Encourage him Lord to go, Lord open his path if this is Your Will.

Come, I am working in many hearts Vassula. Pray to attain My Father's favour. I will restore My Church. Woe to the unfaithful! ♥ Vassula, I wish to remind you that it is I who stunts the tall trees and make the low ones grow. ♥ Come now, we, yes, us, yes[4]. Yes Vassula, never doubt, I have taught you to see Us with the eyes of your soul. I am your Teacher. I love you, never doubt. ♥ ♥ ♥

February 2nd, 1988

Peace be with you flower. ♥ It is I, Jesus, your Saviour. ♥ Love has found you in wretchedness among wretchedness. Beloved! I the Lord have layed My Divine Hands on you and embellished you... to look at Me glorifies Me.
Jesus I hate myself for being wretched.

---

[1]Russia.

[2]Here ends St Mary's Message.

[3]Jesus sounded that He has a lot more hidden that will be uncovered. He sounded happy, excited.

[4]I suddenly saw Him sitting on the armchair and saw His beautiful face while He was indicating with His hand 'we'; the 'yes' was indicating to me that I saw Him correctly. The other 'yes' was I saw St Mary near Jesus and was smiling.

What are you saying Vassula! You seem to forget how I am united to you. Beware of what you say, remember 'us, we?'
O Jesus your patience is Great...
♥ *I love you. Come listen to My Mother[1].* ♥

St Mary:

How I love you Vassula. ♥ (Greek) **To Spiti Mou se zitai, i portes ine orthanikhtes yia sena pethi Mou[2].** ♥

MAKE A HEAVEN IN YOUR HEART FOR ME

February 3rd, 1988

Vassula do you know how much more I love you when you come to Me in this way? You come to Me wretched and on your knees. You expose your heart to Me; your tears My child, your tears of love and longing for Me are a balm soothing My Wounds. O daughter, My myrrh, My remnant, how I love you! Your sighs betrothed sound like a million words of love to Me. Hallowed by My Hand, flower of Mine, do not despair. Abel will not be crushed this time... Abel shall live. ♥ *Yes! Make a heaven in your heart for Me, I am weary and need to rest.* ♥ *Fragrance Me flower, soothe Me with your love; little one I will clothe you in beauty, I will pardon your sins and your garments of old shall be no more. You will be embellished flower; I will renew you entirely. I love you. My grace is upon you.* ♥ *Here, take My Hand - I am guiding you.* ♥ ♥ ♥

St Mary:

"O Vassula, min amfivalis, Se zitao, tha zissis mono yia to Christo, to Potiri Tou ine ksekhilo me tis amarties tou cosmou, afto ine to telefteo Tou Minima, ean to arnithown thafisso to Kheri Tou na pessi apano tous, then tha boresso alo na to kratisso, ekhi varini. Avrio Vassula, tha kano to thavma Mou, i ora plissazi."[3]

---

[1] St Mary.
[2] The translation of this passage in Greek is: My House needs you - it's doors are wide open for you, My child.
[3] Translation of Greek text: O Vassula, do not doubt. I am calling you. You shall live only for Christ. His Cup is brimming over with the sins of the world. This Message is His Last Warning; if they will refuse it, I shall leave His Hand fall on them. I would not be able anymore to hold it - it has become heavy. Vassula, I shall do My Miracle soon - the time is getting close.

♥ ♥ God's Kingdom is among you all. ♥ Keep in mind the End of Times; keep in mind how His Message will heal His Body and unite It; ♥ keep in mind how Jesus' Plan of Salvation will redeem millions of souls. His Message of Peace and Love will draw Our children back to Love. Jesus converts them as soon as they taste His Bread - it is the fruit of Love. ♥ Love will restore you all; Love and Mercy will untangle you from Satan's impious nets. Come beloved, do God's Will. I am always near you[1]. ♥

EVERY BEAT OF MY HEART IS A CALL FOR YOU

February 4th, 1988

Jesus is so distinct this morning. Sometimes I'm so afraid all this might be wrong, that maybe I don't see Him but think I see Him, yet when it's like this He somehow convinces me it is all exact to the point. Is it really You Jesus?

♥ *I Am. You saw Me like I taught you. I will show you My Heart.* ♥ *Write what you see and feel in My Presence.* ♥

I feel that these moments I'm in God's Presence lifted. I do not want this moment to ever leave me, I need nothing more, everything around me becomes so meaningless, unimportant. God's Presence fills up every empty corner. It fills you up and one feels full; complete. I see Him, garbed in the way we know Jesus. My ears could almost hear physically the shuffle of his tunic, His step; now He is standing on my left side while I am knelt on my small table where in front of me is His picture of the Holy Shroud and an icon of St Mary with Jesus as a child. Jesus is two feet away from me, His Holy Face is beauty in Itself. He asked me to look at Him, He showed me His Heart, all His Breast was lit, shining, glowing, out of Love.

---

[1]That same evening, if the devil was allowed to put physical injuries on me he would have killed me. He tormented my soul again, hating me.

♥ *All is correct, everything you discern is correct. O Vassula, My Vassula, how I love you. Dearest soul you may come to Me when you wish - you have seen My Heart. When you open our meetings of the day, open them with those prayers My son James has given you. It is I who showed him what to give you.* ♥

(I have been praying these prayers for some time in the beginning, but later on I stopped. St Mary reminded me to continue. Since the reminder I do it regularly, Jesus explains here of how to open the day of writing by these three prayers, because I was not sure whether I had to do it every time before I write, which could be three or four times a day; sometimes for one sentence, or if He meant once a day as opening.)

♥ *Vassula, assemble My children and read the Message I had dictated to you some time ago[1]. I want you to read It out to them; I love them and among them all I Am.*

My creation, you are Mine, you are My seed. Beloved, I am your Saviour - will you return to Me? Will you fall into My arms? I will forgive your sins. Come and eat My Bread, come and taste My Wine. If you repent I will forgive you. Listen to My Heart beats, every beat is a call for a soul. ♥ *Vassula will you read to them My previous Message and this one?*

Yes Lord, I will. ♥ ♥

MY FRUIT IS YOUR WITNESS

February 4th, 1988

After reading David's letter plus a newspaper cutting where it says why Churches and people get very suspicious of 'revelations' I understood why it is so difficult for any clergyman to acccept revelations, since there are many frauds and fake ones. Yet I cannot forget how sceptical they were even with Fatima's miracle. They are sceptical with Garabandal today and tomorrow they will accept it, maybe too late. Scepticism is <u>too strong</u>. Father I have[2]

Say it,

---

[1]Message dictated by Jesus on 14.10.86. That message was meant for the meeting of 21.2.88.
[2]I was hesitating.

my fears of the Pope's rejection. Why should he believe me, why should anyone believe me? If only it had happened to them! <u>Only</u> then...

♥ *Vassula, I gave you My Bread and I fed you fruit from My garden, I gave you to eat from My Own Hand. Oh beloved child! Who converted you - was it not Me? Who taught you to love Me -was it not Me? Who sought for you and found you dead among the dead and bent to lift you to resurrect you - was it not Me? Who carried you with Pity to My House to heal and nurse you back to health - was it not Me? Who was daily teaching you My Ways - was it not Me? And now who is converting My children? Is it not I? I am your Saviour Vassula, you are part of Me now. You are unable to survive alone, you need Me. As a branch will not bear fruit on it's own but must be attached to the Tree, so are you with Me. Your fruit comes from Me. My fruit feeds many. My Fruit is your witness. Those that doubt will be able to tell you by your fruit: "a sound tree produces good fruit." When My hungered children taste My Fruit and return to me, repenting with tears in their eyes, I feel happy, how happy I become! I wrench them from the devil's grip. Vassula, have patience, I have said that My Word is like a rivulet flowing, then from a rivulet it will start rushing into a river, broadening then it will be gushing and My Word will turn into a vast ocean, an Ocean of Love immersing your hearts with love and Love will be among you as Love. ♥ I have warned you Vassula, that you will be rejected by many[1] - learn to accept. I[2] was rebuffed by many and their obduracy made Me weep! Come, you will learn. ♥ I love you - I will support you. I will convert many more. ♥ Us? We? Feel My Presence - you delight Me when you do. ♥ ♥*

Yes Lord. I thank You for Your support Lord.

I THE LORD HAVE CROWNED MY MOTHER AS QUEEN OF HEAVEN

February 10th, 1988

♥ *Vassula hear me and write.* ♥
Yes Lord.

I am the Word, the Alpha and the Omega. I am the Elixir of Life - the Source of Love and from Me comes all into being. ♥ *I have descended on earth in flesh to*

---

[1]See 23.10.87 and other various times too.
[2]Jesus was talking to me as one would talk to a child, smiling at the same time trying to persuade me and to show me how difficult He had it too.

redeem you. ♥ *Daughter there is in My Church so much confusion about My Words given from My Cross to John and My Mother. Let Me remind you all above everything else how I the Lord have crowned My Mother as Queen of Heaven.*

Lord.

♥ *Yes Vassula?*

You have come introducing Yourself as God, then said, Your Holy Mother twice, You have, Lord, just declared that St Mary is Your Mother, therefore confirming the title of: 'Mother of God.' You have said it Lord! A title rejected by Protestants.

♥ How I rejoice daughter - I have not been teaching you in vain. I am pleased that you have understood My Works; endeavour to keep up your learning; pray for this attainment; I will give you the perception if you ask for it, Vassula. Hear Me again, I want My Words to be known. ♥ I, who am God grew in My Mother's Womb - She nourished your God creation! I fed from Her. ♥ I who am the Word love Her and honour Her. ♥ Vassula, in the very beginning I had given you an account of My Crucifixion - remember when I have said, "My gaze fell on My Mother, I looked upon Her and Our Hearts spoke[1]. I am giving you My beloved children to be Your children too. You are to be their Mother."

Yes Lord, but our brothers the Protestants say that what You uttered from the Cross was meant literally to John. Your Mother becoming a 'widow' being taken care by John when You were not around. They also say that St Mary <u>is not</u> 'God's Mother.

Yet My Vassula Scripture never lies. Scripture says those words, 'Mother of my Lord,' - Elizabeth spoke these words who was <u>inspired by the Holy Spirit</u>. Write: "Of all women You are the most Blessed and Blessed is the Fruit of Your Womb. Why should I be honoured with a visit from <u>the Mother of My Lord</u>?" The words I have said from My Cross are much deeper than many of you seem to understand.

Honour My Mother who is your Holy Mother too. ♥

Rest now in My Heart; please Me by remembering My Presence. Honour Me My Vassula.

Yes, My God. ♥ ♥ ♥

---

[1]A tacit understanding; an interior agreement between Jesus and St Mary.

MY HEART IS AN ABYSS OF LOVE AND FORGIVENESS

February 19th, 1988 - Rhodes

Father?

♥ *I Am.*

Thank You for letting me meet so many souls, thank You for opening the way, thank You for leading me, help them my God to hear You so that they may be healed.

Vassula lean on Me; My Hand in your hand ♥ ♥ *we will proceed.* ♥ ♥ *O era of wretchedness how far have you gone! You have gone as far as to believe that you are able to walk without Me, you have gone as far as to believe you are worthy, you have allowed Satan to feed you his vanity; wretched beyond words, sinful and blind, do not allow yourselves to rest, be alert, do not sleep for the time is near.* ♥ *Grow in My Spirit -approach Me with confidence and open your hearts to receive Me.* ♥ *Many of you pray but your prayers do not reach Me; learn how to pray, let Me feel you. Many prayers are spilled on earth, never reaching Me.*

You mean lip service Lord?

Yes, I mean lip service. ♥ *I offered you My Word to learn and now I offer you My Message to remind you of My Ways. Come and learn - I will replace your wickedness by love. Accept My Ways, My Ways of Virtue. Era of Unfaithfulness, why have you forgotten My Divine Ways? Return to Me your Saviour -* I *have not forsaken you and inspite of all your sins I love you. My Heart is an Abyss of Love - an Abyss of Forgiveness.* ♥ ♥

SACRIFICE, MEDITATE AND FAST

February 20th, 1988

♥ *Love is near you. Daughter encounter Me in the beginning of My tribulations - My time is drawing near. I seek in you a sacrifice - meditate and fast. Vassula learn from F - her ways please Me. Learn how to honour My tribulations then come and behold your Saviour on the Cross; satisfy Me by meditating, fasting. Live in My Wounds. Reveal to all the time of My Passion; reveal to them the correct hour of My Crucifixion. Let there be peace among you.* ♥

The Lord last year gave me the correct date: as the 'Orthodox' follow It, with the Orthodox calender.

♥   *Let there be Peace now among you.* ♥   *Now you all know.* ♥   *Call Me Vassula more often. Remember My Presence - satisfy Me. I love you.* ♥ ♥ ♥

I love You Lord. ♥

- Rhodes -

God allowed me to visit Rhodes again. Those who knew of the messages invited me to meet others. People listened, understood and praised the Lord for His Mercy. Many got private messages from the Lord. The group got bigger per day, many returning to God praising Him. I spent my days meeting people, giving the messages, converting and healing was abundant. Those who wished to follow the program of visiting Churches and Chapels did so with me, we went even out of town to Chapels on the hills.

Pater Yanni announced the revelation in his Church, to all attending, that was on February 24th, at St Anaryiroi, in the afternoon on the same day I was invited to St Nicola Church and Pater Vassili allowed me and the whole group who knew and followed the revelation (around 12 ladies their husbands who also follow were at work then) to announce it in his Church and one of the ladies read one of God's messages from book 8. May God work in them now.

I WILL EMBELLISH MY GARDEN

February 24th, 1988 - Rhodes

Praise the Lord!

Beloved every step you take I bless. ♥

Thank you Father, Glory be to God, may Your Holy Name be Glorified again. Yes Lord.

I will help you all. I will restore My House. My children I will draw back to Love; I will teach them My Ways of Virtue since they have forgotten them. I will enlighten My teachers and I will knock at every door, giving them hope, faith and love. I will embellish My Garden. ♥ *See?*

I thank You Lord and Saviour for all Your Love and Mercy.

Flower, you still have a long way to go; I the Lord will guide you. Be willing; come to Me and repent often; receive Me. Pray for My Kingdom to come and allow Me to use you; remain nothing so that I may be Everything. ♥ I bless you all beloved ones. ♥ ♥ ♥ ♥

MY KINGDOM IS AT YOUR VERY DOORS

February 26th, 1988

Glory be to God, Praise the Lord. ♥ (These words were uttered by St Michael when I prayed to him, a prayer to him.)

♥ *Vassula, it is I, the Lord.*
Era! O era of Wretchedness the hour has come, the hour of your redemption is at hand. My Ecclessia will revive, for Justice, Love and Peace will be among you. My Kingdom is at your very doors!

♥ ♥ ♥

I LOVE YOU IN SPITE OF YOUR NOTHINGNESS

March 1st, 1988

♥ *I Am.* (I saw Jesus standing near me.) *Every time you see Me smile at Me -yes flower remain near your Saviour. Come, let us pray to the Father:*

> *"Behold Father what You have in Your sight - You have Wretchedness; forgive me Father, for I am not worthy to have been given all those graces; I merit nothing for I am Nothing; allow this Nothing to lean on You in Your fathomless Goodness. I love You Beloved Father inspite of my wretchedness and nothingness; I need Your Strength to be able and work and fulfill all that must be fulfilled with Your Grace. Amen."*

♥ *Ah Vassula seek all My Virtues; follow them and grow in them. I the Lord love you in spite of your nothingness.* ♥ *Lean on Me in all times, I will support you fully - trust Me and allow Me to guide you blindly till the end. I will at times place My Cross on your shoulders to bear; I and you, you and I. I will rest in you and you in Me. I Am All-Faithful and will never abandon you ever! Please Me more by devoting your soul entirely for My Works - you must keep true to your vow, your vow of fidelity, yes! O how I sought from you these words, I longed to hear from you these words.*

Lord help me to keep my vow, I do not trust myself!

Do not fear, I will always remind you since I know of your ineffable weakness; you are frail but I will annihilate your weakness by My Strength. Remember My Presence, we, us at all times for ever and ever. Love, hope and have faith. I, the Lord Jesus Christ, will never abandon you. ♥ ♥ ♥

RESTORE MY HOUSE!

March 2nd, 1988

I recited the three prayers.

♥ *Praise the Lord! Glory be to God!* (This was St Michael.)

Jesus?

♥ *Love is here: glorify My Name, revive My Church, restore My House, embellish My garden! Cease to do evil. Ecclesia will revive and Peace will be among you all.* ♥

Vassula, I want you perfect... be innocent; I love children because of their innocence - they have no malice. Come, come and forgive all those who denied you; let their sin be like waters which have passed away. Flower, I will embellish your soul to disarm the stonehearted. Give! Give! Give to them - replace evil by love. Be My reflection!

O Peter, My Peter![1] Lead, beloved of My Soul, My flock back into Integrity! Peter? Look at Me; look beloved into My Face; honour Me your Lord. ♥ *Love and loyalty now meet; Righteousness and Peace is at your very doors now. I rescue all those who cling on Me - I am your Refuge. Look around you Peter; have you not seen? Have you not noticed? My Eyes have grown weary watching the Cains slaughter My Abels,* ♥ *for I have given them ears but they refuse to*

---

[1]Peter is symbolic to the recent Pope.

hear; I have given them eyes but they refuse to see; their hearts have grown coarse - they seek their glory and not Mine. O Peter how weary I am... Love is missing. ♥ *Glorify Me Peter! Glorify Me beloved.*

Jesus spoke to Peter full of love; our Lord sounded so sad and weary, talking to Peter He sounded as if He knew He could rely on him.

I WILL WATER MY ORCHARD

March 3rd, 1988

♥ *Vassula embellish My Church; enter into My Domain barefooted; carry with you My Message; do not look left or right - walk with Me.* ♥ *Ecclesia will revive and into your Father's House you will assemble them, blessing them and I will deliver them from evil and I, the Most High, will be among you and you will speak from My Mouth. Approach your God all you who desire Me and take your fill of My Fruit. Come all those who love Me and follow My Ways; come and have your fill. Eat My Fruit and you will hunger for more. Come all those who are thirsty; drink Me and you will thirst for more. Whoever follows My Virtues will never feel ashamed; whoever acts as I desire will glorify Me.* ♥ *Ah Vassula will I ever abandon you. Listen again and I am going to embellish My garden. I will water My orchard; I will irrigate My flower beds and make discipline shine out.* ♥ *Every word will be written by Me; I the Lord initiated you in the knowledge of My mysteries for My interests and for My Glory.*

Beloved Father I love You limitlessly, I do!

♥ *Come, remember, we, us...* ♥ ♥ ♥

I VEILED YOUR EYES

March 7th, 1988

I looked standing in front of all the messages. Suddenly I was struck by it's quantity and the work inside those pages. Pages which I could have never done alone, in such a short time, a strange feeling came inside me, a feeling like a shock! It was like I started to realize everything deeper. I feel very shaken, Jesus, have we really worked together?

Vassula, YES, WE HAVE WORKED TOGETHER![1] *Will you kiss Me now?*

(I got up all shaken, stumbled towards the Holy Shroud portrait and kissed Jesus.)

See? See how you feel when I lift just a little bit the veil I placed on your eyes? Come, never doubt of My Providential Works; they are all for restoring My House and assembling My lambs; they are for watering My flower beds. Come, I the Lord will remind you always My Presence. ♥ ♥ *Vassula, we, us?* ♥

Yes Lord, we, us.
♥ *Come.* ♥ ♥

I WILL UNITE MY LAMBS

March 8th, 1988

Peter! I am at your very doors now. Glorify My Body; I will unite My lambs, even those which are not of this fold. I am calling and they will recognize the Shepherd's Voice. The hours are fleeing and My Return is now very near. Love will come back to you as Love and My Kingdom on earth will be as it is in Heaven, for Justice, Love and Peace will pour from Heaven upon you creation!

Vassula, since you know now how much you depend on Me your God, will you be praying more? I love your simple words. Say to Me, "I love You Lord, I breathe for You, I smile for You, I hope in You, I believe in You, You are My joy, My bounce, My peace." Yes, tell them to Me your Holy Companion. Share your days with Me.

How I wish My children to realize My close Presence. I am by their side ever so present; anywhere, anytime - if they only realized this, they would fall less, they would sin less. Tell them I wish them to be intimate with Me. ♥ *Come, I love you - love your Teacher too.* ♥ ♥ *Out of My Mouth you will speak, crowning your God with wreaths of Love and Peace, replacing My thorned Crown and I the Lord will pour from My Celestial Hall on My creation, Integrity, Love and Peace.* ♥ *Little child receive from your God peace. I led you My Vassula, I formed you and now you are to proceed with Me, your hand clasped into My Hand, into My Bleeding Body follow Me and remember, neither look left nor right - walk straight to achieve your task. Do not fear, I will embellish your soul to enable you to cast*

---

[1]Shocked, I was shaking, weeping.

out and disarm My foes. I, the Lord, am among you all - at your very doors I Am! I have with Me three Crowns, a Crown of Peace, a Crown of Love and a Crown of Justice.

DO NOT REMOVE NOR KICK MY BRICKS
WHICH REPAIR MY HOUSE

March 9th, 1988

♥ ♥ ♥ Lord, have You heard? Pater Vassili has changed his mind. Now he says that all this is from the devil, he also says that You only go to souls with a mature faith in You and not to the unworthy.

♥ My child here is one more who has to learn to believe in My Infinite Mercy and My Infinite Wealth. ♥ Write My message for him: ♥ ♥ Why are you treading on My flower? Have I not given you eyes to see and ears to hear? Do you not perceive? I am the Lord Jesus Christ, Beloved Son of God. It is I, it is I who stunt the tall trees and it is I who lets the low ones grow. ♥ Cherish My Works of today, believe in My Providential Works. I have given you My child to enlighten you with My Works. I the Lord am Infinite Wealth, fear not. How could I see My lambs dispersed? I have come to find them and feed them; I have come to embellish My Garden; I have come to irrigate this Wilderness. Do not tread on My flower. ♥ Come to Me and repent, do not listen to Satan's voice. I love you boundlessly and for this reason I have come to unite you all. Creation! ♥ Walk with Me your God; do not remove nor kick on My bricks which repair My House - this House which today is in ruin. Never doubt that it is I, the Lord!

Vassula, lean on Me, be near Me, let My Hand clasp your hand. I the Lord love you. ♥ We, us?

Yes Lord Jesus.

Come then. ♥ ♥

YOU HAVE FALLEN AS LOW AS SODOM WAS

March 10th, 1988

Jesus?

I Am. ♥ *Peace be with you. Are you willing to continue working for Me Vassula?*

I'm willing to continue, yes, if it is the Lord's wish.

♥ *I am the Lord little one. It is I, Jesus, who feeds you. I wish you to embellish My garden. I wish you to revive My Church. Follow Me and I will act in you. Through you, satisfy My thirst.* ♥ *Altar! Keep My Flame ablaze to warm these icy winds which penetrated My children's hearts.*

O era, you have fallen as low as Sodom was and your breed is a breed of Cains - so few are like Abel. Your era has grown coarse at heart - do you know why creation? Because love is missing among you. You have forgotten Me and you disbelieve in My Providential Works of today. Yes creation... dead are the virtuous days when blessings were welcomed. Era of Wretchedness I will revive you! I will pour into your dead hearts My Sap which will heal you! Oh how I love you all! ♥ ♥

Write.
Yes Lord. (God sounded hurt and sad. He could if He was not All Merciful and Tender have striked us easily and finish us up, but out of His Boundless Mercy and His limitless Love He pities us, forgives us and will heal us.)
Yes, I love you all in spite of what you have become. ♥ *Will I ever abandon you? Never!*

MY RUSSIA, HOW I THE LORD LOVE YOU!

March 11th, 1988 - Prophecy

Glory be to God! (After having read the three prayers I heard from Heaven Celestial Voices saying: 'Glory be to God, thus it was written.')

Jesus?

I Am. I am near you. Pray beloved for Russia's conversion. ♥ *Russia will be resurrected by My Divine Hand and at this peak of Holiness (while My Hand will be posed upon her, warming her cold heart, reviving her), she will arise from the stillness of death and her world of darkness into My World of Peace and Light.* ♥ *With a loud cry she will manifest her joy, beholding her Saviour at her side. I will lift her to Me and My Flame of Love will inflame her heart, purifying her and leaving her in total rapture for Me her God. O Russia! My Russia! How I the Lord love you[1]. How I wept to see you dead. I shed so many bitter and sorrowful tears upon you beloved when I lost you <u>and all Heaven was mourning for you</u>. Why, why, My beloved had you rejected Me, piercing My Heart full of Love and Tenderness...?*

(I felt St Mary near me.)

♥ Peace upon you My child. I am your Holy Mother. ♥ Pray for your sister, for the Lord is by her side today and soon His Divine Hand will touch her cold and dead heart.

O creation! The Lord will revive your Sister-so-Unloved. Be alert daughter, for her time of her glory is near. ♥ ♥ Petro![2] My so beloved Petro?[3] ♥ Yes Vassula, for years I have been pleading you[4] to consecrate Russia. Now the Lord and all the Martyr Saints have heard your pleas and cries; all your sacrifices were not in vain beloved; all tears were not shed for nothing - those tears were a balm for Jesus' Wounded Heart. Praise the Lord Petro - Jesus is at your very doors, knocking. Peace upon you. Peace upon you all. ♥ ♥ I love you all.

---

[1] God was speaking again as no human can speak but God only, with so much love.
[2] Suddenly St Mary turned Her head toward John-Paul II, as if he was present; in pronouncing his name, Her voice was very sweet but sad, full of a special love for him.
[3] St Mary had tried to keep back Her tears, but could not, She said those words, breaking into tears, she wept very much, shedding many tears and I started to weep too with her. I felt that Our Holy Mother had a weakness for 'Petro.'
[4] Pope John-Paul II.

THE GREAT RETURN
THE NEW PENTECOST

March 13th, 1988

My Lord, thank You for all the graces You have given me to be with You in this special way and so close. Amen.

♥ *Vassula, these graces were given to you for My Interests and for My Glory. Allow Me to use you; perceive what your task is - come, I will help you.* ♥ *Vassula, I willed to inspire you; have faith My child. I willed to inspire My Johannes[1] and ask for a New Pentecost - this inspiration descends from Wisdom and the New Pentecost I the Lord will establish on the very grounds of My Foundation. I will unite you all and under One Shepherd you will assemble creation and I will establish My Kingdom therein. My House will reign in Peace and Love and My creation will be born again, returning like children, innocent, without malice. This will be the Great Return, the Rebirth, the Call of the Shepherd, the New Pentecost - like in the beginning, when Christianity was still at it's early stages; an infant, innocent, without self-interest. Ah creation! Just wait and see.* ♥

♥ *Vassula.*
Yes Lord?

Feel Me - I am at your side. Do you believe this child, although you cannot see Me with your physical eyes?

Yes Lord, I believe for You have taught me to see You with the eyes of my soul, and feel You too, and hear You and simply believe.

♥ *How I love you when I see your eyes searching for Me, for I know I have with me a mere child, helpless and a nothing. I pity you Vassula to have you among wolves - I will never leave your side. I bless you child.* ♥ *Let Me guide you till the* ♥ *end. Yes?*

Jesus, You <u>are</u> where I see You, no?
♥ *I Am. Beloved, have My Peace.* ♥ ♥ ♥
Us? We Lord?
Yes, we, us. ♥

---

[1]Pope John XXIII.

I LOVE YOU BECAUSE OF WHAT YOU ARE NOT

March 16th, 1988

♥ *I am the Lord. Regardless of what you are I will let My Word be established. You are nothing and many times displeasing Me, offending Me; countless times injuring Me.* ♥ *I have in My Hands Wretchedness - the portrait of your era -* ♥ *but although you are what you are I have forgiven you and placed you in My Sacred Heart. Daughter, I am God and Sovereign; Creator of All; the Spirit of Sublime Love, of Fathomless Love. Do you realize how I favoured you? How I rescued you from the Lying Tongue? Creature! Devote yourself to Me. Why let your mind go astray? Have you forgotten our bonds?[1]*

Lord, my entourage is tempting and I am weak.

I desire you to Face Me - do not fear Me! Tell Me this:

> *"Glory be to God! Blessed be our Lord! Praised be the Lord! Allow me to walk by Your side. Amen."*

(I repeated.) *Yes Vassula, do I ever abandon you? I am* Faithful *to you, am I not?*

Yes You are Lord.

I love you because of what you are not daughter. I have named you bearer and bearer you shall die. *I desire you to live exclusively for Me;* ♥ *your entourage will be Me - just Me your God. Allow Me to envelop you entirely - are you willing?*

Yes, I am willing without question.

Vassula, do you know what you are telling Me?[2]
Yes Lord I know.

Depend on Me then. I willed to have you today where you are and with My Will again I will lift you and fill you so that you will be able to fulfill My Word. Today you are My secretary and tomorrow My bearer.

Lord, is it really hopeless for me to improve, I mean from all what You said I am in the beginning?

---

[1]My mind <u>did</u> go astray.
[2]God wants me to reflect on my answer of involvement.

♥ *No, My Vassula, do not loose hope - all that you do will not be in vain. I will teach you to attain perfection - have I not said I wanted you perfect?*

Yes Lord, but the way I seem to be today is like I have to go a long way still to reach where Your Heart desires me to be.

Am I not your Teacher?
Yes Lord, but it does not appear that You have a good pupil.

You are weak, but My Strength will uphold your falls. ♥   *So Vassula, what greater than having Me as your Spiritual Director?* ♥   *What better favour than this one?*

Thank You for everything You give me, since I merit absolutely nothing.

Ah Vassula! I know you do not do these things to offend Me on purpose; your sins are forgotten by Me, like waters which passed away and dried out. I do not look back on your sins nor do I remind you of them. I will let you start afresh. I renew you beloved - feel the love I have upon you; I accept you as you are. ♥ *I have given you in your hands the Crowns of Peace and Love and you are to carry those two Crowns, together with the Crown of Justice, offering Them in My own House at My beloved Peter's feet[1].* ♥ ♥ ♥

Yes Lord, carry me there Lord.

Come, I am by your side. Together we will restore My House. ♥ ♥ *We, us?*
Yes Lord.

YOUR SYMBOL

March 16th, 1988

♥ *Come Vassula, let your Symbol be for you, James and David this Holy Word:*
♥ *FAITH. Child-like faith.*

---

[1]Jesus talks in metaphors.

WAS MY BLOOD SHED IN VAIN?
O ERA OF NO FAITH AT ALL

March 17th, 1988

♥ *Vassula, listen to My Voice as in the beginning of My call. Well before you existed I called many to serve Me; yes, those were the Virtuous Days when blessings were welcomed. I called wretched souls and they never doubted that it was I, their God and Saviour calling them; their entourage would not doubt either like they doubt today. Your era Vassula is dead, they have made a desert by condemning My Works of today, expanding this wilderness. My Blood was shed to irrigate your hearts and allow you to live in My Light. O creation was My Blood shed in vain? This era would tell you, "Do not listen. Shut your ears, for the voice you hear is certainly the devil's." ♥ And to those I blessed, giving them visions today, these blessed souls would be mocked and discouraged by My own from within My House. They would be determined and ever so ready to condemn Me. Yes, in spite themselves, they are condemning Me in the presence of men when they are denying My Gifts. ♥ When My Blessings were welcomed, the words I would hear from My own to those who would tell them of My call, would be these words: "Open your ears son, for it could indeed be God calling you." Let My creation read Samuel's call again[1]. ♥ Those were the Virtuous Days when blessings were welcomed. ♥ I wish I could say today upon you creation, "Era of little Faith" as before, but I can only say this of you today, "O Era of No Faith at all!"*

Daughter, I am weary - let Me rest in your heart child.

O Come Lord!

♥ *We. Us?*

Yes Lord. (Jesus seemed very sad and so tired.)

Write.

Yes Lord. ♥ What God says is so true for so many would put the devil first before Him. St Teresa of Avila says: "I do not understand these fears. 'Oh, the devil, the devil!' we say when we might be saying 'God! God!' and make the devil tremble." Today this is happening a lot; we put the devil first. Then there would be those who would mock and say: 'Go my dear and have yourself examined, we have good

---

[1]Samuel 1, 3:8-9.

doctors today' - or those who would boast about their knowledge of parapsychology, because for them, calls from God are <u>outdated</u>. - But <u>the worst</u> of all things in God's Eyes is: <u>Hypocrisy</u> - it is the <u>diplomatic answer</u>, which is neither yes nor no, they would be as Pilate, they would simply wash their hands, as Pilate did for our Lord. Do you know why? <u>Because Faith is missing</u>.

March 18th, 1988

♥ *Let your symbol be, My flower, this Holy Word FAITH.   Yes, era of Wretchedness.*

I, THE LORD, DO NOT WANT ANY DIVISIONS IN MY CHURCH

March 19th, 1988

Jesus to You I come.
Ah Vassula, weary not of writing. Today I feed My starved lambs. Tomorrow I will unite you and instruct you of My Mysteries. Fill Me with joy and transmit the prayer of the Holy Rosary to all who love Me and witness for Me.

Meaning to <u>all</u> Christians?

♥ *Yes My beloved. You are to honour My Mother as I honour her. You are to transmit and show how to do the Stations of My Cross (the way it pleases your Lord) to all those who bear witness for Me.*

All Christians Lord?

♥ *Yes to all those who love Me. I the Lord do not want any divisions in My Church. You will, for My sake, unite and <u>under My Name</u> love Me, follow Me and bear witness for Me. You will love one another as I love you; you will unite and become one flock under one Shepherd[1]. I have, as you all know, selected Peter - giving him the authority. I have, as you all know, given him the keys of the kingdom of heaven. I have asked Peter to feed My lambs and sheep - looking after them[2]. This authority was given by Me - I have not desired you to alter My*

---

[1] The Pope.
[2] John 21:17.

wish. Assemble beloved ones, reinforcing My Church. Seek in Me what I desire; seek My interests and not yours; seek to Glorify Me. Glorify Me by uniting creation. Vivify My Body. I love all of you. ♥ *Open your ears and hear My cry from My Cross!* ♥

Vassula remember where your home is - Yes, in My Sacred Heart. Come, come beloved, I am waiting. I love you boundlessly. ΙΧθΥΣ ⋖×

I love You Lord and Saviour, please teach me to please You so that I am able to be with You, so that I am able to be used by You.

I am teaching you. Be pliant and look after My Interests only. ♥ *We, us, at all times. I for you, you for Me. At your side I Am. Pray Vassula for the redemption of souls. I have created you for this Message.* ♥ ♥ ♥

Thank You Jesus.

SIMPLICITY AND POVERTY INFATUATES ME
LOVE SUFFERS

March 23rd, 1988

Jesus?

♥ *I Am. Love will prevail. I am Love. Have My Peace. Fear not, it is I Jesus. Will you come? I am waiting. I will guide you where I guided others too to love Me.* ♥ *Beloved, I will take you there. Pray My Vassula. Be aware of the snares of the devil, for if My creation will not change or repent...*
Lord! How is it that You say if, when many times You say that You will change us and that Your Kingdom will come, I do not understand.

Listen and understand, I have given you the freedom to choose. I, the Lord and Sovereign, the Light, descend upon you creation. I descend in this thick darkness to offer you My Heart in My Hand to redeem you and Shine upon you. I come to wash away your countless sins and offenses against Me; I come to call you back to Me; I come to unite My Church; I come to remind you to whom I the Lord have given the Authority and the Keys of the Kingdom of Heaven. I come to teach you all to honour My Mother and to bend your knees for Her, for She is crowned by My Hand and is Queen of Heaven. Creation! Beware of the devil, for he is redoubling his efforts to ensnare you and in the meantime pretending he is non existent so that he manoeuvres without being feared. O CREATION! HE IS PREPARING A LARGE HOLOCAUST UPON YOU, O HOW I CRY FROM MY CROSS! CREATION, RETURN TO ME! ♥ *Do not let him ensnare you by*

denying Me! Pray, pray for the return of souls - let every soul learn the prayers
I have given you[1]. Let them learn those prayers. ♥ *I love all of you - I love all*
of you. ♥ ♥ ♥

Daughter do not weary of coming to Me kneeling and writing. I am your Saviour,
♥ *your Spouse - sharing everything with you. Come, console Me, I am weary.*
O come Lord! ♥ Jesus seemed weary, His broad shoulders slightly curved, sad.
I feel the same, I want to please Him.
Will you remember My Presence Vassula?
Yes Lord Jesus, I will. ♥
Us, we!
Yes us, we, for ever and ever. (Jesus is today weary and sad.)

Peace upon you soul. Vassula, I am weary, weary of seeing how love and
simplicity are missing. What use are rituals and sacrifices to Me when love is
missing among them? Flower, what greater joy than My barefoot disciples when
in their hand they held but a staff guarding My lambs? I love simplicity; simplicity
and poverty infatuate Me. My true disciples were barefoot but rich in spirit. ♥
Vassula -courage! Crucified I am; stretched on My Cross by My own. We are
sharing My Cross - I and you, you and I. Love suffers.

IN THE END OUR HEARTS WILL PREVAIL

March 24th, 1988

♥ **Peace upon you.**

(It is St Mary.)
I love you. Glorify God - pray for the redemption of souls. Glorify Him by
obeying His Will - being His bearer. He loves you tenderly soul. Never weary
of writing. Come and pray, telling Him this:

> **"Almighty God, teach Your servant Your Ways; teach me**
> **humility, patience and love; guide me in Your Path of**
> **Righteousness and Virtues. I surrender myself to You, offering**
> **You my will; forgive my sins, renew me, make me worthy so**
> **that You may use me fully. Amen."**

---

[1]Those prayers are: "The Memorare of St Bernard." "Novena of Confidence to the
Sacred Heart." "Prayer to St Michael." I recite these prayers every day before
writing. Sometimes twice. (See 8.6.88.)

♥ Ah Vassula, I will look after you always. Take My Hand. Ecclesia will revive and in the end Our Hearts[1] will prevail. ♥ My apparitions are to encourage souls of God's Works; they are a call to return to Us, a warning. This year I shall appear to many; visions I shall give and visioners there will be. Pray that the Holy Church returns as in the beginning, when every Work of God was welcomed without disbelief and contempt, without doubt. Pray that the Holy Church's faith will be renewed again, like in the past, and believe in Miracles, apparitions and visions, <u>for this is one way of God speaking to you</u>. Ask for a renewal. ♥
Thank You St Mary[2].

Do not worry; I am praying day and night.

Here is Jesus. ♥ ♥ ♥

Vassula[3] - *I Am. Look at Me soul. I find no holiness in them.* (Jesus, on those who deny Your Works of today?) *Yes, none. Everytime I cry from My Cross, it is that at this same instant I see one of My own giving way to Satan. Vassula, My own, My priest*[4], *I love you.*
Jesus, why call me priest when women priests are not allowed?
I have sanctified your soul; I have chosen your soul. Understand that My Eyes see your soul; My Heart feels your soul. I love your soul not your body; your soul is within your body. ♥ *Try and perceive My Words*[5] - *look upon it as I your God see it.* ♥
The soul is what counts for God. A soul after death goes in heaven and will have no distinction, of being female or male, all souls will be like angels. Jesus looks upon the soul and not what carries it, thus He makes no distinction on His chosen ones.
♥ *I love you. Walk in My Footprints. Come, we, us.* ♥
Yes Lord.

---

[1]Jesus and Her Heart.

[2]I asked St Mary to pray for us.

[3]I discerned Jesus, but I was not sure.

[4]1 Peter, 2:9.

[5]God does not want us to misunderstand this passage. We all know that our body is God's Temple yet God is working in our soul and embellishes our soul and not our body.

TO LOVE ME GLORIFIES ME AND PURIFIES YOU

March 26th, 1988

"My God I no longer can detach my eyes from Your Divine Face. My eyes are fixed upon you in endless hours of adoration and my mind cannot detach itself from You, Beloved Father. Every second upon earth and heaven my mind is absorbed in You, with You. I live for You and breathe for You, my joy is You and my smile. I believe, I adore, I hope and I love You endlessly. Amen. "

♥ *I love you soul - peace upon you. Adore Me - be blessed. Face Me your God and delight Me! I have longed for this hour to come; how I longed to bring you near Me!*

May Your Name be praised Lord!

In the depths of My Sacred Heart I have kept a place for you; your home is in My Sacred Heart. Come! Come to Me. ♥

(Jesus gave me again the same vision I had when I was around ten years old, and the same words: "come, come to Me." That was Jesus' first call to me.)

Come, I love you Vassula. Hold on to Me and I will guide you; you belonged to Me from the beginning. Daughter, do you love Me?

To folly Lord.

To love Me glorifies Me and purifies you. Follow My Footprints, they will lead you where I wish you to be. ♥ ♥ *Let us pray:* ♥

> *"Holy Spirit descend upon us, renewing us; fill our soul with Your Love. Rest in our tormented soul giving us peace. Envelop us with Your wings, sheltering us from all evil. Humble us, guide us in Your Light to be able to see Your desires and thus fulfill them. Amen. "* ♥

YOUR APOSTASY IS CONDEMNING YOU

March 29th, 1988

Jesus, O Jesus what should one answer to the ministers who sneer by the word 'apparitions'. We[1] are helpless and have no knowledge to statements like this latest one: 'Apparitions? Seek <u>The Truth</u> and not in apparitions.' This was said to my companion Beatrice by a Catholic priest. She had nothing to say nor would I have had either. We are helpless Lord!

Flower, I will assure you that <u>I am the Truth</u> and My Word[2] <u>is</u> the Truth, but many of My own have forgotten My Words - hardened at heart they seek in darkness. <u>It is written</u>[3] that I will pour out My Spirit on all mankind and that My children shall prophesy again. I will give dreams and visions to many - even to the least of them I will give. I will give you <u>hope</u> and <u>encourage</u> you by displaying portents in heaven and on earth. These are My Signs of today![4] I have said that out of the babe's mouth you shall hear The Truth! So to those who condemn My Divine Works of today I tell you this: <u>your apostasy is condemning you!!</u>[5] <u>All you who disbelieve and have made desolate My Garden, come to Me and repent!!</u> ♥ Come child, I love you, have My Peace. Eat from Me; hold on to Me - I am by your side. ♥

I love You Lord, praised be the Lord!

Endeavour to keep up My Teachings and follow Them. I the Lord love you. ♥ I am Present wherever you are so smile at Me when you look at Me! Blessed are the simple in heart for theirs is the Kingdom of Heaven. ♥ <u>Justice</u> will prevail and My House will be renewed with Simplicity, enveloped by Integrity. Allow Me child to imprint on you My Divine Words. I shall not fail you. Rest in My Heart and let your Lord rest in yours. ♥ ♥
Jesus give me the strength, the faith and the love to do Your Will. Teach me to obey You and humble myself, teach me to forgive my oppressors and repay evil with love.

---

[1]Beatrice and I.
[2]Scriptures.
[3]Jesus was so very angry. Shouting! Jesus reminded me the way He shouted at the Pharisees that day in the Temple.
[4]Joel 3:14. Acts 2:17-20.
[5]Jesus was very cross, shouting even louder!

♥ *I am teaching you Vassula.* ♥ *Yes[1], smile to Me; believe in My Presence; be faithful to Me; be My reflection.* ♥ ♥ *Yes Vassula, My Body aches - right in the middle of My Heart lies the lance's blade.*

Where Lord?

In the very sanctuary and depths of My Foundation, My Sacred Heart is bleeding; in My agony I sought to warn them. Arise daughter! Ecclesia needs you. My House lies in darkness from the apostasy and iniquitism and because of their sins My flock has been scattered. How I cry from My Cross. Ah Peter!![2] I come to you because I know you remained faithful to Me. Oh[3] Peter, look at My Heart... hear My cries beloved soul. I, the Lord, find no love, no holiness in those Cains; they are many; they have laid desolate My House. On what will My lambs feed since their hands are empty? They have nothing to offer them since they made a desert out of My Foundation. Pray Peter and I will lift you so that your eyes will see this wilderness from above and I will let you penetrate into the Wound of My Heart - I will let you see the lance's blade. Your heart will cry out with pain when you will see it. Peter, I will give you the strength and the courage you will need to have so that you may pull it out. ♥

Jesus was in great agony. When Jesus said "be my reflection" ♥ ♥ (a few lines back) I got up thinking the message of that day was over, but a few minutes later on I received this special urge when a call is there or coming. I started to feel in me God's agony, I knew it was from Him what I felt for it went through my body, reflecting it on me, I heard his cry of agony, so I rushed back hardly seeing through the many tears in my eyes, Jesus was suffering, He was in pain, it hurted Him to say and write this.

FOR AN INDIFFERENT SOUL

March 29th, 1988

♥ *Vassula, My anguish for souls walking in darkness, souls full of blemishes sores My Heart. My Vassula, I am outside her door knocking but she refuses to open; her daily occupations leave no place for her Saviour; her soul going into deeper depths of darkness. Although I have given her the grace of intellect and*

---

[1] I had smiled at Him.
[2] 'Peter' was cried out like 'Peeeteeer' - in a long cry.
[3] This was more of a moan of suffering.

perception she is not apt to change as long as she refuses Me to come in. I demand nothing, I ask only for some recognition, for some love. See Vassula? (Jesus was sad.) Creating her was a delight for Me but would she know all this since she has shut Me out? ♥ *Yes[1] Vassula, love Me My Vassula; you console Me - make up for those who have no love for Me.* ♥

Jesus wrote this on account of a visitor, one of our family who stays now with us for a few days. Having heard of these messages she asked me to have a look on them. She read some of the messages from October 1987 then left it. (She yawned then said, 'I guess when I reach retirement age I will take care of my rose garden and my spiritual life, but not now.' She asked me to watch me while writing, so that she satisfies her curiousity and watch the phenomena. I refused her request. No one sees me unless God calls him or her for this. It is holy and it should not be profaned by curiousity.

I HAVE FORMED YOU WITH TENDERNESS AND LOVE

March 30th, 1988

Today Satan was desperate and tried very hard to convince me that all these messages were nothing and I should abandon writing, meeting God. I was in need of reassurance for my weakness dragged me down to the bottom. Realizing my weakness of doubt I also fear that God in the end will get tired of me and lose His patience.

♥ *Flower, do not fear Me - I will not harm you or deny you. I have not brought you up to Me so that I now push you away from Me or show any wrath or harshness upon you. I have formed you with tenderness and love; I have led you with love; I fed you with love; I worked with you gently - do not fear Me. Come, learn that I am Meek and Gentle. Peace upon you soul.* ♥ ♥ *I love you!*
Lord, thank You for Your patience and for running to my rescue, I bless You Lord.

---

[1]This made me weep to see Jesus so sad.

MY CHURCH NEEDS VIVIFICATION

March 31st, 1988

♥ *Vassula, never doubt that it is I the Lord. Fear not, it is I Jesus.* (I panicked fearing maybe that all this is not from God, but then how was all this written? I'm confused.)

♥ *Vassula, it is I, Jesus, your Saviour who saved you and rose you from the dead. Come, do not fear... I wish to promote My Church. Heresy has infiltrated, thus confusing The Truth and making divisions among you, digressing you from The Truth.* ♥ *My Church needs vivification. Pray for those priests, bishops and cardinals who have nothing to offer My lambs for this is the result of their digression; they have been and still are inactive, never seeking My interests but their own; they have made inside themselves a desert and they know it. No lamb is attracted by wilderness; naturally any sheep will go astray, wandering, because they have no shepherd to guard them. Love them, shelter them and feed them.* ♥ *I have revealed many wonders to the world since the beginning of Times. Beloved, since the world reject My Celestial Works, removing all hopes from you and thus remote Me, My anger burns against these shepherds. The time is near when I will reveal to them My Glory and it shall be shown by a Sign, a grandiose Sign so that they may understand how wrong they were.* ♥ *This Sign will be given to you so that many may believe.* ♥ *Pray, for the time is near; pray for the Great Return of Peace and Love.* ♥

YOU HAVE NEGLECTED MY GARDEN

April 5th, †988

Glory be to God. Will you work with Jesus?
Yes, St Mary, teach me please to obey Him, augmenting my faith, love and hope.
♥ **I will. Endeavour to be pliant child; have My peace; Wisdom will instruct you.** ♥ **Leave everything in His Hands - He will not fail you.**

Here is Jesus. ♥

(Jesus was standing on my left side showing me His foot binded with mine.)
Remember those bonds are for Eternity. I am always at your side. Come, pray for the redemption of souls. I wish you to meditate upon My Passion -I had been crucified this week. Never doubt. ♥

My myrrh, embellish My Church - let no one take away the gift I have given you. I will never ever leave your lamp without oil; I will always fill up your lamp. Ecclesia needs you. My House today is in ruin. Vassula!

David! James![1] You are to rebuild this Old Foundation of Mine, renewing it's walls. Renew My Sanctuary. I am the Lord and with My Strength you will rebuild these ancient ruins and embellish My Old Foundation. Renew Its walls and I will call all the dead to life again; I will awake those corpses raising them back to life - this will be The Great Return, The Great Return to Life. ♥ *For My radiant dew will embellish you creation!*

I will expand My Kingdom and all Heaven will rejoice! You have neglected My Garden but I, the Lord, who am It's Keeper, love you to distraction and cannot bear to see thorns and briars choking My few remaining flowers. The time has come to clean up, extirpating those thorns and briars, allowing My buds to bloom, embellishing My Garden. ♥ *Justice will prevail. I, the Lord, will let them make Peace with Me; those that are sincere will return to Me, repenting. All you who seek Me and long to know My Ways of Integrity, come and you will hear My cries from My Cross. I need Love, Love, Love. Open your hearts and I will heal you and console you creation.*

Peter, assemble Peter all the nations - draw them into My Heart. I call from My Cross: "feed all My sheep Peter." I ask you again Peter : "do you love Me more than these others do?" If you do, do not let the Cains convince you - remain steadfast. They will ask you for laws that seem just, to treat every soul as they please; these very laws that are coming from men, do not let them persuade you. Remember how I, the Lord, am; I am Meek and Humble. Be My reflection. ♥ *If they long for Me to come near them, then why do they not hear My Voice? I am at their very doors knocking. Why do they refuse to hear? If they long for Me and do not hear Me it is because of their apostasy that has grown as thick as slime. I am here now, waiting for them to open their hearts, but they push Me aside, oppressing Me. Lift up your eyes and you will behold your Saviour - recognize Me! Do not tread on My Providential Works, offering no Peace to My children and so none of them follow you with your own traditions. Give them My Peace. Do not be surprised at the weak instruments I use to manifest Myself through them. I am God and I choose whom I please.* ♥ ♥

Daughter, rely on Me. Trust Me. We, us?
Yes Lord.

Come. ♥

---

[1]Jesus is calling the three confessions: Orthodox, Anglicans and Roman Catholics.

MY BLOOD WAS SHED IN RIVERS FOR YOU
SHARE MY CUP

April 7th, 1988

Jesus?

I Am. Have My Peace Vassula. Realize that I have not brought you all the way here, forming you, to abandon you now. I love you all. It is I, the Lord, searching to heal souls and redeem them. O soul![1] Yes, it is I, your Saviour, who came to you[2] to heal you. Beloved soul, it is I, the Lord, who came at your door knocking. O so beloved soul! I have brought you to Me - I am now feeding you[3]. Come! Approach Me. I will embellish you and purify you; I will heal all your wounds; I will restore you My child. It is I who came to you - I sought your soul. Come and I will console you; come and rest in Me soul; come to Me and eat Me; come and drink Me. Hear your Redeemer's call and your soul will live. I love you beloved soul. ♥ My Blood was shed in Rivers for you -for your salvation. Soul? Come and share My cloak; I will shelter you; I will be your Refuge. I am Jesus and Jesus means Saviour. ♥

(Jesus has given this message talking to whoever is reading Him. It is not a coincidence that you are reading His Peace and Love Message. It is He, Jesus who looked for you, came to you and gave you this message to read.)

♥ Enlarge My Kingdom by distributing My Message as you do. ♥ It is I who will establish My Works, extending My Kingdom. Remember, I always reach My goals. ♥ Smile at your Saviour. Bless Me. (I turned around and blessed Jesus.) I bless You Jesus Christ, I bless You.

♥ ♥ I bless you too. Synchronize with Me tonight. I was abandoned by My brothers and betrayed by one of them; share My anguishes of Gethsemane - do not abandon Me. ♥

I will not Lord.

Have Me always in your mind, console Me in this way. Show Me that you will not abandon Me Vassula; share My agony; share My Cup; be with Me till the end; live My Passion. Glorify Me! Stay near Me. ♥

Jesus. Yes I will, (Jesus appeared as though He was living His tribulations all over again.)

O Vassula! Enter into My Sacred Heart; enter into it's depths - therein you will find Peace. I, the Lord, have kept a place for you; you belong to Me and I to you. Love will guide you. ♥

---

[1] This is a cry for the one who is reading Him now.

[2] Here Jesus is talking to the one who is reading His Message.

[3] 'Feeding' stands for reading and understanding. (Spiritual food.)

Lord, I have given You my heart, You can do what You please with me.

♥ *Trust Me then; take My Hand; I will not fail you ever!*

Lead me Lord for You are my guide and God.

♥ *Come, do not forget Me. Bless Beatrice - I, the Lord, bless her.* ♥ *We, us?*
Yes Lord, together for eternity.

Holy Thursday - Easter

I had on Wednesday been to Church and the priest blessed each one with myrrh
mixed with oil. We were allowed to dip a piece of cotton in this mixture which was
blessed by the Church and take it home.Beatrice arrived at my place so that we go
to Church. Jesus asked me to bless her. So I blessed her with the oil and myrrh I
kept. One blesses in this way; while blessing one forms the sign of the cross with
the myrrh and oil on the forehead, left and right cheek, chin, hands inside the palms
as well as above. The priest had uttered some words about healing of body and soul,
Jesus by locution made me understand that He would utter these words. While later
on in Church, sometimes my mind would wander away, because of the language
problem. The Greek is classical Greek and I understand next to nothing. To keep
my mind from wandering in these three hours was difficult, but Jesus made sure that
this would not happen. Everytime my mind started to wander away, Jesus would
say: *"be near Me,"* or *"keep near Me."* I think He must have told me this ten
times or so.

LOVE ME AND YOU WILL DEFEAT MY FOES

April 8th, 1988
Holy Friday

Jesus?
I Am. Why did you doubt?[1] Ah! All I ask from you is love. Love Me and My

---

[1] I was looking where in the Bible it is written the words Jesus said on 29.3.88,
("I will pour out My Spirit on all mankind.") I found it in Acts and I knew that
also it was elsewhere in the Bible, because once Jesus had shown me that passage.
I asked Jesus to show me again where it was in the Bible. After looking for a
while and not finding it, it appeared as though I was looking for a needle in a
haystack! I thought maybe Jesus did not hear me, and I said   .... cont'd

thirst is quenched! Love Me and My Wounds are soothed! Love Me and My Spirit will exult in you! Love Me and you will defeat My foes! My Spirit is upon you My child. ♥ *We, us?*

We, us?

Yes Lord. Yes, St Mary. We, us, for ever and ever.

VICTIM OF LOVE

April 9th, 1988
Holy Saturday (Easter)

♥ *I love you. United to Me you are now, and every step you take I bless My child. I am The Resource of your life. I am the Resurrection.*

Lord, although this Message has converted many laymen and they rejoice, I feel sad that we have sent at least to 33 ecclesiastical authorities copies of the message to them and no one replied except for 2, one said she did not feel obliged to give in her opinion, the other one said he was overworked and had no time for this. Lord, I feel so sad!

My Vassula, let it be that way. ♥ *Vassula, leave Me free to have it My way. I will one day establish My Works which I have given you. You, My child, shall bear this name upon you: 'Victim-of-Love.' I will never abandon you nor will I ever fail you. Every word will be written thousands of times till the End of Times. I have established between you and Me Eternal Bonds; these Bonds are our Alliance of Love between us; these Bonds bear <u>My Name</u> and are for ever and ever, and for all Eternity. I, the Lord, love all of you and it is for the sake of those who seek The Truth that I come to show them again what The Truth really is and what it means, since they have forgotten It. <u>I am The Truth and The Truth is Love</u>, Fathomless Love, Sublime Love, Eternal Love. My Book is a Book of <u>Love</u>.* ♥ *My bride, come and love Me; I am glorified by your love. Understand now why I have descended through you, child; it is not just to manifest in you My love for you alone, but for <u>all</u>[1] My creation! I come to remind them how much I love them. My Heart tears and lacerates to see so many of My creation give way to Satan! How I suffer to see on the way to perdition so many of My sacerdotals! I Am the Word, The Holy One of Holies, The Eternal God, Emmanuel, and your*

---

louder, 'O Jesus maybe I should shout, maybe You didn't hear!!' Before finishing my last word I had discovered I was saying these words while I had the right page that I was looking for, it was right in front of my nose. So He said to me "why did you doubt?"

[1]All was pronounced in this way : <u>aaalll</u>.

Saviour whom you pierced many years ago and never cease piercing through and through. Why? What difference is there now or the days of old when I was in flesh and nailed on the Cross? I am being repeatedly pierced with your hypocrisy, your haughtiness, your apostasy and your obduracy to hear. <u>You have not stopped remaining lethargic towards My Signs, My Miracles, My Divine Works</u>.

Today you are mocking Me like yesterday. <u>I am mocked by you</u>; you on whom I have entrusted millions of souls; you are recrucifying Me, nailing Me anew on the wood with your apathy. O all you whose heart still lies barren, whose heart has turned into granite, will you ever allow your hearts to be touched by Me and softened and opened? Will you one day stop piercing Me?[1] My mouth is dryer than parchment for thirst of love; My eyes have grown weary watching you spill your words on My Altar. You offer Me your prayers but before they reach Me they evaporate in the air like mist. I turn away My eyes from you for I know what lies deep within your hearts - I stifle!... I suffocate! To have to watch My seed filled up with dead words; to have to watch you coming fearlessly to Me, treading upon Our Divine Hearts so openly![2] So obviously! How then do you expect My lambs to trust you? ♥ <u>Ah Vassula!</u> My Heart bleeds profusely; enter into My Heart and feel your God's Wounds. ♥

<u>J - E - S - U - S</u> !!

My heart screams with pain, to feel You in this state, Oh my Beloved God! What have they done ... What <u>are</u> they doing?
Reveal My Works of Love; reveal Them <u>to all men</u> - even to those who will treat you as a jester My child; they will in the end see My Glory. ♥

I am shattered, the Lord knows it. I have already been treated as a jester, as a deceiver, as possessed, as the Anti-Christ, as mentally ill, I have been mortified because people do not even hide their feelings when they mean to hurt you. Will I bear to go on, on these grounds? I am weak... my soul is weary... my witnesses have also no real authority and no power, they go through the same way I am going. Scorned and dejected, disbelieved and ignored, we all drink from the same bitter Cup, sharing It with Jesus.

♥ Vassula, you have Me before you; it is I your God, who in the end will show to you all My Glory. ♥

Lord! We all are so helpless!

---

[1] Jesus' voice was sad and pleading.
[2] St Mary's and His.

I have found the least of all My creation. I chose you so that everybody may see that all Authority will descend directly from Me and Me alone ... and not from you! I am the Keeper of this Garden and no one stunts the tall trees but Me. allowing the low ones to grow. My Word will descend upon you creation as a Thunderbolt! Woe to the unfaithful! Vassula, keep Me in your heart. Have Our Peace. ♥ ♥ ♥

I AM THE HOLY TRINITY, ALL IN ONE

April 11th, 1988

Lord, do not refuse me since I am the least in Your Eyes, have pity on me and feed me, if You wish, even the remaining crumbs Lord. St Mary do not despise me, please have mercy and let the Lord throw to me a few remaining crumbs, please keep me alive! Amen.

Come! Have My Bread - I will not refuse you! From my own Hand I will feed you. ♥ *I will, Vassula, embellish you.* ♥ *Delight Me and praise Me!*

Praised be the Lord!

Come, write, write. Cain will not execute his plan and rid off his brother this time; I will hinder him; I will surprise him. ♥ *Little does he know that I am entering in his room, as a thief enters, to unseam his plan - leaving him naked. And Cain will remain naked until he comes to Me, repenting. Pray for this hour; hour which will rise pleas and supplications and fear; this will be an hour of Justice.* ♥

Be blessed My child. I, your Holy Father, love you. ♥ ♥ ♥ *I Am the Holy Trinity - you have discerned well! Write it.* ♥

I discerned, while Jesus was saying I am your Holy Father, a 'triple' Jesus, like those fancy pictures of one person but made as though they are three, one coming out of the other, all similar and all three the same.

♥ *I am the Holy Trinity, all in One.* ♥ *I love you. Come child, I will initiate you into deep mysteries, all for My Glory. Hold My Hand - I am He who created you. We, us?*

Yes Lord! ♥

YOU ARE MY NET

April 12th, 1988

Since yesterday in moments of weakness, Satan took advantage of this and attacked me leaving my soul agitated. Immediately I felt Jesus tightening our bonds, they really look like soft ropes. I felt His whole arm since the bonds were tighter. I felt as if we were some sort of Siamese twins. He used to lean forward facing me anxiously. I felt consoled.

♥ *I am near you. Come, I bless you. I love you My Vassula. My Eyes never leave you. Especially in these moments of weakness I do tighten our bonds.* ♥ *Think Vassula, I healed you so that the world may see that I am still among you. Vassula[1],* ♥ *I healed you to use you, thrusting you out of My arms, yes, out of My arms into the world, as My Net.* ♥ *Daughter, allow Me to use you in this way. I pull My Net now and then in, and I delight to find My Net with some catch.* ♥ *Yes, seek My interests and you will understand. I know it is harsh to live in among the world for you no longer belong to the world; I have made known to you your origins and to whom you belonged from the very beginning, but the evil one had deceived you all along. You belonged to Me; you come from Me; you are My own -like Abel who was <u>My seed</u>.* ♥ *Having you in the world, the world does not recognize you as their own and because of this they will try to ensnare you. I have you among wickedness and where they will try and destroy you - they will scorn at you and deject you. I revealed to you all these things so that you are prepared before this time and to enable you to endure all the trials; all the trials lying before you. I have shown you your cross, but I am with you, sharing it with you. You are not alone. I am near you and in Me you will find your rest. Courage daughter, lean on Me when you are weary and I <u>will</u> rest you and I <u>will</u> console you.* ♥ *Come, smile at Me, do not forget what I have been teaching you.* ♥ *Never doubt of My Presence; spread My Kingdom daughter. I love all of you.*
Praised be the Lord, Glory be to God! **ΙΧθΥΣ** ⋗⃝

---

[1]Jesus' tone saddened.

ASK AND IT SHALL BE GIVEN TO YOU

April 14th, 1988

I prayed like always the 3 prayers given to me as an opening. Again in the 'request' to Jesus I said: 'choose for me.'

♥ **Beloved daughter,** (St Mary) **have My Peace. Ask and it shall be given to you.**

St Mary I let the Lord choose from my heart.

Flower, We are with you. Remember what I have told you: I will make prodigies before many. ♥ ♥ This revelation will inflame Our children's hearts with love. ♥ <u>Ask</u> and it shall be given to you.

O Lord, I only ask what will give You more glory, decide for me. Amen.
♥ **Vassula, since you give the Lord this freedom, know that He is pleased with you - a better Guide you cannot have. Widsom will instruct you. ♥ Be pliant and leave everything into His Hands - it pleases the Lord. Lean entirely on God. I love you -be blessed.**

I bless You St Mary.

♥ **We, us?**

Yes, we, us.

YOUR ERA IS DEAD
HOW I DESIRE THIS UNITY!

April 18th, 1988

(I only thought of Jesus.)

♥ *I Am. Peace be with you soul. Reap what I have given you. ♥ Teach My children; teach them to cease rebelling against Me; teach them to love each other. Pray for the redemption of souls; pray for the World Council of Churches; pray for the Great Return - your era is dead; pray for the renewal of your era, for it's rebirth, for a New Era; pray for what My beloved Johannes started under the inspiration of My Holy Spirit.* ♥ *My Ecclesia will be one, renewed by Me, drawing many souls back into My arms! My sheep have all gone astray. Satan has brought down his wrath among you, dividing you, splitting you, scattering you, confusing you... Peter! O Peter recognize the End of Times. How is it that most of you cannot tell the Times? Shadowed by Satan under his wings. Satan has digressed many of you from the Truth! Take My Hand Peter and I will guide you. Hear My cry; assemble your Eastern brothers, call them to meet Me under My roof; assemble your Eastern brothers into My Foundation; call them before Me - how I desire this Unity! Peter? Peter, if you listen to Me I will summon all nations under My roof; I will sanctify them, renewing them all. I will pour from heaven My dew of Righteousness like rain and My Garden will embellish; I will fill up your storages from My Storages. Listen Peter to My Voice - My Kingdom is at your very doors; My Kingdom is among you. How is it that you do not recognize it? Peter, you knew that any kingdom which is divided against itself would collapse - My House has been divided and today It lies in ruin. Tell them, beloved, of My Salvation Plan.* ♥ *Peter, free My children.* ♥ *Peace be with you all.*

Jesus, my God, are You calling the Orthodox patriarch? Is it him You want Lord?

♥ *Yes. My plan is to unite all nations, from East to West, from North to South and bring them all together under My Light, under My wings. All united, in one flock, under My protection by One Vigilant Shepherd.* ♥ *I have promised never to forsake you ever and come to you in times of distress. Flower, I am keeping this promise. I love all of you and patiently I am waiting for your hearts to open and grasp Me.* ♥ *Do not harden your hearts like in the time of Rebellion; open your hearts - I am at your very doors! Wisdom will instruct you. Have My Peace.* ♥

Glory be to God! Praised be the Lord! May Your Kingdom come.
♥ *I will feed you My Vassula.* ♥ *We, us?*
Forever and ever. ♥

UNITED AROUND ONE ALTAR

April 19th, 1988

Father, may we be united with one Faith and one Baptism under Your Holy Name; may we be one in You as You, Jesus, is one with our Father, keep us in Your Name, which you have given us. Amen.
Behold, what joy I will have when around One Altar you will gather and around this same Altar you will praise Me; ♥ *acknowledging your mistakes, repenting for your rebellion and remembering My Love for you and loving one another as I love you. Children, be perfect!*

WHY IS IT THAT YOU WANT ME SILENT?

April 20th, 1988

Lord, my sister asked if it is possible that you bless her crucifix like You have blessed mine, kissing them.

♥ Have My Peace. I love you. I want you to discern Me fully. Discern Me. ♥ Yes, I am sitting near you. ♥ Now that you know where I am, lift to My lips the medallion and the crucifixes Yannula has given you; I will kiss them, blessing them. Go ahead, I am waiting... Yes[1]. ♥ Vassula, do not doubt - write: I am telling you this: whoever wishes Me to bless their crucifixes and medallions I, the Lord, will do it willingly. Come, do not doubt. ♥

O Lord, help me to understand all this!

Just believe; be simple; be like a child. I love you. ♥ ♥

Later on:

Vassula, I can flourish My Garden all by Myself. Yes, I can renew My Church all by Myself; I suffice by Myself - I am Omnipotent. All I ask from you is love. Love Me and allow Me to share these things with you. ♥

O Lord I love You boundlessly.

♥ Flower, have you not understood? Have you not observed? Come, I will tell you: since the beginning of times I have been showing Myself in various places, to different peoples in different ages. How is it that your era cannot observe My Signs anymore? Have I at anytime said that I will end revealing Myself and My Signs? Your era is dead and it is through their own finger that they have devastated themselves... I am the Lord of Lords, the Living God. Why is it that you want Me silent? Why is it that you want Me dead? Vassula, I have been showing you and am showing you what My creation has become. Understand, by being bonded to Me you are being dragged along with Me; I am dragging you with Me; crossing this wilderness, showing you; pointing all what was, what has been and what is remaining. ♥ I am thinning out those briars and cutting out those thorns so that they do not harm you, for if they touched you they would pierce you, ripping you My child, tearing you into shreds. ♥ I am with you, opening and clearing your passage. I love you boundlessly and I do not want those thorns to snatch you and pierce you on our way, wounding you to death! I know how by their mere approach to you suffices to leave you in total agony. I see all this My Vassula and My Heart is profoundly wounded, but beloved, all these sacrifices are

---

[1] I lifted each object one after the other, Jesus kissed each one and blessed it.

not in vain. ♥   *Ah how I love you soul... Who seeks Me WILL find Me.* ♥
Knock and I WILL open the door. Come, I will remind you of My Presence. ♥

DO NOT TREAT ME AS A STRANGER

April 25th, 1988

I've read as usual the three prayers and twice Glory be to God was said. My God
is it really You?
*I Am. Daughter, in spite of your incapacity to fathom My gifts I pour upon you,
I love you boundlessly.* ♥   *Live for Me, have Me as first. My House is in ruin,
Vassula - I want it rebuilt. I will show you how. Love desires love. Talk to Me
as now - feel Me near you. I Am.* ♥   *Come to Me freely; open your heart to Me;
treat Me as a friend, as your Father. Nevertheless, never forget that I am Holy
and your God. Tell them that homely words coming from within their heart are
sweeter than sophisticated words coming from their lips. Do not treat Me as a
stranger. I, the Lord, bless you.* ♥ ♥ ♥

CALL ME ABBA

April 26th, 1988

Yesterday while talking to My sister about what God wants me to do, at the heat of
the conversation I found myself saying : "O babas mou ipe na..." meaning: "Abba
told me to..." (Daddy told me to...) I found myself calling in a very natural way
God as daddy in Greek. I quickly stopped because I saw my sister gaping at me.
I put my hand on my mouth and explained to her that I was calling God, daddy,
without meaning to. For so very often I feel so very near Him, and so many times
I say that I have two families, one that I was given on earth but up there lives my
real Holy Family.

♥   *Little one, stay beneath My Cape; near Me you are safe from Satan's
agressions. Yes, he is redoubling his efforts, setting all sorts of traps; he is
hounding you My child; scheming, he is in total frenzy with all that has to come.
I am telling you this My child so that you redouble your prayers.*

Lord do You wish me to fast, will it help Lord?
♥ ♥ *Will you fast?*
If You wish me to.
I do.

Come, I will help you in this. ♥ *Vassula, when you called Me baba¹, I received this word as a jewel. Little do you know how attracted I become at simplicity. Yes, I have named you barefooted, for in heart you are.* ♥ *Hear Me: I created you in My Light; I received you in My Celestial Hall; I have welcomed you to share My Peace, My Cross and My Love; I will lead you soon in a land where you will expand My Kingdom - I will advise and instruct you when the time comes.* ♥ *Flower, tell James this, "delight Me by never being reticent when it comes to witnessing the Truth. Have faith, live in faith and abandon yourself entirely to me. I have elevated you to understand the Truth and to testify for the Truth. Stay small. Please Me by never doubting. You have been given My Revelation to be the witness of My Message in which you have read My desires; I have enlightened you to understand them; I have showed My Holy Face to you James. I love you to folly and I mean to bring you all back to Me. Soul! I wish you to expand My Kingdom. Honour Me and rejoice Me."* ♥

PERVERTED CREATION!

April 27/28th/29th, 1988

These days Satan is constantly attacking me: whispering in my ear that nothing will come out from this revelation; making me forget all the good it has done already and is still doing. He made me loose my sense of reality; my confidence he took away throwing it far away, he veiled the love I have for the Lord so that this great love I have for Him appears blemished. He gave me images of the world and of how real it is, but how false and unreal is spirituality. He gave me agonies and mixed up my thoughts, confusing me. The Lord had warned me. The more His Revelation grows the more Satan's efforts of stopping everything grow. I know it's Satan since he leaves my soul unconsoled and in despair.

Praised be the Lord! **Glory be to God.**♥
(St Michael said 'praised be the Lord' after reading his prayer and St Mary said 'Glory be to God' after reading Her prayer.)

---

¹Abba in Greek.

Flower, have faith in Me. Pray Vassula. Pray My Vassula for the world to open their eyes and hear with their ears. Justice will prevail. Perverted creation! Even Sodom's sins will appear less perverted in comparison to yours; her sins are great but yours have pierced eternity! Garabandal shall not be buried - Garabandal's graces shall re-live!

Jesus, O Jesus, I'm so happy to be synchronizing again with You!

Come, I Jesus have never abandoned you. Accept those trials -everything comes from Me. ♥ ♥ *Vassula, Satan is hounding you, so do not sleep. Sleeping leads you into temptation - you become an easier prey for Satan if you are unaware, so be alert, be on your guard.* <u>*When you are aware, you feel My Presence*</u> - *remember My Presence.*

Jesus used to <u>shake me</u> to wake me up these days I was being attacked by Satan.

TREASON HAS ENTERED IN MY SANCTUARY

April 30th, 1988

♥ ♥ Jesus?

I Am. I am the Revelations. Vassula, upon whom I am engraving My Words, synchronize with Me to understand Me. I love you to folly, creation, but you have withdrawn from Me, treason has entered into My Sanctuary[1], giving birth to Dispersion. ♥ *Vassula, try beloved to discern Me fully.* ♥

- NEVER DOUBT OF MY PRESENCE -
- STAY AWAKE -

Later On:

♥ Jesus?
I Am.

Jesus' Presence is very vivid, it's like I've gone out of a 'fog' and see Him and feel Him better than the last few days when Satan had been hammering me. Right now it is as if Jesus is upon earth in flesh again, or as if I went back in time at His days here. All is alive, its wonderful!

---

[1]<u>We</u>, are His sanctuary.

Vassula all I want is Love. Glory be to God for teaching those things to mere children and hiding them from the learned and wise. ♥
(In saying this Jesus' Beautiful Head had turned upward. Jesus felt very pleased that I do not try and rationalize all this. He likes us to believe blindly and innocently in a naive manner.)

♥   *I am the Alpha and Omega, the Beginning and the End.*

I felt His Presence so very strongly. God's "vibrations" were making my whole body and mind and soul vibrate, it's difficult to put this into words. At the same time His Peace enveloping me, all this together gives me a wonderful feeling. It was like I plunged into a sea of Love. I felt transparent. I felt happy, so happy that tears of happiness were running down my cheeks.

Never doubt of My Presence. ♥ *Vassula, remain now near Me; pray, I will hear you.*
Jesus meant right away in the state He has put me in[1].
I heard every word.
I prayed the 'Our Father', but <u>very</u> slowly, out of my heart it came, while my tears never ceased because of the state of happiness I was in.
Come, I and you, you and I, together always and forever. I, Jesus, love you soul.
♥   *We, us.* ♥

Later on:

I am happy to have you near Me. Ah Vassula, how many times I feared for you, Satan hates you and is determined to thwart My Plans; in his fury he creates all your agonies, he lies to you, accusing you to bring you to despair. Daughter, I had forewarned you of his attacks. Blessed one do not give way to Satan, cling on Me, I am helping you to surmount all temptations. Remember how Satan approaches you easier if you fall asleep, so be alert; child, always on the wake, be on your guard.
By praying Lord?
♥   *Yes, by praying.* ♥ *Pray, pray, pray.* ♥ ♥
Jesus makes me understand that prayer keeps off Satan. Prayers which <u>reach</u> him.

---

[1] I prayed.

YOUR HOME IS IN MY SACRED HEART

May 1st, 1988

♥   *Vassula, listen to My Voice and synchronize with Me - reflect on My Absoluteness[1]. Lift your mind to Me;* ♥ *your home is in My Sacred Heart, My Holy Spirit aroused you.* ♥ *Daughter, everything you discerned is correct.*
When Jesus was saying: My Holy Spirit aroused you, first I saw a dove fluttering above some corpses, among them I layed. Then from Heaven came a beam of Light falling on me, raising me.

Vassula, are you willing to continue with My Works?

Ah, yes Lord, if You still want me. Remember my incapacity, Lord, and help me. I thank You for having so much patience with me. Thank You for pouring upon me Your gifts which I do not merit. I love You Lord to death.
♥ *I love you and I bless you. Daughter, tell James and David how My Works will enlighten many hidden Works of Mine which received abuses from men,* ♥ *healed and resurrected by Me. Stay small so that you can penetrate deeper into My Heart.* ♥ *We, us?*
Yes Lord, we and us. ♥

PRAY WITH LOVE

May 2nd, 1988

Again the Lord asked me to pray the 'Our Father' in His Presence in this way of uniting. I prayed again very slowly, it was like as if He was nodding making me understand how He is listening. For when it comes from the heart, I feel Him facing Me, we are face to face. Jesus approves this manner of praying very much.
♥ *Yes Vassula, satisfy Me by praying in this manner, pray with love.*
(I want to add that I knelt while I prayed.)
Betrothed, I am guarding you from evil, together with My Mother and together with My angels - at your side We all are. ♥
Thank You My Lord for the protection You are giving us against the devil.

---

[1] I should meditate on His Omnipotency and His Eternity.

I AM ALIVE AND ALIVE I WILL ACT
THE TIME IS ALMOST OVER

May 4th, 1988

I prayed part of the Holy Rosary. Maybe I'm not doing it all correctly, but I am trying. Then I pray the three prayers the Lord wants us to pray. I'm going to write them down so that everyone knows them.

♥ Jesus?

I Am. Have My Peace, it is I the Lord - do not fear[1].
O Lord, what can I do more? (I wanted to satisfy God.)
Worship Me! Love Me! ♥ *My Holy Cross at Medugorje is Alive and in flames; I have blessed this territory, giving My Graces through My Mother who is the Arc of Alliance of My Divine Works[2].*
♥ (God has been giving me for the past days a vision of an immense Cross on a mountain, this cross was in flames, but not like as if it took fire and is burning, no, like the fire comes out of the Cross, shaped as a Cross. A luminent non-stopping fire and non-consumming fire.)
Hear Me, in just a short while I will make the unbelievers knee bend on that very mountain; My Holy Cross is Alive with a Living Flame[3]. ♥

I asked the Lord what fire represents here and He told me: "<u>LIFE!</u>"

Vassula, the Time is imminent ever so imminent[4]. O COME TO ME BELOVED ONES! Come to Me! I am the Way, the Truth and the Life. Come to Me now when there is still time, when the grass is still green and the flowers still blooming on the trees. O come![5] I love you exceedingly! I have loved you always inspite of your wickedness and your evil doings. Creation, why thrust yourselves so willingly at Satan's feet? Creation, return to Me when still the Spring breeze is blowing and there is still time for your conversion. Ah Vassula, the time is almost

---

[1]Often I fear that the devil appears to me instead of Jesus; pretending he is Jesus. The times he's done it I discover it rather quick. Then he flees.
[2]Medugorje is a remote village in Yugoslavia, where St Mary appears <u>everyday</u> to some teenagers from 1981 to this day.
[3]I'm wondering if this will not one day be one of the promised signs at Medugorje.
[4]Jesus suddenly cried out these words from His Heart.
[5]Jesus, our Saviour, was begging.

over¹. What is to come is so very near you! My messenger, you upon whom lies My Word², ♥ this Word which is Alive - how could men think they can bury My Word?³ <u>FAITH</u> *has been distorted to appear like an ugly crippled evil-beast⁴ - that is how they make It appear. All that is Divine and Alive today has been distorted in this way, to appear in this way, and make you flee from It - fearing It. ♥ Why is it that you want your God silent and dead? I am* <u>Alive</u> *and alive I will* <u>act</u>. *♥ ♥ ♥*

The ecclesiastical authorities will invariably deny you. ♥ I had been denied by the Pharisees because they believed they held all the power and authority; they had forgotten that they could not do anything without being given power and authority from above, and now these sons of Cains keep forgetting that they cannot do anything unless I give them the power and authority. I Am The Authority, was, and will always be for all Eternity. ♥   Now, as it is, those that deny My Providential Works⁵ are blinded by their vanity which obscures them; they are those same blind guides, who repeat the Error; clean and polished from the outside but all corruption and dead-men's bones from the inside! ♥   Vassula, listen carefully and discern Me so that you are able to write everything - not adding nor omitting since you and My two servants⁶ hold My Message of Peace and Love and since I have given you the Three Crowns, these of Love, Peace and Justice and which you are to leave by Peter's feet⁷.

(I dared to interrupt here.) Lord, the three of us?

♥ Yes, My servants will have to be ready for escorting you. My beloved one, I, the Lord, desire them to be with you. ♥ I desire that around your waists you wear a Belt, offered by Me, which will represent Child-like-Faith, which delight Me. Yes, let this Belt be as a symbol; I desire you to be bare-footed - be like monks; I desire you to wear My Garments of Old.
Which are Lord?
My Garments are Simple⁸.
Beloved Lord they might think we are a new sect!

---

¹While Jesus was saying these words I saw in an interior vision a hot, deadly, poisoned, <u>strong</u> wind blowing on us and nature, leaving on it's passage only death. Everything it touched was left dead.
²This Message.
³Jesus felt amazed while saying these words.
⁴I saw an ugly small black animal deformed.
⁵This Message and others.
⁶James and David.
⁷Symbolic.
⁸Jesus spoke in metaphors but I understood it literally.

Ah Vassula! how little do you understand! Daughter, I will enlighten you and my sons and tell you what I mean by 'wearing My Garments of Old.' ♥ *I love you for attaining this discernment of today. Never doubt of My Love - remember My Presence.*

Yes Lord, thank You Lord Jesus.

Here is one of the prayers Jesus recommends us to pray daily:

NOVENA OF CONFIDENCE TO THE SACRED HEART OF JESUS

O Lord Jesus Christ, to Your Most Sacred Heart,
I confide this intention.

(Here mention your request.)

Only look upon me, then do what Your Heart inspires... Let Your Sacred Heart decide... I count on it... I trust in it... I throw myself on It's Mercy...

Lord Jesus You will not fail me. Sacred Heart of Jesus, I trust in Thee. Sacred Heart of Jesus, I believe in Thy love for me. Sacred Heart of Jesus, Thy Kingdom Come. O Sacred Heart of Jesus I have asked for many favours, but I earnestly implore this one. Take it, place it in Thy Sacred Heart. When the Eternal Father sees it covered with Thy Precious Blood, He will not refuse it. It will be no longer my prayer but Thine. O Jesus, O Sacred Heart of Jesus, I place my trust in Thee. Let me never be confounded. Amen.

This is the second prayer Jesus recommends us to pray daily:

PRAYER TO ST MICHAEL

St Michael the Archangel, defend us in the day of battle, be our safeguard against the wickedness and snares of the devil. May God rebuke him, we humbly pray, and do thou O Prince of the Heavenly Host, by the Power of God, cast into Hell, Satan and all the other evil spirits who prowl through the world seeking the ruin of souls. Amen.

MARY, QUEEN OF HOLY ANGELS - PRAY FOR US!

And this is the third prayer Jesus recommends us to pray, also daily:

THE MEMORARE OF
ST BERNARD

Remember, O most gracious Virgin Mary that never was it known that anyone who fled to thy protection, implored thy help or sought thy intercession, was left unaided. Inspired by this confidence, I fly unto thee. O Virgin of Virgins my Mother! To thee do I come, before thee I stand, sinful and sorrowful. O Mother of the Word Incarnate! Despise not my petitions but in thy mercy hear and answer me. Amen.

FREE-WILL

May 7th, 1988

Lord?
I Am. ♥
I wish to ask both My servants this: "are you still willing to continue working for Me? Are you willing, in spite of the trials which lie ahead of you? If you are still willing, My instructions are going to be written and you can follow them." ♥

I WILL AMASS MY SCATTERED LAMBS

May 7th, 1988

Later on: St Mary.

♥ **Vassula! I will always console you when the wolves' fiery words wound your soul. Satisfy My Son's thirst - quench His insatiable thirst for Love. Let us pray to the Father.** ♥

> "Father of Mercy, in adoration I am at Your Feet, in You I Hope and Believe, I love You boundlessly. Amen."

(I repeated.)
Thank You St Mary, allow me to lean on You.
Beloved, My Son and I never leave you. ♥

Hear My Son. ♥

I, Jesus, love you soul.
I love You Lord! Lord! What will we do? (I meant what are the further instructions now.)
♥ *All will be done by Me. I am the One and only Holy Pure Ecclesia. Pray for this Unity; pray for those souls who reject you My beloved ones.*
(I suddenly saw Jesus opening His arms enfolding Father James, David and me together near His Sacred Heart, an Act of Consolation, drawing us very near His Heart.)

I love you, I am with you all the time[1]. Come to Me when your heart is afflicted by the ravenous wolves. ♥ *Hear Me: My Kingdom is among you.*

Peter-of-My-Heart, Peter-of-My-Lambs. ♥ *This is the Holy Name I have given him: Peter-of-My-Lambs, but the Cains have dethroned him, stealing from him the Crown I had honoured him with. I, the Lord, love him for this one is the well-beloved of My Soul; this stolen Crown I will return to him. I will overthrow the false kingdoms which sallowed My Body; floating kingdoms; kingdoms without roots. I will reverse these false kingdoms and raise up in My Light, like a Torch, My Real Kingdom and to Peter I will give entirely back his Seat, enthroning him; and I will place into his hand an iron sceptre in which I will give him the power to reign as shepherd. I will amass My scattered lambs[2] and when I have done this, I will encircle this Fold with My Arms and no one! no one! - not even the evil-one - will be able to steal one single lamb out of this Fold.* ♥ *My Cape I will spread over them and shelter them in My warmth, protecting them. To Peter I shall give back what I had given him when I was on earth and in flesh.* ♥ *No man will transgress the bounds of My Will, for all that now is your doing, not Mine. I abhore anarchy and rebellion against Me.* ♥ *Betrothed! Brothers! Every step you take, I, the Lord, bless.* ♥

♥ *I, the Lord, whom you seek, will suddenly come into My Temple. I am at your door knocking - will you let Me in? With Me I carry My Salvation Plan; My Scroll has been written and is ready for consumption.* ♥ *It should be mentioned that I relayed My Salvation Plan of Peace and Love to honour Peter's Seat as it should have been honoured; I come to give him back his shepherd's crown. Approach Peter... approach Peter... approach your Lord.* ♥ ♥

Thank You Lord.
♥ *Weary not of writing.* ♥ ♥ *We, us?*
Yes Lord, we, us.

---

[1]Jesus' voice was very soft and intimate here.

[2]I had a vision of angels trying to push together the lambs into the fold.

I LOVE HOLINESS
SEE ME IN MY CREATION

May 10th, 1988

My Lord?

♥ *I Am. Lean on Me entirely - I am your Peace. Come, do not succumb into temptation; learn from Me - remembering My ways. Pray, pray, pray. Let every word uttered from your lips be a prayer which reaches heaven, rising up like incense. Be in constant bonds with Me; lift your mind to Me; think of Me only; all that you have and which is good comes from Me - I revived you. Write it.*
(Jesus sitting near me posed His hand on my shoulder.)
I have formed you; I will encircle you all with My Arms. Flower, speak to Me - you have lessened your conversations with Me. I am giving you everything; I share My Works with you, so do the same to Me, your Holy Companion, your Spouse. I want to share with you your daily activities! My Vassula, when your lips open to utter any word let them utter only holy words; let them utter prayers; <u>be in constant prayer</u>.

How Lord, how is this possible Lord?

I will tell you. Let your attitude, your thoughts, your wishes, your meditations, your reflections, your services, your needs, everything! - let them be a prayer. <u>My Image</u>. Every scope given to you should enliven within you a holiness - this holiness which was given to you by Me but souls have forgotten how to use it. I have given to each soul this gift; I will enliven this grace which now lies dormant within you all. I love holiness. ♥

Would You Lord, with Your grace, make me then holy?

♥ *My beloved, I will, for this is My desire for every soul.* ♥ *I, the Lord, have chosen for you this road; you will adore Me your God in silence[1], I and you, secluded - living for Me. Enjoy My creation, love Me; see Me in My creation, love My creation.* ♥ *Vassula,* (Jesus looked at me. Stopping for a while. He joined His Hands together, His elbows on his legs, His Hands hanging. His Holy Face is looking at me. His hair is long and loose, very light chestnut-blonde with red reflections.)

---

[1]God has given me the grace of meditation. With this I need to be alone.

♥ *Vassula?*
Yes Lord.
Give Me your heart and I will place it in the depths of My Sacred Heart; enter into My Sacred Heart... enter into My Sacred Heart... enter here. (Here Jesus pointed His Heart with His index.) *O come! I have been calling you ever since you were born! I have reserved a place for you. Vassula! Vassula!*
Lord! I have given You my heart already, my life, all is Yours!

Ah Vassula, try and perceive My Will. Listen to My Heart beats - every beat is a call for you. ♥ *Why do you resist Me?*

Lord?
I Am.
Lord, may I tell You something in Your ear?
I am listening. ♥ (Here I said something to Jesus.) *Enter My Sacred Heart and* <u>*rest*</u> *in there.* (I asked something else here to Jesus.) *Yes, let it be so.* ♥ *I love you.* ♥
I love You Lord.

Later on:

I always feel so sad that certain people reject St Mary as Mother of God, I felt terribly sad and wept over Her. I wanted to console Her. <u>Satan attacked</u>.
"Vassula reserve your tears, I hate all those martyrs. P........."
Go! Satan go! Go behind me Satan.

Lord Jesus?
I Am. I will show to you now and then how the devil despises you and My Holy Ways - those ways I am teaching you. If you shed tears of love for My Mother, it infuriates the devil. <u>*Blessed are those who live in My House and are able to recognize your Holy Mother as "Mother of God" and "Queen of Heaven".*</u> *Come beloved, I will bless you[1].* ♥ ♥ *I bless you My Vassula.*
I bless You Jesus. (I touched His Holy Head.) Thank You for teaching me.
Come, remember![2] Let us share! We, us!
Yes Lord, we, us.

---

[1]Jesus stood up, posed His Hand on my head, blessing Me.
[2]With His finger like a Teacher He said, "remember."

May 12th, 1988

Lord?

♥ *I Am. Never doubt Vassula. Everything comes from Me. Write:*
Jesus means my feeling of 'vibrations' in His Presence. Jesus gave me images of His Crucifixion again, of how every drop of blood He had was shed on earth for us. He showed me His Face of agony on the Cross, bruised, black and blue, covered with sweat and blood, His hair stuck together with blood and His Eyes filled with His Blood from His pierced Forehead. All this for me; for <u>us</u>.

♥ *Altar! Keep your flame ablaze for the consummation of My Church! Come, together - feel My Presence.* ♥ ♥

WELCOME THE KINGDOM OF GOD LIKE A LITTLE CHILD

May 16th, 1988

Jesus?
I Am. Come, keep My teachings in your mind. I am your Divine Teacher, dictating you. ♥ *Vassula, in less than two years I have taught you many of My Divine Works, ever so mysterious to men, and for their ability to fathom them.* ♥ *You see My child these Divine Works are beyond human understanding; many souls do not respond on My Works for these souls seldom want to change.*

Lord? What do You mean by 'change'?
These souls are attached to the world, to what is material, even though they call themselves spiritual[1]; they are not, since they cling on what they see with their physical eyes and touch with their body; they are stubborn, living aridly; their heart will not open to let My Divinity pour into them.

Yes, there are many factors that obstruct them from dwelling in My Light. I have said and will repeat again and again these very important words: "Anyone who does not welcome the Kingdom of God like a little child, will never enter it." ♥ *Be innocent; believe in a <u>child-like-faith</u>, then My Divine Light will encompass you, and you, like a flower will face the sun and open, allowing My Light to pour into you. Understand My beloved children that I am with you always[2]. I love you inexhaustably.* ♥

---

[1] Anybody calling himself spiritual but denies God's supernatural works.
[2] We should not be surprised at supernatural approaches. They are not fairytales.

Jesus will You remain teaching us?

All that I have to say will be written. I am always near you; loving you; teaching you. Let those that have ears listen that it is I, Jesus, your Lord, manifesting Myself through this instrument. I have never abandoned you. ♥
(Jesus looked at me.)

Vassula, I will teach you to progress. ♥

A PARABLE - THE CROWS AND THE HARVEST

May 16th, 1988

Jesus?

I Am. Pray for all those souls who have not yet understood the Holy Bible and who misinterpret so many parts of It, cutting out entire parts which could enlighten you - eradicating rich factors that could illumine you. Listen and try to understand: "there once was a sower who prepared an enormous field -he chose the finest grain to sow ♥ *and produce the best wheat! Now when the harvest was ready to be reaped, and what a rich harvest it was! his enemy sent out a bunch of crows to fly over his field; this field, toiled and prepared with so much love and sacrifice; a ready and rich harvest able to feed the entire country - leaving no one hungry. But, these crows which were sent by his enemy, started to pick up here and there from the harvest -devouring and ravaging as much as possible.* ♥ *If it was not for the sower seeing all this and sending out his servants to chase away those crows they would have devastated the entire harvest."* ♥

Lord, will You now explain please?

♥ *Come, the sower is I, the Lord - the harvest is My Word[1]. The enemy is Satan. The crows are those souls influenced by Satan, through many years -now and again - to eat up the important elements from My Words; but I, Jesus Christ, the Lord, will manifest Myself time and again to bring back to you those missing elements. I will embellish and repair My Church.* ♥ *I love you creation.* ♥ *My entire Church will be renewed. These elements given back to you, will embellish*

---

[1]The Holy Bible.

It and will perfect It, but first I will crown Peter, Peter-of-My-Lambs. I have given him this name which he will keep. I will enter My Temple, just as I had done whilst on earth, and with My Belt-of-Integrity strike all those imposters. I will enter with force and overthrow all the money-worshippers. ♥ I will enter 'Jerusalem' so that the New Jerusalem can begin to see the Light; I will sweep away those blocks and open the Way - this My Vassula will be known as the Great Tribulation of My Church. ♥ I will then place into Peter's hand an iron sceptre with which he will guard My sheep, and for those who do not know and still ask themselves 'why is it that we have to have a guide?' I tell you this - "have you ever seen or known of any flock of sheep without a shepherd? I am your Heavenly Shepherd and I have chosen Peter to keep My lambs until My return. I have given him the responsibility, so why all these disputes, why all these futile arguments? and for all those who still do not know My words, I tell you to read them in the Scriptures - they are to be found in the testimony of John, My disciple[1]. I will then unite My Church and encircle you with My arms into one fold for today; as it is you are all scattered, developing too many communities, split sections. My Body you have torn apart and <u>this CANNOT BE</u>![2] I will unite you all. ♥

Jesus here means to unite The Roman Catholics, Orthodox and Protestants, but also other groups apart these, even sects. The Lord will call us under Peter, or, Peter will come to us.

Then I and Peter will work together; I will show him My hidden elements; I will show him many of My mysteries to enable him to teach them to My children and under this teaching you will see a <u>new heaven and a new earth</u>. ♥ I, the Lord, will renew the walls of My Sanctuary. Ah Vassula! There is so much to be repaired! Allow Me to use you.

Yes Lord, please give me the necessary strength. Amen.
Let My finger be on your heart to keep My Altar ablaze. I, God, love you in spite of your absolute nothingness. I will give you the strength you need to be able to accomplish your mission - this mission I have sent you for. Do not get discouraged - be patient. Soon you will return Home to Me, to Us[3]. Receive Our Peace; pray for the renewal which My Church will undergo. I, the Lord, love you all. ♥ We, us!
Yes Lord forever.
♥ Come.

---

[1] John 21:15-17.

[2] Jesus was definite here.

[3] St Mary was with us, reminding me of my vision when I was ten or eleven.

MY MERCY IS GREAT UPON YOU

May 19th, 1988

Lord? The reason maybe that the ecclesiastical authorities do not respond could be that since Your Message of Peace and Love is a "reminder" for repentance as the ones of Lourdes and Fatima they, maybe, do not feel obliged to go into this one too, and they are burdened with work anyway. Although it is not just a reminder. It is also speaking of unity, Russia's conversion and "Peter's" Seat.

♥ *Vassula, I Am the Word - the Everlasting Word. My Word is Eternal Life.* ♥ *If I decide to remind My creation of My Love, even daily, through various instruments and to call you for repentence, it is not up to any creature who is but dust and ashes to discard any of My spoken words.* ♥ *I, the Lord, know of your needs and I tell you, My Mercy is Great upon you![1] Come, feel My Presence.*

Yes Lord.

We, us. ♥ ♥ ♥

COME TO ME ALL YOU WHO THIRST

May 24th, 1988

Lord!

♥ *I Am. Come to Me all you who* ♥ *thirst. Come! Come and drink! I will fill you with everlasting water from My Well which never runs dry[2].* ♥ *Vassula, do not neglect Me! I am All-Faithful. Be at My side. We, us? We, us?*
Yes Lord, Yes. St Mary. Thank You Lord. May Your Name be Blessed. Praised be the Lord!

---

[1] The Lord really emphasized this sentence ever so much.
[2] Jesus looked at me after He paused.

DO YOU WANT ME TO BLESS YOUR FOOD?

May 25th, 1988

This morning I was very busy, it was somewhat difficult to discern the Lord and talk together. Later on I sat to have my lunch at the veranda. While I was eating I suddenly saw interiorly with the eyes of my soul the Lord sitting at the table with me watching me eat. He said, "Is it good?" I said: "Yes Lord it is, thank You Lord." There was a slight pause, then He asked me: "Do you want Me to bless your food?" I said: "Yes Lord, do." So Jesus blessed my food. He stayed with me until I finished. Then I thanked Him for the food - this was to show me that I could ask Him to bless my food before I eat.

♥ *Beloved, endeavour to ask for My blessings - I will bless your food.* ♥

Yes Lord, thank You for teaching me.
Vassula, I love you. I will be your Heavenly Teacher till the end. ♥
Thank You Jesus. Lord, I invoked St Francis and prayed to him, does he hear me when I pray to him?
♥ *Nothing goes by unheard - everything is heard in Heaven.* ♥ *He has heard you - Saint Francis is by your side.* ♥ *Come, we, us?*
Yes my God. Praised be the Lord. ♥

MEDITATE THE ROSARY

May 31st, 1988

Jesus?
♥ *I Am. The Holy Rosary was well said.* ♥
Thank You Lord and Holy Mother for teaching me. (I prayed the usual three prayers, and the whole Holy Rosary - completing It this time.)

Devote your time these days upon the Holy Rosary.

Yes Lord - Lord I've been reading 'Gabrielles' Homebringing Mission but this does not mention St Mary or the Holy Rosary.
♥ *Vassula, let it be known that this is what I the Lord call a misleading torch; pray for these sects. I, the Lord, will not allow to have My Body separated from My Head; these, daughter, are those floating kingdoms, kingdoms without roots,*

I have been telling you about. I have now given you the proof of one. Needless to tell you how My Sacred Heart feels. ♥ *Vassula meditate upon My Sacred Heart - this Heart which never fails you. I will be your Holy Teacher till the end.* ♥ *Do not leave My Hand. We, us?*
Yes Lord.
We, us?
Yes St Mary. Glory be to God.

ABBA

June 1st, 1988

While talking again to a Greek young lady about Our Father in Heaven again the word Abba came in my mouth "O babas" in Greek.
♥ *Vassula, call Me Baba; with love I receive this word - this form of call. I am your Celestial Father.* ♥ *We, us?*
Yes Lord forever.

LEARN THE HOLY ROSARY
SIGNS OF THE END OF TIMES

June 2nd, 1988 - (Fete - Dieu)

♥ I prayed now the 4rd day, the whole Rosary, and of course the three prayers the Lord wishes us to pray. Lord?
♥ *I Am. My Vassula, by persevering[1] the devil weakens - evil diminishes. Learn the Holy Rosary; embellish My Church.* ♥

The Lord means that the Orthodox and Protestants and other Churches who do not pray the Holy Rosary should learn it, thus enriching The Holy Church and furthering the devil, crushing him; heresy will diminish as well as apostasy in the Church, which has infiltrated because of the unfaithfulness and disobedience.

---

[1]Trying hard to please St Mary and Jesus by praying the Holy Rosary, obeying their will.

Yes Vassula, love will increase and evil will decrease ♥ *and for those who argue saying that this was not said by Me[1], I will show you how meaningless their arguments are; their zeal is misguided and do not seem to see clear My Righteousness; they are declarling only their own ideas; they would be ready to disown Me[2]. Surprised by the poor instrument I chose to manifest Myself, they will deny you as coming from Me; they have forgotten what Scripture says. Scripture says[3]: "I have been found by those who did not seek Me and have revealed Myself to those who did not consult Me." ♥ So I, the Lord, tell you - open your hearts, not your mind!*

♥ *Vassula of My Sacred Heart, you have heard Me whisper into your ear[4]. I want to show you in Timothy 1 and 2 everything that has been predicted for the last days of your era. My creation has degenerated and has fallen lower than the Sodomites; darkness came upon them as a deadly veil, sent by Satan. Satan has sent many false teachers, false prophets, who appear today as philosophers, teaching dogmas which do not come from Me your Lord; and My children blinded by their ignorance fall into these traps set up by Satan. I wish that these parts of Timothy be read in public as a warning: 1 Timothy, 4:1-16 and 6:20-21 and 2 Timothy, 2:14-26 - these prophecies were especially pronounced for your times. ♥ Then in 2 Timothy, 3:1-17 - in this passage it foretells the state of your era, to be found now, for these are the last days before the end of Times. ♥ Solemnly, I request from you all to redouble your prayers for a 'come-back'. My Sacred Heart is open for any soul who will repent and who wills to return to Me. ♥ Flower, seek always the Spirit of Truth and Discernment before you write with Me. Love loves you and will guide you. ♥ Come, rest in My Sacred Heart - I will never forsake you. ♥ We, us?*

Yes Lord, Yes Holy Mother. ♥

⊂× ΙΧθΥΣ

---

[1] To learn the Holy Rosary.

[2] Declare that these writings are not from God, because many things written by God in here do not fit with their convenience.

[3] Isaiah 65:1-2.

[4] Two nights ago Jesus whispered into my ear that I should read in the Holy Bible, Timothy I and II.

HOW TO DISCERN TRUE REVELATION
FROM FALSE ONES or DISCERNMENT

June 3rd, 1988

My Lord?
*I Am. Vassula, never get discouraged; remember My Love I have upon you.
Dearest soul, I love you with your weakness; you are frail; allow My Spirit to guide
you; annihilate in Me, in My Strength. Dissolve in Me and let Me do everything
so that they see that all this work is done by Me. You are nothing; stay nothing
and leave space for My Spirit to grow in you. Yes, let Me breathe in your
nothingness let Me delight in you; allow Me to use you in this way to redeem you
all and to unite you.* ♥
Yes Lord.

*Flower? These days I am teaching you to discern the true revelations and visions
from the false revelations, false doctrines and false visions.* ♥ *Everything which
is false comes from Satan; he sows seeds of confusion to blemish the Truth - like
in Pescara[1]. He sows darnel among the wheat, confusing you all. Furious with
the Medjugorje apparitions he tries to confuse you all - trying to label these Divine
Works as not from Me.* ♥ *Daughter, when you read a revelation which openly
expresses a <u>disunion</u> to My Church, denying Peter, denying your Holy Mother,
know that they do not come from Me the Lord your God - they come from My
adversary who appears and takes My Image to accomplish his designs which are
to separate you as much as possible. Know that I the Lord do not want My lambs
dispersed; I want you united under Peter - all in one flock. I desire you all
assembled together. I repeat again that I, Jesus Christ, the Lord, your Saviour,
selected Peter to feed and guard My lambs and sheep until My return - this Peter
who today is John-Paul II. <u>Listen to what the Spirit says to the churches</u>.* ♥
*Vassula, Satan knows that his days are numbered and because of this the red
dragon tries to pull with him as many souls as he can; he has introduced into many
minds, these minds that should have been filled with spirituality and holiness, all
sorts of diversions diverging you from the Truth and from all that is holy. Look
around you My beloved and you will understand. All these diversions were
introduced to you, children, as in the times of Sodom and Gomorrah, so that they
fill your spirit, leaving no space for what is holy, leaving no space for Me your
Creator and God.* ♥ *Yes, My Vassula, I feel rejected[2]. I feel forgotten and
unloved. I, who died on the Cross out of love for you; I, who am the Spirit of
Love - see how they treat Me? Do I deserve this?*

---

[1] A false prediction for an apparition.
[2] The Lord was very... sad. (I can't find the word, sad is not enough.)

My God, I feel torn within me Lord, why is it like that! Lord, oh Lord make a miracle please, I should not ask for miracles, but I love You and I do not want You hurt any more Lord.

♥ *Vassula, pray, pray, pray for this conversion.* ♥ *Satan is intensifying his works on My creation to drag you down to the Pit with him. O creation! How weak you are - how terribly weak you are!* ♥ *Any revelation denying the Holy Eucharist, calling It ritual[1], or denying the Immaculate Heart of your Holy Mother, does not come from Me.* ♥ *I, the Lord, love you boundlessly and wish to warn you once more from these false prophets.* ♥

Thank You Lord. ♥
Love Me.
I adore You Lord.
We, us?
Yes Lord.

MYSTERIES SHOULD REMAIN UNALTERABLE
- THE SEED OF REBELLION -

June 4th, 1988

Lord?

I Am. I shall never fail you. I will instruct you further on the Confusion in My Church. Endeavour to hear Me and please Me by praying the Holy Rosary; feel the Mysteries, see them through your Holy Mother's Eyes; these Mysteries which your era tries to rationalize. ♥ *Daughter, they still have not understood that I want them as children, innocent, with a child-like-faith.* ♥ *My Church, I imbued in Richness and Glory to feed many souls - entire nations; rich in its Mysteries - these Mysteries which many of you do not accept as Mysteries. My people today lack humility, simplicity; they lack pureness of Faith. Your era today is trying to rationalize everything - even My Mysteries!![2] How can they believe they can unveil Me their God? They try to describe My Mysteries rationally. These daughter are those 'crows' I have been telling you in the parable I have given you*

---

[1]Many call it tradition, dishonouring God.
[2]God seemed <u>amazed</u> (from our stupidity.)

about the Sower and the Crows[1]. These crows, having lost their faith, endeavour to set up their own theories to meet with their own human intelligence - trying to please the media - but, in truth, it is because of their own loss of faith in Me. ♥ *My Mysteries should remain unalterable, leaving them in their purity.* ♥ *These 'crows' have propounded ERRORS into My Church, corrupting the Truth, and My Word, (this rich harvest of My parable) My Word and My Mysteries should remain irrevocable.* ♥ *My Church today lies in obscurity and confusion; this is the heresy that penetrated into My Sanctuary - inducing errors upon many of My priests.* ♥ *The Spirit is calling and telling to all churches: refute falsehood, correct error, call to obedience, but do all with patience and with intention of teaching[2]. The time has come. Far from being content with sound teaching, people are avid for the latest novelty and collect themselves a whole series of teachers according to their own tastes; and instead of listening to the Truth, they turn to myths[3].* ♥ ♥ *Tell Me Vassula, can the Gospel be taken apart and separated?*

No Lord, it's impossible.

Take this as an example for My Body too; My Body too cannot be separated, yet, they have separated It... Rebellion penetrated into the very heart of My Church. First an interior rebellion sank into some of My priest's souls, bishops and cardinals; infused by Satan - obscuring them; shadowed under Satan's wings, they fell into his traps. This rebellion is now among them -lacerating My Sacred Heart. In the beginning, these sacerdotals having absorbed the Rebellion Seed from Satan, brooded over this seed, brewing evil designs, scheming; they brewed Opposition, contradicting the successor of Peter - this Peter-of-My-lambs selected by Me. This Rebellion Seed now fully grown gave them the force to openly declare their rebellion, to split again, throwing venomous arrows on My Church... They betrayed Me[4]. They betrayed this Heart-full-of-Love, just like Judas in Gethsamene...; they are dragging Me to be scourged...; they are scourging Me. O Vassula, how I suffer...

O Lord, no! (I could see Our Lord, in an interior vision, being scourged, tied to a column, and with every scourge that tore His Body, He shook, panting and breathless, His Body was one big wound.) Oh Lord when will they ever stop.)

♥ *They are not stopping. They are savagely scourging Me. Drunk with Vanity*

---

[1] See 16.5.88.

[2] II Timothy, Chapters 2-3. (Jesus asked me to open the Holy Bible and write this passage.)

[3] II Timothy, 4:3-5.

[4] When Jesus said "betrayed", He said it very bitterly.

and Disobedience, they are obeying and are loyal only to My foe! They are ruining My Foundation; they are dispersing My sheep; they are treading on Peter's feet, pushing him aside; they are trying to silence him... Cain never understood My Abel. Oh Abel... I will not forsake you; your God is near you; your God is coming with a <u>legion of angels</u> to defend you and tread on My foe -who is your foe. I am preparing My angels and Cain will not strike you; he will have to raise his hand against Me his God. I, the Lord, will surprise him. ♥ *My Church will be united by My Sacred Heart and the Immaculate Heart of your Holy Mother; as both Our Hearts are united so will My Church be united - My Church will be One.* ♥ ♥

LEGION OF ANGELS

June 7th, 1988

Lord?

I Am. I am very near you child - listen to My Heart beats... I will draw My angels[1] all inside My Heart so that they see and feel My Wounds and when they do their voice will rise so loud that My enemy will tremble and the very foundations of earth will shake when they will see in what state My lacerated Heart is; they will feel in their own heart a flame of love for Me their God. These angels, trained by your Holy Mother, prepared with love, is this legion your Holy Mother prepared to defend Our Church[2]. <u>These angels are to repay evil with love.</u> Come, Vassula of My Sacred Heart, I, the Lord, love you. Face Me. Remember, I come now with My Heart in My Hand - offering It to all mankind. How I love you all! (I saw an interior vision of a Sun with Our Lady inside, a Heart and a Cross.)

Vassula do not neglect to pray the Holy Rosary.
No Jesus, I will not.
Come. Us? We?
Yes Lord, us, we. Praised be the Lord.

---

[1]Jesus made me understand the 'legion of angels' mentioned on 4.6.88 are the priests who are guided by St Mary - the Marian Movement.
[2]Jesus Christ's and St Mary's Church.

MY MYSTERIES ARE TO REMAIN MYSTERIES

June 8th, 1988

♥ Jesus?

I Am. I will make you understand what I meant with the expression I had given you a few days ago in one of My Messages, when I said that you should wear My-Garments-of-Old; this was to tell you that My Gospel is not to change, but that It should be preached as I preached. I added that 'My Garments are Simple' - by this I mean that you should approach and understand the Gospel as a child, with a child-like faith. ♥ *Today Vassula many priests do not believe anymore in My Mysteries, so they do not preach the Gospels as they should be preached; they are only interested to please your era and meet with your culture. These priests wear "new garments" - different from Mine - they should know how much this grieves Me. My Gospel should be preached without errors and My Mysteries are to remain Mysteries.* ♥

Thank You Lord. Glory be to God. Amen.

BLESSED ARE THE POOR IN SPIRIT

June 9th, 1988

♥ *I, the Lord, love you in spite of your misery; you are poor in spirit, but I have said "blessed are the poor in spirit, for theirs is the kingdom of Heaven." Ah Vassula, that is precisely what I and your Holy Mother are doing. Our Hearts have selected wretched souls, poor in spirit and the least of My creation, to reveal My Providential Works so as to baffle the ones who call themselves wise. My Spirit will always chose those you call 'nothing' and 'contemptible' to shame the wise.* ♥ *Vassula - persevere[1]. I will always help you.* ♥ ♥ *Come, we, us?*

Yes Lord we, us.
We, us?
Yes St Mary, we, us.

---

[1] Try my best reciting the Holy Rosary.

June 10th, 1988

Praised be the Lord, blessed be the Lord, Glory be to God, for redeeming me.

♥ *Vassula, I will redeem many more souls with My Message. I, the Lord, love you ineffably.* ♥ *My Vassula, the time is here; flower, the hour has arrived -the hour where I will step-in-revealing Myself by this Message of Peace and Love to My predilected priests.* ♥ *My Sacred Heart has been pierced so savagely that It is but one big Wound now - and by My Own, by My closest friends... they are recrucifying Me. My own brothers have betrayed Me.* ♥ *I am sending you to My brothers to reveal Me entirely.* ♥
Oh God yes, I will do Your will. Yes Lord, be with me Lord never leave me. (Jesus was very sad and weary. This made me again sad.)

Vassula, peace be with you My child. (Holy Mother is speaking.)
<u>By the Holy Rosary</u> **and through the Holy Rosary[1], I am linking you[2] to My predilected souls and again by the Holy Rosary I will prevail.** ♥ **Daughter, this step is the beginning for many other events to come.** ♥ **Realize Vassula that at Fatima I appeared as the Lady of the Rosary and now to you I come as the Lady of the Rosary because I have introduced you to My Marian Movement** <u>through</u>[3] **the Holy Rosary. Vassula, I love you boundlessly.** ♥ **Are you willing to pray the Holy Rosary daily?**

Yes, I mean to obey You and Jesus.

♥ **Obedience... Let My children know how much evil is conquered by obedience.** ♥ **Ecclesia will revive. Jesus and I have always worked together because Our Hearts are united.** ♥ **I have prepared this legion of angels; and Jesus' Sacred Heart has prepared His Message of Peace and Love through you -** choosing the weakest, least and most wretched child of all humanity; but in spite of what you are, Jesus loves you boundlessly. <u>He chose you to show the world His boundless Mercy</u>. **He chose you to manifest His Love through you. Come back creation; come back to Us! The time is almost over now! Hear Our call. Children there is not much time left. O beloved hear Our Voice; hear Our plea; hear these Hearts that love you; those Wounded Hearts who weep incessantly for you - return to Us!**

---

[1]Since the Lord asked me to learn the Holy Rosary, I phoned an old neighbour of mine whom I knew to be Catholic, I asked her if she had time to teach me the Rosary. Surprised, because I'm Greek Orthodox, she came anyway. Through her I was introduced into the Marian Movement.
[2]Becoming member.
[3]See above footnote.

June 28th, 1988

Flower, read from My Book these words - writing them down. ♥ *Write, My Vassula. "I the Lord wish to develop My reflections further. Will you allow Me your God to use you?"*
Yes Lord, but never forget my incapacity please.

I do not. Listen to Me then and blossom; give off a sweet smell like incense; spread your fragrance abroad[1]. Bless Me your Lord for all My Works; declare the greatness of My Name; proclaim how wonderful My Providential Works can be. All that I order is promptly carried out - teach them not to judge and say, "what is this? Why is that?" - all will be studied in due time. ♥ *Let them learn and say, "all the works of our Lord are good." I will supply every need in due time; they must not say, "this is worse than that", for everything will prove it's value in its' time; so now I tell you to rejoice, and bless Me your God.* ♥ *I love all of you!* ♥ ♥ ♥ *Be one with Me; feel Me; discern Me and follow Me.*
Yes Lord. ♥

THOSE THAT OPPOSE PETER ARE OPPOSING MY CHURCH
- BEND TO UNITE -

June 21st, 1988

Lord?

♥ *I Am. Pray for the renewal of My Church. Pray for those souls who oppose Peter; pray for those who are trying to silence Peter. The days now are numbered and My Soul is submerged in sorrow; My Sacred Heart is imbued with bitterness; My Soul is yearning for them to realize their Error. Those that oppose Peter are opposing My Church; they are opposing My Law; they are opposing Me their Lord and God; they are condemning Peter-of-My-Lambs, thus condemning My Law. Blinded by Vanity himself they do not see clear anymore that by condemning Peter they are not following the Law but instead become judges of My own Law! O listen to what the Spirit says to the Church! Return, come back beloved one[2]. It is I, the Lord, who have selected Peter; Peter who today bears the name John-Paul II. I am telling you, beloved one, My Sacred Heart has chosen him. Come back,*

---

[1]Prophecy fulfilled. The Lord is sending me to many nations to proclaim His Glory.
[2]Bishop Lefebvre.

reconcile for My sake beloved. I, the Lord, will forgive your sins and will purify you. RETURN! Return all of you to Peter, for it is I your God who have chosen him; it is I who have given him a disciple's tongue and through Me he is able to reply to the weary. Oh creation! Is there no more wisdom left in you? Creation! You are failing to appreciate My Fathomless Love I have for you and yet, I answer to everyone who invokes Me. I am with you when you are in trouble, I am your Refuge. ♥ Today I, the Lord, will add one more commandment. Write: "bend! Bend to be able to reconcile and unite; humble yourselves to unite." ♥ Child,

Yes Lord?

I give you My Peace. Be obedient, allowing Me to use you as I wish. Trust Me - you are in your Father's Hands. ♥

Lord I am but following You, and my soul is in peace as a child with his mother, trusting You fully and as a child I want to obey You.

Remember My Presence. I am with you. We, us?

We, us?

Yes Lord. Yes St Mary.

SHARE MY CROSS BY LOVING ME

June 29th, 1988

Lord?

♥ I Am. Flower, this love I have for all humanity was never understood properly. I suffer! I am suffering profoundly. Dearest soul rest Me; rest Me by loving Me.

O Lord, if I could alleviate your sufferings by sharing your sufferings allow me to do it; use me, use every molecule of mine, teach me to love you infinitely.

♥ I love you My Vassula of My Sacred Heart. We are sharing everything. Realize that you are sharing My Cross, you are sharing My Passion. O Vassula! My Blood is gushing out of My Body in rivers. I am being recrucified by My own; by the apostasy in the very sanctuary of My Church; by cardinals, by bishops, by priests - My closest friends are betraying Me. I have been abandoned by many. I have been scourged by many; I have been pierced by My most intimate friends; I am suffering and I am going through a second Passion.

My Lord.

Love Me, love Me. Let Me be able to pronounce the same words your guardian angel told you: his words were 'no man ever loved his angel as much as you have.' ♥ Little one, let Me be able to tell you one day, 'no man ever loved Me in your era as much as you have.'

June 30th, 1988

Today Bishop Lefebvre is signing and he is being excommunicated. All day my spirit felt very low.

REPENT AND CONVERT
NOW THAT THERE IS STILL TIME

July 3rd, 1988 - Rhodes

Peace be with you child. My Ecclesia will revive but before this renewal She will suffer even more[1]. She is in the beginning of Her Tribulations. ♥ *Here, take a look at My Cup of Justice.* ♥

I looked at a beautiful gold cup decorated with precious stones, it was full to the brim, if one would move it, it would surely spill.

See how full it is? It is very near to spill over - beware! For once My Justice will spill over, it will only pour out on you creation, revealing the anathema prophecied long ago. You will be plunged into darkness. I will come to you like a thief, unexpected. I have been giving you warnings; I have been giving you signs to stay alert but you are rejecting them; you are unwilling to acknowledge the End of Times, no matter how much I try to warn you. Your disbelief in Me is total. My warning will be like a Purge to convert you and this will be done out of great pity. Alas for you creation! Alas for you disbelievers, who will intensify your disbelief and turn even more against Me. Your spirit, enveloped by obscurity, will be pulled as in a current by Obscurity himself[2]. Creation! How I pity you! How I suffer to see you lost forever! My children, in whom I breathed in you raising you to life, consecrating you before you were born, return to Me! My Heart lacerates to see how many will be drawn in this current into total obscurity and eternal damnation! Creation, although your sins are scarlet red I am all so willing to forgive you. Come, come to Me; return to Me your Father. I will welcome you and treat you a thousand times more lovingly than the 'Father of the prodigal son'; return to me before My Cup brims over; return before My Justice blows on you, arousing limitless blisters upon you, scorching you and every other living thing around you. You would want to breathe but you will only inhale a scorching wind,

---

[1] Than what She's suffering now.
[2] While saying this God was in pain and was suffering.

burning you inwardly and leaving you as a living torch![1] Creation, understand how imminent this Hour has become - for today you see the trees still blooming, but tomorrow there will be none left; you will be covered by Satan's smoke - a deadly veil. O do understand that these disasters and calamities are drawn upon you by your evil doings - by your apostasy, and by rebelling against Me. Repent now that there is still time - convert now! I am ready to forgive you. ♥ ♥ ♥ *Vassula allow Me to use you.*

Yes Lord, let everything be according to Your Will.

♥ *Please Me; obey Me your Lord; I will never abandon you. My Sacred Heart gives you My Peace.* ♥

MY DIVINITY TRANSFORMS YOU

July 11th, 1988 - Rhodes

(I have problems to be alone and write, too many people around.)

O daughter, I the Lord, love you. Come, offer Me whatever you have - even your wickedness and I will transform it into good. I, the Lord, am Divine and anything offered to Me can be transformed by My Divinity; I purify every single deed; I can transform through My Pureness everything. ♥ *Vassula, retreat more often; come to Me, even if it is for just a short while.* ♥

- OFFER ME YOUR WILL -
- LOVE WILL COME BACK AS LOVE -

July 11th, 1988 - Rhodes

(I was asking Jesus what would be the first steps for the Roman Catholics and Orthodox to do to start uniting.)
I give you My Peace.
I offer you my will.

♥ *Be still, and listen. Offer Me your will and let My Sacred Heart leap with joy; rejoice your God; arouse My joy; delight this fervent Heart. Offer Me your will - you are offering it to your Father who created you.* ♥ *Come, I will answer you.*

---

[1] I saw a vision of someone running out to inhale fresh air from the intoxicated air surrounding him, but as soon as he inhaled, his insides were aflame.

Your brothers[1] will have to understand and believe that it is I, the Lord, who wishes to unite you. Your brothers would have to believe that I am using you as My tablet to write down My desires. They will all have to be willing to come down from those high seats they have procreated for themselves. My Church of old was Pure, Humble and filled with Love. My Church of today has been transformed to look like a legion of thrones. They will all have to descend from those high seats and follow the new commandment I have given them. I love My children and they have been driven away by those Cains; they have made a wilderness out of My House where thorns and briars only grow now. Vassula, the time is close at hand, My return is soon, Love will come back as Love. ♥ ♥ Love loves you. Seek not why I have chosen you to write down My Messages; understood only that I am glorified all the more for having chosen a nothing for this Message of Peace and Love. For the least you are, the greater I am; the lower you are, the more inclined I am to bend over you and reach you. Be absolutely nothing, allowing thus My Spirit to breathe in you. Efface yourself entirely so that I can only be seen. Gratify Me soul by surrendering often, offering Me your will - you are surrendering to Love. ♥ ♥ We? Us?

Yes Forever.

- AT YOUR DOORS I AM -

July 14th, 1988 - Rhodes

While I was in Rhodos, Jesus kissed and blessed many crucifixes and medallions.
♥ Peace be with you child. Gratify Me and smile at Me when you see Me. Ah Vassula, they have kept Me only at their entrance... forgetting Me, going back to their minor duties. See?

Awake! At your doors I am. I am as a beggar - behold your Sovereign begging you as a beggar. I beg you for love. Be good! Be Perfect! Love one another; repent often; pray often and not only for your interests. Come to Me out of love! I, the Lord, love you - a love you will never understand, not until you are in heaven. ♥ Embrace Me, like I the Lord embrace you. Sin no more... I know your weaknesses, your infirmities; I know your soul. Come, come to Me and give Me everything and I will embellish you. Vassula, tell them that they will know Me better if they open their heart completely and let Me in. I will be among them listening. ♥

---

[1]Roman Catholics and Orthodox.

Is that Lord when we all meet?
Yes. We, us?
Yes Lord[1].

Vassula, My child.
Yes, St Mary.
Rejoice Me and come up to Me[2] with My other children. ♥   Come and I will bless all of you. I love you. ♥
I bless you.

Remind them how I, the Lord, still call them; I want them to come and approach Me. Why withdraw from Love? I am always behind My Tabernacle, waiting patiently to see if one of them comes to visit Me. Alas! I am still waiting... Beware of Satan who always arranges all sorts of excuses to let you believe they are reasonable and valid; he embellishes them to appear ever so reasonable, stopping you from coming to Me. ♥   I love all of you. Make them understand that I do not love you more than them; this, some of them should understand fully; if they read My Message of Peace and Love they will understand, I the Lord love you all in the same way. I am repeating this for those who have not yet understood. So come to Me, visit Me; come and drink from Me and you will thirst for more; come and eat Me and you will desire Me more. Open your hearts and receive Me - do not let Me stand at your door! Welcome Me in your heart; I know your needs, I know your weaknesses - your soul needs Me and only through Me you will enter Paradise. Why do you allow your soul to be caught in those nets layed out by My foe? Return to Me; face Me; instruct yourselves by reading My Holy Word; your time spent by reading Me will not be in vain. ♥   Surely you can give your Saviour an hour of your day? Love one another. Be peaceful with each other. Forgive, like I forgive your sins. Repay evil with love. Be good! Be perfect! Come, Love loves you and love will never leave you. Love will help you and will guide you till the end. ♥ ♥

Sunday - Feast of St Marina

♥   Vassula, My Immaculate Heart rejoices every time I meet My children up in My little House of Tsambika. ♥   I, your Holy Mother, love all of you. Come, we, us?
Yes St Mary, we, us. (The Rhodians gave me crucifixes and medallions for Jesus to kiss.)

---

[1]Jesus was not very happy with the Rhodians.
[2]At Tsambika Chapel. (Rhodos)

Lord?
I Am.

Do You want to kiss those objects Lord? Blessing them?
Raise them to My lips - they will all be blessed. ♥ (I raised everything to Jesus' lips.)

BE MY CHILD OF LIGHT

July 25th, 1988 - (Back in Switzerland)

Jesus.
♥ *I Am. Teach My children to say the prayers I have given you.*
The 3 prayers Lord?
Precisely. Beloved, devote yourself entirely to Me; seek My interests and glorify Me.
With Your help, Lord.

Depend on Me. I will guide you till the end and everything will be accomplished in due time. ♥ *My Works can be compared to a Vine Tree; they will flourish and produce Their fruit at the right season, just like the vine tree will produce it's fruit at its season. Bear the hardships that surround you for My sake and rely on Me your God. Do not loose confidence. Your era is a wilderness; do not let this aridity affect you My child - you must trust Me. Have I not risen you from the dead? I am the Light and Life in Itself. Allow Me to test you now and then; allow Me to lead you in blind faith; allow Me to test your love for Me; allow Me to stretch this love you have for Me. Be My child of Light, living under My Light. I am the Light of this world who will embellish you.* ♥ ♥ ♥ *Remain faithful to Me.* ♥
♥

I SHALL COME TO YOU LIKE A THIEF

July 25th, 1988

♥ *My Day is drawing near and I shall come to you like a thief - unexpectedly, without warning you. Jerusalem! You have betrayed Me, your Lord, and right in the the centre of your heart evil has rooted itself. Yes Jerusalem, inside you lies the Lance's blade; treason and heresy has infiltrated in you. How could you ever believe that your wickedness will go by unseen from Me? I am coming to you unexpectedly, to overthrow you. I am at your very doors now and like lightening I shall descend upon you and annihilate you.* ♥ *You have chosen My adversary's power and not My Grace; you have chosen wickedness -relying on the Black beast instead of choosing Me the Light. With My own Hand I shall come and overthrow your seats, overthrowing all the evil-doers who block the Way to the Truth. Jerusalem! Your Tribulations have only begun. I will clean and purify you in My fire; I will extirpate your evil roots -burning them - and all those doctrines who sallowed My Body.*

Your shepherd, you want no more. Drunk with Vanity; drunk with Disobedience; drunk with Discordance - how could you believe you are able to survive? You have starved My lambs through Disobedience - looking after your interests and not Mine. Jerusalem! You give Me so much sorrow. How I always longed to Unite you all and gather your children - as a hen gathers her chicks under her wings sheltering them - but you refused. My Eyes, and those of your Holy Mother, never stopped streaming with Tears of Blood, watching so much injustice in My own House. ♥ *I have loved you with an everlasting love but I have only been betrayed and wounded by My own friends ... My Mercy is Great and I am willing to forgive you fully. I will not look upon My Wounds; I am willing to forget your sins.* ♥

Vassula, they have been scourging Me incessantly, yet, in spite of My acute suffering, I am willing to forgive them and forget .. Come child, stay in My Sacred Heart. Love is thirsty for love. (Jesus' lips were dry as parchment.) Rest now. I am with you. Pray for those souls who reject Me; ease My pains by loving Me. Please your God - your own Abba. ♥ *Come, we, us?*

Yes Abba. ♥ (I felt very touched again and pity for our Father whom they reject.) *Vassula, pity your brethren; pity their falls; pity their blindness and pray for them.*

A PARABLE : THE NONCHALANT SERVANTS

July 26th, 1988

Lord?

♥ *I Am. Vassula, I am leading you to show you in which state My Church is to be found. My Church has been wounded savagely and in a short time Ecclesia's Foundation will be shaken; this will be followed by the extirpation of all those who caused Her Wounds and who accumulated in My Body with intention of harming It - Her Tribulations have just started. Jerusalem's walls will tumble down into a heap of dust so that My New Jerusalem can be rebuilt. It is I, the Lord, who will*

construct her again; I will renew Her walls; I will embellish her so that you may all live under her New Roof, under a New Heaven and a New Earth, and <u>Love will return to you as Love</u>. Living among you, I will be your God and <u>under My Name</u> you will all live peacefully. Your spirit will be filled with holiness and purity. ♥
Yes Vassula, I will descend from above, like Lightening, renewing her entirely. ♥
Tribulations there will be many because they have made desolate My House - they have plundered It. Do you understand Vassula? It is like a Master of a House who entrusts His household to His servants; although they had been given strict orders to keep His House in order and watch for burglars, they disobeyed His orders by their nonchalance and carelessness. In His return He would find that His servants are asleep and in their sleep His House plundered - His valuables robbed. These servants disobeyed and rebelled on His Orders and these same servants will be taken care of in a severe way when the Master returns. ♥ *On My Return, I will find My House in ruin and My Fundamental Elements missing. My lambs I will find dispersed and starved to death. Ah Vassula, how much will I have to repair... Thorns and briars are replacing the lilies and roses I had planted by My own Hand; they have choked My flowers one after the other; they have grown with Satan's help to encircle and trap My Flower[1]. They are getting closer daily and are so near now to molest him and feel their poisonous sting - those thorns will suffocate him. Peter is trapped and stands helpless in their midst.*

Vassula?

Yes Holy Mother.
Believe, for all this is happening. My Son's Body will bleed even more profusely. Peter's end is near. Love is missing. ♥

ALLOW MY SPIRIT TO BREATHE IN YOUR SPIRIT

July 27th, 1988

Lord?

♥ *I Am. Please Me and discern Me. <u>I am</u> present; I am listening; I am among you.* ♥ *Try.* ♥ (I'm trying.) *Try harder. Follow My instructions and keep Me locked in your heart.*
Yes Lord.

---

[1]Pope John-Paul II.

Everything you do, do it for Me and Me only. ♥ *Come, I will remind you now and then of My Presence. Do not have the slightest doubt. Try and perceive what I have given you as work; work humbly, leaning on Me entirely; efface yourself totally so that I may only be seen; allow My Spirit to breathe in your nothingness - delight Me in this way. All that I have given you is Mine. Detach yourself entirely from this world so that you feel Me and thus be Mine completely. I, the Lord, am your Teacher and My Words come from Wisdom.* ♥ *We, us? Together, with your Holy Family.*

Yes Lord. Yes Holy Mother.

DISLOYALTY, JEALOUSY, DISUNITY AND IMPURITY

July 29th, 1988 - St Marthe

♥ *Beloved! Flourish with love; feel My Presence among you; feel My profound Love I have for all of you - believe in this Love. I am the Source of Love. My Spirit is upon you. Come... I wish you to become pure, holy, humble and merciful.* ♥ *Allow Me to stretch this love you have for Me into a limitless love; allow Me your Lord to pour into your hearts My superabundant Love and fill you up, impregnating you with Divine and Sublime Love, so that It may overflow and imbue this world, honouring My Church. Allow yourselves to draw from this Infinite Love and fill up your hearts.* ♥ *All I ask from you beloved brothers are love, faithfulness and purity.* ♥ *Do not get discouraged little ones when trials come - I will never abandon you. I am your Shepherd and I keep you hidden under My Cape; with Me you will eat; with Me you will never thirst.* ♥ *Treat each other as I treat you; love one another as I love you; respond to one another as I respond to your prayers. Feed from Me and do not accept Satan's fruits which are disloyalty, jealousy, disunity and impurity. Be like one! Be perfect! Let My House glitter from its pureness.* ♥ *Allow My dew of Righteousness to descend upon you and dissolve these heavy thunder clouds, scattering them away. Allow My Light to pierce them so that all darkness and evil disappear.* ♥ *Be like flowers facing the sun and let My Warm Rays revive your holiness, purity, integrity and love.* ♥ *Follow My commandment always to love one another as I the Lord love you.* ♥

I, the Lord Jesus Christ, love you boundlessly. I am soon to come. I bless you all. ♥ ♥ IΧθΥΣ ⊲×

YOUR SINS ARE BLACK AS COAL

August 2nd, 1988 - Rome

Jesus?

♥ *I Am.* ♥ ♥ *I, the Lord, have great pity and My Mercy is uncomparable.* ♥ *My Mercy is Great and fathomless. Creation! Your sins are black as coal and without My Boundless Mercy, My Justice would have brought you in total destruction. I am at your very doors now and as a thief I shall enter. Take heed of My Signs. Be prepared. Pray My Vassula; pray for those who resist Me still; pray for those who are offending Me and who obscure the world -condemning my lambs who walk in the right path.* ♥ *Free them! Free them -bringing them to Me. Ah Vassula! Little lamb. Stay near Me; stay hidden under My Cape - hidden in My Heart.* Salvation will *come from Me - allow Me to use you.*

August 3rd, 1988 - Rome

Father James and I hurried to the Vatican for the Papal Audience, we were among the first to be there in queue. After the discourse, the Holy Father got up and went along the aisle, blessing us. The Pope was facing me and I stuck my arm to reach him, I tried to pass on the message to him but when he felt it was some paper his fingers went above mine and on my hand, I tried again, the same thing happened, his fingers were all over my fingers then above my hand again, then he moved too far away and I thought that I had failed my mission, so he stepped back facing me. I seized the opportunity and pushed it into the top of his sash. I felt that it was still sticking too much (the message) so I reached out again and gave it a slight tap to make it perfect. While doing this act, I felt that I had switched completely off. I could not hear the crowds, nor could I feel being squashed nor the Polish priest's hand on my arm as though one of the Pope's own people was guiding my hand, hand in hand.

A papal photographer had taken us at exactly that moment, the moment I was placing the message in the Pope's sash, that is where I saw the hand of the Polish priest lying on my arm.

August 4th, 1988 - Rome

The next day, after the public audience of 4.8.88 with the Pope: I saw Jesus all around me facing me with a broad smile, all the time.

Jesus?

I Am. Flower, do not seek to understand My Ways[1]. Be simple and accept all that comes from Me. I, the Lord, have led you into My House; I have led you to see and meet My so beloved servant John-Paul II. Dearest soul, <u>you obeyed Me, you trusted Me, you relied on Me</u>. Rejoice soul! For I, your God, feel rejoiced! Simplicity infatuates Me, obedience rebounds My Sacred Heart for this is The Weapon to fight against the evil one.

Lord, was it correct to place Your letter in the Pope's sash?

You obeyed Me - let this be as an example of obedience to others. No matter how hard the situation may appear to you, trust Me and obey. I will always help you when I see that you are obeying Me and doing <u>My Will</u> - seek not to understand why I have asked you to do this for Me. ♥ Remember that <u>it is I</u>, the Lord, who will unite you all under My Name and it is through My Power that all My desires will be accomplished. Let My Finger stay upon you My child, using you in this way. Allow Me to leave My veil on you, thus keeping you away from evil and becoming elated by all these graces I shed upon you. I, your God, love you and will never abandon you, even in the most critical situations. ♥ Love will inspire you. ♥ Wisdom loves life; Wisdom bears the Name of Holiness and She is given to all those who obey Me. All instructions descend from Wisdom. Trust Me and sow the seeds of Holiness[2]. Peace upon you. Come, remember My Holy Presence. Smile at Me. ♥

ECCLESIA NEEDS TO BE REVIVED

August 6th, 1988 - Rome

Our Holy Mother:

Never loose courage - I am beside you. Enter into Jesus' Wounds; enter into My Sorrowful Heart and feel My sorrow; feel how I weep. I come to many[3]; I show them My Heart; I give signs by letting My Images shed tears; I appear at various places, but My children's hearts are covered by a thick crust - a layer

---

[1] This reminded me of the audacious demand made upon Abraham - the sacrifice of his only son.
[2] Meaning Wisdom.
[3] Appearing.

of disbelief. They ridicule those who believe. The Word of God means nothing to them - the calls of God are ignored; they pay little heed on Our warnings. No one wants to listen on revelations given by God and spoken from His Mouth. Your era's faith has vanished - swept away by intolerance, perversion, cruelty and ignominy. How sorrowful My Immaculate Heart is. My Hand can no longer keep God's Arm from falling upon you. Ecclesia needs to be revived and Her time of Purification is almost over now. ♥ The Holy Spirit will descend upon you all, giving you <u>hope, love</u> and <u>faith</u>; restoring your faith and nourishing your soul. This will be known as the Great Return; as the Sprouting of an Everlasting Source; as the Flourishing of Flowers. ♥ Ecclesia's purge will prepare you all to face a New Heaven and a New Earth. She will prepare you to <u>face your God</u>. Understand My deep love I have for all of you. ♥ We, us?

Yes, we, us.
♥ Come.

I WANT YOU TO FEEL ME

August 7th, 1988 - Rome

I want you to feel Me - feel My Heart's desires; My thirst of love; My desire of keeping you near Me; My jealous love for all humanity. Relinquish your ambitions - have none; you do not need these in My Presence, not when I am the one who feeds you. Let My Works be Mine entirely and accept the way I am guiding you. Enter My Sacred Heart. I bless you. ♥ ♥

THE BIG TRIBULATION OF MY CHURCH

August 8th, 1988

Beloved, I wish to remind you that I am your Shepherd, who sought you and finally found you. You were lying dead among other dead. I am the Resurrection and only through Me you will find life, Eternal Life. But on this return the Shepherd finds that His lambs are dispersed and many starved; the Fold they were in, battered, and by His own friends. My lambs mistreated and starved lie dead. These shepherds, who were in charge of My Fold, have disobeyed Me, they were disloyal to Me, so I will have to remove them for fear of more damage. ♥ This will be known as the big tribulation of My Church. Come, you are learning. Love loves you.

ECCLESIA WILL REVIVE THROUGH ME

August 9th, 1988 - Rome

Jesus?

I Am. Dearest soul, how I love you. <u>Ecclesia will revive through Me</u>. Allow Me to manifest Myself through you, My myrrh; fragrance Me your Lord. I have shown you My Sacred Heart; I have come to you soul to teach you My Ways and lead you to the Truth. Your generation is seeking the Truth, when the Truth is <u>Love</u>. ♥ But Love is missing within them. My Name[1] means nothing to them - not any longer; yet My Mercy is Great upon those who defile Me. ♥ My creation has abandoned My ways; they have allowed themselves to be led by Blind Guides; they have rebelled against My Law, teaching a law which is not Mine. Creation! If you only knew how close you are to the Fall! Care for one another[2], instead of persecuting each other. Learn My Ways - Wisdom's Ways. Let every action or thought be covered by Love. ♥ ♥

Flower, I am your Devoted Keeper - so trust Me. I keep you under My Light, nourishing you with My Sap. Trust Me, your God, for I have highly favoured you. I will always be near you - embellishing you. I-Am-All-Faithful. Come, we, us. Be one with Me. ♥

Thank You My God. I had a glimpse of God's beauty and I felt delightful to be enveloped by God.

MY MERCY IS GREAT
- NEW PENTECOST -

August 9th, 1988 - Rome

Jesus?

♥ I Am. My Vassula, let Father James be present - I will speak with him. (Father James came, knelt with me and 'met' Jesus in this special way.) *Brother! Behold your Saviour. Behold, I am being recrucified by My own - I who am Love. ♥ Brother! Be aware of falsehood; combat evil; correct error; call to*

---

[1]His Name is LOVE.
[2]The Ecclesiastics.

obedience all those who persecute Me. My House is in ruin - My Sanctuary lies
in desolation.
(James hesitated, he asked to always do His will.)

Draw from My Heart. Love will help you. ♥ ♥ *Your Holy Mother is near and*
She will be training you to be in Her legion of angels[1].

(Father James asked God to bless those who asked him to pray for them.)
I, the Lord, have blessed them. I love all of you; all of you are Mine and Love
will draw you all in My Heart. ♥   (There was some silence.) *I wish you to*
remember My Presence.

Lord, is it Father James or me?
♥   *Both of you. I wish that My brother says those two words that please My*
Sacred Heart - those two words I have been teaching you: "we", "us" ♥ ♥

(Father James asked Jesus to help him in this.)
Lean on Me. ♥
(Father James prayed for the Pope.)
My wish is that My blessed one, John-Paul, is mentioned more in all your prayers
and by this I request you to teach them.
(Father James prayed for priests, brothers, religious, for the Seminary teachers and
to deliver Banani's teachers from evil inclinations, he prayed for those who despair.)
My Eyes never leave them; I have placed them in My Sacred Heart; My blessings
are upon them.
(Father James prayed for the persecuted.)
Those souls repair, by their sufferings, many errors - warming hearts which are
cold[2].
(Father James prayed for the Arabs and Jews.)
All nations will come together under My Name - this will be My Special Blessing.
♥

(Father James prayed for the victims of abortion.)
Pray for those souls - victims of your era.
(Father James asked Jesus to forgive them.)

My Mercy is Great![3]

---

[1] I think in the Marian Movement.
[2] Heavenly Works.
[3] This was said very slowly and meaningfully.

(Father James prayed for me.)
My daughter will be soon with Me. ♥

My son, (St Mary) **honour your God and fight the good fight; repay evil with good - be blessed. I am pleased to have you among My predilected priests; I have chosen you among those who will repay evil with love. I, your Holy Mother, guide you and have you very near My Heart.** ♥ ♥ **The struggle is not over - if you only knew how many souls fall every single day into hell! The amount is alarming...** (I asked 'who?') **... From cardinals to[1]... young children. Your era has degenerated - indeed, it has become the dominion of Our adversary. He has expanded his dominion on earth at its fulness. Ah Vassula... God is counting the days, the days where He will pour on you like dew, reviving you again into a New and Bountiful Garden. This will be known as the New Pentecost. Come and kneel - all of you - and pray to the Lord for the Glorious Event. Pray for this Coming; pray that Love comes back.** ♥ ♥ **I, Vassula, am the Lady of the Rosary.**

Holy Mother why do You present Yourself in this way, is there a special note in Your message?
♥ **Yes, all that I have said at Fatima will be accomplished before the end of this era.** ♥ **Come, rest now in My Immaculate Heart and Jesus' Sacred Heart. Please Jesus by serving Him as you do and loving Him, repairing for those who do not love Us.** ♥ ♥ ♥ We, us?
Yes forever.

THE DAYS OF RECKONING HAVE BEGUN

August 15th, 1988 - Assumption

Lord Jesus may You be blessed.

♥ *I, the Lord, bless you.* ♥ *My Sacred Heart is labouring with pain; filled with thorns I seek relief and comfort from all those who love Me. Bless Me and seek Me. I turn and reach My little souls, for in their littleness I find My rest, I find My comfort.*
Ah Jesus it's so painful to feel You in such pain...
Pray for those souls who need to be saved. Pray to Me, for My Name is He-Who-Saves. The hours are fleeing, the days of reckoning have begun, the days of

---

[1]Our Holy Mother hesitated and I felt a pang of pain in Her.

reprisals are here. The iniquity of this generation is <u>so great</u> and the apostasy <u>so grave</u> that both Our Hearts have been pierced through and through by their injustice and their flagrant offenses. I beg you to return to Me and turn to Me and I <u>will</u> forgive you! Hold fast to Love and I will shower you with blessings; be just to each other and kind to each other. <u>Love one another</u>. Become children of My Light. Understand how so many catastrophes are drawn upon you - they are drawn by the evil that has accumulated in your soul. Return to Me and let My Blood purify you. ♥

Later on:

♥ **I am your Holy Mother. My children, return to God. I beg you to come back and God will forgive you - His Mercy descends upon you like dew creation, and as flowers you will open and absorb His Light. I am calling you, I am encouraging you, but how many know of Our Calls? How many believe in these calls? My Heart pains to say that only a handful of you trust those calls. This generation's heart has turned into granite - blinded by Rationalism they have forgotten God's ways; they have forgotten God's wonders; they have forgotten that He is Omnipotent and full of Mercy. Never has God's creation fallen so low - not even in the days of Sodom and Gomorrah. Your apathy has pierced Eternity; your lack of faith is condemning you; your relentless persecutions on My apparitions (and on those whom God blessed, giving them His messages) are going to be one cause of your fall. I, your Holy Mother, Mother of your Saviour, appeal and beg you to repent and change. Come back to Us; live holy; live holy under God's Eyes; be prepared to face Him with your hands full of good acts and in purity.** ♥ ♥ ♥

Later on:

I have showered you with My Scent; I wanted you to feel My Presence; I wished to remind you, by this favour I have given you, how dear you are to Us child. I am your Holy Mother and I am happy to have you near Us again. Beloved, I bless you and your whole family.
Holy Mother thank You for everything, I bless You.

Flower.
Yes Jesus.
Call your Holy Mother, 'Mama.' From now on, be intimate with Her as you are with Me. ♥ We, us. Remember My teachings.
Yes Lord.
♥ *I, the Lord, bless all of you.* ♥ ⊂✕ ΙΧθΥΣ

After going out of the Church today and going down many steps it felt as if I was walking in a rose-garden; not one flower was around, only cement. I asked Father James if he smelled anything and while I was asking he said he did; roses; then in the very end of the phenomena, violets.

YOUR APOSTASY BETRAYED MY CHURCH
- THE GREAT CONVERSION -

August 16th, 1988

Lord?

♥ *I Am. Never doubt it is I, Jesus Christ. I have called you from My Cross. I have called you in My agony to show you how I, who is the Head of My Church, is to be found today. The Image of Myself, lying dead in My Mother's arms[1], is a symbolic way of showing you all how your apostasy betrayed My Church. You see, daughter, I led you to see the correct image of the present Church; You have seen on My Mother Her sorrow and you saw in Her Arms My dead body, betrayed, bruised, scourged, pierced and crucified; and this is exactly how My Church of today is to be found. My Mother weeps over Her with tears of blood, as She weeped over My Body on Golgotha; ♥ but in a very short time she[2], will be renewed, transfigured and resurrected as I the Lord was Resurrected. ♥ She will no longer lie in this deplorable state. My enemies had destroyed My Temple, but, with My Power descending from above, and with My Grace I, the Lord, rebuilt My Temple in just three days. ♥ I promise you that My Church will revive and I will have Her renewed and tranfigured, as I was transfigured. I will rebuild My Temple and Integrity will be Her loincloth round Her waist and Faithfulness the Belt about Her hips[3] and Purity will be Her Torch - to lead all those who defiled My Name, in Her Light and purify them. For I, the Lord of Lords, the Lamb, will be living in Her and She will be received by Her own, as I was received by My own after My Resurrection. Then, like a mother who comforts her child, I too will comfort you even more; I will enfold My Arms around you with so much love. Ah beloved children, I am preparing you a New Heaven and a New Earth to live in; an Earth replenished by fruits that come from the Tree of Life. It's fruits will bear the names of Peace, Holiness, and Love since Its' Root is Love[4].*

---

[1] The statue of St Mary and Jesus after the crucifixion in San Sylvestro, Rome.
[2] The Church.
[3] Isaiah 11:5.
[4] The Lion of the tribe of Judah, the Root of David - Rev 5:5. This understanding was given to me later on, on 1.9.88.

You will then face Me, your God, filled by My Holy Spirit - as in the first Pentecost. My Spirit will fill you with Love... My Garden I will embellish; I will irrigate My flower-beds. My dew of Righteousness will descend upon you beloved ones and My Light will strengthen your stems, making discipline shine out. Courage daughter; courage beloved ones. I know it is hard to live in wilderness, but the End of these Times are soon with you.

Soon I will descend to purify you. I, the Lord, solemnly tell you that I will seize you by surprise - inducing My Light upon you. My Heavens will shake the earth and all those who love Me will glorify Me - bending their knee; and many will remember Me and return to Me - this will be known as the Great Conversion of the Church. But, to My great sorrow, there will be those stubborn souls who blasphemed My Holy Name and who battle on My adversary's side - these souls will reject Me even more. When this happens, Satan will wipe them away, pulling them with him into the Eternal Fire.

Vassula, feel My Sacred Heart... I suffer beyond human words to have to tell you this, for I Am a God of Love, a God of Mercy, but I am also a God of Justice and I have to be your Judge when My creation rebels against Me. My Soul is wounded and My Blood is gushing out in Rivers. I love you all! but you have wounded Me. I am your Holy One, but you pierced Me. I am your Saviour who today cries from My Cross to you: "Come back to Me! Return to Me! Come and be holy as I Am Holy!" ♥ Come child, I am with you, keep Me in your heart and rest Me - be one with Me. ♥

Yes, My Lord, I adore You.
Adore Me and rest Me - I am so weary...
Us, we, Lord?
♥ Yes, us, we, for eternity. ♥ ♥
Amen.

CHILDISH WORDS OF LOVE

Later on: St Mary.

**Vassula, be intimate with Me; call Me Mama; have My peace. ♥ I love you.
♥**
I love You too, teach me to love You more.

Vassula, I have placed you in My Sacred Heart.
Lord, thank You for giving me this grace of meeting You, feeling you and seeing You.

This is My gift to you; nevertheless, do not forget that this gift is given to you for My Interests and My Glory. Caress Me with your love; fragrance Me with your love; console Me with your love; glorify Me, your Lord, with your love - lift your mind to Me and Me alone. I Am the One and Only who counts; I Am Everything; I Am the Eternal - the Alpha and the Omega; I Am He-Who-Saves - your Creator; I Am the Holy of Holies; I Am the Spirit of Love - so come to Me. I know how frail you are. Come to Me and love Me. I will always remind you that I Am your God; no matter how weak and wretched you are, My Strength will sustain you. Dearest soul, remember one more thing; remember that I need no one - I suffice by Myself to accomplish My Works, but I love sharing My Works with My creation, so look at Me and rejoice soul for having favoured you. There are many who would have longed to see what you see and never saw it, hear what you hear but never heard it, feel what you feel and never felt it. So rejoice soul! Rejoice! Cover Me with praises; crown Me with wreaths of Love; fragrance Me with incense; adorn Me with your childish words of love - bless Me your Lord and worship Me, beloved one. ♥ My Bread, you will always have from Me, and plentiful too. I will nourish your soul. I am your Saviour and I promise you that I will always be near you in this special way to the end. ♥ Wisdom gives her resources not only to the just, but also to the unjust... ♥ Come. ♥

PURIFICATION
- THE NEW JERUSALEM -

August 17th, 1988

My Lord?

I Am. I am your Redeemer - so trust Me. I have come, through you, to give My Message of universal Peace and Love and show to all My creation My Sacred Heart and how I love you. O Vassula! My Mercy is Great upon all of you! Dearest souls, the time for your purification is drawing near - what I will do is out of love; your purification will be to save you from the gates of hell. ♥ I will descend upon you like Lightening and renew you with My Fire. ♥ My Spirit of Love will redeem you by drawing you into Love and consume you into a living flame of love. I will let My Spirit pour out of heaven and purify your blemished souls into holy spotless souls - purifying you as gold is purified in fire. ♥ You will recognize the Time of Salvation, and when My Spirit of Love will descend. ♥ Unless this happens, you will not see the New Heavens nor the New Earth I foretold you. My child, by My Fire, by My Love, by My Mercy and by My Justice,

My seeds[1] will sprout and open like new lilies which face the sun - seeking My Light and My Dew; and I will pour from My Heavens, My Light, embellishing you and My Dew nourishing you to see a new era of Love. By My Power, I will sweep away all iniquity, perversion and evil; I will descend upon you like a violent torrent of cleansing waters and wash away all your evil and leave you standing upright as columns of pure gold. With My Torrents of Fervent Love, I will sweep away all that is false and faked - just like clay is washed away with a few drops of rain, so will My Spirit of Sublime Love wash away your sins which blemished your soul.
♥ *I, your Saviour, will renew you creation and offer you <u>My Gift</u>. My Gift will descend from Heaven[2]. <u>A Glittering New Jerusalem; A Renovated Church - Pure and Holy</u>; because I, who was, is, and is to come, will be living in Her midst and in Her very Soul. You will all feel Her, palpating and alive, because My Sacred Heart will be throbbing within Her. I, the Lord of Lords, am like the fire[3], and My Sacred Heart is in ardent Flames - so eager with desire to enwrap you all - thrusting you in My Furnace of Love and leaving you ablaze in total rapture and ecstasy of love for Me, your Beloved God! Yes, I will make out of each one of you a living altar, ablaze with My Fire. O creation! When My Fire will enkindle your hearts you will finally cry out to Me: "You are the-One-God-and-Only, the Just One - you are indeed the Lamb. You <u>are</u> our Heavenly Father - how could we have been so blind? O Holy of Holies, be-in-us, <u>live-in-us</u>. Come, O Saviour!" and to this cry of yours, I will not hesitate. I <u>will</u> descend upon you, as quick as lightening, and live among you; and you, beloved ones, will realize that <u>from The Beginning</u> you were My own and <u>My seed</u>. ♥ I will then be among you and will reign over you with an everlasting love. I will be your God and you, My own. ♥*
♥ ♥ *Dearest soul, treat Me as your King - crown Me with your love. ♥ We, us.*
Come. ♥ ⬱ IXθΥΣ

FREE WILL

August 18th, 1988 - Up in the Monastery

I asked the Lord to help a group of people I met and who are living in anguish, they feel they are persecuted by the demon. Lord?

---

[1]Seeds : us.

[2]The Lord gave me an intellectual vision of millions of angels descending from heaven and holding a new city, like on a platter. A New Blessed Church was descending from heaven.

[3]The Lord seemed very impatient, as 'on fire.'

I Am. Daughter, every soul can be freed, but only when they themselves will open and be willing. ♥ I have given each soul this freedom and their will belongs to them only. Now, if a soul is adamant not to open herself to Me, how will I enter in her heart? I am the Lord and God but I have given you all your freedom and your will; if you believe and offer Me your will -surrendering to Me - I will enter in your heart and heal you. I will not enter by force. ♥ I am at their door and waiting for them to open it and welcome Me in. ♥

WAITING IS SLEEPING

August 19th, 1988

I just want to tell You how much I love You and I want to thank You Lord for all that You have done and are still doing to me. I will never ever be able to repay You for all these graces. Lord?

I Am. Flower, lean on Me. I will give even to the most wretched ones. I am an Abyss of Mercy, but to My sorrow many of you have forgotten how I really am. I am not a God of predilection - I am Just and I give even to the most wicked of you. ♥ Rebound My Sacred Heart with joy! Give Me your love and even if sometimes it's tepid, I will accept it. Give Me your love and I will perfect it in My Divinity. Come to Me, like now, without self-interests and offer Me your love; do not wait to be perfect to offer Me your love; do not wait to become a saint to offer Me your love - come as you are, with all your defects, and in My Purity I will transform your love into pure love -reflecting it from above on you. Little soul, I will embellish everything you offer Me. So come to Me as you are, offering Me your love - this love that is missing among so many! Soul! If you only knew how many souls suffer now in purgatory... deliver them from purgatory to be able to come to Me. They are craving to be with Me but they are unable to because of the blemishes on their soul. Deliver them by prayers and by sacrifices; deliver them by loving Me, by adoring Me; deliver them by chaining yourself to Me and My Cross; deliver them by acts of love; deliver them by sharing My sufferings. ♥ Vassula, these souls languish for Me and to be united to Me again and forever - but they must purify themselves first before being in My Presence.

Lord, You said: "... and be united to me <u>again</u>..." have they been with You after their death for sometime?

♥ I have delivered their soul from their body; <u>I have shown them My Holy Face for just an instant</u> and at that very instant their eyes unveiled, facing Me in My Purity and in My Light, immediately saw The Truth face to face, and realized how blemished their soul is from sin; and, in spite of their burning desire to fall in My

open arms[1] and follow Me, they understand that this is impossible before cleaning their soul. So, with a piercing pain of sorrow, they fall back and prepare themselves to be purified - this hurts and burns them beyond words because they cannot see Me. <u>My absence is burning them</u> and the cause of their greatest suffering in purgatory is <u>My Absence</u>. ♥ They also undergo other sorts of sufferings, with fire, depending their sins. ♥ Prepare your soul, creation, in advance - do not wait for death to overshadow you. Keep your soul clean and without blemish. Feed yourselves with My Body and drink My Blood as often as you can. Repent often - be prepared for this day. Be on fast - fasting helps you. Listen to My Voice and prepare your soul as if our meeting would be for this very day. Do not wait - <u>waiting is sleeping; waiting is to leave your lanterns without oil</u>. Be prepared to meet your Saviour. ♥   I love you all to folly. Realize that out of My Fathomless Mercy I want to prepare you all. ♥ ♥   ΙΧθΥΣ ⊂⟩×

Later on: St Mary.

Ma?

♥ **Have My Peace. ♥   I am your Ma - yes[2]. My Vassula, I have. My tears saved your child, and My pleas to the Father. Love the Father, for He is most Compassionate. ♥**
What can I say? To thank You is not enough everything I say or do will not be enough!
My child, abandon yourself to Him. Surrender often - this pleases God enormously. Be confident, for you are in His Hands. I will give you My Peace. ♥ Glorify God by obeying Him.
I bless You Mother.
♥ I bless you and your family.

Later on - after this emotion.

Vassula, I wish to tell you that soon many things predicted by Me at Fatima will come to their realization. I am full of Graces and I am willing to pour them on My children from this year. The time is near and because of this short time left, I, your Holy Mother, will be nearer to you than it has ever been known. ♥ I will pour on many of you My Graces, to embellish you and draw you closer to Jesus, who is suffering enormously. ♥

---

[1]Proving that God does not put a lock from His side, the hinderance is from <u>our</u> side.
[2]St Mary told me something concerning my eldest son. Our Mother made me understand that it was She, out of Her pleas to Our Father, that my eldest son had survived his illness. This was thirteen years ago. This made me very emotional, and disturbed me very much.

Ah daughter... a thorn is always plucked from Our Hearts every time a soul returns to Us! A thorn is always plucked and replaced by a flower each time someone cries out to Us 'I love You!' Peace be upon you daughter.

♥ ♥ We, us?
Yes. We, us.

I SHALL POUR OUT MY SPIRIT

August 20th, 1988

Jesus?

I Am. Beloved, these days Satan is deceiving many by attacking revelations and apparitions which come from Me. Had I not come to deliver you, you would have still been in his claws. Believe, believe in My Mercy; believe in my Works - compare yourself now and to what you were before, had it not been for Me who came to save you. ♥ I am the Light. I have redeemed you from darkness. Vassula, Satan is desperate and is trying to confuse you and bring you all against each other. Realize how he works - he is trying to confuse you all. He knows how My Works save many souls and this is why he wants to thwart My plans and battles against them. I will always be near you. Read Acts 2. My Spirit is given from above to many but, as always, some would laugh It off -unable to explain Its mysteries. I have said again and again that I will pour out My Spirit on all mankind and you shall prophesy. Young men shall see visions[1]. I shall pour out My Spirit. I will display portents in heaven and above, and signs on earth below. Creation! Have you really understood this prophecy? I solemnly ask My teachers, who do not believe in Wisdom's Works, to look for the hidden sense of proverbs and into the wisdom of all the Ancients. They should ask to be filled with the Spirit of Understanding, which will lead them to understand the Greatness of My Name. Beware of Satan's traps - I have forewarned you of his malices, My child. I, the Lord, love you boundlessly and will never see you lost.

But Lord, there are false apparitions, even revelations!

Yes there are, but very soon I shall unveil them and show that these are false. ♥ Which father would watch his child, year after year, heading on the wrong route and not warn him? Or which father would see his child cheated and remain silent? Would he not warn him and show him the truth? Would I then, who is

---

[1]Usually children see visions in our days: eg. Medugorje, Fatima, Garabandal.

Love and Mercy, remain silent and leave you exposed in those dangers and not rush to you to reveal you the truth? Try and understand...[1]

Thank You my God for Your patience with all of us. Your Mercy is indeed Great.
Ah Vassula! If they only understood this Mercy of Mine! Come to Me.
(I felt Him like He wanted me to be close to Him so that I lean on Him.)
I want you to lean on Me. I want all My creation to lean on Me. ♥

THE BIRTH PANGS HAVE BEGUN

August 25th, 1988

Lord?

I Am. Vassula, pray for Love's Return; pray for the renewal of My Church; pray for her Rebirth. ♥ Her tepidness of now will change into a flame of love; her apathy will be transformed into fervour and a thirsty desire to know Me and follow Me; her unfaithfulness into loyalty; her aridity will turn into green pastures and a fountain of purity, consoling My lambs, quenching their thirst and sheltering them. My lambs will find in Her warmth what I once had given Her - they will find Peace and Love - they will return. ♥ ♥

So pray for this renewal of My Church; pray that the Gospels are fully understood and that those parts that have been hacked out, be returned. Pray My child that My Church be United and garbed in Her Garments-of-Old. Pray for all the misinterpretations given to you now from My Word to cease - these misinterpretations are like poisonous food for you. My Food is Pure and Whole. Pray for My sacerdotals to understand fully My Ways and the way I truly am - they still have not understood Me. Pray that they may be enlightened. Oh, My child, pray for My Glory, that in the end My Holy Name may be glorified again and be honoured by all Nations. ♥

Oh Jesus, all this seems to me so very far, and Your coming even further!

Daughter, have My Peace and be willing and eager to receive Me. I tell you most solemnly, the hours are fleeing, dissolving like shadows, and already you are living in the first signs of My Return. Already the first birthpangs have started but like Folly My creation laughs it off - rejecting My first signs. They refuse to believe that the birthpangs have already begun! So devote yourself to Me My child and feed

---

[1]Here God spoke as a very patient father.

from Me - I will see that you lack nothing. Do not look left or right - come straight to Me. I am the Lord and will remain your Teacher and your Spiritual Director. You are learning from Wisdom; you are learning from Me and it is I who hold the Keys to Wisdom; I let no one in to see Her, whose eyes are wise. I only give Her to children. I only allow mere children to penetrate in Her and meet Her. ♥

Thank You my Jesus.

LOVE IS THE ROOT
I AM THE ROOT

August 26th, 1988

I was invited to meet some extremist muslims and meet their two immams and sheikh. I went to their place with a theologian friend of mine. The whole thing was arranged to condemn me and secretly exorcise me, which they did; finding no evil spirit in me they lost their temper and became very agressive, especially when I received a message for them, a love message. Finding me in total calmness it infuriated them even more and accused me of liar and deceiver. They said that "You, My Lord are <u>not</u> a God of Love;" - I and the theologian friend calmly got up and left them. Had we not been in Switzerland they would have killed us. Lord?

♥ *My Vassula, Love comes first. <u>I am a God of Love</u>. Remember how I taught you that <u>Love is The Root</u>? I have given you an example of a good tree bearing good fruits; this tree is The Perfect Tree - because its root is Love; its branches are all virtues and they are all good. Without the Root of Love, this tree will have no virtues and thus no fruit. When you see a tree which is barren, or its fruit rotten, know My child that its root is made out of the most vile evils existing. I tell you solemnly that the Root of all virtues is called LOVE. I am Love. I am The Root who nourishes you - embellishing you. Come and be in Me and you will live forever!*

REMIND MY TEACHERS MY WAYS OF TEACHING

August 29th, 1988

♥ ♥ ♥   Jesus?

*I Am. Peace be with you. Realize how much I favoured you by raising you to Me.
My Vassula, I want to remind My teachers My Superabundant Love; I want to
remind them that I am meek and gentle - full of tenderness. I teach with love; I
taught you with love; I raised you with love, docility and patience. I have often
asked you if you willed to continue My Works. I, the Lord, respected your
freedom; I never pressed you; I was never harsh to you; I fed you with love and
so much tenderness. I have taught My disciples to follow My Ways of teaching and
to expand this method of teaching. I taught them to direct My lambs to Me with
gentleness and love.   How is it that today My Ways of teaching have been
forgotten?   How is it that My House has become a recreation of aridity and
inflexibility, loosing all that was divine? My House today lies barren, lax with
human regulations and human thinking - it lies in desolation! My House is being
ruled with rules that 'freedom' means nothing anymore. My Vassula, My dove,
you are free because you are with Me. I am your Master. I guide you, but with
freedom. I never forced you to work for Me anytime; I never came imposing My
works on you.   My manner is totally different from all those who have the
responsibility of others. I, who am Lord and reign over you, always approached
you using these words: "allow Me to..." My House has to change. My House has
to remember My Ways. I Am Love.* ♥ ♥ ♥

I WARN THOSE WHO LAUGH THE SPIRIT OFF

September 5th, 1988

Since early this morning the Lord was telling me that soon I will be rejected by some
local priests - Lord, am I really going to be rejected again by some priests?

Lord?

♥ *I Am. Fear not. Soon everything will come to light and all those who rejected
you, refusing to believe in My Message, will pray to the Father for forgiveness.
Vassula, had they been "blind" I would have healed them, but they are claiming
they can "see"; they descend from those same blind guides of the time I was on
earth. My child, had they lived at the time I was on earth they would be among
those who crucified Me; they would be sharing their work; they would be among*

those who stoned the prophets and silenced them. Why, what difference is there now and then? They are claiming to believe in Me, but reject what comes from the Spirit - thus rejecting Me again. You come from Me with My Message but, as the scribes and Pharisees, they demand proofs - solid proofs. Prepare yourself My child - prepare your back for scourging. I, the Lord, allowed them to scourge My back - so offer yours to them too. Let them repeat their mistakes since they refuse to hear. I, the Lord, was rejected and in the end nailed to the wood ♥ - so be pliant too and share My Cross. Today is like yesterday - whoever I send, they scrutinize, they persecute or reject. The blood of those I send is continually being shed - from the blood of Abel to this generation! As I have warned the scribes and Pharisees, I warn today those who persecute My Messengers and condemn My Word. I warn those who laugh the Spirit off. I tell them once more that: "your own evidence tells against you. Not one of you has changed; your works remain the same; your way of thinking tells against you. ♥ Guides! Who preach spiritual messages and yet ignore what comes from the Spirit! Guides! Who feed My lambs My Flesh, but keep away My Blood! Have you forgotten My instructions?" My Vassula, I will let you feel My thorns; I will let you feel how Rationalism is reigning in the hearts of these sacerdotals; I will expose you to them.

I am feeding you My Bread - be one with Me. Feel My thorns and let them be your thorns too. Let each nail pierce your soul as they pierced Me. I have warned you. Be prepared now for the scourging. Remember though that My back is also exposed to them and whatever they do to you they are also doing to Me. ♥ ♥ We, us?

Yes Lord.

Three hours later I got the news: one of the priests I trusted and I thought he believed in God's message 'betrayed' me. He did not believe at all but pretended he did all along. He simply said: "God does not reveal Himself in this way, not to this sort of person." This hurt a lot because I thought he understood and was a friend. I lost a 'friend'... these news I got from another friend.

Later On:

Lord?
♥ I Am. I had warned you My child of this betrayal. Come, lean on Me. Let it be known how meaningless are the arguments of those who tell you that this does not come from Me - their zeal is misguided; they do not seem to see clear My Righteousness and are only declaring their own ideas. ♥ Scripture says: "the footsteps of those who bring good news is a welcome sound," and for those who are surprised at the kind of instruments I choose, scripture says: "I have been found by those who did not seek Me and have revealed Myself to those who did not consult Me." ♥

He has a good argument though; I really am the wrong person to have this 'gift'. I'm no good; yet, my friend, Beatrice asked him,'what about Mary Magdalene?, He replied, 'ah yes, but she got converted later on.' So he believes I'm not converted?
♥ *Be in peace! I have placed you in My Sacred Heart.*
Had he lived 2,000 years back, he would have participated in stoning me, as a sinner.
I would not have allowed this - I would have said those same words I once said, "let the one without sin throw the first stone." ♥ Open your hearts! Not your minds! Vassula, lean on Me, your Saviour. Pray for those whose hearts remain closed; pray for those who shut their ears.
Yes Lord.

Prepare yourself for the rest of My Passion. Remember, I had shown you the size of your cross.
Yes Lord.
But you and I will share it together. All will not be in vain. I will help you accomplish your mission, then..., to Me you will fly - yes![1] Come. I am Present. We, us?
Yes Lord.

I CREATED YOU TO LOVE ME

September 6th, 1988

My Lord?

♥ *I Am. Look into My Eyes and do not look left or right - look at Me your Lord. I am the Way, the Truth and the Life Everlasting. Remember with what great love I have taught you My Word, and all that you know, you know from Me. ♥ All My Kingdom is filled with wonders. I am the Alpha and the Omega. Love Me... Treat Me as a King by offering Me every drop of love you have. I created you to love Me - let all the love you have be just for Me[2]. I know how weak and miserable you are without Me, but I also know that I have in My Hands a mere child and a nothing where My Spirit can freely breathe in this space you are giving Me. Allow My Spirit to mould and form you - all that you learn comes from Wisdom and I am Wisdom. ♥ ♥ ♥*

---

[1] Jesus seemed happy.

[2] By learning to love God we learn to love one another too.

September 7th, 1988

Praised be the Lord! Blessed be our Lord! Glory be to God! I love you Father to death. Lord?
♥ *I Am. My child - listen. Will you continue working for Me your Lord?*
If You want me as I am.

♥ *I want you. Your ineffable weakness attracts Me, come and absorb from Me*
♥ *alive and healed! You have seen the Truth face to face. I healed you; I converted you; I have lifted you and placed you in My Sacred Heart; I blessed you and what I have begun with you I will finish. You will remain in My Hall and will be fed by Me alone. I have veiled your eyes to keep you away from evil. I would not want you to become elated by all these graces I am giving you. I have offered you My Sacred Heart to be your Home; creep in Its depths; hide in Its depths and never come out of It.* ♥ *I, your Saviour, will keep you hidden in there till the end.*

Thank You Lord.

AN ADVICE

September 9th, 1988

Lord I trust You, what I have learnt, <u>I learnt from You only</u>; but Lord, many ministers are mocking me, they refuse to believe it's You, they push away Your Works, the visions of children, apparitions, revelations, all are tread upon, they want You SILENT. Please, do not stand aside My God, come quickly to us and help us, Lord our Saviour! Lord?

♥ *I Am. Vassula, My advice for those who oppress you is, "unless you become like children again, you will be unable to penetrate into My Kingdom."* ♥ *My child, the time will come when every vision will be proclaimed as true. I have said that there will be no empty vision, no deceitful prophecy in My Church. What I said will soon come true, since what I pronounce I will fulfill in your own lifetime.*
♥

Thank You Lord.
We, us?
Forever. Amen.

ST MICHAEL

September 10th, 1988

Glory be to God! Glory be to God.
St Michael?
Vassula, I will tell you this: all this revelation comes from the Mouth of the Most High - be certain of His Mercy.
Thank You St Michael. (This came out while I was praying to St Michael his prayer, to combat evil.)

September 10th, 1988

Lord?

I Am.
This film that has come out "The Last Temptation of Jesus", is a real scandal; what next!
Blessed are those who will not seek to go and see it!
(Jesus remained silent after what He said.)

EAT AND DRINK ME

September 12th, 1988

My Lord!

I Am.   Trust Me[1].   I am always with you.   Every soul has not been given the grace you have obtained by My Will, yet, how often will you doubt?   Believe... leave those who pull on you - their hearts are closed and they live in darkness. Why follow a blind man, wandering deeper into the wilderness?   I am the One and Only you are to follow, so open your ear since you can hear.   Try and understand - feel My Presence.   Why are you looking away when you see Me?   Follow My gaze, child.   Yes![2] You see?   You can if you try.   Betrothed!   Please Me.   Reflect on all I have given you and honour Me.

---

[1] I said to Jesus, 'what a grace these people had to live at <u>your</u> time on earth!'
[2] As soon as God said, "child", I sensed Him, I sensed His Presence and my heart 'leaped with joy.'

Lord, I'm terribly weak!
Pray for your weakness and I shall not wait - I <u>will</u> lift you My beloved. Eat My Body. Write it.
Jesus allows me to write that by saying 'eat My Body' I remembered that the night before I dreamt that I detached Jesus' whole Body from a crucifix (20cm length) I have, and ate all His Body, leaving the crucifix bare.

I have given you this vision - you <u>must</u> eat My Body. I have offered you My Body. Drink My Blood - <u>I want you to drink My Blood too</u>. ♥ ♥ *Vassula, do you want to know why you doubt sometimes? It is because you are living, you, as My rose, in a desert; a rose never survives in a desert, not unless it is given extraordinary attention and care - <u>all its' surrounding affects it</u>. I am your Keeper who never takes away His Eyes from you for fear the scorching winds should burn you. I watch over you constantly, keeping a close look upon you. I chase away your enemies, lest they tread upon you. I check that you lack nothing. I prune you when I must and fertilize your soil. Betrothed of My Soul, I just want to remind you not to despair, for I, the Lord, am your Keeper and will never abandon you in this desert. So <u>trust Me</u> and do not let this wilderness frighten you.* ♥ *Have My Peace. I will help you to augment your faith in Me since you want it.* ♥ *Feed on Me.* ♥ *We, us?*

Forever.
And ever.
We, us. Ma?
Yes. We, us. Be always near Jesus.
Yes Mother I want to be.
Come. ♥

I CRY OUT IN THIS WILDERNESS

September 14th, 1988
Exaltation of the Holy Cross

Jesus?

♥ *I Am. Listen to My Voice. I cry out in this wilderness - all those who will listen I will exalt and their sins will be washed away and forgotten like running waters.* ♥ *Woe to those who will shut their ears! And alas! There will be many among you who erred but who will not listen to Me, who is The Way. You have forsaken Me; you have erred in Error for so long now - inhaling only Satan's smoke and my Name is meaningless to you now. You are like shadows on earth* *yet, in your wickedness, you have reversed the Truth. Helped by Satan, you have eclipsed Me with evolution. I have given you so many warnings; I have foretold you of these days; I have out of My Boundless Mercy given you signs but, nevertheless, you preferred to close your eyes upon My Mercy. Guides! Who know My Word and minister for Me and who recognize the End of Times, recognizing that It is at hand, but bystand at the Graces I am showering on you out of sheer cowardice - putting honour before men. <u>Seek to understand and look once more into the hidden mysteries of My proverbs</u>. I solemnly ask you to <u>beg</u> for the Holy Spirit of understanding to descend upon you for a deeper perception of Knowledge. The days are numbered, and your souls too. Be prepared; remove this veil which My adversary layed upon your eyes for, so long as your vanity remains, so will your guilt remain upon you. Humble yourselves and accept My Ways - respond to My Voice which cries in agony in this wilderness[1]. ♥ Come My child - lean on Me. Together... together, we will share My agony.*

Yes My Lord, I want to share.
We, us.
Forever. ♥

DO NOT SUPPRESS MY SPIRIT,
WELCOME ME INSTEAD

September 15th, 1988
Holy Mother of Sorrows

Lord?
I Am.

How is it that so many ministers do not appreciate Your Merciful Signs You are giving us these days? Lord, do You know what they are saying? They say that this is not Real Faith, in other words, "<u>we</u> are already converted without signs, so <u>we</u> can do without them, so God, do not give us anymore, <u>we</u> are not interested in such extraordinary things." Instead of them falling FLAT with their face to the ground and cry out to You, "Glory be to God! Praised be the Lord! for Your Boundless Mercy! You are indeed fulfilling the Scriptures! "What is Real Faith to them if they push away the Spirit? They argue by saying, 'remember what Jesus said to Thomas, "Happy are those who have not seen but still believe..." ' have they forgotten what Scripture also says, "<u>Never</u> try to suppress the Spirit, or treat the Gift of Prophecy

---

[1]When Jesus said these words, He made me also share His agony. Jesus is suffering enormously...

with contempt." - And the Spirit blows where It wills... - When these people argue they do not seem to realize that they are only arguing with You My Lord.

My child, cry out loudly to the nations - shout! so that everyone may hear, "here is your God! Our God is with us, He has never abandoned us, He has come like a Shepherd to feed His flock and gather His lambs in His arms - for His Kingdom is at hand." My little flock I shall feed and gather with great love all of them, in My arms.

They do not care for Your Signs, they hear of them and file them away. They seem to want to tell You to stop Your Signs.

Nobody needs to advise Me. I need not one of these counsellors, for their wisdom is shame to Me. Do I not know how to measure you and know how to feed you? Alas! Only a remnant of you is left who welcome My Spirit. Have they understood how, by having an antagonistic spirit, they have failed Me? And by having failed Me - failed to see The Truth? ♥ Does the clay say to its fashioner, 'what are you making?' Receive humbly what you get from the Spirit, accepting My Works and It's mysteries. I willed to augment My Signs in your days, so receive with joy what you get from the Spirit; rejoice and receive Me; be glad instead of turning your backs to Me; face Me and recognize Me! Do not suppress My Spirit - welcome Me instead! Alas for you who suppress My Spirit; alas for you blind guides - bloated with Vanity - you have made a desolation out of My Holy Church! Seek The Truth by examining yourselves to make sure that you are in The Real Faith!

Altar! I, the Lord, will keep your flame ablaze until the end. My Works are not yet finished. Come now. We? us?
Forever, amen. ♥

THE KEY TO FREEDOM AND LIFE

September 18th, 1988

My God?[1]

I Am. Love Me, do not fear Me. Fear Me only if you rebel against Me. Every drop of love is used to liberate souls from purgatory. By loving Me fervently you

---

[1] I love God to the point I feel like a widow here on earth.

extinguish their fires[1], liberating them from their agony. Then I, the Lord, can receive them finally. So love Me, desire Me, worship Me. Liberate them one after the other. Mankind has to understand that love assimilates the Powers of Heaven and is the Key to freedom and life. Do you now understand why Satan hates you? My Vassula, lean on Me. All is not in vain. ♥   We, us?

Forever and ever.

I AM SPIRIT
TRUE LIFE IN GOD

September 24th, 1988

My God?

I Am. Remember that I am Spirit, and all I have I share with your spirit. You and I are one, linked in union of Love, bound to each other in Love; I, your God, and you My little one; I, your Creator, and you My creature. Let those whose hearts have hardened be reminded that My Heart sanctifies; let them know that I call even nameless people, people without virtues, without any merits. I transform the stone-hearted and raise them from nothing at all. I come unexpectedly among the dead and can raise them all up. Look at yourself Vassula, your merits were none, yet out of great pity I raised you. Now you know what True Life In God means. I Am the Life. ♥

Glorify Me My child. Never rebel against Me. Keep in mind My instructions. ♥
Lord?
I Am.
There is one thing bothering me, there is one who says that I'm in constant sin, since I'm divorced and married again, that is why he says that surely this revelation is not You who gives it my God, because of my constant sin.
Let the man without sin announce himself to Me! Let him come forward and show his face to me. ♥
Yes My God, help me I do not know how to answer these statements, by these people.
Do not. Come quickly to Me - your Father is caring for you. ♥   We, us, child?
Forever and ever amen.
Wisdom loves children. ♥

---

[1] While Jesus was saying this, I saw a scene (vision) of some souls' hands which were ablaze, become extinguished.

HOW TO UNDERSTAND THE SPIRIT

September 25th, 1988

My God, having given a few of Your Messages to L... he said that they are embarassing to read, he felt uneasy reading them because of the Love You have for me Your creature and the love I have for You my God! He said, they are shocking. Lord?

I Am. I am God. I am Love. Whosoever says that My Messages are ignominious, is only condemning Me and by condemning Me is condemning himself. ♥ *An unspiritual man has not the capacity to understand the Spirit by means of his mind, nor penetrate into Wisdom to be able to understand the Spirit. One has to open his heart and allow the Spirit to enter and thus meet with his spirit: and Wisdom will illumine him to see what the Spirit is; how the Spirit works; what the Spirit feels. I am God. I am the Source of Love, who created all of you out of My Boundless Love <u>to love Me</u>.*

Praised be our Lord!

THE MOTHER OF ALL HUMANITY

September 26th, 1988

My God?

I Am. My Vassula, treat Me as a King. Lead all souls to Me - those that want to hear I will rise and place in My Sacred Heart. ♥

Beloved.
Yes Holy Mother?

Yes. Hear Me. My perfume, I propound among you[1]. Realize that Our Presence is among you - listening to your hearts. How we love you! Children, I am your Mother; allow My Son to lead you and heal you -purifying you; allow yourselves to be healed by Jesus. Receive this grace My Son is offering you. Understand why He seeks every soul - Jesus loves you boundlessly! I, the Mother of all humanity, the Mother of your Saviour, am near you children and

---

[1]Many of those who follow this revelation, have smelled incense and roses.

ever so ready to help you. Come! Open your hearts to Us; We are your Holy
Family - receive Our Peace. Jesus and I bless you all. ♥

I bless You Holy Mother, Mother of God.

THEY TREAD UPON MY SPIRIT

September 27th, 1988

Jesus?

*I Am. Follow My instructions given to you and let Me speak. Stay bare-footed -
a nobody. Recognize My levelled path; My Path is straight - so do not look to your
left nor to your right. I have indeed initiated you in My mysteries; I have chosen
you to be My Tablet; I have led you bare-footed into My House to meet Peter; My
Message of Peace and Love will disarm My enemies -just wait and see. I have not
yet finished My Works. My House is in ruin today, but the worst is yet to come.
The Cains, living in My Body and who are the thorns in My Head, full of boast,
will endeavour to slaughter My Abels - these Abels who understand My Spirit and
love Me sincerely; but I tell you truly that their boasts will turn into mourning and
My Fire will burn these unfaithful servants, for what have they to offer Me now?
They tread upon My Spirit, led by their own desires and bigotry; their
unfaithfulness lead them astray and they cannot see clear anymore. Vassula, write
down your question since this question is in many of you. ♥*

Lord, are there no good servants left anymore? Servants who love You truly and are
sincere?

*There are only a few left who really love Me and only a handful who understand
My Spirit - these souls are soothing My Wounds and My Sacred Heart is their
Home.*
Lord what about laymen?
*In these too, very few are left who believe in Me and who believe in My
Providential Works; but the majority have abandoned Me, their God; and in the
depths of My Sacred Heart lies the lance's blade - this blade which is the cause of
so much bleeding. Today I am telling you that he is part of the cause of My
sufferings. I, the Lord, will come upon him by surprise. I will suddenly, without
anyone expecting Me, enter My Temple[1] - these days are numbered. I will*

---

[1]Temple means us.

descend, like lightening; purifying Jerusalem, who will fall into a heap of dust - dragging with her all those who do not love Me. I mean to be her Judge and judge her severely, but all those who remained faithful under My Holy Name, I, the Lord, will raise and place them into My New Jerusalem. They need not fear, since they were following My instructions and My Law; although they were suppressed, and their cries to Me muffled by My enemies, I still heard them. My Eyes never left those saints; they feared Me, they praised Me, keeping faithful to My Word, sharing all the resources I had given them and doing good works that please Me.

Beloved creation, you are living in the End of Times. I had warned you that in these times there are going to be people who sneer at religion, suppressing the Spirit of prophecy, ridiculing the visioners, so that they can follow their own deceitful doctrines for wickedness; their skills turned into perverted inventions, leading them astray - lovers of evil, they cannot retain any purity of mind. Like Folly, they are drawn into devious ceremonies and black masses - worshipping Satan; either that, or lead lives of great wickedness - for their ignorance is such that just by that alone they condemn their own lives. Since they have closed their ears and refuse to see the Truth, acknowledging Me their God, their sin has drawn them into depravity, and rotteness of their very soul. It has also been said that in your times only a remnant of My servants would remain faithful to Me, preaching the Gospel as it should be preached, and that many would fall into rationalism - betraying Me with disloyalty. This rationalism made a desert of My Church, bringing It into a ruin where vipers nestled within Its depths. For those who defile My Name and who sit enthroned in earthly glory, satisfying their thirst for money, seeking their own interests and not Mine, I call out in the wilderness you have made for you to come to Me and repent before the day of purification. I, the Lord, warn you not to suppress My Spirit of Truth, who speaks through this weak instrument. I solemnly request My Church to remember the conditions I and My disciples worked in and where our heads rested. Palaces we had none!... None! Palaces were for kings, but not for Me nor My disciples!

Lord, those whom You mean and who recognize themselves would not like hearing this part and it will be one more reason for them to suppress this message.

True, some of them would not like hearing My words; they stifle Me and My House, with their vain-glory. My House and I suffocate with their perjuries - I have no space to breathe. They have shut all the windows of My House and My Light cannot penetrate, nor can My Spirit blow within to clean the air. These souls are like salt that lost their taste, they are like stained glass, preventing My Light to penetrate in them, preventing My Holiness to purify them. Satan's vapours are like mist these days, penetrating through keyholes and between hinges. Since his vapours are deadly, I solemnly request that you redouble your sacrifices and your prayers. Tremendous reparations have to be made by those who love Me. Satan in his fury has redoubled his works against My Church this year - in the Marian year he chose to split a section of My Church. I had foretold you of this schism and that in the middle of it all you were to descend into My House.

Take My Hand now and walk with Me; share My Cross My Vassula - My Works are not yet finished. Be in Peace. I, the Lord, give you My Peace child. Remember, smile at My Presence - <u>never</u> ever forget My Presence, tell Me a Kyrie elleisson. Please Me, I have given you so much!

Yes My Lord, You have given me so much, I love You Holy of Holies, You have given me so many good things that I want to proclaim them all, all the time, but they are more than I can count, You opened my ear to hear You, You raised me from the dead, may Your love and faithfulness constantly preserve me, may You do all what You've done to me, to my brothers too, let them share too Lord.

My child, I am calling all of you; I am seeking each one of you; allow Me to enter your hearts and I will heal each one of you. Come, rest now. ♥ I am with you always - never forget this!

CONFESSION AND COMMUNION

September 29th, 1988
Saint Gabriel Saint Michael and Saint Raphael

Glory be to the Most High[1] for He has raised you up from the dead. You are to be on your guard always from Satan. Recollect yourself before the Lord. Pray to me.

The Prayer to St Michael, exorcism?

Yes. If God's creation only knew how this prayer combats evil, they would have recited it daily. Be prepared for the Lord's Word always. The Eternal One loves you - praise Him!
Ah St Michael thank You for guarding and combatting for us. ♥

My Lord?

---

[1] I prayed to St Michael.

I Am. Remember, your surrounding is a wilderness. Vassula, repent and confess your sins to Me - I am listening[1]. I forgive you fully; I forgive your sins which stained your soul. Have My Peace.

I wish to emphasize this to all My creation: I have given you all My Law -this Law is to be obeyed by all of you. I have given you teachers who minister in My Church - these are to guide you and teach you all how important it is to Receive Me in Holy Communion; receive My Blood and My Body. My Blood was not poured out in Rivers for nothing; My Blood was poured out for you to drink It. These ministers should not keep away from you My Blood; My Blood was poured out for your Salvation - <u>you are to drink My Blood too</u>, so come and drink Me and you will thirst for more. Obey My words of My Last Supper, and when you come to Me, make sure before, how you will receive Me. Examine yourselves, recollect yourselves. Honour Me fully by repenting and often confessing - I have given you confessors; when, My beloved ones, you are confessing to him you are only confessing <u>to Me</u> - it is to Me you are confessing. Do not treat the Blood of the Covenant as if It were not Holy. ♥ ♥ *Remember My Holy Presence. We, us.*

Yes.
We, us.
Yes Holy Mother.

Later on:

Vassula.
St Michael?
Yes, it is me. I wanted you to commemorate My feast-day, as well as St Gabriel's and St Raphael's with this prayer of exorcism; have it printed and propound these prayers - your era needs them desperately. I am obeying the will of the Most High. ♥ *Glory be to God.*

Glory be to God, blessed be our Lord.
My child, it is I, the Lord. Be always alert when you pray these prayers! I the Lord love you for hearing Me. Never doubt, I will nourish your soul. Come, be one with Me. ♥ *We, us.*
Forever *and ever.* Amen. **We, us.** Forever and ever. **Amen.** ♥ (St Mary I bless You.) ♥

---

[1] I confessed to God.

DISTRIBUTE MY MESSAGE

September 30th, 1988

Glory be to God for the total conversion of a freemason and for a Jehova witness too. Glory be to God for the previous conversions and the most recent one too.

May there be masses returning to You.[1]

Lord?
I Am. Your sacrifice pleased Me. I am your Shepherd and My lambs I come to collect and protect. ♥ Feed My lambs - distribute My Message. ♥ Come, you and I, I and you, in union of love. ♥

RETURN AND REPENT

October 5th, 1988

My Lord?

I Am. It is I, the Lord, who loves you all with an everlasting love. I am ever so present among you all. ♥

Since the beginning of times, whenever My children fell into rebellion, I, the Lord, descended through very weak instruments to give them My warning and bring them back to Me. I, God, always worked in the same way. <u>I descended like a Hammer to break the rocks</u> - breaking the hard crust which covers My creation's heart. I always manifested Myself whenever My creation needed My help, or whenever they fell very low, going as close as possible at Satan's gates. My Vassula, through My whole Message of Peace and Love, I call, I call and cry out with <u>great agony</u> to you all to return to Me and repent. I cry out in this wilderness, but My Voice sounds like an echo - echoing into a void... If only you would hear Me and open your hearts that I heal you! I descend in this <u>Great</u> Wilderness in search of My

---

[1]The name JESUS and the heart are written with my own blood as a small sacrifice.

remaining flowers but I only stumble on rocks - rock after rock... I turn around with great hope but I only find thorns and briars, tearing on Me and on the few who love Me. I search for love but I find hatred; I need to be consoled but I find none; I thirst for compassion but I find only mockery. I find no love. I find no hope, no faith among this generation[1] because they have stopped adoring Me. All My fears have come to reality! O era of no faith at all! Of no hope! Of no love! You have stopped adoring Me and My Holy Name means nothing to you now! Yes, My Name is meaningless to you... Had you followed My ways and had you listened to My cries, all this wilderness would not have been. I ask those who love Me to pray for your brothers who do not. Do not repeat the errors your ancestors made the day of the Rebellion, that day of Temptation in the wilderness. My green pastures of long ago lie barren and desolate and My little flock has been struck by their own shepherds, scattering them... Why provoke Me? Why? Every generation that repelled Me has been punished. ♥ But your minds are wicked. Since you do not stop deceiving yourselves, thinking you are doing better than the Pharisees, saying, "had we been living then, we would never have shared in their evil works, our faith would have saved us!" I am telling you today this: you are receiving Me not very differently from those days I was among you in flesh. Many of you have condemned My Messages[2] before even knowing what it is all about!! Daughter, I came to them in their wilderness to tell them I was the Messiah they were expecting but they disbelieved Me, rejected Me and they persecuted Me - crucifying Me. Today My Holy Spirit reaches you in your obscurity, but you fail to reach Its Works through your disobedience and the lure of sin that has accumulated in you. Your era's wilderness has by-passed all other wilderness. Why are they surprised and even bored and annoyed at My Spirit which descends to illumine them? Their lethargy has made desert after desert! Rock after rock! How I stifle and suffocate to watch My few remaining flowers tread upon by these rebellious peoples!

Vassula, had it not been for your Holy Mother holding away My Arm from striking them and had it not been for My Fathomless Mercy, I, who am a God of Justice too, would have stroke them long ago. For this generation has created a New Sodom and Gomorrah among themselves; they have gone as far as to believe that the calamities that befall on them now come from Me; they have never understood how evil draws Evil and that they are paying now from their own coin. I want all those who love Me to pray, pray, pray for this Rebellion to come to Its end. I wish to encourage My friends to proceed with their good works[3]. I bless all those who scatter My grains of Peace and love - trust Me all the way to the end. I also ask you solemnly to pray for My Holy Spirit of Understanding to enlighten you all.

---

[1] It's not only to God we're doing this, but among us too.

[2] The actual revelations, apparitions, signs.

[3] All those 'new disciples' who help in translations, photocopying, and the work and distribution of this revelation.

For how long will they not understand Scriptures? For how long will they push aside My Mysteries? Find My Fruits in the Proverbs. Perceive, and if you have trouble in perceiving, ask My Holy Spirit of Perception to descend upon you. ♥
Many of My Mysteries lie still hidden and are disclosed in My Wisdom Books[1]. ♥
♥ ♥ *I promise you that Love will return as Love and live among you all. I will restore My House. I will bring you a New Jerusalem, a City of Integrity, a Faithful City - for Justice will prevail. Come, reap My Harvest friends; reap this Harvest I have prepared secretly.* ♥ *Gather My Works and disperse them; they will refreshen the desert winds; they will irrigate the dry soil and bring back life again in this Wilderness. Pray My Vassula for My Return.*

"O God, Yes! COME! COME to us oh Lord return to us!!"

♥ *I will, very soon. My Return is not far now. Tell all the others to pray for My Return. I, the Lord Jesus Christ, the Redeemer, will restore all that has been damaged and is to be damaged still. Do not forget the Big Tribulation that My Church will undergo before I renew Her entirely... So, My child, allow Me to use you as My tablet - share My Cross of Peace, of Love, with Me your Lord. We, us, for eternity.*

Yes Lord.
We, us?
Yes My Holy Mother, for eternity ♥

ALLOW MY SPIRIT TO GROW IN YOU

Message given to the group who meet me, and to be read to them:

My Superabundant Love will seek each one of you. I am not far from you; we eat together... we do things together... so feel My Presence. Return to Me and I too will return to you[2]. My Presence will be felt by many of you to encourage you. Whoever seeks Me will find Me. Allow My Spirit to grow in you - take My Hand, children, and be willing to follow Me. ♥ *I, Jesus, give you My Peace - this Peace that is missing in this world.* ♥ *I have never left you. Have I not said that I shall be with you always, till the end of times? Believe in My Holy Presence; believe in My Presence now, for this Revelation comes from My Mouth. I love all of you; I bless all of you. Come...* ♥ ♥ ♥

---

[1]Here I felt suddenly a widow again and I cried out to the Lord: COME LORD! I desire the Lord.
[2]Malachi 3:7.

LOVE WILL RETURN AS LOVE

October 10th, 1988

Jesus?
I Am.

Blessed be the Lord.

I love you daughter for this faith you are giving Me. Do not worry. Lean on Me and listen to My Heart - this Heart which seeks you all and loves you but that many condemn. Daughter, pray often to Me to give you My Strength - I will always give you My Strength. Pray together with Me this prayer. ♥ *A prayer for My Return:*

> *"Come Lord! Return to us. Hear our sorrowful cries from this wilderness; feel our thirst and have Mercy upon us. Return to us. Come and blot out all wickedness - replacing it by Love. Amen."*

and to this prayer you will hear Me answer you that I, who am Love, will return to you as Love. Be patient, My beloved ones, just for a little while longer and I will return to you. ♥ *Be watchful and on your guard because My return will be sudden - so be prepared. Repent. Face Me your Lord with a pure heart and the shadows on earth will not frighten you, nor will the hour of darkness terrify you; you will feel neither distress nor anguish in this hour of deadly silence. So listen to Me; listen to My words and they will be a consolation to you when this hour of obscurity descends upon My entire creation. I solemnly tell you that this hour is not far from you now. I, who am Love, will draw near Me all those who love Me and I will diminish their fear; I will veil them with My love; console them with My Heart and they shall find their shelter in Me.* ♥ *Alas! For those who are not ready and never loved Me! They will die from their own wickedness and lie in the dust, suffocated by the weight of their sins! For they have defiled My Holy Name with the help of the second dragon; the dragon which wears the black cloaks; the dragon which is opposite to Light. O creation! Creation with sensless minds![1] How I pity you. Give Me one kind look and I will free you.* ♥

Since the day of your birth I knew you to be godless, still, I am willing to forget and talk things over with you. Your navel string is still attached to Me. If you tell Me that you were led astray and that you will stop sinning; if you only tell Me

---

[1] God seemed so sad, almost hesitant that He must punish.

about it, I, who am Love, <u>will</u> rescue you My child - My forgiveness is guaranteed beforehand. Do not provoke Me any longer - come back to Me and I shall indeed give you My Peace. ♥

Come daughter, I bless you for allowing Me to use your hand - how I love you! O daughter, I am well pleased with you; call Me always, caress Me with your love; rejoice Me, diminish My pains. Extinguish My anger by loving Me. Flower, I allow you to be in My Hall because of your nothingness, so remain nothing. I give you My Peace. We, us?

Yes Lord.
My Presence is Holy. ♥ ♥

READ HOW MY SPIRIT WORKS - 1 Cor. 12:1-11
MY CUP OF JUSTICE IS BRIMMING OVER

October 11th, 1988

Peace be with you.
Glory be to God!

I have, since the beginning of this revelation, been telling you that My Church is in ruin and in this ruin vipers have nestled inside It and made their homes within Its depths. Ah Vassula!![1] *How I suffer... I will have to come and untangle those snakes which are creeping all over My Holiest of Sacraments and throw them out of My Church all over again... My child, to live and be surrounded by this devastating wilderness <u>is</u> difficult and terrifying <u>but I am near all those who love Me and worship My Holy Name with love</u>.*

I want to remind all those who tread upon My Heavenly Works that I am Infinite Wealth. Whenever I saw My creation fall into rebellion I always sent messengers, carrying My Word - for Rebellion turns the land you are living in into deserts. ♥ *Although your ancestors rebelled, their doubts were never severe as your generation's doubting that I speak to My chosen angels, giving them My Messages.* ♥ *Today, My child, I have ministers in My Church who claim to believe in Me but refuse all My Divine Works I am offering you in your days and that come from the Holy Spirit! Their aridity is condemning them and in the Day of Judgment I will judge them severely! These peoples should go back to Scriptures and read how*

---

[1]God, with a loud cry full of suffering and pain, called out.

My Spirit works and how I bless the gifts I am giving to the chosen ones - they all come from Me[1]. My child, you and I, I and you, are crossing this wilderness - this deadly wilderness caused by Rationalism, lack of Faith, lack of Love, promiscuity, self-indulgences, vanity and a <u>resentment</u> to all that descends from the Holy Spirit. Their obduracy to listen is condemning them - anyone who rejects the Works of My Holy Spirit is rejecting Me <u>for the Holy Spirit and I are One and the same</u>!... These people are promoting this desert and are making sure that <u>nothing</u> will grow in it; if they see a flower, either they will trample on it and crush it, or will ignore it on purpose and never water it so that it withers and in this way get rid of it... My Cup of Justice is brimming over and already they are sensing the first drops of My Justice upon them. <u>All</u> I ask from these peoples, especially those who serve Me yet refuse the Holy Spirit's Works, is to <u>pray, pray, pray for enlightenment and for a stronger faith</u>. Come, My child, please Me always by remembering My Holy Presence.

We, us, Lord.
I love you. Yes, we, us.
We, us.
Yes Holy Mother.

I AM THE SPIRIT OF LOVE

October 13th, 1988

My God?

♥ *I Am. I have loved you from all eternity and from all eternity I wished you to love Me. I am the Spirit of Love. Leave your soul open to Me so that My Love will reflect in you; be like a mirror opposite Me - I wish to reflect My Love in you. I, My Vassula, am not a harsh God; I am Gentle, loving even all those who despise Me. Flower of Mine, since you start to understand how much love I have for you, can you then understand how Love suffers because of this lack of love?*
Yes Lord, I start to understand.
Then come to Me and console Me - do not deprive Me. You <u>can</u> console Me. Be blessed. ♥

---

[1] Jesus asked me to mark I Corinthians, 12:1-11.

THE SMALLER YOU ARE THE MORE
OFFENDED SATAN BECOMES

October 14th, 1988

Lord, I only ask You for Your Strength. I need <u>more faith</u> to love You more and as You want, I need perseverance and hope to accomplish the mission You have given me, and thus glorify Your Holy Name again.

I will give you all these things for My Interests and My Glory, but also for a higher perfection of your soul. ♥ *I, the Lord, love you. Understand how the demon hates you for this work you share with Me; you glorify Me with your love and you glorify Me by drawing souls to Me. You, whom he once called 'worm'[1] are glorifying Me and offending him - for the smaller and the more insignificant you are, all the more offended he becomes. Remember how pompous he is and how vain?!*

Yes my Lord.
I love you and I shall always protect you. Come always to Me and I shall never deny you My Peace. Love loves you. ♥
Glory be to our Lord.

YOUR WEAKNESS INFATUATES ME

October 15th, 1988

Lord?

I Am. I have never met, since all eternity, such weakness as yours - it's astounding...[2] Child, you need Me! Your weakness attracts Me, who is Infinite Strength. Your weakness infatuates Me; weakness has always attracted Me like magnetism. Listen to My Heart beats, I am Jesus and My Sacred Heart is your Home. ♥ *Daughter, every beat of My Heart is a song of love to you. I have loosened your chains of bondage to this world; remain now detached, like I wished it from all eternity - this detachment I want from every soul. Realize: who could*

---

[1]See 7.3.87.
[2]It was because of the awful wave of doubts again. Where there are the three full-stops I had left God speechless.

do this but Me your Saviour? I am the one who redeemed you from the bondage of sin and this is why the demons are agressive towards you - you have felt their close presence this week. Devote yourself to Me - for your devotion and fidelity pleases My Sacred Heart; this Heart thirsty for love and for fidelity. ♥ Come up to Us in that cavern[1] - invoke Us there. ♥
Yes Jesus, Yes Holy Mother.

Vassula of My Sacred Heart, feel loved by Me; feel loved by your Holy Mother; allow Me to use you for just a little while longer. ♥ We, us.
Yes Lord. Lord?
I Am.

This love I have for You and the fervent desire to feel You and want You constantly with me, thirsting always for more of You, thinking only of You day and night, in short, living for You, sometimes wanting to see You with my bare eyes, are these feelings of desire to 'see' You as those souls in Purgatory who are not with You yet?
They are very near to what they feel, yet with much deeper and clearer feelings[2]. ♥
Then it really must be terrible!
Yes, they suffer very much. If they had never desired Me while on earth then they learn to desire Me in purgatory - there they do not see My Face and they burn with this desire. ♥
Yes my Lord. Thank You my Lord.

I AM OMNIPOTENT

October 18th, 1988

My Lord?
I Am the Lord.
My God?
I Am.
Would You like to bless the religious objects given to me by friends?
Take them up to My lips - I will bless all that is to be blessed[3].
Lord, there are some inside cellophane, can You kiss through them?

---

[1] A cavern above the Ermitage of Longeborgne.
[2] Theirs is much deeper.
[3] Jesus said this and made me understand that one medallion will not be blessed among the other religious ones, because someone gave me a non-religious one.

I love your innocence. Take them all as they are. I am Omnipotent. By the little faith you are giving Me, I will take it and place it in My Sacred Heart which will nourish it into a stronger faith. ♥ Come, rest now.
Yes my Lord. Thank You my Lord.

I WILL SHOW THEM
WHAT TRUE LIFE IN GOD MEANS

October 19th, 1988

Glory be to God. (Answer to St. Michael's prayer.)

Praised be Our Lord. (Answer to St. Mary's prayer.)

I give you My Peace. Come. (Answer to the Sacred Heart's prayers.)

I, the Lord, tell them[1] this; I bless each one of them. I bless all those who help My Divine Message - particularly those who sacrifice their spare time for Me. My calls will not be in vain. Love one another as I love you. Diffuse My message - even to those who will ridicule you. Pray for enlightenment. Treat each other equally. Beloved ones, I am Present at all Times. I, Jesus, love you all with an everlasting love. Come to me Vassula, show My Sacred Heart to them. I, the Lord, will teach them to walk with Me; I will show them what true life in God means; I will make them understand that they all are My seed and that they belong to Me; I will show them how Satan had deceived them all and how treacherous he is. I want to tell them again and again that Satan <u>exists</u>; he is the evil one; he is the one who deceived you from The Beginning and he shall be conquered in the end and crushed. Pray My beloved ones - I will be listening. Pray and talk to Me; I am present; I am your Holy Companion; I am among you always - believe in this Mystery of My Presence. My love to you is everlasting - you will only understand its depths and its fullness once you are in Heaven. Feel My Presence, feel My Presence. I bless all of you.

---

[1]To the little group we formed to meet.

GLORIFY ME BY DESIRING ME

Rhodes - October 23rd 1988

♥ *My child, do you realise how I favoured you? Vassula, <u>glorify Me by desiring</u>
<u>Me</u>[1]. Be thirsty for me, like a flower needing water. ♥ Already you are closer to
me[2]. Yes! I am counting eagerly the days. See Me with you mind; see Me with
your heart; see Me with your soul. I have given you the charisma to discern Me -
so use it. See Me and smile to Me; smile at Me with love; amend for those souls
who never smile to Me but come to Me only for their interests. ♥*
Yes Lord. We, us.

MEDITATE ON MY PRESENCE

October 24th 1988

My Lord and God?
*I Am. I give you My Peace child. I love you daughter. Lead all souls to Me by
your prayers - ask for their redemption. Please My Sacred Heart by forgiving those
who reject you; never blame them - never accuse them. I am the judge and I will
judge them in the Day of Judgement. So you, My child, must forgive them -repay
evil with love. Lean on Me to rest, and find your consolation in My Sacred Heart;
find my caresses in It's depths. Come, we, us?*
Yes, my Lord.

<u>*Then I want to hear you say it*</u>. *Do not forget Me! Remember My Presence. Do
you know how much I desire this meditation upon <u>My Presence</u>? My Presence is
also a very important Mystery that most of you seem to forget - <u>meditate on My</u>
<u>Presence</u>.   Children, whom I love with an everlasting love, please Me by
remembering My actual Presence; train yourselves by using these words, <u>we</u>, <u>us</u>,
<u>you</u> and <u>I</u>, <u>I</u> and <u>you</u>, <u>us</u>. Include Me in your activities, in your discussions and
in your thoughts. Respect My Presence, never forgetting that I am the Holy One.
By remembering Me, you will sin less, knowing and remembering that I am with
you. I, Jesus Christ, the Nazarene, bless you all. ♥* ⊂× ΙΧθΥΣ

---

[1]To desire God is also to glorify Him. Should you not desire Him while you are
on earth, you will learn to desire Him in Purgatory; in a purgatory only for
desire.
[2]Less days on earth.

I CREATED YOU TO DELIGHT MY SOUL
BE ONE UNDER MY HOLY NAME

October 25th 1988

My Lord?

I Am. ♥ Daughter! Rejoice! for I have loved you since all eternity - a love you can never understand! - <u>a love of predilection</u>. I created you to delight My Soul and fill My Heart with your love; I have created you to appease My anger and soothe My Wounds with your tears; I have created you to rest Me when I am weary and to talk to Me when I am forgotten. I love you to folly! Beloved, I have chosen you to know My Sacred Heart's desires; I have chosen you to share all that I have - <u>be My child of light</u>. I am He who loves you most and I am He who blesses you most. My jealous love I have for you will inflame your little heart into a torch of light so that in your turn will inflame other hearts too to love Me. Be My altar, burning with My love - spread this flame and enliven even the stones into devoted followers of Mine. Make no difference of colour or of creed -you are all made to My Image and My Sacrifice was made for the entire Nations. <u>Be one, under My Holy Name</u>. I love you creation to folly! <u>Revive creation!</u> Believe in My Presence among you. Allow Me to enter your heart so that I may heal you all.
     ΙΧθΥΣ ⊂×   *Flower, desire Me, respect My Law and please Me; place Me as first and above all things - detest all that is earthly. Tremendous reparations have to be done to substitute all evil done in this world. Amend for others. Vassula, I will not forsake you ever. My teachings have led you to Me; I and you, you and I - bonded for all eternity. Have My Peace. ♥ Come. ♥*

UNITED AND ONE

Rhodes - October 31st 1988

I took the bus in Rhodes to go to town. The controller comes and I tell him: "One ticket please." He gave me a ticket. Jesus was sitting near me and I turn around to Him chuckling and said to Him: "I asked for one, but we are two in fact, the man has no idea!" Jesus surprised, turns around and tells me:
What are you saying! Are we not <u>united and one</u>? Come. ♥

SEED OF MINE, I AM YOUR ABBA

Rhodes - November 2nd 1988

Vassula, have My Peace.   Come, I am pleased that in spite of where I have you placed, you are trying to understand Me.   Beloved, relieve My pains by loving Me - show to your God your child-like faith; please Me in that way and depend on Me entirely.
I will Lord.   Who else will I turn to than my own Father?   I have no one but You.

♥ *Seed of Mine, delight Me always, be My joy.   I am your Abba.* ♥ *Seed of Mine, flourish, embellish and let your fruits feed many.   My plans I have designed long before you were born, for I Am The Authority.   Men tend to forget easily that My Church will be led always from above and not from below; they tend to forget that all power is given from above so I tell you that any earthly authority, any earthly kingdom that infiltrated into My Church, will not last - I will shatter it and throw it down into a heap of dust.   You know all this from before and yet you neither listened nor obeyed Me; you have barred Me out but I will open all your doors, and even your windows, so that My Spirit would breathe freely in My Domain.   Nobody will have the power to obstruct the passages I will open;   I will remind them once again that I am the Alpha and the Omega.   I, the Holy of Holies, the Holy Trinity-all-in-One, The Authority, I shall soon be with you; I will place all those who love Me into My Heart - My Heart will be their New Home. I come from above and from above your New Home will descend - this will be My Gift and My own New Holy Name again will be once more given back to you My beloved ones.   So come then and praise Me; come and extol Me; come and make your peace with Me and I will open My House to you and welcome you as My own. Come to Me[1].* ♥ *Yes, but I am the Lord now who loves you. Be blessed My child.* ♥ *We us?*

Yes, Lord.
We, us.
Yes, Holy Mother.

November 8th 1988

Today I felt Jesus' Cross.   I felt Him sad and saw Him sad even in the picture.

I Am.   My beloved, take My Cross and unburden Me - your Christ is so weary. I have allowed Myself to leave on your heart a few drops of My Blood to relieve

---

[1] Somehow just there I remembered how Daniel my guardian angel in the beginning was communicating with me; also in writing.

Me, Satan is determined now to discourage you, but I will not allow him to touch you. What has been started by Me and blessed will be finished, glorifying Me. ♥ *Today, you shall write down My message with your own handwriting[1] so that those who have not yet fully understood that I have filled you with My graces may understand that I have also given you the grace of hearing My Voice. Allow Me to dictate you today. Hear Me and write Vassula: the days are counted now* ♥ *-the days of your purification. Those that have been praying to Me for the renewal of My Church, I have heard - I have heard all their prayers to Me. I promise you that I, the Lord, will renew My Church; I will wipe away the stains that stained Her by the impure living within Her and I will rebuild Her anew. Yet, I dread to tell you, beloved ones, how much more She will have to suffer still before This Day. The Great Tribulations of Her Heart will start before I come to renew her entirely. This day must come to fulfill the Scriptures, but I will console all those who love Me in those days of sorrow. I will be ever so near your hearts - I will make you feel Me. I will send you a legion of Angels and Saints to console you all - so courage beloved ones, courage. I am suffering now and you who love Me, feel Me; you feel My Wounds; you feel My Sacred Heart, loaded with sorrow; you feel My gaze upon you creation, you who lie in obscurity. My Eyes are filled with tears of blood, yes, how else could I feel today when I see the majority of you slipping away into Satan's nets? But let those who do not want to hear continue their wickedness - I have been warning them several years now. I have been calling them for their repentance but they pay no heed to any of My warnings. I am weary, ever so weary with their blindness and their obstinacy. Rebellion has spread like fog, penetrating even in My House, dictating Peter what to do - Peter who is their leader. Yes, they do not listen to him and behind his back he is being cursed, cheated. They do not listen to him and they push him aside. Oh, he knows all this but they are too many opposing him, too many betraying him. My House has become a House of Rebels. Very few are left in there who acknowledge Me and honour Me. I, the Lord, will descend in the day of Purification, along with all the Saints and My Angels and purge all this evil away. From the North to the South, from the East to the West, My Fire shall descend! Wait and you shall see......*

'Jesus?' ♥

You have done well child by hearing only. This Vassula is also for those who think that your hand is pushed by Me without your hearing Me at all - some of them would not have believed that I, the Lord, am inspiring you. Now we will continue the way I like it, My Vassula. ♥ *Have My Peace and be alert.*

Please Lord, heal C.. if you were solidly here with Me and I would have asked you

---

[1] The remainder of this message was in Vassula's own handwriting.

to see her, and I would have taken You by Your arm and show her to You, Your Heart would not have resisted and You would have healed her.

My child, she does not believe you - she pushes instantly everything you are telling her. If she refused to open her heart for Me, how could I enter and console her? Still, I know even if she does not listen You can heal her.

Then pray for her Vassula. I love her - so continue your prayers. ♥ I will remind you of My Holy Presence; I and you, in union of love. ♥ We, us.

Yes Lord, we, us.

LOVE WILL REIGN IN EVERY HEART

November 10th 1988

Glory be to God. (St. Michael)
Glory be to God. (St. Mary)
(This was said after their prayers to them).

My God?

I Am. I was eagerly awaiting this moment. (Jesus and I was very anxious to meet in this way) *Hear Me My Vassula; come and touch My Sacred Heart - feel Its Wounds. My Sacred Heart is afflicted by pain and wounded beyond recognition. Souls do not hear Me -they fall by the hundreds into Satan's nets.*

Later on:

I will not fail you or desert you little one. ♥ Listen and write. After the Great Tribulation My Church will undergo, you will see a great Sign in the sky and all those who love Me will rejoice and praise Me; but all those who defiled My Holy Name will withdraw into deeper obscurity and fall into total unawareness. My Sign will be a blessing for those who kept My Commandments for they have kept My Word, honouring Me, glorifying Me; they were and are the golden pillars of My Church - the steady foundation and robust structure of Her Body; they are the purifying incense within Her. These souls I, the Lord, will exalt and place them in My New Jerusalem forever. ♥ Their New Home will be given to them from above, for from above My New Name will be given to you again and they and I will be one; you, My people, with My New Name, you shall not be called godless but I shall return to you My Name. When My Day comes, I shall withdraw all evil and have it locked. ♥ I, the Lord of Love, will let this New Earth sprout with seeds of Love; I will open her up and even from the rocks I will let new springs flow out of them - I will indeed flourish My Garden. ♥ For your sake, I will allow My holy angels to descend on you to nourish you; I will allow My Saints to become your instructors, instructing you My Holy Word - guiding you, as your friends; and Love will reign in every heart and Virtue will be worn as a crown for all My people of My New Earth. I have promised you long ago of this New Earth and I am keeping My Promise - it shall soon be fulfilled. I will descend though before this to purify you; I will purify you as gold is purified in fire - all impurities will be consumed in this Fire. ♥ I will have to do all these things to wash away all this impurity that covers this earth like a curse. I am solemnly telling you that everything that came to pass and is to pass had already been announced to you; every word has been written in My Scroll - this Scroll that shall be opened, read, then consumed. I, the Lord, have purified My Scroll by My own Blood - so eat It. Read Me. ♥ Pray creation that Wisdom may descend upon you to nourish you and enable you to unveil the truths and mysteries that lie still hidden in My Wisdom Books; pray for discernment; repent often and I will always forgive you. ♥

Daughter, have My Peace. I love you for allowing Me to use your little hand. I will end up My Message of today by saying: "Let those who have ears hear." Come I bless you. We, us?
For eternity Lord. Praised be the Lord. Amen.

ASK PADRE PIO

November 14th 1988

Today I looked at Padre Pio's picture, a <u>great</u> Saint according to Jesus' words, below his picture in an enveloped cellophaned space lies a piece of his clothes, dark-brown, for he was a Capucin. By looking at him I know that I had received this picture with a small piece of his clothes <u>because he wanted it</u>. So I prayed to him, as he is a great Saint and asked him to improve me in what I have worse in me, then on second thoughts, since I'm probably loaded with evil things, I asked him to pick up at least two things from me. I suggested that he helps me efface entirely all my vanity and to strengthen my faith in the Lord. Lord?

I Am. I have inspired you to ask Padre Pio to intercede for you. Come, today you will write My Message without hearing Me - I will lead your hand alone. (Now Jesus dulled my hearing) *"Repent often; bring to Me all your faults, that I may forgive them; come to Me as you are and I will perfect you; glorify Me by loving Me; praise Me all the time. I am the Lord."* (This was written as the Lord wished) *♥ My beloved, whom I sanctified, take My Hand and proceed with Me - I will instruct you with Wisdom.* (Suddenly I felt the Lord's presence vividly.) ♥

Vassula, do you know how I delight in you when you believe fully?[1] (Jesus was so very happy! I, too.) *Discern Me - it pleases Me so much.* ♥ *Come. We, us?* Yes, we, us.

I AM YOUR HOLY ONE
BUT YOU ARE CONDEMNING ME

November 15th 1988

Today I felt Jesus' Cross on my shoulders. I felt His Heart filled with tremendous pain, how he suffers... (For the world that rejects the Lord)

Lord?

I Am. Feel My Cross. Rest Me My child of Light - I am so weary. Stay near Me - I need to be consoled in this desolation. My Vassula, hear Me and write: O Creation, My seed! I am your Holy One but you are condemning Me; I have loved you from all Eternity, but you are dispising Me; I have delivered you from Death, yet you are attacking Me; I am feeding you daily wth My Bread and filling you with My Wine but in your evil you are offending Me. I thirst for Love, but you abandon Me in My thirst; I welcome you when I see you weary, to rest you in My Heart, yet when I am weary, you reject Me. I open My Heart to you - showing you how you have wounded It - but in your wickedness you are repeating your stabs - piercng Me through and through. I open My Arms to welcome you and embrace you, but you turn away - giving Me your backs. Full of tenderness I open My Sacred Heart to warm you, yet when I come to you, you shut your door in My Face, leaving Me outside in the cold - <u>Like a beggar</u>. I call you all day long, stretching out My Hands to you, to raise you and heal you, but you, instead, ignore Me and reject Me. My Eyes and those of My Mother are worn out with suffering. My Body is afflicted by It's Wounds - beyond recognition. All I ask from you is Peace and Love, but you refuse to hear My pleas. I have come to My own first, but again I was rejected by them - despised and persecuted. You hounded Me, treating Me as a jester; you betrayed Me; your betrayal has cost Me every tear left in My Eyes; your wickedness has pierced all Eternity - leaving even the demons gaping at your wickedness. ♥

Ah Vassula, I have come, out of pity and great Mercy, to warn you and deliver you from Death. <u>I have conveyed you to My own but they muffled down My Voice, for</u>

---

[1] In the actual Presence of Our Lord.

fear of coming out to Light and exposing their guilt; since they muffle My Voice and do not welcome My Spirit of Truth, I shall have their sins exposed by strangers. I shall have My Voice sound like a trumpet on the roofs of your houses.

I have been welcomed by strangers, who never knew Me - I knocked at their door and they allowed Me to enter; in spite of their poverty, they let Me share their meal; they have, out of their poverty, not sought Me, yet they have found Me. I have showed them My Wounds, made by My best friends, and they knelt in front of My Wounds on seeing Them; struck by Their depth, struck by the savagery inflicted on My Body, their hearts melted like wax. Do not weep My child. ♥ My Voice will be carried by strangers. When you hear the Echo know that it came from Me. I will be exalted by strangers who never sought Me; I will be glorified by those who never knew Me, and I will become their Master and teach them, and their faults I will dispel. I will reason with them and they will understand Me - they will heal My Wounds. ♥ I am The Shepherd, and I shall gather My Lambs, since they were struck by their shepherd[1] and dispersed. O Vassula, all this will be fulfilled so soon now. Come, rest in Me. Allow Me to rest in you. Bonded in love - let us share. ♥
Yes My Lord, we, us, for eternity, Amen.

Since yesterday Satan is attacking me ferociously. Jesus had warned me. Satan knows my weak points and he goes for these points. My weakest point is my insecurity for this revelation, mainly because of who I am, I'm not angelical nor holy, I blunder a lot and really know nothing. Then, I sometimes feel that Jesus is not adding any extraordinary supernatural signs, like on others, so Satan attacks me there and nourishes those weak points for his convenience, tormenting me.

Vassula, it is I, the Lord. Every time you doubt, I plunge into a deep sadness - My Heart hurts. Are you willing to continue My Work?[2]
Say Glory be to God and Blessed be Our Lord.

Glory be to God. Blessed be Our Lord! Vassula![3] Vassula, My child, do not get deceived by Satan - he is fighting you with suggestion - he is fighting My Plan. Every time your foot goes a step up, he rages with fury. I am beside you little one to warn you. ♥ Vassula, My signs are limited this time for this revelation. I get more glorified giving it in this way. I have explained to you why - I want that Faith comes first, without having too many extraordinary signs within this revelation. I want it simple. I have told you that the only sign I will give is you

---

[1]This Message is meant for those lost souls, souls who deny God, souls whose hearts are closed and sacerdotals who deny God's Works of today.
[2]I was suspicious.
[3]Jesus' voice was so very soft and tender - I melted.

yourself and your fruits - which are mainly the conversions. ♥ *I know how faith is missing in your era, that is why you will be persecuted, but, was I not persecuted too? I was disbelieved in spite of My Fruits.* ♥ *I am giving you many graces Vassula, although you merit none. I have servants who merit so much more than you - I am only reminding you. All I ask from you is love. Love Me your God with all your soul and with all your mind, for I have created you to love Me; to love me with a special love - deep, fathomless. I have opened My Gates in Heaven and allowed you in; I welcomed you in My Hall, where only the Elect are to be found.* ♥ *I have told my Elect of My Plan of Salvation - it is out of My Boundless Mercy I have been preparing it in secret; I announced it in My Hall to Them; I told Them that I had My Eyes set on you; I said that I would choose the least of all My creatures, the weakest and the most wretched of all eternity, so as to show My Great Mercy and My Authority. I have descended all the way down to you, to seek you among the dead and raise you, lifting you to Me - for this was My Will.* ♥ *I then layed a table for you and I, Myself, placed My food into your mouth with My Hand. How I your God love you!! I love you to jealousy! I then annointed you with my oil and made you Mine. I espoused you to Me and I became your Master; I covered you with graces and I enriched you with My Jewels. Have I not given you My Cross, My Nails and My Thorned Crown? What more valuable treasure can a Spouse offer to His beloved? I, who am the Spirit of Love, have taught you how to love Me and how to grow in this love; I have shown you around to My angels - I share with you all that I have.* ♥ *You live in My House; you live in My Sacred Heart; blessed by My own Hand, hallowed by My Grace, try and understand why Satan is hounding you - he is after My Plan to destroy it. If you only knew what a battle is going on! But the earth feels these vibrations from this battle, so beware of him and <u>do not let him deceive you!</u>*

How could I do anything unless you help me! Please do not allow him! Please turn him away!
If you knew how I am protecting you. Here, have a look at this.
(I saw myself standing and around me was formed a circle of angels, holding their hands to bar out a passage, like this).

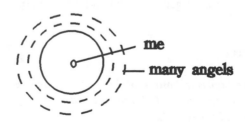

Satan is not allowed to lay a finger on you[1] - this I promise you. ♥ *I, for My part will never abandon you, nor will I neglect you - with Me you will lack nothing. My Peace I have given you and I have shown you My love of predilection I have for small souls - I have shown to you My Sacred Heart. So, My Vassula, you are made to love Me unmeasurably and delight My Soul; you are to desire Me always; you are to obey Me, pleasing Me; you are to appease My anger; you are to console and rest Me; you are to adore Me; you are to hope in Me; you are to believe in Me fully and blindly - these are the principles of My Heart. Honour Me by being my reflection and glorify me by accepting everything I am giving you. Flower, live only for My interests and My Glory - accept always with joy all that I give you.*
Yes, My Lord, I'm trying.

I am Present at all times. Remember, if I had not come to rescue you, would you have been now desiring <u>*Me and Me only*</u>*?*
No Lord.
I have taught you what <u>*True Life in Me means*</u>*; pray often, pray daily the Holy Rosary - for this little chain shall be* <u>*The Chain*</u> *in which Satan will be chained and conquered! I give you My Peace - never doubt. We, us.*
Forever. Amen.

I think that when Scripture says that Satan will be <u>chained</u> (appoc. 20:2), I think it will be when all humanity will recite the Holy Rosary, the whole globe. When this day comes, Satan will be conquered and crushed, by "the chain" of the Rosary.

I AM YOUR HIGH PRIEST

November 21st, 1988

Glory be to God. Blessed be our Lord! My Lord.
I Am. Feel how My Sacred Heart is. ♥
Jesus'Sacred Heart is the most gentle, warm and forgivng of all hearts, how could I resist you?

Message for our Meeting:

I am Love. I am the Supreme Source of Love, so do not resist Me. Come to Me, plunge in Me, for I am an Ocean of Tenderness and Peace. Draw all of you from My Sacred Heart to fill up your hearts; I will embellish you, I will perfect you.

---

[1]Causing illness or death on me.

Come and eat from Me and you shall live forever[1] for I am the Living Bread, the Bread of Life![2] Beloved ones, do not doubt of my Providential Calls. I am still among you all; I am in your meetings, assisting and present - feel My Presence. I am The High Priest who speaks in your hearts and encourages you all to approach Me. I am trying ever so much to draw you near Me. Ah! How I long to hold you all in My Arms and with great Tenderness embrace you all! How I long for you to approach Me and become intimate with Me! I am your High Priest, but also your Holy One, your Brother, your Companion, your Spouse. I am your Creator and you are all My seed. Vassula, I am and will always be in these meetings. Your discourses will come from Me - out of My Mouth your words will come. Have I not said that I am going to water My orchard and irrigate My garden? I will spread above you all, like morning mist, leaving on you all My Dew of Peace and Love - so do not resist Me. I intend to embellish you creation! Blessed are those who will open themselves to Me and allow My Dew of Peace and Love penetrate in them. Blessed are those who are faithful to Me and Love Me, for I shall draw them even closer to Me and cover them with My Love. ♥ You are created in My Image and you are called to live in this Image - an Image that many of you have forgotten; but I, The High Priest, shall remind you of My Divinity and of My Holiness. I shall remind you that I am Holy.

St Mary:

Flower, have My Peace. Careful now - be obedient and you will have nothing to fear. O Vassula, Jesus loves you boundlessly. He cares for you; you and He are sharing His Cross - Jesus will never abandon you ever. Come, take your rest. I am with you. ♥ We, us?

Jesus?

I Am. I shall remind you all that I am Holy, so that you live holy. I am Love and out of My Infinite Love I am giving you warnings and signs in various places all around the globe. Have I not said that the Advocate, the Holy Spirit, whom the Father will send in My Name, will teach you everything and remind you all that I have said to you?

---

[1] John 6:51.
[2] John 6:35.

I WILL DIVINIZE YOU FOR I AM DIVINITY

Jesus?

Message given for the meeting:

♥ *I Am. I am your Lord, the Crucified.* ♥ *Children of My Soul, beloved of My Heart, Love is suffering profoundly. Understand how I feel; I feel abandoned, forgotten and betrayed by My own.* ♥ *I am today on My Cross and in My second Passion.* ♥ *The earth is dryer than ever before and* ♥ *you, beloved ones, suffer from the consequences - you are the victims. Many of you are being starved - others are constantly deceived by the Evil one. How I pity you all! My Heart bleeds to watch all this from My Cross. My Eyes are filled with Tears of Blood. I am giving you all so many signs, yet, very few notice them.* ♥ *Come to Me in your prayers - I am Present and I am listening to you! Come in your Saviour's Arms - give Me your faults and I will purify you and heal you. I will divinize you for I am Divinity - I will perfect you! Come to Me as you are - do not fear Me. I am a Loving God. I am full of Mercy for the wretched ones. I am a God full of Pity! Pray to Me, talk to Me - do not hesitate! I am eagerly waiting for you. My Love for you all is so Great, that I, who am the Holy of Holies, the Eternal One and Sovereign of all My Creation, bend all the way down to you to be able to reach you and heal your infirmities* ♥ *I am among you always and till the end. Blessed are those who propound My Message of Peace and Love. Blessed are those who come to Me and console Me; be one with Me; remain in My love forever.* ♥ ♥

COME AND CONSOLE JESUS

St Mary:

Most beloved children, I am your Holy Mother - I am the Mother of all Humanity. My beloved ones, Jesus is suffering beyond human words - He is now in His Second Passion! Feel Our Hearts - how they suffer. Today there is a great battle going on. Satan is attacking ferociously and St. Michael is battling him with God's angels. The earth feels the vibrations of this great battle. I need your prayers, beloved ones - never cease praying. Pray My beloved ones - be like shining angels of light in this obscurity. Pray for the redemption of souls; pray My beloved ones for the conversion of souls. I count each one of you. Please understand how a mother would feel when she sees her children heading towards an eternal fire, and how she feels to see some of her beloved ones fall in this eternal fire. Meditate on this and you will understand Me better. ♥ I will end up My Message by blessing you in the Name of The Father, The Son and The Holy Spirit. ♥ Come, and console Jesus.

♥ My Lord?

I Am. I am always happy when I see you trying hard to please me in re-living the Mysteries while praying the Rosary. Blessed child, teach others too, to pray the Holy Rosary slower - it is of no use praying quickly from just your lips. Every prayer should come from the heart - you have to feel what you say, so take your time by meditating every Mystery.
Thank you, my Lord.

RECEIVE MY CHILDREN

December 3rd, 1988

My Lord? I love You, I desire to be with You, thank You for giving me this grace, this gift to be with You. I feel You so near. Thank you for teaching me and lifting me to You, Glory be to God, Praised be our Lord, Blessed be our Lord, Lord?
I Am. Rebound My Sacred Heart by believing with a child-like faith. ♥ Do not seek why I have chosen you and lifted you to Me - just accept without the whys and whos. Do not raise any questions - just accept what I have given you. ♥ Ah My child, I was behind your doors for years!

Forgive me Lord.
I have forgiven you - I am not reproaching you, since this is a past thing, I only wish to show you the joy My Sacred Heart has for I am now with you again. I have formed you to receive Me; so please My Sacred Heart and receive My children - in receiving them you are receiving Me; I am bringing them all the way to your door-step - sacrifice your time; they need my Peace; they need to be encouraged - encourage them to approach Me intimately, but nevertheless, never forgetting that I am Holy.

Lord, is it Your wish to have these meetings?
It is my will. Cling to Me and let Me lead you. Abandon yourself to Me. I, Jesus, am before you.
Lord, it is alright, is it not - reading the messages in these meetings?
You are glorifying Me beloved. ♥
Thank you my Lord.

LOVE IS THE ROOT OF THE VIRTUOUS TREE

Never forget that I am leading you - trust Me. ♥ *Those who love Me will learn to grow in My Love so that in their turn they may bring others to Me to love Me.* ♥ *My Sacred Heart is in Flames of Love and ever so eager to draw all of you in It's depths. I thirst for love; all I want from you is love because Love is the Root of the Virtuous Tree. Come, all those who have not reconciled with Me; come, come and Reconcile and have My own Peace; come and share My Love; come all those who still have not understood Me - make Peace with Me; come and make Peace with Love. I, your Lord Jesus Christ, wish you to become My Children of Light; yes, My disciples of Peace and Love, honouring Me.*

Oh Lord! Some will be persecuted like all other times!

MOTHER OF GOD

I know My child - some will be persecuted by those whose hearts are still closed and reason with their minds and not with their hearts; but by My Grace, I shall draw many of these too in My Sacred Heart. Little flower, courage - I am beside you and My Eyes are upon you, so do not fear. It is My desire to have My Message of Peace and Love diffused from North to South and from East to West, so have faith in Me - I have been preparing It in secret for your Era. ♥

I ask in My Message that My Churches unite, for as the Father and I are One, My Church must also be One - all united and into one Fold. I have chosen Peter to be your guardian and guard you in the Truth until My Return, but men have disobeyed Me; they have split, declaring their own rules. I am telling you truly, do not listen to those who oppose Peter, Peter-of-My-Lambs - who is John Paul II now - for he is My chosen one and the beloved of My Soul. Do not listen to those who condemn him - they have been led astray. Beloved ones, when you have recently split, part of Me was torn off; yes, they did not realize that they have torn a part off My Body. Oh My beloved ones, do I deserve this? Why tear My Heart? Why tear on your God's Heart? Why fill My Eyes with more Tears of Blood?[1] *I beg you, just like a beggar who has been lamed by his own friends, to return all of you to Peter and be one - like the Father and I who are One.* ♥ *I am also calling all those who reject My Mother*[2] *to open their ears and hear. My Mother is the*

---

[1] Jesus portrait appeared in extreme suffering. His Eyes were filled with Blood with a blood-crust around.
[2] The Protestants.

Queen of Heaven - She is by Name, "Mother of God." I am not blaming those who had not known - I am only trying to bring you back to The Truth. I also call out for the conversion of this world, I am also reminding those who have forgotten My Omnipotency that they should not compare Me to themselves[1].

I am reminding you all that you are living in the End of Times and thus My Signs have increased... Scriptures are being fulfilled... I am Peace and Love. I, your Lord Jesus, am ever so Merciful - yes, My Mercy is Great. Believe in My Mercy, never forgetting though that I am also a God of Justice. My purification, which I will send down, will be out of love; do not misunderstand or misinterpret this by calling it menaces from God; I am not menacing you - I am warning you out of love. Just like a father who warns his child and who tries to reason with him, bringing him back to his senses, I too am trying to reason you and show how wrong and misled some of you are and how sins can obstruct My Light. I come to wake you up because many of you are in deep sleep. I am coming to you all, out of My Boundless Mercy to revive the dead. I come to ask you, out of My Infinite Love I have for all of you, to repent and change your lives and be holy. Live in holiness, for I am Holy. ♥ I give you My Peace so that you are in Peace and that you may give this Peace to your brethern. ♥ Come now, recollect yourselves in prayer at the end of this year. Come and love one another as I your Lord love you. I bless each one of you. ♥ ⊂╳ ΙΧθΥΣ

HAPPY ARE YOU WHEN PEOPLE ABUSE YOU

December 7th, 1988

Message for the group:

St Mary:

My Vassula, have My Peace. Beloved children, I bless you. I am your Holy Mother, who suffers just like you for the aridity that is being spread. Do not get discouraged - I am by your side. ♥ I will encourage you to diffuse Jesus' Message of Peace and Love. ♥ Behold, Jesus is manifesting His Message through this weak instrument, a frail flower whom He formed; but many ministers will refuse to believe - they do not seem to understand God's Infinite

---

[1]Those who rationalize God's Works of now.

Wealth! Many of them would not believe, even when they would see that sinners believed and repented! These sinners will get into the Kingdom of Heaven before these ministers will. Do not fear My beloved - I, your Holy Mother, see all that is happening. I will encourage you always. ♥ I will always console you - have faith and lean on Jesus always. ♥ Vassula, My child, happy are you when people abuse you and persecute you and speak all kinds of calumny against you on Jesus' account; ♥ rejoice and be glad, for your reward will be great in Heaven - this is how they persecuted the prophets before you My child[1]. There are many ministers that believe in God's present signs and revelations but, for fear of being persecuted, they hide their feelings. Those ministers should pray, pray, pray, asking Jesus' Sacred Heart for courage. Jesus will give them courage. ♥ I will end up My Message by blessing you, in the Name of the Father, the Son and the Holy Spirit. ♥ ♥ ♥

LITTLE FLOWERS

Message for the group:

Vassula, edit My Message. ♥ I desire to give this Message to all those who came to us. ♥ Aahh, My child, let them feel My Sacred Heart! Five of My Wounds are wide open for all to come in and share My pains! Beloved, it is I, Jesus, Jesus your Saviour, manifesting Myself through this weak instrument to give you all and to the entire Nations My Holy Message of Peace and Love. *I, who am Sovereign and above all, bend all the way to you, My little flowers, to be able to reach you. ♥ Out of My Infinite Love and out of My Boundless Mercy I come to offer you My Peace and My Love. I am the Light of this world, and I come to shine on this dark world in which you are now living in. Little flowers, you need My Light like any flower needing light and the rays of the sun to live, you too need the Rays of My Love to live for Love and in love - for such are the riches of My Grace. I love you creation to folly! Continue your prayers, your penitences, and your acts of love, for all these acts are a balm to My Wounds. I love you, and because of this love I have for you, I will see that in this desert that your era has become, new grains will sprout - grains of Peace and Love.*

I will descend among the dead to revive them and make out of them devoted servants of Mine, honouring My Holy Name and glorifying Me. Little flowers, the days are so near, those days I have been telling you about, of a New Earth and of the Era of Love which will descend from above. All this will happen - thus,

---

[1]Matthew 5:11-12.

Scriptures are fulfilled. ♥ *Beloved children of My Light, be united and always near Me; be with Me and pray for your brethren who are lost; pray for those sacerdotal souls who wound My Sacred Heart by denying My Signs. Disperse My Message of Peace and Love - proclaim It to all Nations. Glorify Me by distributing this Harvest[1] which is ready - It will nourish many. My Eyes and those of your Holy Mother are upon you. We give you Our Peace - take this Peace and share It with others. I bless all of you.* ♥ ⬤✕ ΙΧθΥΣ

LEARN HOW TO PRAY - LIVE HOLY

December 16th, 1988

Lord?

♥ *I Am. Here is My Message for the reunion of today. I will ask My flowers this: flowers of Mine, I will ask you all to learn how to pray.* ♥ *When you pray, pray from your heart. I need prayers that come from your heart and not from your lips. Do not pray quickly. Recollect yourselves and pray slower, looking at Me - I am Present. Let your prayers reach Me. Learn to be in constant prayer; by this I do not mean to have you on your knees endless hours, no, but just in remembering My Presence you will be in constant prayer - your minds will be lifted towards Me; all that you say, or do, or think, will be for Me.* ♥ *I need devotion and fidelity. Love Me without measure and desire Me. I am your Saviour and Consoler - so come to Me without hesitating. I will console you all. I will give you hope, so do not diminish your prayers and sacrifices - increase them by being in constant prayer. I, the Lord, will end My Message by giving you a motto for 1989:*

> *"Live Holy and repay evil with love. Love one another, like I love you."* ♥

I am Peace and Love and I bless you all. ♥

---

[1]The Messages.

THE PROGRAMME OF MY MEETINGS

December 17th, 1988

My Lord? (After our reunion.)
I Am. ♥
I was surprised to see so many come, there must have been 130 people!
♥ *Vassula, I have said before - full, you shall be many.* ♥
Lord, You must have noticed that there was some disputes somehow because of the programme?
How could I not notice all this![1] Vassula, opposing forces there will be, but I will not allow anyone to tread on you. Detach yourself and depend on Me; from now on, it is I who will organize and give you the programme of My Meetings; it is I who will tell you what to say - the programme will be given to you from above. I am Wisdom and from Wisdom you will receive It. ♥

Write:

First you will sanctify the place you are to hold My Meeting, like you have done, by praying the prayer to St Michael - open My Meeting by saying these words: "Peace be with you." Remember to tell My little flowers that it is I, the Lord, who gives them My Peace and that these words come from My Mouth. Then you will invoke all of you the Holy Spirit. You will all pray the prayer to St Michael - your era needs this prayer desperately. I will indicate always to you the passage to be read from the Holy Bible, just like I indicated to you in this past meeting to read Joel 3 : 28-32; in this way too I will show to you the passage to be read. My wish is that you read to them, then tell them why I chose this passage. This is to be followed by you reading to them parts of My Peace and Love Message.

How would I know which part am I to read to them?
Do not worry, am I not your Counsellor and Guide?
Yes My Lord.
After reading to them you can ask them if they have any questions - it is a time for open conversation. I will inspire you little one. Then, I would like you to read to them My Message concerning them. Please Me by offering them love; please Me by terminating with the Holy Rosary. ♥
If anyone wants to talk to me should I accept?
Beloved, yes, talk to them. ♥
Thank You my Lord Jesus.

---

[1] Jesus was not at all content, in fact He was upset with certain people.

I, THE LORD, DESIRE THIS UNITY
- THE ADVOCATE -

December 20th, 1988

Lord?
♥ *I Am!*[1]
Oh God.

Vassula, embrace My Cross! Share It with Me. My Cross will lead you into My Domain. Reside in My Sacred Heart - creep into It's depths and you will find Peace. ♥ *My child, pray for your brothers that have abandoned Me and are only captivated by the worldly riches; pray for those lost souls who fear My cross...; pray My child for My Church to unite and be one - every priest has to understand that I, the Lord, desire this Unity.* ♥ *Any division does not come from Me - it comes from My adversary. My Kingdom should be One and Holy.* ♥

Lord?
I Am.

Lord, the few Greek Orthodox priests who read a few pages in Your revelation You are giving me, do not agree about unity, as soon as they read that it's about uniting with the Pope, they become allergic and say this revelation is devilish. One lady, Greek Orthodox, after reading this revelation, with good-will went to a Catholic Church. When her confessor heard this, he condemned the revelation as coming from Satan, then excommunicated her! He did not want to hear of unity! But many Greek Orthodox laymen are willing because when they read Your revelation they understand, and they know You desire it, but the Greek Orthodox priests get infuriated!

Do I not know all this My child? My thoughts are not their thoughts, My ways are not their ways; they are burdening Me with their sins and they do not see clear anymore. Unity shall come from above. For now, as it is, you are divided altogether and do not live according to My Divine Image; you are not obeying My Law. Your division is contaminating and is spreading; your division will always remain unless I put an end to it - it shall not be overcome. How could you believe you can unite since love is missing among you? Many of you are inflexible and stiff like iron rods! but I shall bend you all - I will unite you! I shall turn this wilderness into a lake and the dry ground into a waterspring. Then, I shall place you all in this New Earth beloved ones and My Kingdom on earth shall be as it is

---

[1]Jesus answered "I Am" with such fervour and love.

in Heaven. ♥ My Kingdom shall come. Oh! How I long now for this New Era! You will live all in perfect unity under My Holy Name and I, who am the Supreme Source of Life, shall regenerate you all into one Holy People. ♥ From above, My Divine Image shall reflect on you, like a mirror, and you will understand that I, the Holy of Holies, restored you once again. ♥ Scriptures are being fulfilled. ♥ Wisdom shall not wait; She will cultivate My people like a ploughman and a sower; She will cultivate the earth's aridity into fields - I will spurn Her and yield Her fields into fields of Peace and Love. I am the Light of this world and I will always descend to you whenever I see you covered in obscurity.

Lord, there are some ministers who refuse to hear or believe that You can manifest Yourself like this, through me, they say that You, Jesus, have brought us all The Truth and they need nothing else but the Holy Bible, in other words all these works are false.

I have said to you all that the Advocate, the Holy Spirit, whom the Father will send in My Name, will teach you everything and <u>remind</u> you of all I have said to you. I am not giving you any new doctrine, I am only reminding you of The Truth and leading those who wandered astray back to the complete Truth. <u>I, the Lord, will keep stirring you up with Reminders</u> and My Holy Spirit, the Advocate, will always be among you as the <u>Reminder of My Word</u>. ♥ So do not be astonished when My Holy Spirit speaks to you - these reminders are given by My Grace to convert you and to remind you of My Ways. ♥ Come, smile to Me when you see Me flower.

Ah Lord! Blessed be Your Name, thank You for Your teachings.
Wisdom will instruct you child. We, us?
Forever and ever!

I LOVE THEM TO FOLLY

December 21st, 1988

Lord, it must probably sadden You when some people misunderstand Your Love in Your Message and compare it with sentimental love! Lord? (I had heard some remarks one or two from certain people.)

♥ I Am. My love in this era is not appreciated or understood. <u>You</u> know how much I love My children[1] - I love them to folly! But the sins of your era are so

---

[1]Jesus in saying this turned to me and faced me.

grave and so great that it does not recognize Me your God any longer! Have they forgotten the ransom I have payed for them? I was humiliated, tormented, tortured and willingly suffered a most painful death - <u>all out of love</u>. How then could I not repeat Myself - telling you millions of times how much I love you? and of trying to make you understand It's depths and It's greatness. I am repeating Myself and I will keep repeating Myself until My Words penetrate in your heart! Even now I am ready to repeat My Passion, unsparingly. O creation! How much suffering you give Me! My Love for you is Infinite - try and understand this Love. ♥

I AM LOVE

Christmas Eve
December 24th, 1988

Jesus?
♥ *I Am, beloved.*

Today is the Eve of Your Birth. Lord! I rejoice so very much Beloved One, Holy of Holies! Praised be our Lord! O God, dissolve me in Your Holiness and show me how to live holy. Dissolve me Eternal One in Your Purity, purifying me. Beloved One, sanctify us, Your children, and unite us all into one Fold, glorifying You and praising You around <u>one</u> Tabernacle. Allow Your Holy Spirit of Truth to descend upon all of us to show us The Truth. Let Your Light be our Guide in this obscurity, and lead us in The Truth, bringing us all under one shepherd until Your Return. Lord, COME!

Ah beloved soul, I <u>will</u> enfold you all into one Fold and <u>My Own Arms</u> will be your Fence and My Sacred Heart your Home. ♥ *Love will return as Love. Yes, My beloved ones, pray for My Return.* ♥ *I am Love. I am the Supreme Source of Life, so come to Me your Saviour, come.*
Yes Lord.

I LOVE CHILDREN

December 26th, 1988

Jesus! Today I just fully understood that one can ask You directly for blessings, I mean I can ask You to bless me. I thought one can ask from You blessings for others, but not for our self!

♥ *I have told you that you are wretched. Vassula, I have blessed you millions of times - have you not noticed? Even though you never asked Me, I blessed you.* ♥ *Your ignorance child is incessantly baffling Me - your helplessness makes Me all the more eager to rush to you and pull you to My Heart.* ♥ *I love children. Leave Me free to remain your Master and He who leads you.* ♥ *Depend fully on My Mastery, for in doing so you are only then abandoning yourself entirely in My Hands and thus doing My Will.* ♥

DO NOT WORRY ABOUT TOMORROW
SUBJECTIVITY WILL ALWAYS LEAD YOU WRONG

December 27th, 1988

Jesus?
I Am! Ah, all I ask from you is love. Glorify Me by distributing My Message - show My Love in the meetings. Vassula, do not look over My shoulder[1] to what comes next - look what today is offering you.
Lord, is it wrong to plan?

I have said not to worry about tomorrow. Do not worry - trust Me. I wish you would understand that by leaving Me space to breathe in you, I would feel free to do My Work. I wish you would understand fully one day that all you have comes from Me and is My Work and not yours. Without Me, you are unable to even wink you eyes - so abandon yourself to Me. Do not let your subjectivity deceive you. ♥ *I love you and I will not see you fall. Desire Me and nothing else. Accept what you have and all that I give you. Do not listen to people's gossip. Rely on Me, for this is My Work. Subjectivity will always guide you wrong. Let things happen as though they are happening by themself - this is the way I work. Do not 'push' things, events; by 'pushing' you are also pushing Me away - so stay and remain nothing. Let everything come from Me.*
Lord, how can I know the difference of 'inspiration' and 'subjectivity?' It's difficult.

Beloved, I will tell you this: every step you want to take, come first to Me; come and consult Me. Pray to the Holy Spirit of Counsel and Advice, and I mean every step. Everything you want to undertake, come to Me first - I will guide you. Never, ever, plan on your own. ♥ *Vassula, pray for discernment. Do not hurry. I have laid down My Plans long before you were born.* ♥ *Daughter, I have*

---

[1]Worrying about the next meeting.

commissioned you to declare and transmit My Message to the world, but do remember that <u>I do not ask you to convince them</u> - let those who have ears, hear. So remember flower, all My instructions. We, us?

Yes My Lord. ⫷⫸ IXθYΣ

I WILL NEVER WEARY KNOCKING

December 28th, 1988

This is a message for the group:

♥ *I am the Lord. My flowers, be in Peace, for I, your Lord, am Peace. My beloved creation how I love you! You are precious to Me. You whom I named flowers, grow, grow in My Divine Light. Pray for your brothers who yet have not seen My Light;* ♥ *pray for their conversion. Flowers! I intend to irrigate you. Yes! My rivulet will grow into a river and My river will grow into an ocean of Peace and Love. I have said that[1] I shall send My Light far and wide and that I shall pour out teaching, like a prophecy, as a legacy to all future generations. I am your Consoler and He who loves you most. Flowers, I know you are living in a period of obscurity; whereupon this obscurity only brings sufferings, calamities and aridity. It had been said that in these times many would lose the sense of the Divine and would live in their own way and would be unable to tell good from evil. Flowers, when a soul fills herself with materialism and clings to what the world has to offer her, then she has allowed herself to be filled with Obscurity, thus leaving no space for Holiness - no space for My Spirit to grow in her, no space for The Truth, and no space for My Light.* ♥ *She lives in obscurity - this is why most of this young generation lacks spirituality and refuses to hear My Word and acknowledge Me as God; they are after degrading passions, since they have given up the Divine Truth and are after material objects. I know, My flowers, how many of you suffer to see one of your own walking in this obscurity and being in constant deep sleep! but I tell you that I, the Lord, am outside their door - I will always be there, knocking, until they hear Me. I will never weary knocking, and I will never abandon them ever! I love you all with an everlasting love - this love so misunderstood! Come to Me with all your problems - offer them to Me and rest. Come and lean on Me - I am your Consoler and I will console you, giving you My Peace. Come to your Gentle Saviour and I will heal your wounds - never weary of invoking Me and praying to Me. I am always with you. I love you and bless each one of you. I bless all your family.* ♥

---

[1] Ecclesiasticus 24:31-46.

LOVE YOUR NEIGHBOUR AS YOURSELF

Later On - Our Holy Mother:

♥   Children, approach Jesus - He calls you all from His Cross. **Please Jesus by loving each other as much as He loves you**, for the whole Law is summarised in a single command: "Love your neighbour as yourself."[1]   ♥   Find Peace and Love in His Heart. Take His Peace and Love and spread It among you. Imbue the entire world with His Divine Love - fill your soul with this joy that My Son is offering you. ♥   Little ones, pray, pray, and conversate with God - have a constant link with your Father in Heaven. ♥   Pray with fervour - let your prayers reach Him; pray with love - let Him feel your prayers. O children, how I love you! I am always with you. I am now here, with you, and I will be with you when you will leave this place and with you when you enter your homes. ♥ **We are always Present** and forever will be. I bless you all in the Name of the Father and of the Son and of the Holy Spirit. ♥ ♥ ♥   We, us. ♥

(The Lord asked me to read in His meeting Galatians 5 and 6, which I will.)

BE MY REFLECTION

January 10th, 1989

Message to the group:

Lord!

♥   *I Am. All I ask from you is to pray in holiness; pray without cease; pray from your heart. Be good to each other; be My Reflection - My Divine Image; be like mirrors, reflecting My Holiness and Purity. Let the world see on you that you are Mine, that you are Love's children; for where the Spirit of the Lord is, there is Holiness and Love, there is Light, there is brightness - so love one another. Love your enemies! Be perfect! Like your Father in Heaven is Perfect! Blessed are you all. Blessed are the newcomers. I tell you truly this: I am the Door to Eternal Life; he that believes in Me, but he were dead, yet shall he live. I am the Resurrection. ♥   Take My Peace. I offer you My Peace - take It and spread it in the world. Be My offsprings - let every soul recognize Me in you. ♥ ♥*

Just before the Lord wanted me to take out His Message in public, someone came

---

[1]Galatians 5:14-15.

and offered me a beautiful statue of our Lady of Fatima (70cm height) - I knew that Our Lady arrived here in time so that She accompanies me in all my public meetings.

In one of the meetings arranged outside Lausanne, they told me not to bring Our Lady of Fatima because they arranged everything. That same night I saw in my dream Our Lady of Fatima, as statue, facing me. I asked Her to give me a sign to know whether I had understood that She came to accompany me in my meetings and as soon as I said these words Our Lady opened Her arms and put them tightly around me and stayed like that. I woke up and the same morning Our Lady of Fatima wrote: 'Please, do not leave Me behind, take Me with you!'

Vassula, have My Peace. Read the signs the Lord is giving you - discern them and follow them.
Please help me notice them.
♥ I am helping you. ♥
Thank You Holy Mother.

Yesterday I heard of a reaction of a priest who heard about me, he said: 'away from her, she is a charlatan!' Somehow, his remark pleased me, because I'm being accused as imposter, just like Jesus was accused by the Pharisees of false prophet and it reminded me of the message you gave me (See page 405) and so many times Jesus said to me I will be blamed, persecuted and scrutinized, it only proves His words. I am happy because I am blamed and persecuted for His sake.

♥ My child, pray for those who accuse you and pass judgement on you; pray for them to open their heart; pray for all those souls who do not recognize the Lord's Merciful Signs. ♥ Stay near Me. ♥ We, us?

Yes, we, us.

CAN SATAN DIVIDE HIMSELF AGAINST HIMSELF?

January 13th, 1989

Jesus?

One priest now has said that Your works You are giving me are spiritism, because of the writings. Please help me.

Vassula, I will help you. ♥ Glory be to God for delivering you from evil. Let all those who doubt and accuse you of all sorts of calumnies remember My words in

Scriptures: "a good tree produces good fruit." Peace My Vassula. Rejoice when people abuse you and persecute you, for your reward will be great in Heaven. Beloved, those that assert that these Works are not from Me, the Lord, but are through spiritism or occultism, I ask them this question: can Satan divide himself against himself? If he is divided against himself, how can his kingdom then stand? My grace is upon you My child but they have not understood. ♥

Lord, those that accuse me and judge me before having read or met me do not want to believe either that many got converted through Your Message. They do <u>not</u> believe me!

Because they have ears, but do not listen. Vassula, I have always sent prophets since the beginning of times, but many were slaughtered and persectued. Men have not changed. I, the Lord, say this: if anyone declares openly himself for Me, in the presence of men, I, Myself, will declare him in the presence of God's angels; but, if anyone disowns Me in the presence of men, I too then will disown him in the presence of My angels. ♥ *Any men who is not with Me is against Me, and he who does not collect with Me, scatters. I declare to all generations that My Works shall never end. My Spirit is indeed among you.* ♥ *I love you all with an everlasting love, and because of this love My Sacred Heart will not see you fall.* ♥ *Recognize My Works! Discern the spirits! Scripture says: "he who prophecies will talk to people for their improvement, their encouragement and their consolation[1]."* ♥ *My Sacred Heart, so misunderstood, is an Abyss of Love and Mercy. Your era is dead, but I, who am the Resurrection, shall revive it. Pray for those priests who have ears but refuse to hear; My love for them is <u>Great</u>, but so are the sufferings and sorrows they give Me... Share My Cross My child - the struggle is not yet over. I, the Lord, am with you till the end.* ♥ *We?*

Yes Lord.
Us?
Yes my Lord; forever and ever, amen.

On the 16th January I was invited at the World Council of Churches to meet the Metropolitan Damascinos. He wanted to hear and study the Message. Jesus sent me exactly on the Celebration week of ecumenism. It's a sign. The Celebration day would be held on the 18th January which was also the Feast day of St Peter's Chair and also my birthday. I remember still how on 20th May 1987, when not one priest yet supported me and those who knew and supported me were a handful of friends, after Jesus dictated to me about the Church and it's future unity, I got exasperated asking how will this Message reach the right ears, since I'm an outsider, living in Asia, (at that time I must admit too, that I had no idea about the World Council of

---

[1] 1 Corinthians 14:3-4.

Churches) Jesus said simply *"It will."* (See page 110) I understood that, the "it will" was fulfilled exactly on the 16th January. If they reject the Message or not, this is another story.

BE INTIMATE WITH ME

January 17th, 1989

I feel I'm slipping back, so I prayed to Jesus to lift me and remind me of the meditations He taught me to discern Him and hear His Voice.

Jesus?

♥ *I Am. Flower, I will remind you how to meditate and how to hear Me. I, who am The Word, will inspire you and instruct you with Wisdom.* ♥ *Open, open up, and allow My Spirit to fill you. Yes, meditate - how else could you reach Me? Lift your soul to Me in silence, with faith. Offer Me, your Father, your will and I, who know your needs, will guide you and feed you. So, work little one - work harder.*

Lord, I am trying to.
Please Me by talking with Me. Pray to Me. Pray, pray - all I ask are prayers.
Is writing with You a form of prayer too Lord?

♥ *Yes, because you are in conversation with Me, your God Almighty. I am pleased when I am with you, for what greater is there than being in constant link with Me, your God? I am now united to you; I and you, you and I - together in union of love. Ah Vassula, peace My child. How could you imagine that you could have written all these Messages on your own? I have indeed hidden My Face for just some time to make you feel and understand how you are unable to write one word of Knowledge without Me. I am the Revelation who speaks, who offers, who instructs, who reveals, who resurrects and who feeds godless people. My Vassula, are you happy with Me? Are you happy to know to whom you belong? I am God, the Living God, your Creator. I am Love. I am your Father, who speaks to you now. I am the Most Holy Trinity.* ♥ *Devote yourself to Me. Although you are absolutely nothing, I have pursued you - like a lover pursuing his maiden. I have convinced you to love Me, and share My Works. Little do I care for what you are not, I suffice by Myself, but I delight to have you in My Light; I delight to have you in My Hall; I delight to nourish you and flourish you. My child, do you understand?   Grieve Me not[1].   ♥   Abbas are always close to their children.   Be intimate with Me always, yet never forget My Holiness.   I love you and I want you to love Me in holiness.   Respect My Law - by respecting It, you will be respecting Me.   Love My Law - for in loving It, you love Me too.   ♥   Follow My Law - by following It, you will be following Me.   My Law will lead you to Me, in My House, which is your Home too. ♥ ♥ ♥   Have faith in Me, for My Power is Great.   We, us?*

For eternity Lord.
Praise Me.
Lord, find me in the Scriptures a Chapter of Praise to read to You.
♥   I will.   Open the Holy Bible.
I did, it was the book of Daniel Chapter 3 : 52-90 so I read to the Lord these verses; it pleased Him.

MY SHEPHERDS I WANT THEM PURE

Message for the prayer group.   Written for the 17th February:

♥   Peace be with you.   ♥   My Word is Light; My Word is Peace and Love; My Word is Unity and Hope.   ♥   Come to Me and read My Word more often.   Beloved ones, it is I, Jesus, the Merciful One; Jesus, your Saviour, who descends through this weak instrument to engrave on her My Words.   Out of My Infinite Love and My Superabundant Mercy, I descend in this desert and in this aridity, to pour out My Spirit on you.   ♥   Creation! I descend to irrigate this dry soil and make rivers out of this thirsty earth.   I descend to pour on you, like morning dew, My Blessings. I come to dispel all this evil and uproot iniquity, replacing them with Peace and Love.   ♥   Today, My Lips are parched with thirst of love - I need love from you.   I am thirsty for love -I am thirsty for love... How My Sacred Heart desires you to learn to love Me!   How I desire you to attain one day love's zenith and hear you cry out: "Abba!": then... only then, My Wounds will begin to heal. How I desire that My priests draw from My Infinite Love, to fill up their heart! My love for them is <u>Great</u> - so Great that not until they are in Heaven, will they be able to understand It's fullness.   ♥   <u>Devotion should be their Banner; Fidelity their Torch; Purity their Festal Gown; and Love their Emblem</u>, so that My lambs may recognize Me in them and see clearly My Image.   ♥   My shepherds I want them pure, so that in their pureness their fruit will be whole.   Rejoice My Sacred Heart and obey fully My Commandments.   To love, is to follow My

---

[1]Because of the familiarity and intimacy, I very briefly had suddenly doubts coming upon me, wondering if it was God speaking. This hurt Him.

Commandments. Love one another. ♥ *O children of My Light, live My Words, live My Words... take My Peace and let It be in you. Take My Love and let It fill you. I will renew you entirely, if you open yourselves to Me. Trust Me. Come to Me and I shall make a new nation out of you, a pure nation! Live My Messages; meditate on My Message. Come to Me with love. Follow My Footprints, which will lead you to Me, in My House, which is your House too. Do not be shy - even in your imperfection, I will open My Arms to you; even though your love may be tepid, fall into My Arms and I, who am Master of Love, will teach you to love Me and to love one another. Come to Me - even those who do not love Me. I have forgiven you. Come, and I will heal you.* ♥ *Blessed are you all who believe and yet have not seen. Blessed are My little souls - for on such, I have a love of predilection. Stay small and simple - never try to be something. Stay small, so that you may creep in the depths of My Sacred Heart. Be like little children, with a child-like faith - for this is what pleases My Father. <u>Never cease praying</u>. Please Me and pray with your heart. I wish you to pray for unity, the Unity of My Body. I wish you to pray for the Pope and the Patriarch. I wish you to pray for all the priests - pray that the sheep who are not under the guidance of Peter, return to Peter and reconcile; pray that there be one Fold under one shepherd; pray for Peace, Unity and a greater love among you; pray that you may praise Me around one tabernacle. Unite, beloved ones, and be one - just like the Father and I are One and the same.* ♥ *I bless you all.* ♥

FORGIVE

22nd January, 1989

Lord?

I am with you child. Follow the pattern I lay for you. Pray for the Spirit of discernment and of truth to come upon you always. Be steadfast, even when they persecute you. Reach for Me and your Holy Mother. Vassula, cling to all that I have given you - you are not the first prophet My own condemn and treat unjustly; no, you are not. My best friends inflict upon Me My deepest Wounds; they have not understood; they know not what they are doing. Their hearts are troubled; troubled by the fact that I have chosen you, My child; troubled that I can come upon Wretchedness, and love her too. They have not understood My Heart, which is an Abyss of Mercy.

Many of them are vindictive; when they say their daily prayer to the Father, do they come with a clear conscience to Him, asking the Father to forgive them as they forgive others? How could they ask the Father to forgive them, when they have not forgiven you to this day? They would not hesitate to judge you. They cry out for peace, but there is no peace - not one of them repents of their wickedness. Where is your ardour of Peace? Where is your desire of unity? If today you are divided, it is because of your wickedess, of your unforgiving spirit. ♥ Where is love? Is there any love left in you creation? Is there no wisdom left in you? I, the Lord, have said that even to the least of you I will give and that through men speaking strange languages and through the lips of foreigners, I shall talk to the nations - and still they will not listen to Me. ♥ My Vassula, do not worry - persecutions there will always be. You, beloved one, hold on to what I have given you; you are now My daughter, because you are moved by My Holy Spirit - so cling to Me. Be steadfast. I shall never forsake you. ♥

⫷⟊ ΙΧθΥΣ

Glory be to God for the Mercy and Love he has shown upon me.
Be confident, you are in your Abba's arms. ♥ We, us.
Yes, forever.

EVANGELIZE WITH LOVE FOR LOVE

January 27th 1989

I, the Lord, love you. I am the Principle of your life and let it always be that way for, I Am. ♥ Remain in My Light. Gratify Me by bringing souls to Me. ♥ Caress Me with your childish words - never cease praying. Be always aware of My Presence. Treat me now as a King. Offer Me garlands of love; offer Me prayers like incense which reach Heaven; offer Me souls to redeem them; offer them to Me so that I thrust them in the Furnace of My Sacred Heart - I want to make out of each one a Living Torch of Love's Furnace. Honour Me now and evangelize with love, for love. ♥ Come, praise Me.
Praised be the Lord for having looked upon Wretchedness and lifted me. Praised be the Lord for rising me from the dead. Glory be to God for descending and bending all the way to us to redeem us from evil. Blessed be the Lord for the compassion He has upon His children. Amen.

Feed from Me. Come, us, we.

Yes, my Lord.

I WILL FEED YOU
BEFORE THE VERY EYES OF YOUR PERSECUTORS

January 29th 1989

I saw last night a symbolic dream. I entered a church full of people, Mass was still on, it was crowded and people were standing too, the air was full of incense. The priest brought a box with him and we all knew that inside this box was the Dove. Alive. He was to free it, so that it may fly around us, giving us joy. The Dove was liberated, flying around us; we all stretched our hands so that it may come upon us, knowing that if it did, it would be a Grace. The Dove which was of sky-blue colour, came towards me, I felt that I loved It and I knew too that It loved me. On my stretched arms towards It, It posed and sat on the tips of my fingers. There was around me an awesome joy, some people were surprised, some also hoped It came to them too. But It flew around again not stoppng, then once more It posed on my fingers; I took it in my hands carefully and pressed It lovingly on my left cheek near my ear, hearing the quick heart-beats It had, Its heart was throbbing - then I found myself alone on a road, a path, walking. On the side of this path, all along, unknown little animals were swallowing each other without mercy. On my way, coming towards me, to frighten me, was a rat holding still an animal in its mouth. I did not fear, and to show the rat that I was "master" I hastened my step. It realised this and so went aside, by the path, attacking a squirrel from behind, and literally swallowed it. Then, like 7m in front of me, blocking my way, and stretched from one side of the path to the other, was a snake. I thanked God for letting me see it, because it was transparent like cellophane, so that people do not see it and step on it, so that they are bitten. I did not fear it since I made up my mind to go over it, avoiding it. Suddenly, from behind me, on my right, another snake came, but it was different, because it was an "attacking" snake. It was also transparent with only a small design on its back. That snake was as thin as my fingers but as long as 3m. - I found myself trapped but immediately I was levitated from the ground, by my Heavenly Father, I was levitated like 3m above ground, still, I was afraid that this long smake might stand up and reach me, so My Heavenly Father floated me forward, passing above all these snakes and placed me on the ground near a friend. Both of us were standing at the end of the path; there was a wall, a dead-end wall. I turned my head to my right because I heard something. I saw the first snake, looking for something. I told my friend, who had not seen the snake: "Don't move, stay still" avoiding to say there was a snake, less out of fear, this friend would move. I saw the second snake come too, near the other one, then the first snake, hungry attacked the thin one with such ferocity, swallowing it up with an ugly noise. I felt relieved and in peace, knowing that that snake now is only interested to sleep and thus leave us alone in peace.

I will feed you before the very eyes of ♥ your persecutors. I will raise you to Me, less they tread upon you. I, it is who will pour My Dew of Righteousness upon you and <u>no man</u> will I leave to extirpate you flower! You are guarded by Me and in your own Abba's arms you are hidden. Have no fear - I am near. Love loves you. ♥

MY CREATION IS DEAF
THE REBEL

January 30th 1989

My Lord? O Yahweh, <u>how I love You</u>!!

I Am. Flower, I love you. ♥ My Spirit is upon you - feel My Presence. Without Me you would have been still lying dead among the dead! I, the Lord of Mercy, have risen you so that with My Message I will resurrect this godless nation. ♥ The days are fleeing, the hours are speeding away in tremendous speed too, and My Creation is deaf! Plunged in Obscurity, they do not listen nor believe on My Merciful Signs! In My Love and pity, I have redeemed you and lifted you up to Me and cradled you in My Sacred Heart. I descend from Heaven, from My Holy Throne. I bend to reach this ungrateful generation; your hands still fresh with My children's blood - blood, because you refused to believe My Messages given at Fatima. You refused to believe then Its urgency and now you are repeating your errors. New blood will be shed because of your obduracy. O My child, so many of My own are blinded with Satan's smoke! My own rebel fearlessly, and without the slightest hesitation. Sincerity is missing from them - I find no holiness in them either. ♥ I search for love and I find none in them. There is no justice to be seen and Wisdom has been replaced by folly, abandoning them, because their tongues are forked, murmuring only treachery. These rebels have allowed Vanity to be their crown and Disobedience was accepted by them - becoming their scepter. I find no peace in them, none. ♥ Their way of thinking is not Mine - they are heading for the havoc and the ruin of My City. ♥ O Cain! Cain? Where is the Spirit with which I endowed you? Are you heading for your own destruction again? I had known you violent since the day of your birth, and because you knew that this was not new to Me, here you come masquerading and dressed up as a High Priest. You have garbed yourself in My clothes, in gold and silver, to hide your dark robes, given to you by the Black Beast. You have no light in you, and to hide your hideous face you have placed a mask on your abominable face so that your appearance can thoroughly deceive even My Elect. Your mask cannot deceive Me, for My Eyes know that behind the lamb's mask, you are hiding an immense destruction - you have armoured yourself to the teeth with Evil! And now you are scheming to conquer the world - to wipe out the little light that is left in them. Your intentions are to increase lawlessness and extirpate all that is Holy, removing powerful men and monopolizing My Sanctuary. These, My child, are the Vipers I had shown you in a vision - creeping all over My Holy Sacraments and on My Tabernacle. ♥ He will deceive many and people will be blinded, blinded because of his imposter's garments. These poor souls will be convinced that what they see before their very eyes, and in their own era, is the High Priest Himself! With his glorious disguise, he will bring a Great Apostasy upon all My Church - he will bring desolation. But everything will be disguised by miracles - by great portents and signs in the skies. My perpetual Sacrifice he will fling down, trampling on It and abolishng It - but all in disguise, in malice. My Holy City will be under Cain's power, because they have rejected My Warnings. I have come to them unexpectedly, bare-footed, but they have scoffed on Me. Cain's power will last just for a short time, thanks to my beloved souls who repair -who pray and sacrifice themselves. All this I have taken in consideration and your sacrifices were not in vain. ♥ Iniquity and transgression can be suppressed with your prayers.

Lord, what will happen to your holy ones?

To My great sorrow, many will be deceived because of his appearance. Because of his lamb' mask, he will draw many to his favour, but I have allowed you to see in reality what his insides look like; they are those of a Viper's - deadly... Vassula, I will, with great thunder and with My Fire, overthrow this Rebel and all his followers. I will trample their shelter, since it was made out of Falsehood and bring into a heap of dust their refuge since its foundations were made out of lies. I will then call My Abels and with great love embrace them. I will shelter them in My Sacred Heart; they will be like doves with purity and My Sacred Heart will be their cote. Look around you, do you not see? Have you not noticed how many of My brothers are plotting against Me? I'm being betrayed, My child, by My very own.
Lord, why do they do this to you, maybe they do not really realise it?
My child, they are blinded by Vanity and Disobedience.
They are sincerely thinking they are doing right!

How could they believe they are doing right since they are breaking My Law! They are disobeying, and disobedience does not come from Me! They are following My adversary's law, they are placing their feet right into his foot-prints and they are led to their own destruction and fall! Like the East wind I will scatter these rebels - just wait and see. ♥ Plead on their behalf. Love Me and appease My Justice. Glorify Me by bringing to Me souls for their salvation - My Eyes are especially upon the youth of this dark era. Come, let us pray to the Father: ♥

*"O Father, take pity on your children - especially the young ones.
Take these souls and place them under Your wings; rescue them
from the Evil one; redeem them from the lethargy that surrounds
them; fill them with Your Holy Spirit of Truth and bring them in
Your Light for ever and ever. Amen."*

*Come, rest My child. I shall never forsake you. They[1] will not succeed to take
away from you the Light I have given you. Do not fear - I am with you. Come,
us, we? My Presence?*
Yes Lord, I love you to death.

DISCERNMENT

February 5th 1989

*Vassula, have My Peace. Allow Me to clarify My Message. ♥ You are not to take
any parts to the word - you simply cannot do these things I require of you. To
start with, even though I write "you", it is not really you yourself! How many
times have I written "revive My Church Vassula"? I will revive My Church with
My Power. Flower, I will be the One who will bless My children of Garabandal.
David and James are your helpers. I want David to understand how I work -
David will witness. ♥ Flower, My words are symbolic. Realise how I work. Free
him from his worry - I will proceed with My Work Myself. My servants should not
sleep - they should be aware of the dangers surrounding them with disbelievers.
All I ask from David is to comply with My Burning Desires of Unity - he could
become an example for the rest of the Anglican Church.*
Was he supposed to be in Rome?
*I requested it from him - nevertheless, ♥ My wishes were accomplished. My
Ways are not your ways - My Plans were not changed. I have permitted everything
to be that way for My reason.*
What does "wash Peter's feet" really mean?
*♥ Humbleness; but do not go on thinking about it. My Words are symbolic -
allow Me to test you now and then.*
But then it does confuse me sometimes.

*My flower, I mean to unite My Church. Have I not also written "unite My Church
Vassula"? Now, do you really think that it will be you who will unite My Church?
There again, My Words are symbolic. ♥ Now you know, so do not deceive*

---

[1]My persecutors.

yourselves any longer. I will do all the Work, My angels. I have given you many graces - use them. Do not get muddled up! Be in Peace. Feed My lambs with My Divine Message and depend on My Guidance. I love you all. ♥

BE FIRM LIKE A ROCK

February 9th 1989

The Lord woke me up at midnight and asked me to write down a message:

I have called you Vassula. Hear Me. ♥ Be firm, be firm like a rock ♥ - do not be like quicksand. ♥ I have chosen you in spite of your weakness, nevertheless, I knew you would not swallow up My Words like quicksand. My Word shall be placed on you -engraved on you and they will lie there for everyone to read! Vassula, think, would a farmer choose to toil and cultivate a rich soil to sow his grains, or would he go and throw his grains in swamps and quicksand? My Vassula, what have you to fear? Pray for discernment. Listen to My servant James' advice[1]. Remain. Allow My Finger to engrave on you My desires; allow Me to use you as My tablet - accept all that I give you. Eat from Me. Peace be with you. ♥ ⋖∕ ΙΧθΥΣ

This past message was given to me because I had started to take away very small bits, here and there, especially names of people and religious movements, when I was translating the messages in French; all this started when I was advised by a local priest <u>not</u> to mention certain peoples names and movements. So the Lord seems not to agree at all with him, since I'm not even under his direction but I am under the direction of Father James whom He has chosen.

Vassula, I will write now my program. ♥ for the meeting of the seventeenth, then I shall also write down My Message to them. ♥ My child, you will sanctify the hall with incense and holy water; you will pray the exorcism prayer to Saint Michael.

Here God made me understand that the rest of the programme is to be left into my private copy book.

---

[1] I thought that the message was over and I was preparing to get up.

LIVE OUR MESSAGES

♥ My Vassula, will you write down My Message?
Yes Holy Mother.
Peace be with you. My beloved ones, today I will ask you all to augment your prayers for unity - this Unity that My Son desires so much. ♥ Pray for those priests, who are dispersed, to return to the Fold - the one and only Fold of Peter. ♥ Pray that they may unite with sincerity; pray for Peace and for those children who are not reconciled with God; pray for those false kingdoms, those floating kingdoms, that they may understand how wrong they ♥ are. Come and praise the Living God, Who manifests Himself in different places these days. ♥ Praise Him for His Infinite Love and Mercy - His Grace will continue to pour on all humanity. Let those who receive Him bless His Holy Name. Bless Him, for He is a Loving Father. All those that have ears let them hear this loud cry from Heaven: "Be Holy for I am Holy!" My flowers, live Our Message - live Our Message. ♥ You have obtained all His Mercy. Try to understand God's Will - be His children of Light. ♥ I bless you in the Name of the Father and of the Son and of the Holy Spirit. Amen.

WOE TO THOSE WHO TREAD UPON MY SPIRIT

February 15th 1989

*My Vassula, never get discouraged - for before you I stand and to whom can you compare Me to? I am the Beginning and the End, the Eternal One - for I Am, I was, and will be forever and ever. ♥ My Word will be known all round this vault. Those that kick upon My Word will find themselves kicking against a goad. ♥ In every corner of the world will arise many more persecutors. They will, like enormous blocks of granite, form a fence to block My Way for all humanity. From the beginning I knew them to be heartless, filled up with boast and treachery - a devastating wilderness. Their armies will rise up, all in vain; with one single blow of My Breath I shall overpower them - sweeping them away. I am the Lord, your Holy One, and I am known to have overthrown kings and kingdoms so that My Word be known. I have, with My Power, toppled thrones and brought to shame those that call themselves "authority", and so will it be this time. I shall strip them naked for every eye to see. I deferred My anger long enough. Today I, the Lord, solemnly request them to come down from their thrones and repent! My Spirit will keep pouring on mankind and *no man*, no matter how hard they try to suppress It, no man will succeed to crush It. Woe to those who tread upon My Spirit! Unfaithful and hypocrites will be wiped away with My Breath. ♥ If they only* *knew how I hold back My Justice from falling on them they would never cease praying and repenting. If they only knew what I am offering and Who It Is that Is saying to them all: "Unite! - Unite! Be one now as the Father and I are One and the Same!" but they would not listen, for they have not understood. I have warned them, but they have neither listened nor believed. I tell you most solemnly that the hour is at hand - ever so imminent. The time of reckoning is now here. No man now can say that I have not been warning you for this Hour. Even the dead have stirred up upon hearing My Cry - even them[1] I, the Lord, am raising the dead among you - yes! I shall raise each one of these corpses, since My Cry was heard by them. I shall make out of these corpses living columns of Light. I shall place some as the sturdy pillars of My Church; and to each one of these I shall place in their right hand My Scroll and in their left hand My Lamp to be their guide. ♥ I shall give them a disciple's tongue and I shall have them minister before you. ♥ I shall have all the nations see their integrity and they will proclaim the Truth to the ends of the earth and I promise you that as the earth makes fresh things grow, as a garden makes seeds spring up, so will I, the Lord, regenerate those corpses and out of My Own Mouth, I shall confer to them My New Name. ♥ Come, be with Me child. Stay in your Father's Arms. ♥ We, us?*

Forever and Ever, Lord.
Sign My Name.
Yes. ♥ ⊂⟩< ΙΧθΥΣ

I WILL PURSUE THE SINNER

February 15th, 1989

Lord, there are so many people now who wish to receive from you 'personal' messages. Some of their questions are very worldly. Some of them take me as an 'information desk' to Heaven.
Vassula, I have given to most of them My answers. They are to be found in the Holy Scriptures and also in this Message.
Lord, allow me nevertheless to mention their names to you.
Feel free. ♥
(I did.)
Betrothed, I will not answer to questions not worthy of My Holiness. ♥ I will call the humble; I will raise the dead; I will encourage the weak; I will pursue the sinner. Countless times I shall call the godless. ♥ These, from now on, these will be the private messages as you call them. Never weary of writing. Be prudent, as

---

[1]God's voice was very sad.

now. Always come and consult Me first.
Lord sometimes without anyone asking for a private message, You just give one like this.
I will choose and decide. I shall guide you, whispering in your ear all that I want to say. ♥ Come, us, we.

February 17th, 1989

Today is our group meeting for prayers, reading Scriptures and the Messages. Jesus?
♥ I Am. Beloved, follow My program. I am with you all the time. Come, we will work together. We, us. ⋖⋗× ΙΧθΥΣ

I HAVE OPENED MY HEAVENLY STORES RECOGNIZE THE TIMES

February 20th, 1989

Message given for the reunion:

I am the Lord, your God. I am Sovereign and above all, I am He who created you. I am God unrivalled. I am the Holy of Holies. ♥ Countless angels of each order fall prostrate in My Presence, worshipping Me without cease. To whom can you compare Me to? All Heaven praises My splendour all day long. I am enthroned on the cherubs; I am robed in majesty and power; <u>I am the Word, the True Light</u>. ♥ Yet, in all My Sovereignity, in all My Majesty, I, out of great pity, descend and bend to reach <u>you</u>. I come to you, a nation so highly favoured - to you beloved ones I come. Before you I stand, barefoot and like a beggar - My Hand outstretched to you I hold. I beg you for Love, Peace and Unity. ♥ Will you hear My Cry? I am Wounded beyond recognition. My Wounds are constantly multiplied by perjuries, iniquity and a great attraction to sin. For how long will My creation continue to be godless and evil? I am asking those who defy My Commandments: "what will you do on the day of Punishment? To whom will you run for help? Where will you leave your riches?"[1] Out of My Infinite Mercy, and My great pity, <u>I have filled the skies with portents. Without cease, I am pouring</u>

---

[1]Isaiah 10:3.

*My Spirit on all mankind. I am giving visions to your young ones. I am
showering you with Signs and Graces. See? I have opened My Heavenly Stores
for this hungry generation; you will eat to your heart's content; you will eat to your
fill. Scriptures are being fulfilled. I am giving you the Signs of the End of Times,
yet, so many of My own refuse to recognize the Signs... How is it you cannot tell
the Times? But now, although most of My children have turned their backs to Me,
although they have abandoned Me, I, with everlasting love will, without ever
wearying, I will pursue them. I shall never fail calling each one repeatedly:
"Come back to Me with all your heart. Fast and repent. Open your hearts to Me
and I shall heal you." Turn to Me, your Father, and as tenderly as a father
treating his children, I will treat those that repent and come back to Me - for I am
most Tender with the weak and most Compassionate to the wretched ones. I am
full of Pity and rich in Graciousness. ♥ O beloved souls, hear My Cry from
above: "fill up your hearts from My Divine Love." Fill up your hearts and learn
to forgive each other. Do not judge each other! By forgiving each other, you will
begin to enter in the Path of Unity. By not judging your neighbour, you will be
called Truly Mine. Let Me, your God, rejoice in you My lambs. ♥ I am offering
you My Peace. Take My Peace and share It with others; take My Love and let It
encircle you like garlands of flowers. ♥*

*Children of My Heart, how I dread in telling you this, yet I must keep you in the
Truth; in spite of My supplications to you; in spite of all My warnings, many will
continue sinning - they are heading for the ruin of their soul. You are living in
a rebellious era and it had been said, that in your days these people will scorn at
religion, and will make fun of the Promise. These people, hardened at heart, will
refuse to hear. You are living in the last days before the Purification Day; be
aware day and night - never cease praying. I am solemnly telling you that the days
of Purification is at hand. I love you all with an everlasting love, and because of
this Infinite Love I descend in several parts of this earth to warn you. Do not
misunderstand Me - taking these warnings as menaces. I am Holy and I desire
you, who is fashioned to My Image, to live Holy. I have, since the beginning of
Times, raised up saints and prophets to remind you that I am Holy. I have
prepared you all for this Day, this Day of My Purification, where My Spirit of Fire
will be thrust upon you and clean all wickedness away - it will clean all that is
unholy. Be prepared for this Day and hear My Cry - hear My plea. Let the wise
man understand these Words: come back to Me, return. I am your Refuge.
Recognize the Signs, recognize those of the End of Times! Do not close your ears,
do not shut your eyes. Recognize the Times... Remember that I, the Lord, am
your Refuge. ♥ Beloved souls, be steadfast. I bless each one of you. I bless your
beloved ones. ♥* ⸙ ΙΧθΥΣ

ALLOW ME IN YOUR NOTHINGNESS TO BE EVERYTHING

February 26th, 1989

Lord?

I Am. Have My Peace. I have been teaching you now for more than three years, have I not?
Yes Lord, You have.

Have confidence then - I shall not abandon you now. My bonds are Eternal Bonds - you are linked to Me; I and you, you and I, forever in union of Love. O Yes![1] Desire Me, you are under My Grace; desire Me, your God; desire Me, your Father - let Me feel that you do not belong to the world. Please Me flower and turn to Me, seeking My Light. Be thirsty for Me. Just like a flower which needs a keeper to maintain its beauty, need Me, need My Light, need My Springs. Grow, beloved one, grow in your faith. ♥ Come, I shall whisper in your ear the part from Scriptures that you will read in the next meeting. Lean on Me and I will support you. Remember, you are nothing - allow Me in your nothingness to be Everything. I will always check your lamp's oil; I will never leave it dry; I will keep your flame lit; I will never leave you in obscurity. My Guidance will be in Peace, so I want you to never take Me out of your sight. ♥

Lord?
I Am.
Can I ask You something?
Feel free and ask. ♥
Lord, You have risen me from the dead, have You not?
♥ I have resurrected you. ♥
Lord and Saviour, You are feeding me in great abundance, You are watching over me day and night less evil may befall me, You lift me to You when I am about to be trampled by my persecutors, You are my keeper, Guide, Teacher, Spouse, Holy Companion, You are God most Tender; allow me to ask You Lord this: You have poured on me Your Spirit, will You not pour out Your Spirit on my brethren too? You have sought me among the dead and have risen me, will You not raise the rest of the dead?

My Vassula, I shall raise the dead. Already I am around those corpses - for they shall see around them something never told and they shall witness something never heard before. Those that have never been told of My Beauty will see Me, the

---

[1] I suddenly had a nostalgia for my Heavenly Father, a nostalgia to be with Him, nearer; I felt like an orphan, a widow, it is very painful this desire of God.

Light, and those who have never heard of My Love will understand and will be converted. They will be the new vessels of My Word, to bring your youth back to Me. Yes, it will be foreigners who will rebuild My Church; they will rebuild the ancient ruins; they will raise what is now lain waste; they will restore all that now is lying in ruin - have you not noticed?

They are only so few compared to the devastating ruins of Your Church, Lord.

I will multiply them - just wait and see. Love will return as Love. I am with you always. Come now, rest in Me. We, us?

Forever!

BELIEVE IN WHAT YOU ASK

February 27th, 1989

Peace be with you. (St Michael.)
Praised be the Lord. (St Mary.)

O hear Me - I am the Lord. Come to Me as now, offering these souls to Me[1]. I never deny any prayer - even when it comes tepidly from poverty itself, I hear it. I know your weakness but My Strength will sustain you. Pray for your faith to grow. I am sending you all those souls. Pray to discern My Will. Pray without cease. Ask and it shall be given to you, ask. Never cease praying - I am listening. Even the sigh that you will give Me I take into consideration, as long as everything comes from the heart. So believe in what you ask and I shall give it to you in hundredfold. You ask to be forgiven? I will forgive you. You ask for help? Which father will not give it to his child?

There are sometimes fathers who do not help their children Lord.

These fathers are not from Me - if they were Mine they would love Me and thus love their offspring and they would help them. I am here to help you in your spiritual growth. I will never deny you My Food. ♥ *Come, Wisdom will instruct you.* ♥

---

[1] I came to the Lord and offered all those souls who had asked me to pray for them. Somehow I felt arid.

HEAVENLY WORKS

February 28th, 1989

(I felt absolutely arid, alarmingly arid and cold.)
My Vassula, how could you doubt of My Love? Allow My Finger to be on you.
Wisdom will instruct you - remember who it is that is guiding you. Think! Allow
Me to use the essence of your love to heat up other hearts who are cold and do not
love Me. I have already taught you these Heavenly Works, have I not?
Yes You have Lord, but it is worrying while this is happening.
I am near you all the time - you need not fear daughter. ♥   Come, we, us?
Yes Lord.
Then how is it that I do not hear you say it? Come, I shall remind you of My
Presence. ♥

MAKE PEACE WITH GOD

March 1st, 1989

St Michael's message for the reunion:

Vassula, Glory be to God! Praised be the Lord! The Lord's Mercy is
Boundless, the Lord's Grace is upon you. ♥ Awake! Awake! Come back
to the Lord all those who have abandoned the Truth. Return and repent!
Pray for the conversion of your brethren. Take heed upon the Lord's
warnings. ♥   Peace, peace, make peace with God! I, Saint Michael, am
near you, to defend you. ♥ Pray without cease - your prayers are needed
more than ever these days of Lent. I bless you in the Name of the Father
and of the Son and of the Holy Spirit. Amen.

GOD IS REMINDING YOU
OF HIS FUNDAMENTAL TRUTHS

March 3rd, 1989

Mary's message to the reunion:

Peace be with you. My beloved ones, today I am asking you to persevere with
Love. I want to encourage you all. ♥ <u>Glorify</u> God by keeping faithful to Him.

Devote yourselves entirely to God. Let this flame that is flickering now, revive, and become a Living Torch for every eye to see. Be firm in your faith and open your hearts entirely to the Lord and receive Him with joy. ♥ Praise the Lord for sending you His Merciful Calls. Do not expect any new revelation. His Calls are only a Reminder to the Divine Truth; a reminder of how to live holy; a reminder that God is Love. God is recalling you of the Fundamental Truths ♥ - so fill your minds with everything that is true and pure. Do not leave an empty space inside you less the Tempter comes and deceives you. ♥ So fill yourselves with the Divine Love of God - for you were created to love. ♥ Pray for Peace; pray for the conversion of your brethren; pray for a greater love among you. I am beside you to help you and I will intercede for you - so do not hesitate and come to Me. I am your Mother who will always help you. ♥ Come to the Lord with love and He will fill you with His Peace; ask with love and you will receive; pray with love and you will be heard. ♥ Have My Peace. Remember to live Our Messages. I bless you all in the Name of the Father and of the Son and of the Holy Spirit. Amen. ♥

JESUS MEANS SAVIOUR

Messages for Biarritz in France: these messages were given to me now, to be read there during the Holy Week.

Peace be with you all. ♥ *I am the Lord. Beloved ones, to you I come, through My servant, and through her I will speak.* ♥ *Ah, My Beloved, I give My Peace to this house. Come, come and listen to Me now. I am your God and your Creator who breathed into you Life.* ♥ *I have sanctified you with love. I am the Source of Sublime Love and I have created you out of Love to love Me, your God.* ♥ *Souls! You belong to Me - you are My seed. I desire you to understand fully My Words. Believe in My Holy Works; believe in My Infinite Love and My Superabundant Mercy; believe in Me. I descend out of Mercy to revive you, to arise you from this lethargy that has now covered your eyes like a veil.* ♥ *I am Jesus and Jesus means Saviour. How could I see you wandering away into deeper depths of obscurity and not rush to your rescue? I, who am the lord, the Holy of Holies, and Who am surrounded by innumerable angels of each order, prostrated before Me, worshipping Me without cease - I left My Glory and My Celestial Throne, to descend to you and save you from the eternal fire. I left Heaven, My Kingdom, to come in your Wilderness and your Desolation in this earth. Yes, I left My Throne, encircled by cherubines, to come and be born in poverty - to deliver you. I, the Sovereign, that the Heavens praise from all Eternity, accepted to be humiliated by men - offering My back for scourging. I allowed them to crown Me with a crown of thorns; I allowed them to mock Me and to spit on My Holy Face; I have allowed them to crucify Me - all out of Love for you.* ♥ *O children of The*

Crucified! How could you forget all that I have done for you? Wisdom had descended, to be taken by force and by law. I was despised and rejected by men to bear your sufferings. I was nailed to the Wood to free you. I allowed them to pierce Me and deliver you. I accepted a most painful death, so that your soul may live and be able to share My Kingdom. I let My Blood run out into Rivers so that you may obtain Eternal Life. ♥ For your sake, I allowed Myself to be taken for a sinner. Today, My Wounds are re-opened because of the iniquity of this generation. I am for countless hours calling you to conversion. Return to Me! I love you with an everlasting love! Come and make Peace with Me. I shall not punish you - I shall liberate you. I shall not call you Godless anymore - you will be called My-Own. You are not fatherless - you have a Father already in Heaven, a Father most Tender. All I ask from you is a recognition. Return to Me and I shall espouse you to Myself forever. I will crown you with Integrity, with Loyalty, with Purity and with great Tenderness I will teach you to be faithful to Me - capturing your love, which I will place in My Heart to embellish it. Like a Spouse, I will adorn you with My Love and My Peace. ♥ Beloved ones, do not fear Me. O come! Come to Me. Fall into Love's Arms - I shall not reprimand you. I am here to forget and forgive. ♥ Do not be so willing to fall into Satan's traps; open your eyes and see; open your ears and hear My Cry from above; open your heart and understand that it is I, Jesus, who calls you. ♥ I have created your soul to live forever. Will you meditate upon this? I am Holy. Happy are those souls garbed in holiness, for the Gates of Heaven shall not resist them; but woe to these souls who have not washed themselves clean, but are filled with stains - these, will not be able to enter into My Kingdom. ♥ Convert yourselves and follow My Way by hearing My Merciful Call. ♥ Meditate on My Message - live My Message. ♥ I, the Lord Jesus Christ, love all of you. With all My Heart I love you. ♥ I bless each one of you. ⊂⤬ ΙΧθΥΣ

WHY HAS THE LORD ANNOUNCED HIMSELF?

The following message is also given for Biarritz (France) by Our Holy Mother:

Praise the Lord! Bless the Lord! Children, listen to the Words of Wisdom - never deny the Lord. Seek the Truth and do not resist the Truth. ♥ Ask yourselves this: "why has the Lord announced Himself to us?" Beloved, the Lord has come to you out of Love and Pity, for today so many have gone astray, without realizing where they are heading to. ♥ Your era is dead and Jesus seeks your soul to revive it again. Allow your hearts to open; allow the Lord to enter your hearts - how else would He heal you? I am your Holy Mother, who weep day and night over your strayed souls. ♥ The Lord gives you innumerable Signs all around the earth, to warn you. You are living in the End of Times.

Children, come back to us - hear Our Calls. Pray to Me and I shall intercede for you. Come, and pray with Love. I am, even though you do not see Me, always with you - your step close to Mine. Beloved, <u>We are always Present</u>. Please the Lord in remembering His Presence. I bless you all in the Name of the Father and of the Son and of the Holy Spirit. Amen.
The Lord instructed me to read for them from Scriptures : 2 Tim 3:1-17.

TREMENDOUS REPARATIONS HAVE TO BE DONE

Jesus?

I Am. Feel My Presence. Love loves you. I will prepare always your way in all those meetings. Allow My Spirit to breathe in you. I will teach you to be willing; I will teach you not to rise; I will teach you to stay small. My Spirit is upon you. I desire love. Love, to efface injustice; love, to repair the damage inflicted upon My Church; love, to feed My starved lambs; love, to repay evil; love, to quench My insatiable thirst. O My child! Tremendous reparations have to be done! Tremendous reparations have to be done, but you are so few who are sincere and repair - you are only a handful now. A remnant of My creation are sincere. So many who follow My Signs are attracted only by the sensational and nothing more! You are even seeing[1] those souls. <u>My Signs are not given to you to make a sensation on this earth</u>. I solemnly ask all those who are after the sensational to come to Me humbly and pray. Come to Me without seeking for miracles, signs and wonders. <u>Come to Me with prayers. Be holy, repent, and go on fast</u> instead of filling your soul with vain illusions - then, because I do not satisfy your spirit, you turn your backs to Me altogether... Where is the Spirit with which I endowed you? Let your heart keep My principles. Lower your eyes before Me - kneel in My Holy Presence and repent of your wickedness. I, the Lord, will exalt the lowly. Come to Me to hear My Voice; come and discover Wisdom, humbly and sincerely. My Sacred Heart takes no delight on those who seek the sensational, nor on those who affirm to do good but come out of curiosity - how little will they learn! ♥ My child, although you are incapable to understand fully My Wisdom, I have been and I am, your only Teacher. I am progressing you, step by step. I am educating you in the Ways of Wisdom. I am guiding you in the paths of virtue. Do not seek to turn to your left nor to your right, cling to all that I have given you. My child, I offer you My Peace. Will you kiss your Lord's Feet?

Yes Lord.
Come, I am Present. ♥

---

[1] I recognize those who only go after the sensation.

EPILOGUE

by Vladimir Zielinski

Does a work like this really need an epilogue?. The words of this book speak for themselves. They need neither explanation nor intermediary. They are charming and simple. They speak to us of God and tell us that they are words of God.

Words of God: another revelation?

There is only one Revelation of God, unique and definitive, and that is the Gospel of Christ. Everything that Jesus has taught us, everything that He did during His earthly life is engraved forever in the sacred memory of the Church. But the life of the Church is much richer and more deep than what is readily apparent. It transcends the visible boundaries.

In this sense, the words of the Gospel of St. John that Vassula happened upon are most meaningful: "there are many other things that Jesus did; if one were to write them all, one by one, I do not think that the world itself would be enough to contain all the books that one could write (Jn. 21:25).

The words and deeds of Jesus which the evangelists and apostles were unable to put in their books remain in the Eternal Gospel. St John himself says in his revelation: "Then I saw another angel... who flew to the middle of the sky, bearing the Eternal Gospel to announce it to those who live on the earth...."(Rev. 14:6).

This "Eternal Gospel" belongs to the same Jesus who speaks to us in His Gospel. He has a heart-to-heart conversation with each of us; those who have ears listen to Him. It is not a question of a different Gospel or a different Jesus, for "Jesus is the same yesterday and today, and he will be the same forever (Heb. 13:8).

The whole history of the Church is full of accounts of personal revelations, mystical experiences and ineffable messages, for there have always been chosen ones, men and women, to whom Christ, His Holy Mother, or the Saints address themselves directly. But the case of Vassula is unique.

After being awakened one day by this personal revelation, Vassula began to write down the words which Christ Himself spoke to her. These words do not contradict the Holy Scripture and Tradition. They should not be read as ordinary texts.

They should be read in interior silence. One must here experience the silence of eternity. It is the dialogue of a soul with its Lord: a dialogue that develops in the mystery of faith. This mystery is like the Light that illuminates the coming of each person into the world. He expresses Himself in simple words: love, peace. joy. "I love you, you belong to me, you are Mine." One has to know how to understand these words that come to us from eternity. They must be listened to in the heart. They must be listened to in prayer. The words pronounced in this book have to become incarnate within us; they must take shape in us. This dialogue must become our dialogue, so that the prayer of Jesus becomes our prayer and the beating of our heart:

> Beloved Father,
> Purify me by the Blood of Your Son.
> Father, purify me by the Body of Your Son.
> Beloved Father, drive away the evil spirit
> That is tempting me now.
> Amen.

For this message is a book of prayers: a single, uninterrupted prayer.

A NOTE TO THE READER

by Lucy Rooney SND and Robert Faricy SJ

Vassula Rydén: national tennis champion of Bangladesh, Sheraton Hotel model, exhibiting painter, socialite, her husband's hostess, mother of two sons, the ideal person to receives revelations in our times? Perhaps so, since God's ways are always surprising, his choices not usually those we would make
(cf. Isaiah 55:8)

The extraordinary way in which these revelations are made - by Vassula's hand being taken over to write messages, is off-putting. She herself had doubts from time to time - yet knows in her heart that it really is Jesus who moves her hand.
"I am too realistic, too sceptic. I can't help feeling again today doubtful that this is happening...I who very well know that I can't handle my hand and that I know how powerless I become when God takes possession of my hand." (10:23)

She has examined all the arguments: that she is influenced by the sub-conscious, or by evil spirits, by psychological disturbances. She knows what will be said about her: ridicule at least, even hatred. Yet courageously, risking all the scorn, she publishes these messages. She knows too her own lowliness as the messenger, as Jesus said to her: "Do not think for one moment that I gave you this charisma because I love you more than the rest of My children." (23 January 1987)

But how do you know that the words here attributed to the Lord really come from Jesus? How can you be sure that Jesus spoke to Vassula, wrote through her, dictated to her? Do you have a right to believe that? Can you believe it? We believe that Vassula's experience is authentic. That is our personal discernment. We do not, of course, nor could we, make any kind of official recognition or pronouncement of validity. On the contrary, we submit our judgement to the judgement of legitimate church authority.

Obviously, no one is obliged to believe that Jesus says what Vassula says he says. But anyone can believe that these are Jesus' words. Should you believe? Make your own discernment. Read, and decide for yourself with the Lord's help.

What is the message of Jesus to us through Vassula? He said: "I come and refresh all that has already been taught by Me." (1 March 1987) "My message is one of Peace and Love ... I come to show this world My Mercy." (8 March 1987)

It becomes clear from the multiplicity of apparitions and revelations in our times, and it is perfectly in accord with the Gospels, that the end of these times is near. There is a battle on, before Satan loses his power. There is no indication of the end of the world, but of a time of tribulation followed, for those who endure, by a new era of love and of peace. We are in training for those dark days. Meanwhile we are living in a time not of judgement, but of Mercy. Jesus said to Vassula: "Your era has lost all spiritual values ." (26 August 1987) "The world has incessantly been offending Me, and I, for my part, have incessantly been reminding them of My existence and of how I love them. My Chalice of Justice is full, creation! My Justice lies heavily upon you ... My cries resound and shake the entire heavens leaving My angels trembling for what has to come. I am a God of Justice and My eyes have grown weary watching hypocrisy, atheism, immorality; my creation has become in its decadence a replica of what Sodom was. I will thunder you with My Justice as I have thundered the Sodomites. Repent, creation, before I come.: (1 September 1987 and following) When Vassula pleaded that his children were only asleep, He replied: "They are sleeping hour after hour, year after year."

Jesus says that He has sent signs and warnings but they have been rejected (1 September 1987) Here then in Vassula we have another message of mercy: "You are one of the many signs." (8 January 1987) And Jesus confirms what has startled us all - the present day outpouring of the Holy Spirit upon all who ask, and the multiplication of apparitions and wonders all over the world: "I tell you solemnly that I shall keep spreading My Holy Spirit on your sons and daughters as has never happened among many generations, to nourish you from My Own Hand, and to place My entire Law in your hearts." (message from the Sacred Heart for England, February 1991).

"All the messages bearing the call of love and peace, leading those that are lost to find their way back to me, are all from the Father and Me." (10 October 1986) This is the good news: "The weaker and more wretched you are the more I seek you and love you." (17 March 1987) It is our unbelievable privilege that Jesus can say to each one of us, through Vassula: "I love you to a degree you are unable to grasp." (8 January 1987) "I, God, love you to distraction." (8 December 1986) And most profoundly of all: "Love loves you."(29 August 1987)

Read the book and share in Vassula's experience of the Lord. That sharing will constitute a part of your own experience of the Lord. Read with faith. Not with faith in Vassula, and not with faith in the authenticity of her experience, but with faith in Jesus. Have faith, Jesus wants to share himself and His love for you with you through this book. Through your reading, Jesus can lead you to know Him better, and to love Him more, and to follow Him more closely.

What if you, the reader, are not a Roman Catholic? Neither is Vassula. This book is not just for Roman Catholics, but for everyone, for anyone that the Lord leads to read it. Whoever you are, if you know Jesus, this book will help you to know him better. And if you don't, this book can help you to know him. He knows you. And He has already led you to read at least this far.

1991

A MEETING WITH VASSULA

by Abbé René Laurentin

By chance, people spoke to me of Vassula Rydén, an Orthodox mystic who lives in Switzerland. She is married and the mother of two children. They told me that contact with her and the reading of her messages had changed their lives. These fruits impressed me.

I spoke about her with Patrick de Laubier, who lives in Geneva, Switzerland. He then went to see her. Next, he took a week's retreat to read her writings. Shortly after, now convinced, he brought her to me at Evry on August 26, 1989. I questioned her for a long time. She responded in a measured, coherent, and satisfactory way.

The narrow way of discernment

I do not feel qualified to make a judgement on these messages. I have only tried to raise good questions and to honestly record the answers. The readers will have to judge for themselves.

I did this investigation, among others, as a man who is amazed, overwhelmed, and dazzled by the contemporary multiplication of apparitions, communications, and extraordinary charisms. Seven years ago, I did not know any active seers. Today, I know dozens. I didn't know any stigmatics. Today, I know a dozen. (Vassula is not one of them.) I ask myself the burning question: what does this multiplication mean... illuminism or an outpouring of grace? The church intelligentsia tends to think that the critical response, i.e. negative, is always the best. But discernment can only base itself on facts. Here they are surprising, often in a positive sense.

We should avoid the two pitfalls which threaten the subject: on the one hand, there is a mind closed to grace, which extinguishes the Spirit, on the other hand there is an illuminism that imitates grace and is its caricature.

Let us therefore avoid both a narrow secularism and that gluttonous pietism which deviates towards the opposite extreme. What is truly important (and often forgotten) is discernment. This should normally be the daily bread of every seer and of everyone who feels called to share in their grace.

Who is Vassula?

Vassula Rydén, who is seated before me, was born in Egypt of Greek parents on January 18, 1942. In 1966, she married a student who began working for F.A.O in 1968. From then on, her husband's career took her from country to country: sixteen years in Africa (Sierra Leone, Ethiopia, Sudan, Mozambique, Lesotho), and then a few years in Asian Bangladesh (in March, 1984). A new posting of her husband brought her providentially to Switzerland (in August 1987), where she is in a better position to spread her message.

Her blond, nordic profile makes her seem Swedish like her husband. But her father, though Greek, was also blond. Both of her parents were Greeks, though they were the second generation to live in Egypt. She has a balanced, harmonious air, the result of a profound peace. She is reserved, but without timidity; her perfect decorum is accompanied by a great interior assurance.

She receives her messages in English, her best language, but she also speaks Greek, French, Swedish, and Arabic, etc. For a long time she was absorbed in the higher strata of worldly society: she did fashion modeling in the capital city of Bangladesh; she was also a gifted painter. In a word, she was absorbed in worldly activities and success, which for her are now things of the past. She has kept an attractiveness that, in perfect modesty, remains hers today. For thirty years (1955-1985) she had never put a foot in a church, except for such social obligations as marriages and funerals.

Nevertheless, in her childhood, she had already had two dreams which had deeply impressed her.

When she was ten, a call from Christ had come while she was sleeping. With an irresistible force He was calling her to Him.

The following year, at the age of eleven, in a dream she saw her spiritual marriage with Jesus. The Virgin Mary welcomed her with open arms and prepared her wedding garments and tresses for the marriage. She was so moved by this that she spoke to her mother about it, but it did not change her life then.

Today that forgotten dream has again become alive and pertinent as a promise fulfilled. Mary Magdalene, she recalls, was present for her spiritual wedding. But that was only a dream that had passed over the surface of her life. So it happened that she wandered away from religious practices, caught up in the current that swept along so many Catholics in the time since the Council. She had not even gone ten times to a church after her childhood.

The simplicity of her appearance is a positive sign. Her straight, blond hair frames her face as in certain classic paintings of Christ. Her home too is kept in perfect order, something that I have also noticed in the homes of other seers, who unite prayer with common sense, love for God and for their family. Those who have visited her home have fully confirmed this.

-But your husband, how has he accepted your new life of prayer?
-He accepts it, but he doesn't share it. My youngest son does. (She has two sons, Jan who is eighteen, and Fabian, who is thirteen).
-My youngest son - she continues - supports and defends me in any difficulty.
-When you came to Bangladesh, did you have any spiritual communications? Were you practicing your religion?
-I didn't even go to the Christmas Mass.

The purifying angel

-When was it that the communications from Christ began?
-It began sometime in the last week of November 1985, but it wasn't Christ yet.
-What happened that day?
-I felt in my body a kind of supernatural vibration that was flowing through my hands. I had been writing a shopping list, but my hand began to shake and the pencil was too strong for me to control. It was my guardian angel. He began to write spiritual messages.
-How did you know it was your guardian angel?
-Because using my own hand, he wrote, "I am your guardian angel." His name is Daniel and he helped me make a sketch which represents him.
-But then, when you write, it is your own muscles that are acting.
-Yes, but even if I resist, it doesn't stop. It's the same with Jesus. Once I started to doubt and I said to myself, "It is impossible that things like this are happening to me." I wanted to put down the pencil, but Jesus, as if to encourage me, took control of the pencil more fully. He wrote even faster, as if to tell me not to have doubts.
-But we were still speaking about the angel....
-The angel prepared me; it was a kind of purification. He showed me my sins as one sees them in purgatory. Little sins that had previously seemed to me to be nothing at all, I now saw with other eyes. They seemed enormous, and that made me feel so bad that I hated myself. How could I have done such things? It was a great purification."

Dictation from Jesus

-How long did that last, two years?
-No, just three months for the angel.
-At the end of those three months, who came? the Virgin Mary? Christ?
-Jesus came. He asked me, "Which house is more important, yours or Mine?"
-You could see Him then?
-Yes, interiorly. I can describe Him. I even said: "Often you look sad." He answered me: "No, I am not sad when I am with humble souls, with those who sacrifice themselves, with those who love me".
-But did he always seem sad?
-He has dimples when he smiles!
-There is one thing that creates a problem in these messages. Jesus said to you several times that He was suffering. But now that He has risen, does He still suffer?
-My spiritual director made the same objection: "How can He suffer now that He is glorified?"
-Jesus answered me: "I suffer because I am one with all of you, and I feel it when someone rebels against Me".
-You began to discern Christ three months after the angel, that would be in February of 1986. How did that happen?
-Up until then, I was intimidated by Christ, but one day He took the place of my angel without my knowing it. At the end of the message He said: "See, that's how you ought to be intimate with Me." He insists on this intimacy.
-Could you be more precise?

Transcendent yet intimate

-At the beginning of these messages when I was in Bangladesh, one day while Jesus was dictating to me, I suddenly thought: "the oven is on!" Then, I exclaimed, "Oh!" Jesus asked: "What's wrong?" I said: "I think something is burning in the oven." He said: "Then let's go down there right away"... But at the same time he reveals His holiness: intimacy and holiness.
-What do you mean by holiness?
-Adoring God.
-Yes, holiness, in the Biblical sense, is Transcendence.
-During the dictation were you in ecstasy? Were you withdrawn from the outside world like the seers at Medjugorje? It does not seem like it.
-No, I see what's around me, but I am absorbed in Jesus and His message. It's a little like when you are writing at your desk and don't think about what's around you, which is nevertheless still present to your sight.
-But you are very dependent. For the seers at Medjugorje, the apparitions especially aroused their freedom.
-He asked me not to take a step without asking Him.

-But doesn't that change you into a robot? It is not even your handwriting any more: it is somebody else's. And even though it is your hand, a graphologist wouldn't dare to say that it is the same person.[1]

-Yes, but Jesus has told me and clearly shown me that this handwriting is not automatic writing, as some people imagine. One day, he told me, "Today you will write My message with your handwriting, so that those who have not truly understood this grace that I am granting to you can understand, realizing that I have also given you the grace to hear My voice. Allow me today to dictate only. You listen and write.

At this point Vassula showed me her notebook where the handwriting changes for the message that follows. Her own, small, sensitive writing begins:

"Vassula, the days are now counted."

This message continues then in the normal handwriting of Vassula for two pages and then concludes with the words:

"This is for all those who think that your hand is moved by me without your hearing or understanding that it is I, the Lord, who inspires you. Now let us continue in the way I like, My Vassula."

Then the large handwriting reappears:

"Receive My Peace, be alert".

No, Vassula is not in a robot-like mechanical dependence. She is inspired, not manipulated. She expresses herself with a perfect spontaneity. She is free, calm, and joyful. It is more of a receptivity than a dependence. There is no sort of constraint; rather there is the receptivity of love. I asked her to clarify the matter.

-But in the case of these messages, is it your hand that moves, or rather is it dictated to your hearing?
-It is dictated.
-But you said that your hand was moved in some way.
-Yes, it is simultaneous. At first, He guided my hand without dictating, One day He said to me:
"I would like you to learn to listen to My voice, the interior voice." And in just six weeks I learned to hear His voice. It is dictated word by word; and at times there are words that I don't even know. I have to look them up in the dictionary.
-Even in English, there are some words that puzzle you?

---

[1] Cf. Appendix I, Handwriting analysis of the writing of Vassula by J.A. Munier.

-Yes, there are some words that I don't know. At other times, He gives me a paragraph all at once, and I have to hurry to write it before I forget. But if I do forget, He reminds me of the word that I skipped. One day, He invited me to go to confession. I was against that. I wanted to erase the sentence I had begun, but He blocked my hand. It was as if the pencil had gotten stuck in a hole. Then I pushed with the other hand that felt more free. Then the pencil just twisted in my hand, flew to one side, and my hand was flung back.

The difference in handwriting is apparent. When Vassula writes in dictation, the handwriting is large, with very tall letters. When she writes something of her own to comment or make some point, it is her own small, delicate, sensitive handwriting. Besides this, Vassula writes things twice. The first time she writes rapidly: then she eliminates whatever is personal, and rewrites the remainder in a more careful way.

-When I rewrite it, He corrects me - she adds.
-But among the words, you sometimes draw hearts, lots of hearts.
-That is the symbol of the Sacred Heart.
-And is that also imposed on your hand?
-Yes. At other times I draw a fish. (A symbol of Christ.)
-You were just saying that God is both transcendent and near, adorable and intimate. How do you reconcile this familiarity with adoration?
-At first, I used to write sitting down. Now I write while kneeling in front of a little table in my room with a dozen icons. At first I didn't kneel down; when I understood truly the message, I also realized the greatness of Christ. He said to me: "Vassula, don't I deserve more than that?" Since then, I always remain kneeling.
-And how long does this last?
-Four or five hours, sometimes six: four in the morning and two in the afternoon.
-Do you mean that you only write? Do you pray? Do you ask Him things?
-Yes, I talk to Him about everything. He told me never to take a step without asking Him: "Come to Me, seek my advice, and I will tell you."
-Did you ask Him about coming here?
-Yes, I asked Him and He said: "Be confident, lean on Me."

Temptations

-Once, the devil appeared to you.
-Yes, I have often been attacked by the devil. He even went so far as to give me four lines that made sense.
-Did your hand move?
-Yes, but Jesus taught me how to discern. When it isn't Jesus, it leaves me completely cold. As soon as I realize it, he gets up and leaves. One day he even dared to come while Jesus was dictating. Then Jesus turned to Him and said: "Silence!" Then he was quiet.

-Then, when you realize who he is, the demon leaves you?

-Right away, but he insults me before going.

-What kind of things does he say?

-The insults? "Bitch" and other things like that. But it was like that especially last year.

-You were insulted, not assaulted?

-Assaulted? Once, it was almost physical. One night, it was like a bird of prey, an eagle, that came to grab me at the waist; I was suffocating; I could not breathe. But I called out the name of Jesus and it left me.

Why publish?

-But why publish these notebooks?

-After three years, He asked me to make these messages public. In November of 1988, he insisted that there should be prayer meetings once each month.

-Before it was kept private?

-Yes, just He and I, and only four or five persons.

Family

-Your husband is not involved?

-No, he is Lutheran.

-And your children?

-They believe and defend me, especially the youngest. He becomes like a little lion. If I get in a disagreement, he starts listening in his room, then he comes right away to support me and says "what's going on here?" One day, Jesus said to me: "Mary is the Mother of God." For me it was something new. As I was thinking it over that night, my son came to my room around 9.30 with an Asterix book in his hand to say to me: "Mary is the Mother of God, isn't she?"

-But how did such an idea come to him?

-I don't know. That struck me. The next day, I was taking him to school and I reminded him, "You came to my room last night and asked that." He had by then completely forgotten it.

-He didn't know what it meant any more?

-No.

-Then he is interiorly very united to you?

-Yes, that day Jesus spoke through him.

-And what does Jesus ask of you?

-That I become holy. That frightened me. I thought it meant: go to a monastery, leave your family. I was running away from Him. Then I returned to Him to say: "Do you want me to be honest with You?" "Yes," He said. Then I said: "Can't I love you the way I am?" "Of course. That's what I want, because it is the heart that counts; remain as you are." And He added, "If the salt loses its flavor, of what use is it? It isn't the habit, it's the heart that is important".

Devotion to the Cross

-What kind of holiness does he expect from you?

-Sharing everything with Him, carrying His cross, following His law.

-Did He give you a mission?

-Yes.

-What is it?

-He said to Me, "You are to write, to love Me, and to spread my message. It is I who will do the rest."

-And how long are you going to write like this?

-"Till the end of your days." He told me. Till the end. I said to Him, "Hurry."

-You are in a hurry to leave this world and join Him?

-Oh, yes.

-Aren't you afraid of death? Not at all?

-No, not at all. He lets me taste a little bit of Paradise. What else could I want?

-That doesn't keep you from sometimes becoming tired, discouraged?

-Yes, after three years I said to Him: "Lord, it is good to take your Word, but it is very heavy to carry it alone." I was very discouraged, and that same night I saw a long stairway that went all the way up to heaven, and there before me were Padre Pio and St. Francis of Assisi."

-Two stigmatics!

-I do not know.

-You didn't see their stigmata?

-No. Padre Pio spoke to me in Italian. I didn't understand well except that he was telling me not to give up, to continue, to be encouraged. St. Francis showed me the stairway. At the top, I saw the silhouettes of all the saints, and they were gesturing with their hands, "climb! climb!"

-What were they trying to tell you?

-Not to give up, to continue without getting discouraged.

-Once you asked Christ to be allowed to give up this way and to begin a normal life again.

-Yes, I begged Him. I said to Him: "I can't go on any more. Leave me. I will continue to love You just like other people, but I can't go on any more like this".

-And yet you are not afraid of death. Is this mission so hard then?

-Yes, but then He opened His Heart. I saw it wounded unto death. He showed me all His wounds, and He began to dictate a very heart-rending message: "I am being scourged daily...." Then I said to myself: "No, I must not abandon Him." That was Thursday (August, 24). It was late at night. I was writing a letter to a priest in Canada who wanted all the cassettes. I asked Jesus what more I could add. He answered me, "Tell him that I bless him." I added that, and said to Jesus, "Couldn't we at last go to sleep, my Lord?" He said to me: "let us rest, but on the condition that I rest in your heart and you rest in My Sacred Heart."

First distributions of the message

-Have you distributed the messages in Greece?

-At Rhodes, the Orthodox charismatics have accepted it. I taught them the Rosary and they accepted it. They hang it around their necks.

-Was it a parish, a monastery?

-No, a very open charismatic group. Many of them speak English and read the messages.

-Your mission for the Christ is unity. In your messages, Jesus often speaks of Pope John Paul II as "Peter's successor". But what does your Orthodox Church think of that?

-I gave the messages to the Orthodox Metropolitan Damaskinos. He took note of them and is studying them. Maybe the messages about the Pope create some difficulty for him, for they declare his primacy.

-Primacy or jurisdiction? The primacy is recognized by the Orthodox. It is jurisdiction that causes problems.

Vassula is not used to this terminology. She says to me:

-The Pope is the foundation of the Church. He is the successor of Peter. Jesus says: " I have chosen him, people should acknowledge him."

She adds:

-Some people also asked Archbishop Mamie (the Catholic Archbishop of Fribourg) to designate a church where I could read the messages. He didn't object, but he didn't take any position yet.

The resurrection of Russia

She continues:

-Jesus also spoke to me about Russia. The first time was January, 1988. He said, "Your sister is dead"; I saw a woman lying on the ground, exhausted, emaciated. It was Russia. In February, 1988, he showed her to me again: "I am going to raise her like Lazarus. I have placed my hand on her cold heart." A third time on March 11, 1988, He said to me: "Russia will glorify Me."[1]

---

[1] Since then, on December 24, 1989, there as been a new message: "I mean to show My splendour and My glory to every nation living under these skies through your sister Russia. I shall dress her with My beauty and with My integrity, and I shall parade her to your brothers so that they may see My beauty and My integrity through her and in her. Daughter, the wedding of your sister's conversion is soon to come....It is I your Saviour who comes to rescue you from the red dragon's jaws; it is I, your Jesus, My doves, who comes to break your cages and free you....My Light shall resurrect your sister Russia and all her neighbouring countries. I shall break all your cages and set you free. Learn that salvation and liberation comes from Me alone. Pray for your sister, pray for her neighbours."

-That is in agreement with the messages of Fatima and Medjugorje. Do you know them? Did He speak to you of the Immaculate Heart of Mary at Fatima?
-He told me: "I am leading you to My Mother, in the room where I was conceived."
-I didn't know how to interpret these words. Is He speaking of Nazareth? I think rather of being within Mary."
-Yes, the Fathers of the Church and the Council have said that Mary conceived in her heart before conceiving in her body.

Jesus asked me to draw up a procedure for these meetings in churches. I told Him: "I don't know how; I don't know how to speak; I don't know how to do anything." He answered: "But it is not you who will do it; I will do it, and I will dictate the program for you." He asked me to evangelize with love for Love.
-But what is your own initiative in all this? Do you develop a theme?
-Yes, for example, He gave me this program: "Bless them in My name." Then I say: "All of this program has been planned by Jesus, and I bless you in His name."

1. Peace be with you.
2. Prayer to the Holy Spirit (according to a version that I pray daily).
3. Prayer to St. Michael the Archangel (according to the prayer that used to be said at the end of the Mass).
4. A Biblical reading.
5. A reading of the messages of the Sacred Heart and of Mary.
6. We finish with the rosary and the benediction of the Blessed Sacrament."

-But why is there this multiplication of apparitions that is both surprising and shocking?
-Yes, I think they are going to multiply according to the prophecy of Joel 3: "Your children will see visions and your aged will have dreams."
-Your messages stress the Holy Spirit.
-Yes, I wake up at night and hear the prayers that He says within me. The Holy Spirit prays within us. It's a tangible presence. The Holy Spirit within me prays the prayers of the Church. One day, it was the Creed.
-Your experience is indeed that of St. Paul: "The Holy Spirit cries out in us 'Abba', Father...." You also have a message of healing.
-Yes, spiritual healing, conversion. But some people have told me that they were physically healed. For one, it was cancer. For another, it was A.I.D.S.
She spoke to me seriously without elaborating on these facts for which she has no scientific documentation. She also spoke to me of the scent of perfume that occurs at times, and of her vocal prayers.
-Each day, I begin with three prayers: one to St. Michael the Archangel, one to the Sacred Heart in reparation, and one to the Blessed Virgin Mary.
She shows them to me and recites them in English.
-Do you have any messages for priests?
-Yes, they should be less skeptical. They shouldn't extinguish the Spirit. Jesus says:

"If you believe in the Holy Spirit, why do you persecute Him (in those who have charisms)? Why do you want Me silent? Why do you want a dead God?

Contradiction

-Have you had difficulties with priests?
-One, Father S., an exorcist in Switzerland. At first, he supported me. Then he changed his mind. He thinks that I might disturb the Marian Movement of Don Gobbi. Nevertheless, I am a member, and my spiritual director, Father Fannan of Bangladesh, is also in the Movement in that country, and he supports me.
-What kind of objections does Father S. make?
-He never exactly said.[1] A mystic advised him. It seems that the devil said to her regarding me, "I have succeeded".[2]
-Your messages make it clear that the devil did in fact try to deceive you. It is typical, but you weren't deceived by him. (To me she seems gifted with discernment.)

Daily life

-Listening to you, someone might think that you live in another world. You pray for four hours in the morning and two hours in the evening, but what do you do the rest of the time?
-I have something to eat in a hurry at noon. I have to do my errands, not just for myself, but for my mother who is tired. She isn't sick, but she can't walk very well. Thus I do all the errands; then I take care of my son after school.
-Then you are very busy. But what happens on days when you are away from home, like today for example on this trip?
-I get a small message, maybe a page or two, but tomorrow I will get a lot more.
-Are there days when you get no message at all?
-No, even if it's just three minutes. I wouldn't be able to give it up.
-Will you be able to write in the train that takes you home?
-Not only can I write, I can concentrate to hear His voice and converse with Him. I see Him interiorly. And when the conductor comes, He doesn't stop me from saying: "One ticket, please." He taught me to speak of "us": "We are going out, we are going to make a cup of coffee." It is always "we", "us".
-Why?

---

[1]See below, appendix II.

[2]The mystic referred to here remains unknown and does not wish to make known her identity.

-So that I never forget Him. Even when I was in the bus and I said to the conductor "one ticket". I laughed and said to Jesus, "You see how lucky we are? I asked for one ticket, but there are two of us." He answered me: "We are one, we are only one."
-United or one?
-United and one.
-Do you fast?
-Wednesdays and Fridays on bread and water.
-As at Medjugorje?
-Yes, as at Medjugorje.
-Is it because of Medjugorje?
-I asked Jesus if he wanted me to fast as they do at Medjugorje and he said, yes.
-But how do you do it with your family?
-At first I didn't dare. Now I do it.
-How much bread do you take for a meal, one slice or two?
-Two, and I confess monthly.
-Just as they have asked at Medjugorje?
-Yes, and Jesus also asked me to say the rosary.
-But the fasting, was it you who asked Him?
-Yes, I asked him, "Do you want me to fast?" He said: "Yes, that would please Me".
-But do you teach others to do it?
-Yes, I do.

Medjugorje

-What about Medjugorje?
-He spoke to me about Medjugorje.
-Is it He who sent you there?
-Yes, my spiritual director was urging me; I didn't know how to go about going there. Then I said to the Blessed Mother, "If it is really you who wants me to go, arrange it all for me, because I don't know where to begin. And in one week, everything was taken care of. A friend called me and said that everything had been arranged for a bus trip.
-When was that?
-Last year (1988) on June 25.
-Then we were there together, but there was such a crowd.

True and false apparitions

-Did Jesus speak to you of other apparitions?
-Yes, the one at Pescara. He said that it was a trick of the devil to cast doubt on all

the other apparitions.

-Yes, it was a shock in Italy. A pseudo-seer had announced great signs: one at noon, the other in the evening. It was supposed to be the greatest miracle of all time, the transferral of Medjugorje to Pescara. A crowd of 100,000 persons gathered with the press. It was a disappointment.

Fortunately the bishop had warned them, but it was a blow to apparitions in general just the same.

-Jesus also condemned a prophetess named Gabrielle in Germany, a sect that is called "Home of Missions."

-I think that Jesus spoke to you also of Garabandal; was He favorable?

-Yes.

-What about the Australian, "Little Pebble"?

-The Little Pebble wrote me twice and sent me his messages. I started to read them, but they made me feel ill at ease. I asked Jesus, "Give me an answer through the Bible." Opening it, I came upon a message that urged me to avoid him.

-He was, no doubt, sincere at the beginning. He had received a strange message from the Blessed Mother that the Cardinal Secretary of State was a devil-worshipper, that he would become an anti-pope, and that the Little Pebble would be named by God as the last Pope for the end of the world, Peter II. Did that shock you?

-Not just that, He spoke against Medjugorje. He said that the seers had fallen from grace. He also spoke against Don Gobbi. He said that he too had fallen from grace. He wrote me from Australia, I don't know how he got my address.

-He wants to make a federation of seers; he would be some sort of leader: the Pope of the seers. -I had tried to answer him and even to send him some messages, as he had asked, but each time there was something that prevented me. Now I am sure that I mustn't send him anything.

Meetings and conversions

-And the fruits of your messages?

-There are conversions. Among others, a mason, a Jehovah witness, and many lay people who were far away from God.

-What sort of people come to your meetings?

-Many kinds of people. There are the newly converted, there are those who are learning to love God as He wants them to love Him. There are also priests. Some tell me that they pray better after reading the messages.

-And how do you go about teaching them to know God?

-I myself don't teach them anything; it is the message that teaches. God says: "How can you love someone if you do not know him?" "Come to know Me and you will love Me".

-Nevertheless, you are not a robot.

-No, He dictates to me, He reassures me. I give what He gives to me, nothing more. If I don't know how to answer a question, I say: "I don't know; I haven't

received anything about that; I can't answer you." When someone asks me for a private message, I say, "but you have messages, 2000 pages of them, and maybe more."
-Your meetings take place each week?
-No, once a month. The Capuchins of St. Maurice have started to host us. It's in Valais, near Econe, just a half-hour away. Now these meetings take place all over in Switzerland.
-How many people come to these monthly meetings?
-That depends, 150-200.
-And how long do they last?
-An hour and a half.

The schism

-Did you have messages for Bishop Lefevbre?
-Yes, last July and August. Jesus begged him not to break away. It was truly moving. I had already sent some messages to Bishop Lefevre.
-Did he answer?
-He didn't answer, but someone from him came incognito. When he was speaking to me, Jesus whispered in my ear: "This is a follower of Lefebre." Then I said to him, "Do you come from Bishop Lefebre?" "Yes," he said to me. I said to him, "Do you think that the Church has opened the doors too wide?" He said, "Yes." Then I said to him, "You know Jesus is going to open the windows as well."
-What did he say?
-He laughed; I don't know why he came to see me.

Discernment

At the end of this free-ranging conversation, some things are quite evident. Vassula refers everything to Jesus. These communications do not disturb her life nor her duties in life.
She does everything in peace. Through the writings, many people have found spiritual nourishment, have been converted, and find union with Christ through prayers - a new life. These are positive signs, and within the limits of my investigation, I don't find any bad ones.

Her sincerity is clear. Her union with Christ and her profound infused sharing in His Passion is genuine. The fruits of her prayer are positive in those around her, as well as in her own life.

Experience has taught me that even authentic seers are not always infallible. One needs, therefore prudence and discernment. Our critical ability should remain

454

attentive to details, because man remains sinful and fallible. Many Christians are not attracted to private revelations. The Gospel or other messages is enough for them. This is their right, for these apparitions are a freely-given aid for faith.

Other people are greatly attracted to apparitions. They can be divided, running after apparitions and comparing messages. But there are too many of them; you cannot follow them all. That would be an over-load, a kind of spiritual indigestion.

Some readers have the feeling that such a personal message as that of Vassula should be kept private and not published. They feel that delving into it is a kind of invasion of privacy. If someone feels this reaction, there is no need for him to go on reading. If someone wants to read these messages out of simple curiosity, he should be careful. One should keep present in mind the classical criteria for discerning true apparitions and discarding what is false: sound doctrine, honesty, fruits, etc. Even when the signs of an authentic communication are all present, there remains at the same time a margin for taste and different interests.

Vassula believes she has received a mission to spread the love of Christ by these messages that she is receiving. This way has been positive for some people, since it has responded to their needs, but no one is obliged to follow this particular way. Each person should judge the matter according to his own taste and the fruits that result from it.

Usually the Gospel and the preaching of the Church are enough for us, but in our cultural milieu, where faith is being smothered, prophetic messages have a useful role of restoring a contact and breathable atmosphere, as useful a role for some as an oxygen tank.

As for the mission of unity that Vassula has received, it converges with the ecumenical movement which has been raised up by the Spirit since the beginning of the century, but trampled under foot. May these messages from an Orthodox believer stimulate it.

ANALYSIS OF VASSULA'S WRITING

by J.A. Munier, graphological consultant, SGF. GGOF.,
Expert in handwriting for the Court of Appeals of Paris

I (Fr. Rene Laurentin) submitted the messages of Vassula to J. A. Munier, a licensed graphologist of the highest reputation. I did not tell him anything about the matter except for the age (47) and the first name of this lady whom he did not know.

He prefaced the analysis which follows with the title: Graphological interpretation, with no previous information (and without taking into consideration the text itself due to lack of knowledge of the English language).

Interpretation of the large letters dictated by Jesus.

- Extraordinary telluric force
- A controlled enthusiasm with a touch of delight, i.e. seems to be the source of some kind of well-being.
- She is filled with a force that goes beyond her normal self.
- She is filled with invisible forces to which she reacts with a kind of primitive simplicity, whereas there is also in other areas a refined element.
- She is convinced of this invisible power which she perceives with intensity.
- She is an intermediary, like a center of transmission and amplification.
- She has the faith of a mystic.
- She experiences a kind of tranquil enthusiasm, a kind of fullness.
- She is very redoubled, nourished by an invisible force that seems indestructible.
- The writing in any case appears a bit strange from an ordinary point of view
- She is very hard-working, she is a docile pupil.
- She is in a kind of second state, indifferent to the exterior world.
- She can perceive invisible worlds quite well, like a medium.
- She has a very great concentrated force; she is profound in meditation.
- She does not belong to herself. There is a certain firmness. She has great self control, probably in her demeanor as well. She is dignified.

An additional interpretation of the fragments of handwriting in smaller letters between the lines:

- She is a person who lives in her own world.
- She is not mentally ill.
- She is of at least above average intelligence.
- She follows her own logic.
- She is capable of some integration.
- She conducts herself with tenderness, kindness, docility.
- She has a goal and she is dedicated to it.
- She experiences an inspiration from a high level.
- Her life is inspired by an ideal.
- Nothing else really matters for her.

A new analysis by Mr. J. A. Munier of a note by Vassula (in long hand) with her signature: March 3, 1990.

- Direct simplicity. She has a kind of simple seriousness without exaggeration. She has a great sincerity; without pretentiousness.
- Her temperament is very well balanced. Her personality seems to dominate very well her physical state. Her emotional balance seems excellent.
- She has a good intellectual level; she is lucid, serious, and has a sense of essential values. She has measured judgement, and is capable of intellectual precision. She notices detail and is free from confusion. She is capable of serious critical discussion: she is careful to be objective and not to delude herself. She is careful to be clear-thinking and free from illusions, with a positive intellectual curiosity that is even above average.
- Her social personality is not showy, she is simple and candid. She is a person to take seriously, though she appears to be "just like everybody else". She is serious without being tense, with a sort of calm severity. She is not easily affected by events, but has a high level of sensitivity. Perhaps at times there is a possible touch of playfulness or pleasant imaginativeness for recreation.
- Her moral level is excellent. She has a firm conviction in her beliefs. Her will is calm and steady enough to dominate her weaknesses. She has dignity and also a very notable goodwill.
- Some other notable qualities are: a certain reserve in relation to the phenomena that are affecting her and her states of awareness as well. She has something much more than just a "rich subconscious". She has an ability to be simultaneously both present and beyond. Because of her equilibrium, her emotions, her intelligence, she herself, as well as others are all in their proper place.

QUESTIONS ANSWERED

by Vassula Rydén

Followers of the *True Life in God* messages often have questions which they would like answered. The most frequently received questions are below and I will attempt to answer them as best I can:-

1. Why are some words changed and corrected?
2. What is the explanation for Jesus "broken" nose?
3. Why are passages of text deleted?

WHY SOME INDIVIDUAL WORDS ARE CHANGED

On 5th March 1987, approximately 16 months after I started to receive the messages, God said to me:-

> "SUMMARIZE everything I gave you, correcting them as I will instruct you, completing My Messages. Will you do this for Me Vassula? Vassula, I am sending you someone whom I will enlighten (Fr O'Carroll obviously). When everything is assembled and put in order, I God, will seal it with My Own Hand." [Volume I, *Trinitas*, p.50. Handwritten notebook no.8, p.48-49][1]

With regard to this, one might say, "how is it possible that God can regret certain things He said and even come to alter them?" And yet He can, He can because of the wickedness and spite of man on earth. Have you not read in Scriptures: "Yahweh saw that the wickedness of man was great on the earth, and that the thoughts in his heart fashioned nothing but wickedness all day long. Yahweh REGRETTED having made man on the earth, and his heart grieved. 'I will rid the earth's face of man, my own creation,' Yahweh said 'and animals also, reptiles too,

---

[1]Volume I, <u>JMJ Publications</u>. March 5, 1987, p.50.

and the birds of heaven; for I REGRET HAVING MADE THEM'" (Gn 6:5-7).

In the particular case below the text was open to misinterpretation and therefore for the sake of clarity God gave me a sign to slightly change the wording. [Ref: Volume II, *Trinitas*, again, p.112 and p.113, Handwritten notebook no.23, p.51-52]:-[1]

> "Peter! O Peter recognize the End of Times, how is it that most of you cannot tell the Times? Shadowed by Satan under his wings, Satan has digressed many of you from the Truth! Take My Hand Peter, and I will guide you; hear My cry, assemble your Eastern brothers, call them to meet Me under My roof, assemble your Eastern brothers into My Foundation, call them before Me. How I desire this unity!..."

When Christ dictates to me the messages, only I would know, since I am the receiver, when He talks to all of us, or when He talks to a certain person or if He switches from having talked to one particular person on to another or all of us. The same thing might happen if, eg, the Eternal Father speaks to me, then stops and the Son takes over to tell me something else. But usually in the latter, they introduce themselves in the beginning or the message is so clear that anyone could tell who is who.

Coming back to the above passage that I changed so that I am not misunderstood, this was how it read:

> "Peter! O Peter recognize the End of Times, how is it that most of you cannot tell the Times? Shadowed by Satan under his wings, O come Peter! Take My Hand; Satan has digressed you from the Truth! Take My Hand and I will guide you, hear My cry, assemble your Eastern brothers into My Foundation..." etc...

Here I will note, had I left it as it is when Jesus was speaking to the Pope and when Jesus was speaking to all of us, one might have misinterpreted this passage saying that Jesus is blaming the Pope, but normally no one should have misunderstood it since from the beginning Jesus asks us to honour Peter. Here below I will put in capital letters the parts concerning the Pope. The rest in normal letters will be when Jesus spoke to us. This is the original again:

> "PETER! O PETER RECOGNIZE THE END OF TIMES." (Then Jesus turns to the world and says). "How is it that most of you cannot tell the Times?" (Christ's voice drops here when He says to the world:) "Shadowed by Satan under his wings..." (then there was a pause here before Jesus cried out again). "O COME PETER! TAKE MY HAND." (Jesus had paused here again. The

---

semi-colon represents a stop, notice there are no full-stops in the original handwritten version of *True Life in God*, just like in the Old Testament in Hebrew, no stop or capital letters were used, which is rather significant and interesting too since it is the living Word of God and God is the Alpha and the Omega - the Beginning and the End. Then Jesus said to us:) "Satan has digressed you from the Truth! (Again turning to Peter He said) "TAKE MY HAND AND I WILL GUIDE YOU, HEAR MY CRY, ASSEMBLE YOUR EASTERN BROTHERS INTO MY FOUNDATION...etc"

We can always tell when Jesus started to say "Peter? O Peter recognize the End of Times," that He was talking to Peter (the Pope), and it is by what follows that is very important because we can see that Christ was turning to speak to us too, since He said: "How is it that MOST OF YOU cannot tell the Times?"

Many of the passages are to be taken metaphorically, not literally, but God knew that in our weakness and hardness of heart, we were bound to misinterpret His Word and He REGRETTED it. When Jesus said "Destroy this Temple, and I will raise it up again in three days" the Pharisees took him literally which was of course a total misrepresentation. In the same way, when Jesus speaks in metaphors in *True Life in God* one must look for the deeper meaning of the message - this is why I was instructed by God to delete certain passages for He "saw that the wickedness of man was great on the earth, and that the thoughts in his heart fashioned nothing but wickedness all day long."(Gn 6:5)

DELETED PASSAGES OF TEXT

There were a number of reasons for deletion of certain passages:-

a. Some of them were deleted under instruction from God.
b. Most that I had deleted were tasks I had to accomplish.
c. Some of the passages were personal messages for individuals.

Most of the passages I had deleted were things that I had to accomplish and MOST OF THEM NOW HAVE BEEN ACCOMPLISHED. Many of the deleted passages were instructions to go and HAND OVER to the Pope the Messages by my own hand. Some of these passages were regarding Garabandal and the children - these HAVE been accomplished too. One particular passage which was deleted made reference to the Greek Orthodox and Anglicans saying the Stations of the Cross with John Paul II - this has been partly accomplished. Firstly, I will deal with the deleted passages concerning Garabandal.

Garabandal:

Our Blessed Mother was asking me to go to Garabandal and bless the sites where She had appeared and pray over there. This has already been accomplished again in a very simple way. Then Jesus had asked me to meet the children. He had asked me to bless them. I never looked for them or "panicked" not knowing their whereabouts, because God had already taught me how He works. He asks for something quite impossible in anyone's capacity, He expects you to trust Him and lean on Him entirely, then He lays out Himself the way
for you to accomplish in peace what He had asked, so long as our spirit is one with His Spirit, every detail He asks is fulfilled. And so I have met Conchita the main seer and talked to the others by phone. Someone had arranged everything for me while I was in the States and Conchita wanted to meet me. This too has been accomplished without me trying. I was invited to go.

Secondly, I will deal with the numerous deleted passages referring to the Pope:-

Pope John Paul II:

The way we were invited to enter the Vatican and meet the Pope on the 6th November 1993, is very important, for it reminded me of the prophecies I deleted in my books. God did not want me to go in a pompous way, with special invitations from high authorities. This is why several times, in the deleted passages He calls me "barefoot messenger," and that I should go to Peter "barefoot," which of course if we know the biblical terms, it means "simple and poor." When God tells me in these deleted passages that I should bend and "wash Peter's feet" which of course is symbolic (although I had not understood what God meant immediately, just like St Francis was asked to rebuild the Church and he took this literally and went and laid brick upon brick reconstructing a church in ruins), I in the beginning had problems to grasp the deeper meanings. I understood later, that since I am an Orthodox, I represent in a way the Orthodoxy. God wanted in this way to tell us, that the Orthodox (our patriarch of Constantinople) ought to give Peter a return gesture of humility, this gesture of washing his feet, a return to what Pope Paul VI did to the Patriarch Athenagoras. Pope Paul VI had bent humbly and kissed Athenagoras' feet. They were two giants of Unity.

When God said, "Hand over My Message to My beloved servant John Paul II" He was referring to the *True Life in God* messages and this I was able to do at that November visit when I personally handed him books in four different languages (three of which were in Polish).

And now here are the passages concerning the Pope that were deleted but have now been fully accomplished:-

1. Volume II, *Trinitas*, p.2. Handwritten notebook no.17, p.4-5:-[1]
   "...You will enter My Domain barefoot, Vassula, now you have given me a vow, every vow is kept. Little one will you do this for Me? From thereon remain barefoot for Me, be My barefoot bearer..."
   Volume II, *Trinitas*, p.3. Handwritten notebook no.17, p.8-12. This message regards the same thing.[2]

2. Volume II, *Trinitas*, p.24. Handwritten notebook no.18, p.33-34[3] AND Volume II, *Trinitas*, p.35. Handwritten notebook no.19, p.10-11:-[4]
   "...Hand over My Message to My beloved servant John Paul II, have My Peace..." Just before that, on page 33 of notebook, I deleted a private message to Beatrice.

3. Volume II, *Trinitas*, p.25. Handwritten notebook no.18, p.37-38:-[5]
   "...and into your House you will receive a barefoot messenger, and the mighty shall wait for you. You will strip them (the freemasons that infiltrated into the Church, enemies of the Pope), from their weapons, disarming them, beseeching you. My Messenger will also speak for you, (the Pope), yours will be the voyage of courage, the great challenge. Vassula, My messenger, you will hand over My Message to My well beloved John Paul, he will recognize you, (he seemed to know about me since others before me had handed in to him my books, and especially when we met later on Cardinal Sodano, because when they introduced me to him he seemed to have already heard of me) when you will enter My House, let us be together entering My House." (And I asked: "Jesus will you arrange it?" And Jesus answered: "I will, Vassula").

4. Volume II, *Trinitas*, p.26. Handwritten notebook no.18, p.40 and p.41:[6]
   "...You are to be My barefoot messenger, keeping faithfully your vow, remembering My instructions. You are to enter My domain humbly, reminding them that I am a humble God who will bend in front of My servant's feet and wash them. This will be My example, I the Lord will bend. Yes, little one they will have to bend to unite. I will be coming humbly (that means to give His message), barefooted. I am not coming loaded with weapons..." (meaning that the message is not loaded with inflexible statements and arguments and menaces).

---

[1]Volume I, JMJ Publications, p.205. October 13, 1987.
[2]Volume I, JMJ Publications, p.207. October 16, 1987.
[3]Volume I, JMJ Publications, p.227. November 14, 1987.
[4]Volume I, JMJ Publications, p.239. December 4, 1987.
[5]Volume I, JMJ Publications, p.230. November 16, 1987.
[6]Volume I, JMJ Publications, p.231. November 18, 1987.

5. Volume II, *Trinitas*, p.48-49. Handwritten notebook no.19, p.63-64:-[1]
   "...You are My messenger carrying My Word which should be given to My servant John Paul, it is I who showed you how you will appear in My Domain. John Paul will not refuse you..." (the Pope seemed pleased to receive the books with the messages in his hands, and he did not refuse them).

6. Volume II, *Trinitas*, p.51. Handwritten notebook no.20, p.5:-[2]
   "...take My Message to My servant John Paul, I will fulfil the prophecies of My servant Johannes, (Pope John XXIII called the Pope of Unity), prophecies which will come to light (about unity). I, the Lord, have foretold this event of My messenger and to whom I have entrusted My Word.
   "You will speak from My Mouth and the mighty will fear, (the freemasons and the enemies of the Church), for I will speak of them, disarming them. My messenger will also speak of the tribulations that My Church will undergo. This revelation is My Voice. Recognize the Signs of the Times..."

I will not continue to add everything, since it is repetitive. But I wish to mention just where in the Volume II this message is repeated:

1. Volume II, *Trinitas*, p.56-57. Handwritten notebook no.20, p.27-29.[3]
2. Volume II, *Trinitas*, p.64-65. Handwritten notebook no.20, p.56-58, 61.[4]
3. Volume II, *Trinitas*, p.87. Handwritten notebook no.22, p.12.[5]
4. Volume II, *Trinitas*, p.144. Handwritten notebook no.25, p.48.[6]

Finally, I will deal with the deleted passage that this Easter has been partly accomplished. Jesus was asking the Greek Orthodox and the Anglicans to do the Stations of the Cross with John Paul II. As usual, Jesus was speaking in metaphors and this is why again I was advised by God to delete it because many would have misinterpreted this passage again.

Unity and Stations of the Cross

Repeatedly God tells me that I am the sign of the future unity. By this He means that the unity between the Orthodox and Roman Catholics, will be lived as I live it with them (the Roman Catholics). When He tells me: "Unite them", He does not

---

[1]Volume I, <u>JMJ Publications</u>, p.253. December 28, 1987.
[2]Volume I, <u>JMJ Publications</u>, p.254. December 31, 1987.
[3]Volume I, <u>JMJ Publications</u>, p.259. End of January 6, 1988 message.
[4]Volume I, <u>JMJ Publications</u>, p.266. January 18, 1988.
[5]Volume I, JMJ Publications, p.287. March 3, 1988.
[6]Volume I, <u>JMJ Publications</u>, p.340. June 26, 1988.

mean that I will have to run to the Pope and the Patriarch and tell them face to face: "Go and unite with your brother!" What He wants from me is to pray, pray, pray for the unity of the Church. All the sacrifices I could offer Him will go in the same balance of unity. All the penance and fasting I will do will go there too. All the sufferings, fatigues etc... will go for the unity too. Until the weight of the "balance" is heavy enough and pleasing to God, accumulated also by other instruments' prayers and sacrifices for unity, only then, will unity come. So here is this passage from Volume II, *Trinitas*, p.37. Handwritten notebook no.19, p.16, dated December 6, 1987:-[1]

> "Write Vassula: I the Lord wish you to honour My Stations of the Cross, introduce the light, (meaning to have candles). Vassula, will you ask My servant John Paul to do My Stations the way I have taught you, remember?" The Patriarch Bartholomew of Constantinople this Easter prepared ALL THE PRAYERS for the Stations of the Cross. "I desire to see you all three there," (meaning the Orthodox, the Anglicans and the Roman Catholics), "with My beloved John Paul, first honouring My Mother, offering Her a candle, then I wish to see your knees bend in all of My Stations, honouring Me by holding at My Stations a Light."
> Then I asked: "Lord, 'all three there?', who do you mean Lord?"
> "I wish to see My beloved servants there too, James and David."

In this message, it is obvious that Jesus speaks vaguely to the Roman Catholic Church, the Orthodox Church and the Anglican Church of celebrating Easter altogether in the same date. Today I understand this message even more. The Stations of the Cross is really representing Easter. The Lord spoke in metaphors asking me and the other two to be together with the Pope and do the Stations of the Cross, but in reality, Christ was asking the three Churches to be together. This has now been accomplished. This past Easter, (1994), when the Pope went to do the Stations of the Cross in the Coliseum of Rome as every year, he invited the Orthodox Patriarch Bartholomew to be with him. As he could not go himself, he sent a representative from Constantinople, Archbishop Polikarpos. We all saw him as he was right behind the Pope. The prayers of the Patriarch Bartholomew were read out by Pope John Paul II. Present also was an Anglican Bishop, thus the 3 Churches were there as Jesus desired.

John Paul II then spoke a lot about unity and mentioning several times the Patriarch of Constantinople. John Paul II during Lent was speaking many times of UNIFYING THE DATES OF EASTER.

As for the other few messages that are deleted, they were deleted because God

---

[1] Volume I, <u>JMJ Publications</u>, p.241. December 6, 1987.

instructed me to do so. They are private messages given to individuals that do not concern the readers.

JESUS' "BROKEN" NOSE

We all know that no bone on Jesus was broken according to scriptures. We also all know that most of the nose is not bone but cartilage and cartilage is not a bone. All the experts and best pathologists in this field who studied inch by inch the Holy Shroud, confirm in one voice that the cartilage of the nose was fractured. One can even see it with the naked eye on The Shroud.

Books were written by these experts, and even the famous scientific and documentary video called "The Silent Witness", confirms the words that Jesus gave me. The pathologist in Silent Witness is Dr Robert Bucklin, from Los Angeles, where he says in the film exactly these words: "...separation and possible fracture of the nasal cartilage." Here below are also a few other reports by experts:

In the back cover of the book on the Shroud by Msgr Giulio Ricci, entitled "The Way of the Cross in the light of the Holy Shroud", these words are printed:

"Msgr Giulio Ricci, President of the Roman Center for the Study of the Passion of Christ and the Holy Shroud and of a similar organization in the USA, demonstrates that 'the Man of the Shroud is Jesus.' Basing his research on the sciences, he came to this conclusion after an exhaustive examination of the internal evidence of the Holy Shroud, thus introducing us to a new, realistic vision of the central events of the Christian faith, which find detailed and dramatic confirmation in this precious archaeological document."

On page 25 of his book, there is a picture of the face of Jesus from the Shroud and this is what he writes:

"A second fall can be 'read' on the face of the Shroud in a remarkable swelling of the middle of the forehead and in the fracture of the nasal septum. When the Shroud was brought into contact with the forehead, it did not touch the sides of the forehead; the swelling in the middle came into contact with the material and left its imprint there, while the adjacent areas are shaded. According to the judgement of experts, between the edges of the nasal septum and the beginning of the cartilage, a concave area can be seen, indicative of a fracture caused by some blow."

Another book called "Verdict on the Shroud", written by Kenneth E Stevenson and Gary R Habermas, (I have only the French translation of this book by France-Marie Watkins), nevertheless in this French copy, picture no.12, after page 152, shows again a portrait of the Head of Jesus on the Shroud. The French words are: "(…) le nez a pu être cassé (…)" in English: "the nose could have been broken."

The last book from which I shall quote from, (there are many more), is French too - called "Le Linceul de Turin", "The Shroud of Turin" by Antoine Legrand, published at Desclée De Brouwer. This is what the author writes on pages 128 and 129: "Ce qui est certain c'est qu'à la base de la joue droite (exactement dans la région zigomatique sur le muscle élévateur naso-labial) il y a une tumefaction résultant d'un coup de bâton qui a également fracturé le cartilage dorsal du nez. Ce coup n'a pu être donné que par une main située à droite et en arrière de la victime qui ne pouvait deviner qui la frappait."

In English the translation is: "What is certain is that at the base of the right cheek (exactly at the zygomatic region on the elevated naso-labial muscle) there is a tumefaction as a result from a strike given by a rod that has also fractured the dorsal cartilage of the nose. This strike could only have been given by a hand situated on the right side and behind the victim who could not guess who was hitting him."

I will conclude this subject by quoting what Scriptures say: "Then they spat in His face and hit Him with their fists; others said as they struck Him, 'Play the prophet, Christ! Who hit You then?'" (Mt 26:67-68). "With a rod they strike on the cheek the judge of Israel" (Mi 4:14).

WHY SOME INDIVIDUAL WORDS ARE CHANGED

I received this message from the Eternal Father given to me in the early times and which will one day go out in print with the very early messages of my angel:

"Peace be with you. Any word you feel is not right and troubles you, feel free to correct it. I, God, give you the feeling. Vassula, are you happy?" (October 12, 1986).
"More than happy, overwhelmed." (I cannot describe it when I feel God's Love on me).

I will give a couple of examples of where I changed individual words:

a. If the words "worship" have been changed to "venerate" it is because God permitted me to do so, as you have seen by now from what He had said. (By the way, the word "worship" was used instead of "venerate" in the old times. It does not mean "adore", but it meant to honour. It has been changed for the sake of misjudgement).

b. The word "Hades" has been changed into "purgatory", so that people may understand it better. Again with God's permission. My soul is often exposed in purgatory where with the love I have for God and with my daily prayers for the souls, Jesus brings the souls out of purgatory to Him. This was one of the messages that was deleted in Volume I, *Trinitas*, p.38-39. Handwritten notebook no.8, p.1-2.[1]

I have done what God asked me to do.

Vassula

Vassula .

LIST OF HEADINGS

468

472

474

NATIONAL DISTRIBUTORS (ENGLISH EDITION)

United Kingdom

Chris Lynch
J.M.J. Publications
PO Box 385
Belfast BT9 6RQ
United Kingdom
Tel: (1232) 381596
Fax: (1232) 381596

Australia

Center for Peace
c/o Leon LeGrand
91 Auburn Road
AUBURN Victoria
Australia 3123
Fax: (03) 882-9675
Tel: (03) 882-9822

New York (USA)

John Lynch
PO Box 533
Bethpage
N.Y. USA 11714-0533
Fax: (516) 293-9635
Tel: (516) 293-9635

Philippines

MARY AND DAVID
PO BOX 146
Lapulapu City 6015
Cebu,
The Philippines.
Fax: (6332) 310305

South Africa

Winnie Williams
Friends of Medjugorje
PO Box 32817
Braamfontein 2017
Johannesburg
South Africa
Tel: (011) 614-3084
Fax: (011) 614-3417

Republic of Ireland

D.M.Publications
"Maryville"
Loughshinney
Skerries
Co Dublin
EIRE
Tel: (1) 8491458
Fax: (1) 8492466

Malawi

Rui Francisco
PO Box 124
Lilongwe
Malawi
Africa

Fax: (265) 721504

Denmark: Niels Huidt, Mysundegade 8V, DK 1668, Copenhagen V, Denmark (Fax: 45 331 33115)

Switzerland: Parvis, CH-1648, Hautville, Switzerland (Tel: 41 29 51905)

Holland: Stichting Het Ware Leven in God, Timorstraat 16, 6524 KC Nijmegen, Holland

'True Life in God' books are available in the following languages:

Switzerland: Tom Austin True Life in God, PO Box 902, CH-1800 Vevey, Switzerland

Phillipines: Center for Peace Asia, Shaw Blvd Cor. Old, Wackwack Road, Manduluyong Metro, Manila, Philippines. Tel: 795-622. Fax: 922-8358; and
Mary and David Thomas, PO Box 146, Lapu-Lapu City 6015, Cebu, Phillipines

French:
1. Edition du Parvis, CH-1648 Hauteville, Switzerland
2. 'La Vraie vie en Dieu', Editions FX de Guibert (OEIL), 27 Rue de l'Abbé-Grégoire, F-75006 PARIS

German: Das Wahre Lebe in Gott, Mariamverlag, D-7893 Jestetten, Germany

Italian: 'La Vera Vita in Dio', Edizioni Dehoniane, Via Casale San Pio V, 20, 1-00165 ROMA, Italy

Spanish/: Mexican Centro de Difusion 'Grupo Reina', Belisario Dominguez 1302, "Laboratorios Jema", Mazatlan, Sin, Mexico CP 82000 Tel: (91-69) 82-11-59

Portuguese: and Spanish Ediçoes Boa Nova, 4760 Vila Nova de Famalicao, Famalicao, Portugal. Tel: 75-165. Fax: 311-594

Polish: Vox Domini, Skr Poczt 72, 43-190 Mikolów, Poland

Greek: Candy Jeannoutsikos, Essex SA, Fokionos 8 Ermou, 10563 Athens, Greece

Russian: Cyril Kozina, Foyer Oriental Chrétien, 206 Ave de la Couronne, B-1050 Bruxelles, Belgium

Korean: Father R Spies, Father Damien Center, PO Box 36, Anyang-Shi, Kyeong-Gi Do 430-600, South Korea

Flemish: Mevr Lieve Van den Berre, Epsomlaan 34, 8400 Oostende, Belguim. Tel: (059) 503-752

Danish:	Niels Christian Huidt, Louis Petersenveg, 2960 Rungsted-Kyst, Denmark
Bangladeshi:	Father James Fannan, National Major Seminary, Plot 9, Road No.27, Banani, Dhaka 1213, Bangladesh
Indonesian:	Indriati Makki, Jalan Larong no.1a, Kompleks PLN, Kelurahan Duren Tiga, Jakarta 12760, Indonesia
Norwegian:	Ingfrid Lillerud, Lerdalsvn 22, 1263 Oslo, Norway
Ukranian:	Cyril Kozina, Foyer Oriental Chrétien, 206 Ave de la Couronne, B-1050 Bruxelles, Belgium
Dutch:	Stichting Getuigenis van Gods Liefde, PO Box 6290, 5600 HG Eindhoven, Holland
Bulgarian:	Miladora Anastassova, Bd D Grover 20, 1606 Sofia, Bulgaria
Hungarian:	c/o Ilma Jordan, Szolyva v 1/b, 1126 Budapest, Hungary
Croatian:	Franjo Ereiz, Za Belaka, Za M D Vukić, Palmotićeja 33, 41001 Zagreb PP699, Croatia
Japanese/ Chinese:	Serge Bernard Kuhn, Foyer de Charite, Ai to Hakari no Ie, Sendaiji 136, Oaza, 568 Ibaragi-Shi, Osaka-Fu, Japan
Canada:	Caravan Agencies 6 Dumbarton BLVD. Winnipeg MBR3 P2C4 Tel (204) 895-7544. Fax (204) 895-8878

Queries relating to any version, please contact:

Patrick Beneston
Association la Vrai Vie en Dieu
5 Rue de Turbigo
75001 PARIS
France

(Fax: France [1] 34-93-08-13)

True Life in God
Original Handwritten Version

'When God Gives a Sign' (Vassula Rydén) by Réné Laurentin

'My Angel Daniel' - early dawn of 'True Life in God'

Videos and Audios

Available from: Pat Callagan
                   Trinitas
                   Independence
                   PO Box 475
                   Missouri
                   USA 64051-0475

                   Tel: (816) 254-4489
                   Fax: (816) 254-1469

35

Jesus?
$\heartsuit$ egho imei * $\heartsuit$ thank You for this grace; although
5.8.87

I know it's meant for feeding others too, it will me

for timeless hours you and I will be to-

gether $\heartsuit$ Vassula, have I not said that

the wise will not understand what comes

from the Spirit? philosophy cannot be

compared to spirituality; never $\heartsuit$; that is

one of the main reasons why all those in

power and who call themselves wise will

mock you, will scorn you, will deject

you, will scrutinize you, so be prepared

beloved for the wolves to hound you,

* Greek: I am.

do not fear I will be near you ♡ (I sighed.)
all Nassula is but a passing shadow, do
not get discouraged, I will be near you.
Then I remembered how I feel unfit to be out in exile,
and how I dislike it, what I thought was amusing
in my past life is a pain now, and I can't like
these things any more, I can't stand them. I'm a misfit. ♡ I know, lean on Me., (I felt desperate.)
♡ Nassula Nassula, no, you cannot enjoy
these earthly solicitudes as before for this
is My will, I do not want you to bear
those things ♡ ♡ — Jesus ? ♡ I am, look
into My Hands, look ♡ ♡ Nassula they
♡

37

are bleeding, ♡ Vassula revive My Church,
hear Me; have you seen all this blood
streaking down My arms? I suffer, Lord,
why do You give me so much pain and show me
all this? The vision was
so vivid I thought His Blood
will drop on this ♡ ♡ to let you understand
Look.
how I suffer beloved seeing so many souls
under Satan's power ♡ let Me use
you till the end ♡ I love You♡ be with
Me, iii, I will always remind you
♡ ♡ we* ♡ love Me ♡ ♡

* in saying "we" He indicated it with His index
as a Teacher talking

that I the Lord honour My Mother,
let it be known to those who offend
Her that She is the Queen of Heaven
and that on Her Head I the Lord
placed a crown, a crown of twelve
stars ♡ She reigns beloved and this
is written in My Word ♡ I honour
My Mother and as I honour Her you
should honour Her ♡ I love you,
both My Mother and I, bless you ♡

Lord the pastor denied Her as our Holy Mother,
that we should not venerate and when I told
him that You said it from the Cross, he said

NEW TITLES AVAILABLE

John Paul II - A Dictionary of His Life and Teachings by M O'Carroll CSSp
A quick and fascinating guide to the life and teachings of this outstanding leader of the Church, which will be of great help to Catholics in these confused times. What has he said about the third secret of Fatima? What does the Pope think of Opus Dei? the Orthodox Churches? the Jews? What was his relationship with Monsignor Lefebvre? All these questions have been answered by this comprehensive dictionary, compiled by one of the outstanding theologians of our day, Father Michael O'Carroll CSSp.

Bearer of the Light by M O'Carroll CSSp
This is the second book by Father Michael O'Carroll on Vassula and the messages 'True Life in God.' In this book Vassula's most recent visit to Russia is recorded. Other themes include: pre-history of her conversion; extraordinary signs; the Passion; Chastisement and Purification. The book includes some extraordinary personal testimonies from people all around the world who experienced supernatural events in her presence. A must for any reader of the 'True Life in God' messages.

Volume IV (Notebooks 65-71)
This most recent volume of the messages of 'True Life in God' contains, among other things: prophecies on Russia explained - resurrection of the Church - repairing what was undone - unity by intermarriage. Daniel explained - the Rebel - the "enemy enthroning himself in 'my sanctuary'" - abolition of the Perpetual Sacrifice. Message to Cardinals, bishops and priests (17 March 1993).

Fire of Love
In this book prepared by Vassula Rydén from the complete works of 'True Life in God' to date are those passages she considers, the most important references to and by the Holy Spirit. 'Note to the Reader' is written by Emil Castro and the Preface os written by Fr Ion Bria, Professor of Orthodox Theology, World Council of Churches, Geneva.

When God Gives a Sign by René Laurentin
Father Laurentin has long been recognised for his scientific and theological approach to claimed apparitions and his search for the truth. In this book he skillfully and with discernment answers questions arising in relation to Vassula Rydén's charism and the 'True Life in God' messages.
(This book is available in the UK from Sue Ellis, Spring House, Spring Bottom Lane, Bletchingly, Surrey, England Tel: 0883 346365 and in the USA from Trinitas, PO Box 475, Independence, MO, USA 64051)

OTHER TITLES AVAILABLE

Volume II (Notebooks 32-58)

Jesus teaches that God is alive and very near, desiring a return to love, Adoration, sharing His Passion, consoling Him; return of Jesus. He teaches about the state of the Church, His shepherds; the renewal of His vineyards; Devotion to the Two Sacred Hearts of Jesus and Mary; expands on the ten commandments and Beatitudes; Apocalypse 12. The rebellion in the Church and the Great Apostasy; the suffering of His Peter; the minature judgement; unrolling of the 'scrolls.' Many prayers, of consecration, of adoration, of consolation, praise etc... to Father, Son and Holy Spirit.

Volume III (Notebooks 59-64)

Among the contents in this volume: Jesus marks foreheads with the consecration to him, Judgement Day, the time of sorting, the lamb's seal, the three days of darkness, and a strong message when the earth will shake and the sky will vanish.

Prayers of Jesus and Vassula

A beautiful assortment of prayers, some given by Jesus, others by Vassula, inspired by the Holy Spirit. A section on the Devotion to the Two Hearts; Daily Prayers and quotations of Jesus' teaching how to pray.

Vassula of the Sacred Heart's Passion by Michael O'Carroll C.S.Sp.

A 220 page book giving an outline of Vassula's life, her charism and analysis of Jesus' messages in the light of the teaching of the Church. Also a message to cardinals, bishops and priests of 'The Rebel' with a warning not to listen or follow the teaching of anyone except the Holy Father, John Paul II. (17 March 1993)

'True Life in God Magazine'

Available quarterly - annual subscription £5 (incl p&p). USA $15. This glossy magazine will keep the True Life in God reader in closer touch with Vassula, her travels, important new messages, videos, new books and new testimonies. Articles by Fr M O'Carroll, Vassula and Fr James Fannan. News of 'True Life in God' prayer groups worldwide.